D1567886

Johann Scheibe

Johann Scheibe

Organ Builder in Leipzig at the Time of Bach

LYNN EDWARDS BUTLER

UNIVERSITY OF
ILLINOIS PRESS
Urbana, Chicago, and Springfield

Publication of this book was supported by a grant from
the Henry and Edna Binkele Classical Music Fund and
a grant from the Claire and Barry Brook Fund of the
American Musicological Society, supported in part by
the National Endowment for the Humanities and the
Andrew W. Mellon Foundation.

Library of Congress Cataloging-in-Publication Data
Names: Butler, Lynn Edwards, author.
Title: Johann Scheibe: organ builder in Leipzig at the time
    of Bach / Lynn Edwards Butler.
Description: Urbana: University of Illinois Press, 2022. |
    Includes bibliographical references and index.
Identifiers: LCCN 2021050719 (print) | LCCN 2021050720
    (ebook) | ISBN 9780252044311 (cloth) | ISBN
    9780252053306 (ebook)
Subjects: LCSH: Scheibe, Johann, 1680-1748. | Organ (Musical
    instrument)—Construction—Germany—Leipzig—
    History—18th century. | Organ builders—Germany—
    Leipzig—Biography. | Bach, Johann Sebastian, 1685–1750
    —Friends and associates.
Classification: LCC ML576.8.L45 B87 2022 (print) |
    LCC ML576.8.L45 (ebook) | DDC 786.5/19432122—dc23
LC record available at https://lccn.loc.gov/2021050719
LC ebook record available at https://lccn.loc.gov/2021050720

To Greg

Contents

Preface

Johann Scheibe, who was buried in Leipzig on 4 September 1748, was one of Saxony's most important baroque organ builders, and his work has long merited investigation and evaluation. He worked in Leipzig, a major trade center and home to one of Europe's oldest universities, throughout a career that spanned more than forty years, and he was a colleague of Thomaskantors Johann Kuhnau and Johann Sebastian Bach. In Leipzig he maintained and either newly built or rebuilt all of the city's organs—all of them—demonstrating great respect for what was old and valued while at the same time experimenting with what was new. It is an odd twist of fate that, in spite of his close association with Bach, one of the greatest performers and composers for organ who ever lived, Scheibe's organ-building activity has either been overlooked or unjustly criticized. Attention has been directed instead toward Scheibe's contemporaries Gottfried Silbermann, Zacharias Hildebrandt, and Heinrich Gottfried Trost, perhaps because more of their instruments have survived and are easily available, both to visit and to listen to via splendid recordings. But as Ulrich Dähnert warned, in his magnificent study on Hildebrandt, "The late baroque period was far too rich and artistically significant to be incapable of producing more than just one first-rate master in the field of organ building."[1] Unfortunately, only Scheibe's small but charming organ in the village of Zschortau survives. His magnum opus at Leipzig University, his organ at St. John's, his rebuild at the New Church, his renovations at St. Thomas's and St. Nicholas's, his small organs for other village churches near Leipzig—all are lost. This monograph offers an in-depth study of Johann Scheibe that is long overdue. A gifted and skillful craftsman whose accomplishments can now be seen as ground-breaking and significant, Scheibe deserves our attention.

Like the project to rebuild the organ at Leipzig University, which began inadvertently, my interest in Johann Scheibe came about rather unexpectedly. I wanted to know more about the organs of Leipzig—in particular, what they were like during the years between 1723 and 1750, when Bach served as Leipzig's Thomaskantor and director of music. My search for documentation took me to the Leipzig Bach Archive, to the city and university libraries in Leipzig, to the City Archive of Leipzig, to various church archives, and, most importantly, to the Leipzig University Archives. At the university I discovered a trove of documents—dozens of memoranda relating to the Scheibe organ at St. Paul's, as well as payment records and minutes of meetings—and at other archives I found documents describing Scheibe's organ-building activities at Leipzig's other principal churches. The realization that Scheibe had shaped the organ scene in Leipzig at the time of Bach dawned slowly but inexorably. Along with it came the desire to fully research and tell Scheibe's story, a project that took me 15 years to complete. I never tired of the exploration, and my hope is that, as complete as I have tried to make it, this book will nevertheless inspire further investigation not only into Scheibe's work as organ and instrument builder but into the work of his contemporaries.

A few practical matters should be mentioned:

- Organs were often built or repaired by multiple generations of the same family. Johann Tobias Gottfried Trost (the father) is referred to as Tobias Gottfried Trost; Tobias Heinrich Gottfried Trost (the son) is called Heinrich Gottfried Trost. Johann Gottfried Hildebrandt assisted his father, Zacharias, during the renovation of the St. Thomas organ in 1750–51, but only the father is mentioned in tables 6 and 12. In Leipzig, the New Church organ was built by Christoph Donat I and Christoph Donat II; in Görlitz, the organ at St. Peter and Paul was built by Eugenio Casparini and Adam Horatio Casparini. I sometimes refer to these instruments as the "Donat" organ or the "Casparini" organ or to characteristics of a "Donat" or a "Casparini" organ.
- Readers should be aware that the fiscal year for Leipzig's principal churches began and ended at Candelmas (February 2); for Leipzig University, the year was Michaelmas (September 29) to Michaelmas.
- Regarding terminology, I use the following terms for the organ's manual and pedal divisions: Brust, Brust-Pedal, Brustwerk, Hauptwerk, Manual, Hauptmanual, Hinterwerk, Pedal, Rückpositiv,

Seiten-Pedal, Werk. In many instances, I have retained stop lengths commonly used at the time: 3' for 2–2/3', 6' for 5–1/3', 1–1/2' for 1–1/3'. Formulas such as "II/P/22," which appear in most of the organ dispositions, refer to the number of manual divisions (using a roman numeral), the presence (or not) of a Pedal division, and the number of stops overall. As to the terms "repairs," "overhaul," "rebuilding," "renovation," and the like, I have used the term that I believe best reflects the extent of the work; in a sense, however, these terms are interchangeable.

- Finally, for the text of this book, I have settled on stop-name spellings that reflect the practice of the time but are not unfamiliar to 21st-century readers. In the German transcriptions and the English translations in appendix A, however, stop names are spelled as they are found in the archival documents.

For making this research possible I want first of all to acknowledge and thank the Leipzig Bach Archive, especially its current director, Peter Wollny, but also Manuel Bärwald, Markus Zepf, Christine Blanken, Hans-Joachim Schulze, Michael Maul, and Andreas Glöckner, all of whom have patiently and generously answered questions. For their assistance—and encouragement—I am also grateful to Kristina Funk-Kunath, head librarian at the Bach Archive, and her former colleague Viera Lippold. Truly, this book would not have been possible without the Bach Archive's generous support. At the Leipzig University Archives, my thanks go to Petra Hesse and Sandy Muhl, who always graciously facilitated my searches. At the City Archive of Leipzig, special thanks are due Carla Calov, who generously provided all the assistance I required. Thanks also go to Maik Thiem at the Kirchlichesarchiv Leipzig. As well, the opportunities to present work in progress for discussion at meetings of the American Bach Society and with participants in the Bach Colloquium have been extremely helpful. I am also grateful to the various archives, libraries, and individuals who gave permission for reproductions from their holdings—especially to the Leipzig University Archives, the Leipzig City Archive, the Leipzig Bach Archive, the City History Museum Leipzig, Daniel Zenf (pastor in Zschortau), Konrad Dänhardt (restorer, Hermann Eule Orgelbau), and Marcus Stahl. Several organ builders readily answered my queries; I am particularly grateful to John Brombaugh, Martin Pasi, and Paul Fritts. As well, I am indebted to Manuel Bärwald and Traute Marshall for assistance with transcriptions and translations and to Quentin Faulkner for providing me with hard-to-find copies of baroque organ dispositions and an early draft of his translation of Jacob Adlung's *Musica mechanica organoedi*.

Parts of early drafts of this book were read and commented on by Markus Zepf, Edward Pepe, and James Wyly (who also brilliantly photoshopped Scheibe's organ into an old photograph of the interior of St. Paul's), and I would like to acknowledge their assistance without assigning them responsibility for any errors or omissions that remain. Likewise, my thanks go to Konrad Dänhardt and Jiri Kocourek, who read and commented on the Zschortau chapter. Part of this book was written while I was in residence at the Helen Riaboff Whiteley Center (Friday Harbor, Washington), for which I am deeply appreciative. Kerala Snyder read the entire penultimate draft and made many helpful suggestions; I am so grateful for her encouragement, advice, and friendship. Special thanks for their assistance and support go to Laurie Matheson, director of acquisitions at University of Illinois Press, to Julie Bush, who edited the manuscript with painstaking care, and to Jennifer Argo, managing editor.

Finally, I want to thank my husband, Gregory Butler, for his love and support. He not only read every word of this book—more than once—but never tired of "Scheibe and Bach discussions," no matter what time of day or night I initiated them, and, with a constancy I found inspiring, urged me to do this work.

Events in the Life of Johann Scheibe

(Unless otherwise indicated, all churches are located in Leipzig)

May 1680	Johann Scheibe is born, probably in Zschortau
9 Nov. 1705	Marries Anna Rosina Hesse and becomes a resident of Leipzig; begins working as organ and instrument maker
1706–7	Along with Christoph Donat II, makes repairs to the Thayssner organ at St. Nicholas's; first record of Scheibe's work in Leipzig
1707	Birth and death of son Johann Abraham Scheibe
5 May 1708	Son Johann Adolph Scheibe is baptized at St. Nicholas's
ca. 1709	Builds a new organ or positive for church in Stötteritz, a village now part of the city of Leipzig
1710	Is hired to move, repair, and enlarge the large organ at St. Paul's, Leipzig University
1710	Birth and death of son Johann Gottfried Scheibe
1710–12	First phase of major renovation of large organ at St. Paul's
1712	Makes repairs to the Trost organ at St. John's
1712	Another son, also named Johann Gottfried, is born; he dies in 1715
28 Jan. 1713	Signs contract for overhaul of the large organ at St. Thomas's
17 Dec. 1713	Organ in Gundorf is successfully examined (but will be examined again, in 1716, after an outstanding debt is paid)

10 Apr. 1714	Death of Gottlieb Gerhard Titius, whose bequest funded the completion of the St. Paul's organ
26 May 1715	Johann Burchard Mencke signs contract on behalf of Leipzig University for second phase of St. Paul's organ project
5 Dec. 1715	Council agrees to have the "18 registers still missing" built for the St. Paul's organ
1716	Builds new organ for the village church in Wachau
15 May 1716	Organ in Gundorf is reexamined, this time by Georg Friedrich Kauffmann of Merseburg
29 Oct. 1716	Scheibe requests that the St. Paul's organ be examined and that he be paid for work done over and above the contract
1716–20	Dispute with Leipzig University regarding additional fees sought for organ at St. Paul's
ca. 1717	Builds new organ or makes repairs to the organ in Löbnitz
1717	Makes repairs to organ at St. John's; requests that the window near the organ at St. Paul's be partially bricked in to protect the organ
20 Apr. 1717	Scheibe's wife stands as godmother to a son born to the organist in Zschortau
16 Dec. 1717	St. Paul's organ is examined by Johann Sebastian Bach, who writes a report that supports Scheibe's request for additional payment
1718	Builds new organ for the village church in Glesien
21 Apr. 1718	Is appointed organ builder to Leipzig University, effective Michaelmas 1717
26 Mar. 1720	Signs agreement with Leipzig University, accepting promise of 200 taler
1720–21	Repairs (and renovates?) small organ at St. Thomas's; renovates large organ at St. Thomas's
1721–22	Rebuilds the Donat organ at the New Church
1722	Repairs organ at St. John's
11 Dec. 1724	Signs contract for renovation of organ at St. Nicholas's
1725	Repairs large organ at St. Thomas's
1726–29	Is absent from Leipzig; before leaving, in December 1725 he is paid gratuities from St. Nicholas's, St. Thomas's, and the New Church

1729	Repairs and adds a stop to organ in Zschortau
1729–30	Corrects ciphers in the wind chests at St. Paul's; recommends (but the university postpones) a general cleaning of the pipes; requests 12 taler for an invention used in repairing/ maintaining the organ
ca. 1729–32	Examines, along with Johann Gottlieb Görner, a new organ built by David Apitzsch in Leutzsch (near Leipzig)
1730	Overhauls and sets temperament in large organ at St. Thomas's
1731	Repairs bellows of organ at St. Paul's
1732	Overhauls the New Church organ; publishes article concerning his inventions in *Neue Zeitungen von Gelehrten Sachen* (Leipzig)
Mar. 1732	Provides employment affidavit for his apprentice Christian Francke
1733	Overhauls the organ at St. Nicholas's
1735	Again, recommends thorough cleaning of St. Paul's organ
1736	Overhauls the St. Paul's organ
Mar. 1738	Johann Adolph Scheibe dedicates *Der Critische Musicus* to his father
1739–40	Builds new pedalboard for large organ at St. Thomas's and is paid for tuning on festival Sundays; repairs bellows of organ at the New Church
1740	Evaluates the small organ at St. Thomas's, then removes it from the church
10 Mar. 1741	Signs contract to build a new organ for St. John's; receives the small organ from St. Thomas's and the Trost organ from St. John's in partial payment
Mar. 1741	Along with Gottfried August Homilius, takes Johann Andreas Silbermann, who is visiting Leipzig, to see the organ at St. Paul's
1741–42	Improves the bellows at St. Thomas's
1742	Proposes a positive for Leipzig's Georgenhaus
Fall 1743	St. John's organ is examined by Bach and Zacharias Hildebrandt; Scheibe requests a supplemental fee
30 June 1744	Signs contract for new organ in Zschortau

1744	Installs an 8-stop positive in Leipzig's Georgenhaus
1744–46	Builds new organ for church in Zschortau
17 Apr. 1745	Receives additional payment for organ at St. John's
1746	Overhauls the New Church organ
7 Aug. 1746	J. S. Bach examines Zschortau organ and writes a report
1746–47	Repairs organ at St. Jacob's, Köthen; his proposal for major overhaul is not accepted
26 June 1747	Signs contract to do a major overhaul of organ at St. Thomas's
1748	Provides disposition proposals to church in Stötteritz, which are reviewed by J. S. Bach; tunes the large organ at St. Nicholas's
4 Sep. 1748	Scheibe is buried at Leipzig University

Abbreviations

Bach-Dokumente I	*Schriftstücke von der Hand Johann Sebastian Bachs.* Edited by Werner Neumann and Hans-Joachim Schulze. Kassel: Bärenreiter, 1963.
Bach-Dokumente II	*Fremdschriftliche und gedruckte Dokumente zur Lebensgeschichte Johann Sebastian Bachs 1685–1750.* Edited by Werner Neumann and Hans-Joachim Schulze. Kassel: Bärenreiter, 1969.
Bach-Dokumente V	*Dokumente zu Leben, Werk, Nachwirken 1685–1800.* Edited by Hans-Joachim Schulze and Andreas Glöckner. Kassel: Bärenreiter, 2007.
Bach-Dokumente IX	Christoph Wolff, *Bach: Eine Lebensgeschichte in Bildern / A Life in Pictures.* Editorial assistance from Marion Söhnel and Markus Zepf. Kassel: Bärenreiter, 2017.
BWV	[Bach-Werke-Verzeichnis.] Wolfgang Schmieder, ed., *Thematisch-systematisch Verzeichnis der musikalischen Werke von Johann Sebastian Bach.* Leipzig: Breitkopf and Härtel, 1950; rev. ed., Wiesbaden: Breitkopf and Härtel, 1990.
Dresden Ms.	*Orgeldispositionen: Eine Handschrift aus dem XVIII. Jahrhundert, im Besitz der Sächsischen Landesbibliothek, Dresden.* Edited by Paul Smets, with contributions from Christhard Mahrenholz and Ernst Flade. Kassel: Bärenreiter, 1931.

Fl. (fl.)   Florin(s) or guilder(s).

Gr. (gr.)   Groschen (reckoned at 24 gr. per taler, 21 gr. per guilder or florin).

Minutes A   "Acta, Conclusa Decemvirorum, 1709–1718." UAL, Rep. I/XVI/I 13.

Minutes B   "Conclusa Dnn. Professoren, 1710–1718." UAL, Rep. I/XVI/I 15.

Minutes C   "Acta, Den Gottesdienst in der Paulinerkirche . . . betr., 1710–13." UAL, Rep. II/III/B II 4.

Minutes D   "Acta, den Gottesdienst in der Paulinerkirche, auch Kirchen- und anderen Bau . . . betr., 1712." UAL, Rep. II/III/B II 8.

Minutes E   "Protocollum Decemvirale de ao. 1705." UAL, Rep. I/XVI/I 11.

Minutes F   "Acta, Protocollum Concilii Dnn. Decanor. 1726." UAL, Rep. I/XVI/I 34.

Minutes G   "Protocollum Concilii Dnn. Decemvirorum ab Anno 1732–1743." UAL, Rep. I/XVI/I 36b.

NBR   *The New Bach Reader: A Life of Johann Sebastian Bach in Letters and Documents.* Edited by Hans T. David and Arthur Mendel. Revised and enlarged by Christoph Wolff. New York: Norton, 1998.

New Church Accounts   "Rechnung der Neuen Kirchen." Stadtarchiv Leipzig.

Pf. (pf.)   Pfennig (reckoned at 12 pf. per groschen).

Riemer Chronicle   Johann Salomon Riemer, "Andere Vortsetzung des Leipzigischer Jahr-Buchs." 3 vols. 1714–71. Stadtarchiv Leipzig.

School Accounts   "Rechnung der Schulen zu St. Thomae in Leipzig." Stadtarchiv Leipzig.

SeN   *Sammlung einiger Nachrichten von berühmten Orgel-Wercken in Teutschland mit vieler Mühe aufgesetzt von einem Liebhaber der Musik.* Breslau: Carl Gottfried Meyer, 1757.

Silbermann-Archiv	*Das Silbermann-Archiv: Der handschriftliche Nachlaß des Orgelmachers Johann Andreas Silbermann (1712–1783).* Edited by Marc Schaefer. Winterthur, Switz.: Amadeus, 1994. Silbermann's notebooks are now held by the Sächsische Landesbibliothek—Staats- und Universitätsbibliothek, digitized as Mscr.Dresd. App.3165, digital.slub-dresden.de/id280760329.
St. John Accounts	"Rechnung des Hospitals zu St. Johannis." Stadtarchiv Leipzig.
St. Nicholas Accounts	"Rechnung der Kirchen zu St. Nicolai in Leipzig." Stadtarchiv Leipzig.
St. Paul Accounts A	"Rationarium Fisci veteris Templi Paulini, 1685–1741." UAL, Rep. II/III/B I 3a.
St. Paul Accounts B	"Rationes Fisci veteris Templi Paulini, 1714–1761." UAL, Rep. II/III/B I 3b.
St. Paul Accounts C	"Rationes Fisci veteris Templi Paulini, 1741–1801." UAL, Rep. II/III/B I 3c.
St. Paul Renovation	"Acta, Pauliner Kirchbau-Rechnungen, 1710–13." UAL, Rep. II/III/B I 5.
St. Thomas Accounts	"Rechnung der Kirchen zu St. Thomae in Leipzig." Stadtarchiv Leipzig.
T. or taler	Taler, thaler, reichstaler. In this book, "taler" is both singular and plural.
UAL	Universitätsarchiv Leipzig (Leipzig University Archives).
Vogel Annals	Johann Jacob Vogel, *Leipzigisches Geschicht-Buch oder Annales, Das ist: Jahr- und Tage-Bücher der weltberühmten Königl. und Churfürstlichen Sächsischen Kauff- und Handels-Stadt Leipzig.* Leipzig: Friedrich Lanckischens sel. Erben, 1714.
Vogel Chronicle	Johann Jacob Vogel, *Leipzigisches Chronicon, Das ist: Gründ- und Ausführliche Beschreibung der Churfürstl. Sächs. Welt-bekandten Handels-Stadt Leipzig.* Leipzig, ca. 1700.

Johann Scheibe

1 Bach's 1717 Visit to Leipzig

> If there is anything that pleases me in Leipzig, however, it is the most praiseworthy organ in the incomparably well-planned St. Paul's.
> —Pastor Christian Gottfried Petzsch, Zscheila, 1715

Johann Sebastian Bach had only just taken up his position as court Kapellmeister in Köthen when he was invited by the rector of Leipzig University to examine and approve the newly expanded and rebuilt organ at St. Paul's (Paulinerkirche), also called the University Church. In December 1717, in the third week of Advent, Bach undertook the journey from Köthen, some 71 kilometers/44 miles distant, a trip that probably took three days by coach.[1] Bach was 32 years of age, and this was his first visit to Leipzig. At the University Church was the city's newest organ, and at the New Church (Neue Kirche) was an organ only 12 years old. At the city's principal churches, St. Thomas's (Thomaskirche) and St. Nicholas's (Nikolaikirche), were large "historic" organs that had last been thoroughly renovated in 1702 and 1694, respectively. Bach had met Leipzig's Thomaskantor, Johann Kuhnau, one year earlier, when, in April 1716, Bach, Kuhnau, and Christian Friedrich Rolle, organist in Quedlinburg, had examined the large organ built by Christoph Contius for the Market Church of Our Lady (also known as St. Mary's) in Halle.

Leipzig was Saxony's second-largest city and a thriving commercial, intellectual, and cultural center, with Gothic churches; monastery buildings formerly belonging to the Augustinians, Franciscans, and Dominicans; a spectacular Renaissance city hall; and a large number of imposing homes newly built by

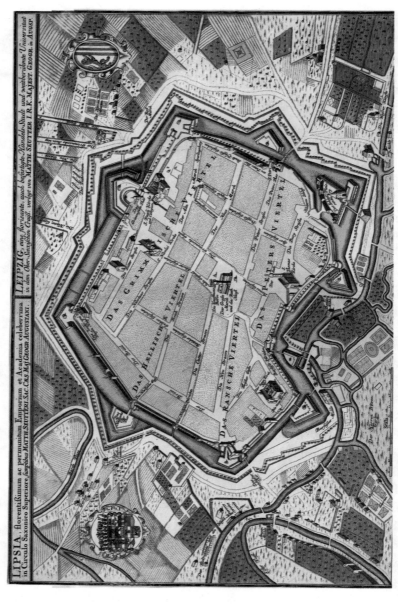

1. Street map of Leipzig, showing the town hall (*center*), with St. Thomas's (*lower left*), the New Church (*lower center*), St. Nicholas's (*upper center*), the Georgenhaus (*upper left*), and St. Paul's (*upper right*). St. John's lies beyond the city walls. Engraving by Matthaeus Seutter (ca. 1723). City History Museum Leipzig, No. L 42 b.

wealthy merchants. Leipzig's population would expand from 20,000 in 1700 to over 32,000 by the early 1750s. A bourse modeled on the Roman Capitol designed by Michelangelo had been built in 1678–79, underground sewers and street lighting had been added in 1700–1701, churches (including St. Paul's) had recently been renovated or reconstructed, and three times each year—at New Year's, Easter, and Michaelmas (late September)—visitors and merchants flooded into the city for the international trade fairs, each of which lasted two or three weeks. Some wealthy residents, such as the Boses, who later would become godparents to some of Bach's children, built immense formal gardens that were open to the public and located just beyond the medieval town wall.

It is likely that upon his arrival in Leipzig, Bach was greeted by Professor Carl Otto Rechenberg, a native of Leipzig who had attended Leipzig University and earned a doctorate from the University of Wittenberg and who, after becoming full professor at Leipzig in 1710, was appointed the university's first professor of public and international law in 1711. In 1717, at the age of 28, he was elected rector of the university for the winter semester. As witnesses to Bach's examination of the organ at St. Paul's, Professors Johann Burchard Mencke, Johannes Cyprian, and Johann Wolfgang Trier would join Rechenberg.

St. Paul's was a magnificent Gothic building next to the Grimma Gate, just inside the city wall. Dedicated by the Dominicans in 1240, it had served since the founding of Leipzig University in 1409 as the location for the university's academic and religious celebrations. The church was enlarged and given characteristic net vaulting in 1485, and in the years 1519 to 1521 the choir was rebuilt with three aisles and rhombus vaulting. Secularized in 1539, the monastery buildings were given to the university by the city in 1543, and on 12 August 1545 Martin Luther dedicated the now Protestant church as the "University Church of St. Paul's."

Academic events at St. Paul's included orations (when, in public and in Latin, doctoral students presented lectures based on their completed dissertations), the conferring of doctorates, funerals and memorial services for university professors, and, at times, services honoring political and royal personages. As well, for 300 years, from 1409 to 1709, religious services took place at St. Paul's four times annually—at Christmas, Easter, Pentecost, and Reformation. In 1710, however, the university began offering services each Sunday, and to accommodate the large number of students and professors who would attend, the interior of the church was completely renovated between 1710 and 1712. In his *Leipzigisches Geschicht-Buch oder Annales*, published in 1714, historian Johann Jacob Vogel described the extensive changes: "Not only were the large organ and pulpit dismantled, the pulpit moved to a column on the opposite side, and the organ moved to the student choir gallery and brought into much better condition in a more convenient location, but in addition, two levels of galleries were built, the steps set up more comfortably, and new chairs for women . . . as well as twenty-four decorated chapels [were built], and the ceiling, walls, and columns were painted."[2] At the same time, the orientation of the church was changed. A new west entrance was constructed using dark red porphyry stone from Rochlitz, and a vestibule was created in the nave's westernmost bay, its ceiling decorated with acanthus leaves. Academic processions now entered through the west portal, proceeded majestically along the broad middle nave, and exited through the north door. For public celebrations, the room's academic role was emphasized; a newly made double lectern, often decorated with beautiful tapestries and velvet draperies,[3] was used for doctoral ceremonies of the three most important faculties (theology, law, and medicine). According to the Institute for Historic Preservation in Dresden, in an evaluation provided prior to the church's unconscionable destruction on 30 May 1968, the university renovation of St. Paul's created an "academic theatre" that would be the "architectural and cultural high point of the building's history."[4]

The rebuild of the organ that Bach had agreed to examine, "partly newly built, partly renovated" by Johann Scheibe, had spanned some six years, from 1710 to 1716. (Scheibe was 30 years of age when he undertook the project.) The organ that dated to at least 1528 had been thoroughly rebuilt three times in the seventeenth century—once by the great Heinrich Compenius II of Halle—and now, early in the eighteenth century, had undergone its most dramatic renovation and expansion so far. Located in the *Schülerchor* (student gallery), also known as the west gallery, with a new, modern facade, three manuals (or keyboards), and 54 stops, Scheibe's organ was one of the largest and most impressive in Saxony, comparable to the monumental three-manual, 57-stop organ built in 1697–1703 by Eugenio and Adam Horatio Casparini for the Church of St. Peter and Paul in Görlitz and to the three-manual, 65-stop instrument built in 1712–16 by Contius for St. Mary's in Halle and surpassing the smaller, three-manual, 44-stop organ built by Gottfried Silbermann for Freiberg Cathedral in 1710–14. Although the project had been overseen by Daniel Vetter, organist at St. Nicholas's, and Kuhnau was the university's music director, there is no evidence that either participated in the organ's examination.

We can be certain that Bach would have been curious about the organs in Leipzig's other churches and that either Vetter or Kuhnau, or both, or perhaps someone from the university, would have shown him around. They could have

started with St. Nicholas's, Leipzig's official municipal church, which is dedicated to the patron saint of travelers and merchants and located just a short
walk north from St. Paul's. The original Romanesque church was rebuilt around
1400 and again in the early sixteenth century, when, as part of a late-Gothic
renovation, it became a three-aisle hall church. In 1555 the church's two towers
were given onion domes, and an eight-sided tower was built in the middle. (A
dramatically larger, 76-meter/249-foot middle tower was built in 1731, eight
years after Bach moved to Leipzig.) St. Nicholas's was one of the city's two
principal churches, home of the superintendent—Johann Dornfeld when Bach
visited—and, together with St. Thomas's, the church where concerted music was
performed by instrumentalists and the most experienced and advanced boys'
choir under the direction of the Thomaskantor.

In appearance, the St. Nicholas organ resembled a Renaissance instrument,
and, indeed, it had been newly built at the turn of the seventeenth century by
Johann Lange, a renowned builder based in Kamenz. Renovated at least twice
during the seventeenth century, the organ received a major makeover from 1691 to
1694—during the tenure of Vetter, who had been organist since 1679—when the
organ was renovated by Zacharias Thayssner. Among the eight reed stops built
by Thayssner was a Posaunen Bass 16', a pedal stop so powerful and penetrating
that it became the standard against which other Posaune stops were measured.

Walking west from St. Nicholas's, Bach and his host(s) would have crossed
the city's busy marketplace, the city hall on its east side, before coming to St.
Thomas's, the city's second church in rank. A three-aisle hall church, St. Thomas's
was built in the period 1482 to 1496, replacing a church built in the thirteenth
century. The nave is square in plan, the entire church, including the choir, 115
feet wide and 258 feet long—that is, about 50 feet longer than St. Nicholas's. (To
compensate, perhaps, in 1731 St. Nicholas's made sure to build its tower higher
than St. Thomas's 50-meter/164-foot tower.) The floor was brick, the vaulting
ribbed. Notable in the church's interior were the elaborately carved pulpit from
1574, newly painted and gilded in 1713; the galleries made with Rochlitz porphyry
that had been added in 1570 and in 1638 had been marbleized, provided with
brass lamps, and their 24 panels decorated with paintings of biblical scenes and
gilded biblical texts; the student choir gallery, extended to meet the new side
galleries; the two organs (described below); the main, carved altar with predella
and four wings from around 1500 (which would be replaced in 1721); the 1615
baptismal font, with a base of black-and-white marble and an elaborate cover
filled with carved figures, the whole surrounded by a railing with two doors; the
electoral pew or box (*Fürstenstuhl*) from 1686, its latticework painted white, its

carvings richly gilded; and the numerous portraits and epitaphs. There were a number of wooden galleries in the church, including two under the bell tower, two on either side of the east (stone) gallery where the small organ had been placed in 1639, and two on either side of the *Schülerchor*, one each for the string players and the wind players. Looking at the church from the outside, Bach would have noted the high tower that housed four bells, the five entrances (one in the west, two each on either side), and the chapels that had been built on the north and south sides by Leipzig's wealthy burghers.

In 1717 St. Thomas's had two organs. The large organ stood at the back of the west gallery, next to the church wall, on its own balustraded balcony supported by three wood pillars.[5] Winded by 10 bellows, the three-manual, 35-stop organ had been renovated by Christoph Donat I in 1657, 1670, and 1702 and overhauled by Scheibe in 1713. No one now knows exactly what the organ looked like—no representation from the time of Bach survives—but it must have retained its Renaissance facade and much of its Renaissance—perhaps even Gothic—pipework; perhaps it was similar in appearance to the organ at St. Nicholas's, for both instruments had been built (or rebuilt) around 1600 by Lange. According to Thomaskantor Johann Friedrich Doles, in a report he wrote in 1772 following the organ's renovation by Johann Gottlieb Mauer, the feet of the facade Principals were built in the old way, with pipe mouths in a straight line.[6] Mauer characterized the old pipework, which he preserved as far as possible, as "transcendently beautiful."[7]

St. Thomas's other organ was located at the east end of the nave, in a gallery at the axis of the middle aisle, above the arch to the antechoir. The gallery was much smaller than the *Schülerchor*, bigger than the galleries used by the instrumentalists in the west gallery—13 *Stände* (pews or seats) as opposed to 10—and smaller than the *Fürstenstuhl*, which accommodated 16 *Stände*. The latticework, carvings, ornamented crown, and large sculpted angel below were all opulently painted and gilded by Hans Richter when the gallery was constructed in 1638; panel paintings of biblical scenes were completed by 1666. The organ, built in the fifteenth century and renovated in the seventeenth century by Heinrich Compenius II and Donat I, was a two-manual, 21-stop instrument at the time its disposition was recorded by Vogel a few years before Bach's visit in 1717. Vogel reported that concerted music was performed in the east gallery on feast days.[8]

Let us assume that Bach had time to visit the city's other churches and organs. Leaving St. Thomas's, walking north along the city wall, Bach would have come to the New Church, formerly the Barefoot Friar's (Franciscan) Church. After a renovation, the church was dedicated in 1699, and its new organ, built by Donat I and his son, was dedicated in 1704 by Georg Philipp Telemann, who served as the church's organist and music director for one year. Bach admired Telemann, had copied and studied Telemann's concertos, among other works, and had chosen Telemann as godfather to his son Carl Philipp Emanuel, born in 1714. Only a few months before Bach's visit, Telemann's Passion oratorio based on Barthold Heinrich Brockes's famous libretto had been performed at the New Church on Good Friday—the first time a concerted Passion was heard in Leipzig. The New Church had an active, modern music program, which in 1717 was led by Johann Gottfried Vogler, who would be invited by Bach to perform in Köthen the following year—probably as violinist—in a musical celebration of Prince Leopold's birthday.

The renovation had preserved the basic hall plan of the old Franciscan building, but there were additions to the outside and the interior, which was lavishly decorated. Double galleries resting on Tuscan columns surrounded three sides of the building. The altar was placed on the narrow east wall; the pulpit and organ were placed in a prominent position in the middle of the south wall, emphasizing that the church was a "preaching" church. In 1703–4, the same year the organ was built, a ridge turret was added to the middle of the roof, bringing the total height to 70 meters/186 feet.

The exact disposition of the Donat organ in the New Church is not known. According to the contract, it was to be a two-manual, 21-stop instrument, but Donat was paid extra at the conclusion of the project because he had built "more than was contracted for," and in 1722, just five years after Bach's first visit, the disposition would be altered during a renovation by Scheibe. Although the organ has not survived, its appearance is well known from Johann Christian Seyler's drawing (see p. 155), and it probably was Seyler who provided the beautifully proportioned and lavishly decorated design.

Would Bach also have visited St. John's (Johanniskirche)? Located outside the city's Grimma Gate, St. John's served primarily patients at St. John's Hospital and those poorer citizens of Leipzig who lived outside the city walls. No concerted music took place at its services; indeed, the fourth, least expert choir from the St. Thomas School performed chorales in unison only on the three most solemn feasts of the church year. (This chorus also performed music for the burial services at the adjoining cemetery.) The organ at St. John's was a 10-stop instrument built in 1695 by Tobias Gottfried Trost, organ builder in Grimma at the time and father of the more famous and similarly named Heinrich Gottfried Trost.

Trost (the son) would later build the organs in Waltershausen and Altenburg. The small, pleasingly designed Trost organ at St. John's would be replaced in 1741–43 by a much larger organ built by Scheibe.

St. John's stood in the middle of a church- and graveyard known as "God's Acre," not far from the hospital. The original church, which dated to at least 1399, had been destroyed and rebuilt in the sixteenth century and had been most recently renovated in 1670. The building was 142 feet long, 27 feet high, and 46 feet wide (approximately 43 × 8 × 14 meters). A small tower held two bells. (The baroque tower that can be seen in so many depictions of the church was built in 1746–49.) The pulpit, which is now owned by the City History Museum Leipzig, had been carved by Valentin Silbermann in 1586; the altar was inherited from St. Nicholas's in 1607; the walls were hung with epitaphs and portraits of pastors; the ceiling was flat and covered with painted panels, the crest of the city of Leipzig in their middle. The Trost organ stood in the *Schülerchor*, which was in the middle of the balcony on the west wall. It had been erected under the authority of master builder and board member Georg Winckler and had been funded "in substantial part"[9] by a legacy from a nurse of the hospital, one Elisabeth Schützerin.

But musical tastes change, and organs are by no means immune from alteration, even when the cost is considerable. By the time Bach died in 1750, two years after the death of Scheibe, almost everything was different. Major changes to Leipzig's organs had transpired even before Bach returned in 1723 to take up his position as music director for the City of Leipzig and kantor of the St. Thomas School, and many more changes occurred over the next thirty or so years. It may come as a surprise that almost all these changes were carried out by Scheibe. When we talk about the organs of Leipzig at the time of Bach, we are primarily talking about organs that were repaired, maintained, altered, rebuilt, built, tuned, and, yes, guarded and sustained by Johann Scheibe, the organ builder who is the focus of this study.

2 The Life and Work of Johann Scheibe

My father distinguished himself by his profound knowledge of
organ building and has for many years now been organ builder to
the honorable University of Leipzig. . . . He successfully built the
large organ in the University Church there, which is without doubt
one of the largest and most beautiful in all of Germany.
—Johann Adolph Scheibe, 1748

On 30 May 1968, in an act that still defies comprehension, the ruling
Socialist Unity Party blew up what remained of St. Paul's Church at Leipzig
University, a building that had been only marginally damaged during World
War II bombing. The organ destroyed that fateful day was no longer the instrument built by Scheibe and examined by Bach in 1717 but an organ built by
Johann Gottlob Mende in 1843 that had been renovated a number of times
since. The large modern organ that Scheibe built for the university is recover-
able now only from a facade engraving, the disposition published in 1718, and
the tantalizing story revealed by the handwritten memoranda, minutes, and
financial records preserved primarily by Leipzig University. Scheibe's magnum
opus is not all that has been lost, however. Scheibe worked as organ builder
and instrument maker in Leipzig for more than 40 years and built or rebuilt
all of Leipzig's organs, but all that remains are his small organ in Zschortau
and an organ bench and the key desk from the organ he built for St. John's.
Even the one remaining pipe from the St. John's organ—74 centimeters high,
a facade pipe of polished tin, composed of separate pieces soldered together
in a spiral shape, a pipe once owned by collector Wilhelm Heyer of Cologne
and that still existed in 1910—has disappeared.[1]

The only sources for the month and year of Scheibe's birth are his burial record and wind chest inscription:

A 68-year-old man, organ builder Johann Scheibe, [buried] at St. Paul's [on 4 September 1748].[2]

Completed 22 August 1742 by Johann Scheibe, currently organ maker at the Honorable University of Leipzig, 62 years [of age] in May.[3]

When Scheibe was buried in September 1748, he was 68 years of age; when he completed a wind chest for the organ at St. John's in August 1742, he had turned 62 in May of that year. The inscription, which first appeared in 1867 in the *Neue Zeitschrift für Musik*, was discovered in the St. John's organ by the organ builder Friedrich Ladegast when he was making repairs and minor changes to the organ. The place of his birth is not mentioned, but an 18th-century Leipzig source refers to Scheibe as having come from "Schorta" or Zschortau,[4] a village about 20 kilometers/12 miles north of Leipzig, and, although birth records for 1680 are missing, there are numerous references to Scheibes in Zschortau: Maria and Martin Scheibe (d. 1700)—who may have been Scheibe's parents—baptized four children in Zschortau in the period 1691 to 1698;[5] in 1704 a young man named Johann Scheibe stood as godfather to Magdalena Barth, of Zschortau;[6] Johann Scheibe's wife stood as godmother to the son of Zschortau's schoolmaster and organist, Georg Heinrich Moyses, in April 1717; and in the same year a payment was made to Scheibe for repairs, apparently to the 11-stop organ that had been built by Johann Christoph Hennig.[7]

Scheibe married Anna Rosina Hesse, a Leipzig citizen, on 9 November 1705. Originally residing in the Querstrasse, by 1710 Scheibe and his family had moved to St. Paul's College at the University of Leipzig. He and Anna Rosina had four boys, all of whom were baptized at St. Nicholas's. Only Johann Adolph survived early childhood. Johann Adolph's younger brother died as a three-year-old in the family's rooms at St. Paul's; the other two children both died within a year of their births.[8]

It is not known with whom Johann Scheibe learned organ building; both Christoph Donat I, of Leipzig, and Eugenio Casparini, who worked in Italy from approximately 1640 until 1697 and whose career culminated with the organ he and his son built in Görlitz from 1697 to 1703, have been suggested.[9] The first evidence of Scheibe's organ-building activity in Leipzig appears in the account books for St. Nicholas's, where in fiscal year 1706–7 Scheibe and Christoph Donat II each were paid four taler for repairs to the organ. Donat I had been buried in Leipzig on 17 August 1706, but members of the Donat family—Christoph Donat

II, his son Johann Christoph Gottlob, and his brother Johann Jacob (known by the surname Donati)—continued to make repairs to Leipzig's organs. Not until after Donat II had died in 1713, and his brother and son (whose last repairs in Leipzig were in 1718) had left, did Scheibe take over the almost exclusive care of Leipzig's organs.

Scheibe maintained all of Leipzig's organs. Except for the years 1726–29, when he was absent from Leipzig, Scheibe carried out maintenance and tuning at St. Nicholas's (with a couple of interruptions) from 1706 to 1736, at St. John's from 1712, at St. Thomas's from 1713, at St. Paul's from 1716, and at the New Church from Easter 1718. Scheibe renovated the organs in the three main churches in the 1720s. He "completely and fully repaired" the large organ at St. Thomas's in 1720–21, he thoroughly rebuilt the New Church organ in 1721–22, and he renovated the organ at St. Nicholas's in 1724–25. Around 1730, Scheibe began retuning all of Leipzig's large organs during major cleanings and overhauls: in 1730 at St. Thomas's; in 1732 at the New Church; in 1733 at St. Nicholas's. Scheibe recommended cleaning (and tuning) at St. Paul's in 1730, too, but it was 1736 before the university approved the work. There were also general overhauls—and some major changes—in the 1740s. In 1740 Scheibe removed the small organ from St. Thomas's and reused some of its pipework for a new organ, built 1741–43, at St. John's. Scheibe overhauled the New Church's organ in 1746 and in 1747 carried out a major overhaul of the large organ at St. Thomas's.

Scheibe also built (or rebuilt) several organs in villages near Leipzig. Records are far from complete, but it is certain he built organs for Gundorf (examined in 1713) and Zschortau (1744–46). He also built or repaired organs in Stötteritz (1709–10),[10] Wachau (1716),[11] Löbnitz (around 1717),[12] and Glesien (1718),[13] although little is known about these (probably) one-manual instruments. There is no evidence to support the assertion that he also built in Zscheila (near Meissen).[14] As was usual for organ builders at the time, Scheibe also built stringed keyboard instruments—at least this is what one infers from his claim in 1732 that his joiner had "two *corpora* and cases" under construction for "an entirely newly invented musical instrument" Scheibe intended to show His Majesty the King of Poland and Elector of Saxony—Friedrich August I—at the upcoming birthday celebration.[15] Also, as is quoted in full below, in 1765 a Leipzig newspaper carried an advertisement for "a *Clavier*" built by "the famous organ builder Scheibe."

The largest project Scheibe undertook was the renovation of the organ at St. Paul's. Scheibe agreed in 1710 to move, repair, and expand—modestly—the three-manual, 36-stop organ. The rebuild and expansion, which turned out to be

extensive, took place in two phases, from 1710 to 1712 and from 1715 to 1716, and
the official examination, by Bach, took place more than a year after the organ
had been completed, in December 1717. As is described later in the book, the
rebuild started accidentally, and other options were considered, including having
Gottfried Silbermann build a completely new organ. No disposition proposal
from Scheibe exists, and it is unclear exactly when the university decided—or
agreed—to expand the organ by nearly 20 stops. Scheibe worked steadily and
with great devotion, even while the rebuild was officially suspended. In spite of
many difficulties, in November 1716 he completed his magnum opus, a three-
manual, 54-stop organ with Hauptwerk, Brustwerk, Hinterwerk (Echo), and
Pedal divisions. When he published the disposition and something about the
project's history in 1718, Leipzig historian Christoph Ernst Sicul remarked that
the organ "can be counted among the greatest achievements in all of Germany."[16]

Scheibe had at least two apprentices. Christian Francke was a joiner who
had been working for Scheibe for 14 years when, in 1732, he got caught up in a
dispute with the joiners' guild in Leipzig. (Carpenters and joiners belonged to
guilds and organ builders did not. The two trades often used the same tools and
did work similar to that done by woodworkers, so it was not unusual for conflict
to arise between them.) In the affidavit he provided, Scheibe certified that he
had employed Francke "in my organ building and instrument manufacture,
both in the country, and in the city, and on the organs of the churches here, and
he has assisted me with handwork, and also, by much diligence, guidance and
instruction, I have brought him to the point that he can build my wind chests,
stop knobs, bellows, pipes, cases, and other woodwork, as well as make tin pipe
sheets according to my wishes."[17] It is not known how long Francke continued
to work with Scheibe.

Another organ builder, Johann Hinrich Jentz, worked with Scheibe in the
1740s. Jentz witnessed Scheibe's signature on the Zschortau contract and worked
on the organ Scheibe built there in 1744–46. He left an inscription in the Manual
wind chest of this organ indicating that he came from Lübeck.[18] In the year or
so immediately following Scheibe's death, Jentz was paid for tuning and repairs
at St. Nicholas's, St. Thomas's, and St. John's.[19] In September 1748 he unsuccessfully applied to the university to be Scheibe's successor[20] and appears to have left
Leipzig in the fall of 1750. J. Adolph Bästel may also have been an apprentice.
Bästel worked primarily in Thuringia, claimed to have been an organ builder
in Leipzig, and proposed building a stop associated with Scheibe, the "Viol di
Gamba naturell."[21]

Scheibe remained in Leipzig as an organ builder until his death in 1748. But there was a hiatus. In 1725, 20 years after he had established himself in Leipzig and only a few months after his son Johann Adolph had matriculated as a law student at the university, Scheibe apparently decided to seek his fortune elsewhere. He had just completed a major renovation of the organ at St. Nicholas's, and, for "a project well done," on 22 December 1725 the city council had awarded him a gratuity of 40 taler. On the same day, Scheibe received a gratuity of 40 taler in recognition of his "demonstrable diligence" during the organ repair several years earlier at St. Thomas's. He also was given 20 taler "as a gratuity for the organ repair recently concluded at the New Church."[22] Shortly thereafter, Scheibe left Saxony in order to "build several organs in a certain principality." No one knows where he went. He returned to Leipzig some three or four years later, promises of work unmet, his son reported, and "in utter poverty."[23] Around 1730 he again took up his work in Leipzig. Johann Adolph would later claim that his father's departure from Leipzig and the subsequent lack of family support caused him to give up his study of jurisprudence at Leipzig University, a program he had begun in 1725. (He thereafter devoted himself entirely to music.)

Johann Adolph grew up in his father's organ-building shop, where, at the age of 10, he lost an eye in an accident caused by the carelessness of one of his father's apprentices. "I was educated in organ building from an early age and witnessed the construction of some of the largest and most valuable organs in Saxony," he wrote in 1748 in the introduction to his detailed and well-informed evaluation of a proposal from Johann Dietrich Busch to rebuild the organ in Gottorf.[24] To Johann Mattheson he reported that "from experience and habit from my earliest years on, I became very knowledgeable about organ building." Johann Adolph claimed to have educated himself by reading music treatises, and there is no evidence that he was a student of Bach.[25] After withdrawing from the university, he was active in Leipzig until 1735 as a teacher, performer, and composer. Many of his compositions were performed at the New Church.[26] In a recommendation provided in 1731, New Church organist Carl Gotthelf Gerlach reported that "on many occasions [Johann Adolph] did a fine job playing the organ for me during church services here and he also played an accomplished continuo in the concerted music. As well, in various musical pieces he demonstrated great success in composition."[27] In his application to become organist on the Silbermann organ in Freiberg Cathedral in 1731, Johann Adolph spoke both of his organ-building expertise, learned from his father, and of his facility and acquaintance with Leipzig's organs: "Also, from the building and repairing of various organs which my father, a well-known Leipzig organ builder, carried out in various places, I have achieved great knowledge of organs, and can play them according to their strength [*nach ihrer Force*], and I know my way around them, and have also, here in Leipzig, practiced on the organs daily."[28]

Johann Adolph's organ-building expertise was on full display in several entries in *Der Critische Musicus*, a journal edited (and written) by him in Hamburg. (The two volumes originally published in 1738 and 1740 were combined and expanded in the 1745 edition.) He defended the existence of mutations and mixtures in organs when they were under attack in the 1740s, arguing that they were essential for filling a church with sound and for supporting a congregation.[29] Two issues (7 and 14 July 1739) were dedicated to an extensive exploration of the qualities that make a "true and well-grounded" organist: knowledge of continuo, chorales, preluding, and the organ. In another issue (1 September 1739) he published a letter dated 12 August 1739 criticizing Christian Lorenz, court organist in Altenburg, for choices made during Heinrich Gottfried Trost's construction of the new organ.[30] (Johann Adolph disapproved of the decision to build a two-manual rather than a three-manual instrument and the attempt, only partially successful, to tune the organ in equal temperament. Johann Adolph Scheibe, Johann Sebastian Bach, and probably also Johann Scheibe visited the Trost organ in Altenburg a short while before its examination by officials from Gotha in October 1739.)

For a while, Johann Adolph considered becoming a professional organist. But he was not appointed in Freiberg, where he submitted testimonials both from Gerlach and Bach—Bach testified that Johann Adolph was "thoroughly at home not only on the clavier and violin but also in composition"[31]—and he also was unsuccessful in 1735 and 1736 in Prague, Gotha, Sondershausen, and Wolfenbüttel. Nor had he been appointed organist at St. Nicholas's when, at a mere 21 years of age, he was one of six candidates who applied in December 1729. On that occasion Bach had been the examiner, and Johann Adolph later described political machinations that had not worked in his favor: "Because of the falseness and back-biting of a certain man, who owed his happiness to my father, and pressure from his friends, on a certain occasion a stranger, whom I still had to teach music to afterwards, was preferred. And a while after this, when another position was being filled, because of 'apron strings,' another [candidate] was preferred to me. So, I finally changed my goal and decided to give up pursuing a career as organist." Johann Adolph did not identify the occasions further, but the first incident no doubt occurred in 1729, when the position of organist at St. Nicholas's, vacant because Johann Gottlieb Görner was moving to St. Thomas's, was awarded to Johann Schneider, a native of Oberlauter (Bavaria). Between Schneider's appointment by the city council on 24 December 1729 and his confirmation by the consistory on 3 August 1730, the position at St. Nicholas's was filled by Karl Hartwig, another unsuccessful candidate for the position. (Hartwig, who later became organist and music director at St. John's in Zittau, was born in Olbernhau, Saxony.) The second incident probably related to Johann Adolph's attempt to become cathedral organist in Freiberg in 1731, but whatever strings were pulled, if any, so that Johann Christian Erselius was appointed instead remain unknown. Johann Adolph went on to serve as Kapellmeister to Margrave Friedrich Ernst of Brandenburg-Culmbach in 1739 and to be appointed Kapellmeister to King Christian VI of Denmark in 1740. He died in Copenhagen in 1776, having remained active as composer, educator, translator, and critic.[32]

Johann Scheibe was not the only organ and instrument builder working in Leipzig. At the principal churches, harpsichord tuning and minor organ repairs were also carried out by David Apitzsch and Zacharias Hildebrandt, and positives[33] were built in 1719 for the Royal Catholic Chapel (in Pleissenburg Castle) by Johann Christoph Hennig and Christian Grimmer[34] and in 1720 for the St. Thomas School by Wahl Friedrich Ficker, of Zeitz.[35]

In village churches nearby, Scheibe, Apitzsch, Silbermann, Hildebrandt, and Michael Bach (of Mechterstädt) built small, mostly one-manual, organs (see table 1).[36] Builders competed for organ contracts and sometimes examined

TABLE 1   One-manual organs built for village churches, District of Leipzig, 1720–1750

Village	Year and Number of Stops	Builder
Rötha	1722, 11 stops	G. Silbermann
Störmthal	1723, 14 stops	Z. Hildebrandt
Liebertwolkwitz	1725, 13 stops	Z. Hildebrandt
Leutzsch	1729, at least 8 stops	D. Apitzsch
Lindenau	1732, 10 stops	Z. Hildebrandt
Eutritzsch	1736, 10 stops	Z. Hildebrandt
Zschortau	1746, 13 stops	J. Scheibe
Wiederitzsch	1748, 10 stops	Z. Hildebrandt
Probstheida	1748, 10 stops	Michael Bach (Mechterstädt)*

*For information on the Probstheida organ, including the examination report by Johann Gottlieb Görner and Johann Georg Hille, see Kraft 1957, 85–86.

the completed instruments of their competitors. Three of these occasions are well known. Silbermann visited Leipzig in 1710 and proposed building a completely new three-manual, 44-stop organ at the university, a proposal sternly criticized by Daniel Vetter, Leipzig's most senior and respected organist, and ultimately rejected. There was the severe examination by Hildebrandt (and J. S. Bach) of Scheibe's new organ at St. John's, and the examination in 1746 by Silbermann (and J. S. Bach) of Hildebrandt's largest organ, at St. Wenceslas's (Wenzelkirche) in Naumburg. There were other occasions as well. Scheibe joined Görner in examining the organ Apitzsch had completed in 1729 for St. Laurence's in Leutzsch (now part of Leipzig), the contract for which Apitzsch had obtained when he underbid Scheibe by a mere nine taler (see chapter 10). In 1731 Schneider evaluated proposals submitted by Apitzsch and Hildebrandt for a new organ in the church in Lindenau and recommended Hildebrandt's proposal and work. Writing to the superintendent in Merseburg with notification of its support, the Leipzig city council dryly noted that Hildebrandt was willing to do the work for less.[37]

It has often been reported that Scheibe succeeded Christoph Donat—either father or son—as university organ builder, but even though Scheibe worked for the university from 1710 on, he was not officially given responsibility for maintaining the St. Paul's organ until April 1718, a few months after the organ's official examination and acceptance by the university, although the appointment was made effective from Michaelmas 1717 and the organ was under warranty for a year before that. Coincidentally or not, 1718 was the same year a last payment was made to an organ builder in the Donat family (when Johann Christoph Gottlob Donat received an annual fee for maintenance of the New Church organ). Builders were not appointed to the position of university organ builder; whoever maintained the university organ assumed the title, and there were no particular statutes or rules governing the post.[38] Donat II had worked alongside his father—in 1703 they jointly signed the contract for the new organ

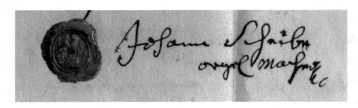

2. Johann Scheibe's signature and seal. Stadtarchiv Leipzig,
Rechnung des Hospitals zu St. Johannis, 1745, fol. 103.

at the New Church—and may have continued to maintain the university organ after his father's death in 1706. University records show that wages were paid regularly (from 1685) up to 1710, the year that Scheibe was hired to dismantle the organ for its rebuilding, and began again in 1720 (with retroactive payments for 1717–18 and 1718–19).[39] Memoranda that Scheibe submitted to the university throughout the St. Paul's organ project are signed "Johann Scheibe, Organ Builder" or "Johann Scheibe, Organ Builder in Leipzig." It is very likely that Scheibe did not refer to himself as university organ builder before 1718.

Scheibe's relationship with Leipzig University was fraught. There was the organ project itself, which started simply and grew ever more complex. Renovations can be unpredictable, as is well known, and moving, repairing, rebuilding, and expanding the three-manual organ at St. Paul's was never going to be easy, but Scheibe's work was made immeasurably more difficult by the university's recalcitrance. During the first phase of the project, decisions were made piecemeal, Scheibe's contract was left unsigned, work was held up for lack of materials, and the project was suspended before Scheibe had finished. His recommendations—whether for protecting pipework from damage from the elements or for timely cleaning and maintenance—were not acted upon promptly. Further, the rooms Scheibe lived and worked in at St. Paul's College were uncomfortable and unhealthy—two of his babies died there—and yet the university was charging him rent at three times the previous rate and did not offer free accommodation during the organ's major rebuild, as was common practice. Finally, in spite of Bach's supportive examination report and his recommendation that Scheibe be paid for additional but necessary work, the university bargained stiffly and then delayed payment. Nevertheless, Scheibe maintained and cared for the university's organ throughout his career.

Scheibe had "a clever mind"[40] and took credit for a number of inventions, such as reed stops that required little tuning and improvements that allowed an organ to operate well at a low wind pressure. He described three of his inventions in an article he published in 1732 in *Neue Zeitungen von Gelehrten Sachen* (see appendix A-31), a semiweekly newspaper in Leipzig that reported on scientific findings. According to Scheibe, he had worked out these ideas during more than 20 years of steady organ building to which he had applied "notable industriousness and ingenuity." He first described the transmissions he had built in the St. Paul's organ, which made six Hauptwerk stops also playable in the Pedal. This was a huge advantage when voices crossed. As he pointed out, even if a note was already being played—in the manual, say—when it was played at the same time in the other division, the pedal, one could "hear a new and distinct attack, making one think that another pipe had spoken."[41] (Although Scheibe took credit for inventing transmissions, they had been built previously—by members of the Compenius family, for example.)

Scheibe's second invention allowed the player to raise or lower the organ's pitch so that it matched a solo instrument (an oboe or traverso, for example). He discovered that he could maintain optimal wind pressure with only about a third of the normal weight on the bellows. Not only did the organ have the necessary "force and sharpness," but the wind supply was more even and accurate. Scheibe described a small two-manual, 12-stop instrument (that included Fagott 16′ in the Pedal) he had built in 1731. With two one-pound weights, one two-pound weight, and one four-pound weight, eight variations of wind pressure (and pitch) were possible. His experiment also showed, he noted, that, depending on the size of the instrument, it could be played without weights entirely and yet one could be "quite content" with its low wind pressure.[42] Exactly such an instrument was advertised on page 10 of the 12 January 1765 edition of the *Leipziger Intelligenz-Blatt:* "An ingenious positive [organ] built by the famous

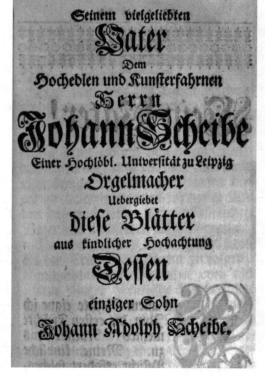

3. "To his much beloved father, the most noble and skillful Herr Johann Scheibe, organ builder to the Most Honorable University in Leipzig, his only son, Johann Adolph Scheibe, with filial respect dedicates these pages." Johann Adolph Scheibe, *Der Critische Musicus,* 1738. Public domain.

organ builder Scheibe, with two manuals and 13 registers, coupler, and a Pedal division with Fagott Bass 16′, which can be played or pumped with or without weights, as well as a *Clavier* by said Scheibe . . . are for sale."[43]

His third invention, also made in 1731, was a stop that sounded like a reed even though it had none of the usual parts of a reed— shallot, resonator, tuning wire, or tongue. It had "the effect of a reed and at the same time it is more delicate, because one hears a flute along with it. It is even more beautiful than the so-called Vox humana," he wrote.[44] Further, like all fluework, it did not require frequent tuning. Scheibe never published the detailed description of his inventions he promised, but a few years later they were briefly described by his son, who observed that such originality differentiated his father from other organ builders: "In truth, organ builders are rare who aside from their scalings, plane, and tuning knife, also possess insight into mathematics and physics."[45]

Not to be forgotten is Scheibe's renowned voicing skill. He was particularly praised for his Viol di Gamba stop, which Sicul called "the most extraordinary stop" in the St. Paul's organ. The Viol di Gamba imitated the sound of the stringed instrument; it was very difficult to build because of its narrow scaling and demanded not only a master builder but a generous budget, for it was expensive. When Scheibe undertook revoicing the existing Viol di Gamba in the Donat organ in Leipzig's New Church, the examiners praised the result. Scheibe had used "his unique art" to give the stop its "proper, gamba-like tone," and the organists were delighted that it was so delicate.[46] In Zschortau Scheibe said he would build the Viol di Gamba stop "gratis, as an everlasting memorial," and although we cannot know for certain, it seems he built this rare and time-consuming register there to honor his birthplace.[47]

Scheibe had admirers among his contemporaries—not only his son, Johann Adolph, but also Johann Burchard Mencke and Bach. Johann Adolph dedicated the 1738 edition of *Der Critische Musicus* to his father, noting that the organ at St. Paul's was a fitting monument to the skill and experience of its builder. In 1748 he wrote that his father, "who is a very well-known organ builder [in Saxony], brought all of the organs in Leipzig into their present condition, partly by building new [organs], partly by making important major improvements [to existing organs]."[48] Mencke, professor and rector at Leipzig University and an advisor to the king, brought his influence and leadership to bear on the organ project, seeing it to completion in 1716. Writing to his fellow professors at the conclusion of the project, Mencke described Scheibe's diligence and devotion and pressed them not only to pay Scheibe for his extra work but to provide this "wretchedly poor man" an appropriate gratuity at the time of the

My father!

With good reason I dedicate to him the first fruits of my reflections. My filial duty requires this, and I give in to this urge with much greater pleasure than those people who, from avarice, add a large introduction dedicated to a rich man.

I cannot request any protection here, for I want to defend my writings myself. I also cannot expect a kind or gracious reception, for I am removed from all self-interest. And I cannot be afraid that it will insult my patron that I have committed my work to my father, my loving father, out of filial love.

Can anything be more pleasant than following the impulses of nature? Can anything be more honorable than publicly showing one's father examples of one's devotion? Is it not right that we should show the first results of our diligence to those who have made it possible through their fatherly care?

However, I enjoy a double pleasure. By fulfilling my duty to my father, I can at the same time show my respect to a great artist, respect he would richly deserve even if he were not so closely related to me by blood.

My father! The fame he earned from his art and his diligence deserves to be honored. The large organ in the university church in Leipzig exhibits so much that is special that foreigners, too, have seen and heard it with the greatest astonishment. The splendor, the energy, and the exceedingly comfortable and harmonious temperament of this large instrument and all other organs built by him demonstrate extensive experience and no ordinary skill. Also, I cannot refrain from introducing some of his inventions, which have come about solely from his ruminations and industriousness.

Who has ever heard, among other feats, of a single pipe that could immediately be made to speak twice? Who knew that with a little lead—yes, without even all the weights—one could give a bellows enough wind that a small organ with twelve to sixteen registers, including one at 16-foot and two at 8-foot, could maintain its full life? And who was it who finally brought about what so many great artists had for several hundred years tried in vain to accomplish, who, namely, invented a reed that has no resonator, tongue or wire but nevertheless is a reed that sounds simultaneously like a flute?

Certainly, these examples, and many others besides, clearly set him apart from other organ builders. In truth, organ builders are rare who aside from their scalings, metal plane, and tuning knife, also possess insight into mathematics and physics.

My father! I could cite so much more that would add to his renown. The role that I assume for myself imposes limits on me, because I do not want to be my family's eulogist.

Rather, I hope he will receive this musical work in the manner I wish—that is, as a father, and that he will continue to see me as he always has.

God keep him and my loving mother for many more years in lasting contentment, no one will be happier about that than,

My father!

Your obedient son,

Johann Adolph Scheibe

Hamburg, March 1738.

Source: J. A. Scheibe, *Der Critische Musicus* (1738).

organ's examination.[49] Bach came to Scheibe's defense as well. As is discussed in chapter 5, Bach's examination report was not so much critical of Scheibe, as has too often been claimed, as it was corroborative of Scheibe's own account of the difficulties he had overcome in spite of the university's lack of support. Bach (and Hildebrandt) declared Scheibe's new organ for St. John's faultless and apparently offered their support to Scheibe's demand for payment beyond the amount stipulated by the original contract (see chapter 9).

It is perhaps important to acknowledge that up until now our opinions of Scheibe as an organ builder have been formed primarily on the basis of Bach's reports and the dispositions of the three Scheibe organs Bach examined—that is, on somewhat limited information gleaned as a by-product of our exhaustive search for more knowledge about Bach as advisor and examiner of new and renovated organs. Because the examination report Bach wrote for St. Paul's has generally been interpreted as negative, despite the fact that Bach "could not praise and laud it enough,"[50] Scheibe's largest organ—"a masterpiece,"[51] an instrument seen and heard "with the greatest astonishment" by foreigners and citizens alike, whose "splendor, energy, and unusually good temperament" were a fitting monument to "the extensive experience and extraordinary skill" of its maker[52]—came to be seen as a "mediocre instrument" compared with what surely would have been a masterpiece in the hands of Silbermann,[53] an example of the decline in the art of organ building,[54] an organ exhibiting a lack of focus in its disposition, seemingly useful only for "*pleno* pieces, and interludes using a variety of stop-combinations."[55] As well, so much attention has been given to the supposition that Bach tested Scheibe's organ at St. John's severely because his son, Johann Adolph, had criticized Bach's compositional style—a "vitriolic" attack, as it was once characterized[56]—that the innovative organ itself has largely been ignored. Similarly, we know that Bach's report on Scheibe's organ in Zschortau was positive—everything was "skillfully, diligently, and well built"[57]—but the organ itself, a lively and charming instrument that is the only organ of Scheibe's to survive, has not received the attention it deserves—in spite of its recent, excellent restoration.

One 20th-century scholar expressed no ambivalence about Johann Scheibe. Paul Rubardt, who was active in Leipzig as an organ expert and writer and teacher of music and served from 1953 to 1966 as curator at the Museum of Musical Instruments of Leipzig University, praised Scheibe as "the most important Leipzig organ builder and instrument maker of the 18th century" and as "the most notable builder in Leipzig during the time of Bach." Scheibe's great organ at the University Church had brought him great fame, claimed Rubardt, and in the 20th century he was still held in high esteem "because of his brilliant technical and tonal improvements and discoveries."[58] Another Leipzig personage, Carl Ferdinand Becker, published a history of the St. Paul's organ in 1842. Becker was an organist, musicologist, music collector, and bibliographer; he served as organist at St. Nicholas's in Leipzig from 1837 to 1854 and was one of the founding members of the Bach-Gesellschaft (Bach Society) in 1850. He had this to say about Scheibe's organ: "Certainly the organ's layout was excellent and it contained a lot of sweet, strong, very unusually timbered registers. For this reason, among the organs in Leipzig, the most important organists chose the one by Scheibe, for it was here that they liked to display their virtuosity and to prove that in fact an organ built properly in all its parts is solely and alone the king of all instruments."[59]

Histories of European organ building rarely mention Scheibe. Only one of his organs, and none of his stringed keyboard instruments, survives in our time, yet when he died in 1748, 25 years after Bach took up his positions in Leipzig, Scheibe had either newly built or significantly improved all of the city's organs. As musicologist Arnold Schering observed in 1926, "For decades, year in and year out, partially in the form of complete rebuilds, [Scheibe] kept up the city's organs, and thereby, as far as resources allowed, was no doubt able to realize all the concepts that were active in the head of his great fellow citizen [Johann Sebastian Bach]."[60] Scheibe's work in Leipzig is described and evaluated in the chapters that follow. The narrative provides a context for evaluating the contradictory viewpoints mentioned above and reveals a builder who was not only reliable and competent—"honest, cheap, and hardworking," as he was once characterized by Johann Kuhnau and Vetter[61]—but an artist deserving of the praise he received for his inventiveness, his voicing abilities, and his devotion to his craft.

Scheibe worked as organ builder in Leipzig for more than 40 years. He died on 3 September 1748 and was buried the next day at St. Paul's.

3 The Organ for Zschortau

The contract has been fulfilled in each and every way, with
everything skillfully, diligently, and well built.
—Johann Sebastian Bach, 1746

The organ in Zschortau, a village about 20 kilometers/12 miles north
of Leipzig, is Scheibe's only surviving instrument. Since most of its pipework
is original, the instrument is of prime importance for understanding baroque
organ building at the time of Bach. With Principals that are "remarkably fresh,"
registration possibilities that "tend toward the romantic," and a bass register
that is strong, and supplied with a large number of 8- and 16-foot stops, this
wonderful organ, built in 1744 to 1746, is "unique among Baroque organs in
the Leipzig area."[1] Although modest in size, the organ is elegantly designed and
beautifully decorated and has a remarkable tonal palette.

St. Nicholas's in Zschortau is charming and very old. Its tower and portal are
late Romanesque and date to the 12th or 13th century, the nave is Gothic and
has vaults traced in red, the choir has remnants of ceiling paintings from the
fourteenth century, and its superb pre-Reformation altar is a carved and painted
polyptych from 1517. Central figures include the church's patron saint, Bishop
Nicholas of Myra, holding three gold balls atop a Gospel book, and the Madonna
on a crescent moon, holding the child Jesus. A heavy hand-forged key opens
the church's massive front door, whose wrought-iron reinforcing bars "end in
elegant curves, softened by the addition of horseshoe shapes."[2] (Horseshoes are
a reference to travelers, said to be protected by Saint Nicholas.)

4. St. Nicholas's, Zschortau. Photograph by Daniel Senf.

Negotiations for the new organ at St. Nicholas's took place during the summer of 1744. The organ built by Johann Christoph Hennig[3] in 1698–99 had become "unplayable and of no further use," and repairs, deemed necessary in order "to keep the congregation on pitch," had proved expensive.[4] (The organ had been renovated in 1729, when Scheibe was paid 70 taler.)[5] The church hoped to sell the old organ but the wood was worm-eaten and rotten and, in Scheibe's view, worth nothing more than the scrap value of its metal. Scheibe proposed building a new one-manual organ the same size as the old one, with eight stops in the Manual and three in the Pedal, for a fee of 560 taler.[6] In the contract signed for 500 taler on 30 June 1744, he promised to provide "a truly good and skillfully built organ with all appurtenances, including the necessary wood carvings, according to the drawing and disposition submitted"; to have the organ playable by Christmas 1745 and completely finished by the following Easter; and to provide a one-year warranty.[7] He was guaranteed transport of his tools and the parts of the organ that he would build in his workshop, as well as lodging for himself and his workers during the installation. As was usual at the time, any work done by a locksmith or blacksmith would be paid for by the church.

Scheibe must have begun work immediately on signing the contract—an inscription in the Pedal chest is dated 1744—but the organ was not ready for inspection until three months after the agreed-upon deadline, perhaps because the congregation wanted the painting and marbling of the case to be finished before the organ was examined. On 13 July 1746 the pastor wrote to his superintendent telling him that as soon as the painter had finished, the organ could be "given over" by the builder. The town's patron, Heinrich August Sahrer von Sahr, had suggested this happen on the ninth Sunday after Trinity, and the pastor asked whether this date was convenient or whether the following week would be preferable and whether the superintendent would like to give the dedication sermon. He informed him that "Kapellmeister Bach of Leipzig has been commissioned to examine the instrument."[8] Superintendent Johann Paul Streng agreed to give a sermon, and Bach's examination took place on 7 August 1746. Shortly thereafter, the pastor sent payment—cash in the amount of 9 taler 6 groschen and barley worth 18 groschen—and asked the superintendent to forward the enclosed "report of Herr Kapellmeister Bach's examination of the newly built organ" to Sahrer von Sahr's administrator, Andreas Christian Brandes.[9] Bach was paid 5 taler 12 groschen for the examination and report.[10]

Bach's brief but positive report is one of only seven organ reports by Bach that have been preserved.[11] He assured Sahrer von Sahr that Scheibe had fulfilled the contract in every way and that the organ was "skillfully, diligently, and well built." Scheibe had already taken care of the few minor problems that had existed, and there was no major fault. Further, Scheibe had surpassed the contract by building three wooden stops, one metal stop, and an *Angehänge* (a coupler between the Manual and the Pedal), none of which was required by the agreement. The report that is deposited in the British Library is dated 7 August 1746 and is in the hand of an unknown scribe but with Bach's autograph signature. Another copy, dated 8 August 1746, also in the hand of an unknown scribe and neither signed nor sealed by Bach, was recently discovered in Delitzsch, not far from Leipzig.[12]

Scheibe's fee was to be paid in three installments: 100 taler on the signing of the contract; 200 taler once the pipes, chests, and bellows were delivered; and the remaining 200 taler after the organ was examined and accepted, but he received the 500-taler fee in eleven uneven amounts, paid between July 1744 and August 1746:[13]

1 July 1744	100 T.
8 December 1744	100 T.
2 May 1745	100 T.
28 October 1745	60 T.
29 November 1745	20 T.

19 December 1745	20 T.
28 March 1746	15 T.
28 April 1746	25 T.
17 June 1746	15 T.
2 August 1746	5 T.
11 August 1746	40 T.

Beyond contract payments to Scheibe, expenses related to the organ and its examination and dedication included these:[14]

For making an organ railing	8 gr.
To the mason for 6 days' labor to make a window and for cutting a hole in the wall (for the organ)	1 T. 18 gr.
To the carpenter and two apprentices for 6 days' labor	3 T. 6 gr.
To the organ builder's apprentices for building the bellows room	18 gr.
For two beams (*Jocken*) for the organ	1 gr.
Housing ("bed and resting place") for the apprentices	5 T.
For wood and boards for the new organ	3 T. 10 gr.
To Bach, for examining the organ and writing a report	5 T. 12 gr.
For the celebratory meal	10 T. 22 gr. 5 pf.
To the superintendent for the sermon (in cash)	9 T. 6 gr.
To the administrator for recording the proceedings	2 T. 18 gr.
To the lacquerer	40 T.
For picking up the lacquerer	8 gr.
To the sculptor	8 T. 12 gr.
To the smith	9 T. 2 gr. 6 pf.
A gratuity to the organ builder's assistants	5 T.
To the bellows pumper for 83 days of labor	12 T. 2 gr. 6 pf.
Subsequent payment to Herr Scheibe	60 T.

Scheibe designed and built the case and, according to his contract, also was responsible for the carvings (such as pipe shades). It remains unclear, then, why the church paid a sculptor 8 taler 12 groschen, but perhaps Scheibe paid for basic ornamental carvings and the church paid for "extraordinary" work. As well, the congregation, not the organ builder, paid for the expense of a bellows pumper. (A bellows pumper not only pumped the bellows while the organ was voiced but also did odd jobs.) Scheibe's 5-taler contribution toward the cost of "painting the organ"[15] perhaps offset the cost of the special marquetry that was done on the key desk (see below), which may have been perceived by the person keeping the records as a kind of "painting" or "decoration."

The church received a number of gifts to help pay for the organ. Frau Mayin contributed 1 taler 8 groschen, Hanß Thierbach gave 16 groschen, Christoph

Bach's report on the organ in Zschortau

Since His Highborn Lord, Herr Heinrich August Sahrer von Sahr, Hereditary Liege Lord and Magistrate of Zschortau and Biesen, as Most Respected Patron of the Church of Zschortau has requested me, the undersigned, to go through and examine in said church the organ newly built by Johann Scheibe of Leipzig; and, in the presence of said Lord of Sahr, I painstakingly went through it part by part, tried it out, and carefully compared it with the original contract put before me, drawn up between the inspectors and Herr Scheibe on 30th June 1744; and have found not only that the contract has been fulfilled in each and every way, with everything skillfully, diligently, and well built, and with the exception of a few minor problems that Herr Scheibe took care of on the spot, there is nowhere a major fault, rather there are the following stops built over and above the contract, namely,

1. Quinta Thön 16', of wood
2. Viola di Gamba 8', of wood
3. Fleute-Travers 4', of wood
4. Super Octava', *Metall*
5. A coupler [*Angehänge*] between Manual and Pedal,

all of which were found and adjudged to be durably made and good.

Therefore, in the interest of truth, and to the renown of the builder, I have wished to attest to the same over my own signature and with my own seal affixed.

Dated: Zschortau, 7 August 1746.

Joh. Sebast. Bach

Royal Pol. and Elect. Sax.

Court Composer

Sources: Wolff and Zepf 2012, 147–48, citing *NBR*, 221 (no. 235); and Bach-Dokumente I, 168–69 (no. 89). The original document, Add. Ms. 33965, fol. 168–69, is held by the British Library, London.

Beyer gave 8 groschen, Hirschberger (the Zschortau ferrier and armorer) gave 1 taler, and the Lords of Sahr, Böltzig, and Egidi contributed 15 taler. Old oak from the previous organ was valued at 7 groschen, and, as just noted, Scheibe contributed 5 taler toward "painting the organ."[16] (Unaccountably, the total received, 23 taler 15 groschen, is remarkably lower than the 111 aßo 8 groschen contributed for the new organ in 1698–99.[17] An aßo [Alte Schock] was worth 20 groschen; a guilder, 21 groschen; a taler, 24 groschen.)

Not only is the Zschortau organ the only Scheibe instrument that has survived, but a large proportion of the pipework—85 percent, or 569 out of 668 pipes—is original. As such, the organ's importance for revealing the tonal character of Scheibe's instruments and for understanding Scheibe's building methods cannot be overestimated, and a detailed description of the organ, based primarily on the thorough report prepared by Konrad Dänhardt, chief restorer for Hermann Eule Orgelbau, the organ-building company based in Bautzen, Germany, follows.[18]

Case and Facade

The organ is splendidly decorated—with marbled panels, gilded carvings and cornices, and a gloriole in the center. The original color palette was revealed in 2009, during one of the most demanding and technologically complex restorations ever undertaken in Saxony, according to the restorers Christine Kelm and Anke Noczinski. (Not only were there approximately six different kinds of marbling but also imitations of blue quartz and burl-wood veneer. Even the gilding was done using various techniques and with different kinds of metal leaf. Also, because the binder for the paints was almost always natural resin, the baroque paints were extremely sensitive to the solvents that were used to remove the imitation wood painting that had been applied in the 19th century.)

The three-part facade is angularly concave—that is, there is a flat middle section with 11 facade pipes that is slightly recessed from the two outer sections, each with 14 pipes, which both project forward a bit at their outside edges. Further, the outer pipe fields have a trapezoidal shape; their cornices are convex while the cornice over the large middle flat of pipes is concave. The largest facade pipe is placed in the middle, the rest of the pipes arranged in alternation to the left and right of the center pipe, so that the smallest pipes are at the outside edges of the facade. (The pipes on one side form a whole-tone scale on C and those on the other a whole-tone scale on $C_\sharp$.) This diatonic arrangement can produce a pyramid shape, but this effect has been reduced dramatically here in Zschortau by the trapezoidal shape of the outer fields and by the lengthening of the pipe feet as the pipes get smaller, their mouths creating a fairly sharp upward curve. Overall, it is a very elegant, fluid design. Because of the decorative distribution of facade pipes in Scheibe's organs, Paul Rubardt described his facades as "ornamental" and saw them as representative of the changes occurring in the rococo period.[19]

Only 39 of the Principal's 48 pipes, from F–g^2, their Roman mouths scribed, are in the facade. Their dark, earthy appearance—they are not highly polished—blends perfectly with the elegant, rococo decoration of the rest of the restored case. The Pedal division is located behind the organ, separated from the main case by a walkway, and while the main case is covered with top and side panels, the Pedal, which is not visible from the nave of the church, has no top, and its

5. Organ built by Johann Scheibe in 1744–46 for St. Nicholas's, Zschortau. Photograph by Daniel Senf.

panels go up only to the level of the moldings. After its recent restoration—the organ itself by Hermann Eule Orgelbau in 2000, the case by the Saxon State Office for the Preservation of Monuments (Landesamt für Denkmalpflege Sachsen) in 2009—the organ is painted with gray and auburn marbling, and its pipe shades and carvings are gilded.

Bellows and Wind Pressure

The wind system originally consisted of three wedge bellows that were housed in the church tower. As the restorers discovered, Scheibe built frame bellows, a construction in which the boards are rabbeted together within a frame rather than glued together to make a board.[20] The two methods for building wedge bellows are described in Johann Julius Seidel's organ handbook, first published in 1844: "Either the top and lower boards are built from two-inch to three-inch boards [that are glued together]—these are called board bellows [*Bohlen-Bälge*]—or frames the same strength as a door frame are filled with 2½″ boards [that are rabbeted together], which are called frame bellows [*Rahmen-Bälge*]. As experience shows, when meticulously built of good materials, both types can be durable."[21]

Frame bellows were favored by Heinrich Gottfried Trost, who stipulated that the boards be three inches thick and that the bellows be built "with rabbeted-together frames [frame bellows], and not from boards that are glued together [board bellows], which are useless."[22] In a contract signed in 1720, for the organ in Großstöbnitz, Trost promised to build "2 large single-fold bellows . . . with a pushed-together frame with three-inch boards covered with horse veins."[23] Trost scholar and organist Felix Friedrich has observed that frame bellows are extremely stable and not as susceptible to changing temperatures and weather conditions as board bellows.[24] Indeed, it was the only construction Trost used for his single-fold wedge bellows. (In Zschortau, not enough of Scheibe's original wind system survived for it to be reconstructed during the 2000 restoration. The restorers constructed two new board bellows using Scheibe's outside measurements. A third bellows, should it be desired, can be added at any time.)

It also appears Scheibe may have employed one of his inventions in this organ: a means by which, from a stop knob at the keyboard, the player could regulate the wind pressure in the bellows and thus the pitch of the organ. The restorers were unable to determine exactly how this might have been accomplished, but they believed the presence of such a system was indicated by the original (frame) construction of the bellows and by the partial remains of a connection between keyboard and bellows.[25] It would have been a great advantage to the organist if the organ's pitch could have been changed—from Chorton to Cammerton, say—thus eliminating the need for transposition. In the article Scheibe published in Leipzig in 1732,[26] he describes a different means of accomplishing this: "On the bellows of a small instrument built here in 1731 by [Scheibe], which consisted of 12 stops, 2 manuals, and had a Fagott 16' in the Pedal, he had not more than 8 pounds of weights: two one-pounders, a two-pounder, and one four-pound piece. These allow the [pitch of the] instrument to be raised or lowered, higher or lower, eight times, and also they can removed altogether, without anything being out-of-tune or false. Thus, if an oboe or traverso is somewhat too high or too low, one can immediately make the organ higher or lower." The wind pressure in the restored Zschortau organ is 55 mm WC.

Wind Chests

The wind chests are divided into a C-side on the left and a C♯-side on the right. Except for the long sides of the grid frame and the pallet box, which were made of spruce, Scheibe used oak for all parts of the wind chest: frame, bars, sponsels, pallets, bungboards, toeboards, bearers, and sliders.[27] Scheibe covered the hinged pallets with a double layer of sheep's leather. The brass wires connecting the pallets to the trackers were given leather pouches or *Pulpeten,* which prevent wind from escaping through the small holes drilled into the floor of the pallet box. Scheibe's wind chests are sponselled—that is, rather than one large glued-up wooden panel, a board, covering the channels, individual wood pieces called sponsels are glued between the channel tops. Here, again, Scheibe built differently than Zacharias Hildebrandt and Gottfried Silbermann, who used table boards. (The boards have to be crosscut boards that are very carefully chosen from the middle cut of a tree trunk.)[28]

There are three inscriptions in the wind chests. "Johann Scheibe currently organ builder at the Honorable Leipzig University 1744" was found on the bottom board of the Pedal pallet box; "Johann Scheibe Orgelmacher Anno 1745" appears in an empty C-side channel in the Pedal wind chest; and "Johann Hinrich Jentz von Lübeck 1745" was discovered on the frame of the C-side Manual wind chest.[29] (Jentz was Scheibe's apprentice in the 1740s; see chapter 2.)

Windkoppel

As one of the extras, Scheibe provided the organ with a mechanical connection between the Manual and the Pedal ("ein Angehänge zum Manual und Pedal"). Homer Blanchard assumed, correctly, that Scheibe constructed pedal channels in the manual chest,[30] a construction sometimes called *Windkoppel* (wind coupler). Any time a register is pulled on in the manual, that same register also plays in the pedal—that is, the pedal is permanently coupled to the manual.

As constructed by Hildebrandt and Silbermann, each channel is divided and closed with two side-by-side pallets, one of which is opened when a manual key is played, the other of which is opened whenever a pedal key is played. The term used by Silbermann for the *Windkoppel* was *a parte Ventile* (separate pallets). For example, in the contract for the Nassau organ, he wrote, "The pedal is coupled to the manual by means of *a parte Ventile,* which contributes greatly to the gravity of an instrument."[31] In larger organs, Hildebrandt and Silbermann often provided a *Baßventil,* a wind coupler that could be turned on and off by means of a stop knob. After Silbermann's death, many of his permanently coupled organs were altered so that the coupler could be turned off by means of a knob at the key desk.

Heinrich Gottfried Trost's *Windkoppel,* which he built in all of his organs and can be turned on and off at will, even while playing, operates in a completely different way. In the pedal range, each note has three pallets: one pallet in the pedal pallet box that is opened whenever a pedal key is played, and two pallets, one each for the manual and the pedal, in the coupler pallet boxes. When the stop knob for the *Windkoppel* is drawn, by means of a roller every pedal coupler pallet in the organ—48 of them in a pedal compass of CD–c^1, 24 pallets for the pedal channels and 24 pallets for the manual channels—is opened at the same time. Wind flows from the pedal coupler channel into the manual channel (on which all the pipes stand); the coupler pallet boxes do not receive their wind independently but only from the wind that is in the channel already from the pedal pallet box at the rear of the chest. (Thus, to prevent a pallet from opening inadvertently solely by the force of the wind, Trost provided each pallet with three springs.)[32]

For the double channels in Zschortau, Scheibe provided one spring for the manual channel and two springs for the pedal coupler channel. Further, he built *Trennschiede,* or channel dividers, for the Viol di Gamba 8′ and the Quintatön 16′. These channel dividers kept wind from the pedal coupler channel reaching these two stops (which stood at the back of the Manual wind chests), so that neither the Viol di Gamba 8′ nor the Quintatön 16′ could be played in the Pedal. Further, the dividers ensured that these two "wind intensive" stops received adequate wind. (Scheibe also provided a channel divider for the Posaunen Bass 16′.) Given that Bach referred in his report to an *Angehänge*—a term reserved only for a pull-down pedal—we can be quite certain that Scheibe's Pedal was permanently coupled to the Manual and that it had no stop knob. A switchable pedal coupler (with stop knob), added by organ builder Eduard Offenhauer during the rebuild in 1870, operates through a set of squares mounted on a rail that is movable by means of a Manual/Pedal coupler knob. When the squares are in the "on" position and activated from the pedal trackers, they pull open the pedal coupler pallets in the Manual pallet box.

Keyboards and Actions

Scheibe built a balanced key action for the manual keyboard and used rollers of forged iron for the roller board. The arms on both ends of the rollers simply bend 90 degrees to receive the trackers and are attached to the board with brass loops, a construction also used by Eugenio and Adam Horatio Casparini in the organ in Görlitz and, in some situations, by Silbermann.[33] According to Christian Ludwig Boxberg's description, "The roller boards [in Görlitz] work especially well and are of good design. The rollers are all made of iron and the loops [*Würbel*] in which they rest are made of brass wire, which does not rust together or wear out. Neither does it cause ciphers, either through expansion or contraction. This device also has the following advantage: one may well make use of such a roller board in a small, tight space, because it is narrow and takes up little room. It is not an eighth as large as a wooden roller board."[34] Scheibe also used iron rollers in the pedal-coupler roller board but used wooden rollers in the pedal roller board.

Scheibe used pear wood for the stop knobs. During the restoration in 2000, the porcelain inserts added to the stop knobs in 1870 were removed and new paper labels provided that used a calligraphic script similar in style to the original stop labels found on the key desk of Scheibe's organ for St. John's. At St. Paul's, the stop knobs were turned and ebonized and had ivory buttons in their centers, just as one finds in the organs of Silbermann and Hildebrandt. The inscribed white parchment labels were placed immediately below them.

Key Desk

Doors enclose the organ's manual keyboard and the four vertical rows of stops, two on each side of the keyboard. The compass is CD–c³ and the manual naturals

6. Key desk of the Scheibe organ in Zschortau. Photograph by Konrad Dänhardt.

are covered with boxwood, the sharps with ebony. The original keyboard was replaced in 1870, during the rebuild by Offenhauer, and while the original place-ment could be determined by the restorers in 2000, other dimensions were copied from Silbermann's Crostau organ or decided on the basis of the key desk from Scheibe's organ for St. John's. Unfortunately, no original keyboard or pedalboard from Scheibe has survived. (The keyboard and pedalboard in the St. John's organ were replaced by Johann Gottlob Mende in 1833.)[35]

The restorers remained uncertain regarding placement of the stops for the Tremulant and the Pedal coupler. If, as discussed above, the organ originally did not have a *Windkoppel* that could be switched on and off, then the place where the Pedal coupler knob is now would have been for the Tremulant, and where the Tremulant now is there probably would have been a stop for Scheibe's unknown invention that apparently affected the organ's wind pressure.

One lovely feature of the key desk is the marquetry decoration in the board placed just behind the keyboard. In the middle is a stylized compass in black and white with four points and an eight-petaled center; to the right, the year the organ became playable, "A[nn]o 1745"; to the left, Scheibe's initials, *J S*, in both correct and mirror images, resting on branches that hold the initials and surround them with six flowers.

7. Detail of manual keyboard and marquetry, Scheibe organ in Zschortau. On the left, Johann Scheibe's initials in normal and mirror images. Photograph by Lynn Edwards Butler.

Disposition

Surprisingly, for a long time little was known about the organ's original disposition. That Bach had examined the organ and written a report was referred to in 1880 by Philipp Spitta, but it was not until 1911 that Bach's text was published.[36] A facsimile of the report was published by Rubardt in 1937, and he also provided the disposition of the organ as it was at that time—essentially the organ after its enlargement in 1870 by Offenhauer (see below).[37] Later publications printed the same 19th-century disposition.[38] Ulrich Dähnert's version of the disposition, published in 1980, appears to be an amalgam in which from the known disposition of the time he eliminated the stops in the secondary division (added in 1870), omitted the Violon 8′ from the Pedal (apparently believing it to be a 19th-century addition), and added registers to the Manual known from Bach's report to have originally existed. (One result is that the Manual appears to have two four-foot flutes, Gedackt 4′ and Fleute travers 4′.)[39]

The disposition set out in Scheibe's contract was first published in 1986, when Hans Wolfgang Theobald gained access to original documents, now lost, held by the church in Zschortau.[40] He had earlier provided photocopies of the documents to Blanchard, who used them for his discussion and disposition of the Zschortau organ in his *Bach Organ Book* of 1985.[41] In addition, Michael Gerhard Kaufmann's article on Bach's testing of the Zschortau organ, published in 2000, includes the disposition and a transcription of Scheibe's original proposal.[42] (For the disposition in 1744 [proposed by Scheibe], in 1746 [when examined by J. S. Bach], and in 2000 [after the recent restoration], see appendix D-1.) Please note: stop names in table 2 are spelled as they appear on the organ's stop knobs; stop names used throughout this chapter follow the standard spelling used in this book.

There are minor but significant differences between Scheibe's proposal and the contract. The contract specified that the manual wind chests be made from oak barrel staves (whereas the proposal did not specify the wood) and that Scheibe would provide a one-year warranty, a common provision in any organ-building contract of the time. Also, although Scheibe had requested free room and board for him and his workers during installation, the contract provided only free lodging. In the proposal, the Viol di Gamba was numbered among the organ's 13 stops (11 registers + Bellows signal + Tremulant), whereas the contract lists 12 stops (10 registers + Bellows signal + Tremulant). The gift of a Viol di Gamba stop was noted in the contract—as "a register already discussed as a gift in memory"—but it was not given its own number.

TABLE 2   Disposition of the Scheibe organ (I/P/13) in Zschortau, 1746

Manual	Pedal
Quinta Thoen 16', wood	Sub-Bass 16', wood
Principal 8', from F in façade, tin; C, D, D♯, E inside, wood	Posaunen Bass 16', wood
Viol de Gamba 8', divided c¹/c♯¹, CD–b, wood; c¹–c³, *Metall*	Violon 8', wood
Grob Gedackt 8', wood	
Fleute doux 4', wood	
Octav 4', *Metall*	Manual compass: CD–c³
Hohl Floet 3', divided c¹/c♯¹, *Metall*	Pedal compass: CD–c¹
Octav 2', *Metall*	Tremulant
Super Octava 1', *Metall*	Calcant [bellows signal]
Mixtur III–IV 1–1/3'	Pedal Coppel

Sources: Pfarrarchiv Zschortau, "Acta die Kirchen und Geistlichen Gebäude betreffend," fols. 194r–98v; Dänhardt 2000.

Note: Stop names are spelled as they appear on the organ's stop knobs. The pedal coupler does not couple the Quinta Thoen 16' and the Viol de Gamba 8'. The organ was restored by Hermann Eule Orgelbau in 2000. Two bellows provide wind. The pitch is Chorton; wind pressure is 55 mm WC.

The Zschortau disposition differs in essential details from one-manual organs of a similar size built by Scheibe's contemporaries Trost, Hildebrandt, and Silbermann. One rather startling difference is the presence of a wooden Quintadena [Quintatön] 16', one of the stops added during construction, over and above the contract. It was unusual to put a Quintadena 16', a cylindrical, narrow-scaled stop, in a small, one-manual organ; neither Trost nor Hildebrandt nor Silbermann ever did so. The Quintadena's sound is characterized by the prominent fifth (third harmonic). Because of its low cut-up, it is difficult to voice, especially when built of wood, and is therefore often constructed from metal and with beards (small pieces of metal attached to either side of the mouth). Casparini is said to have built a wooden Quintadena 16' in Görlitz that was "a masterpiece," not only for its sound quality but for its even voicing. "Accomplished organ builders know how much hard work it takes to voice a metal Quintadena evenly, to say nothing of the diligence required to voice a wooden one," remarked Christian Ludwig Boxberg.[43] The Quintadena 16' had already been in use some 40 or 50 years when Michael Praetorius described it as *lieblich* (elegant, narrow-scaled) in his *Organographia*, published in 1619.[44] Writing over a hundred years later, Jacob Adlung observed that because the speech of Quintadenas, especially 16-foots, was slow, a Bordun 16′ worked better than Quintadena 16′ in passagework on the full organ.[45] Nevertheless, the delicate and elegant quality of the Quintadena was prized in Central Germany—among others, apparently, by Bach. (Quintadena 16′ was included in the disposition Bach drew up around 1742 for an organ in Bad Berka, for example.) The Quintatön 16′ in Zschortau is a welcome addition, adding gravity (but not thickness) to the plenum of a small organ.

The Zschortau organ follows the Silbermann model in having a Principal 8′ in a small organ. (Indeed, it could be argued that the presence of a Principal 8′ makes this *not* a small organ.) Principal 8′ appears in all of Silbermann's organs with nine or more stops, usually along with Gedackt 8′ and Quintadena 8′. Trost never built a Principal 8′ in his small one-manual organs. Hildebrandt followed the example of his teacher in his first two organs, in Störmthal and Liebertwolkwitz, and in 1743 proposed a Principal 8′ for a small organ in Naumburg, but generally, like Trost, Hildebrandt provided his small organs with Gedackt 8′, Quintadena 8′, and Principal 4′. Silbermann's Principals were built of tin, and this is what Scheibe proposed as well. The Principal 8′ in Zschortau is made from *Bergzinn*, a pure tin mined in the Erzgebirge (Ore Mountains) of Germany.

Scheibe's Flute douce—a 4′ stop that imitates the recorder—also was unusual in one-manual instruments. It is not difficult to find Flute douce 4′ in dispositions of the time—in the collection compiled by Adlung, for example—but always it is in much larger instruments.[46] In one-manual organs, Trost built Gedackt as the four-foot flute (although one disposition—for Ossa—called for "Fleut de douce or Lieblich Gedackt 4′"), Silbermann always built a Rohrflöte 4′, and Hildebrandt, too, generally built a Rohrflöte as the four-foot flute. Construction methods varied for the Flute douce and are not always known. Casparini built a stopped, metal Flute douce 4′ that Boxberg described as "only a small metal Gedackt, to be sure, but it sounds exactly like the instrument for which it is named."[47] Johann Georg Schröter built his Flute douce "from metal, open at the bottom, closed at the top"—that is, it was tapered. Zacharias Thayssner built his Flute douce from maple. Johann Friedrich Wender, too, built his Flute douce from wood. "In order to imitate the sound of flutes as much as possible," Adlung wrote, "organ builders prefer to use wood over other materials. The pipes are shaped—as hardly anyone would have thought—so that they get smaller at the top, and are covered at a slant, so that they are neither completely open nor completely stopped." Johann Lorenz Albrecht, Adlung's editor, added that the stop's very narrow scaling resulted in a sound that was "much gentler [*sanfter*] than a normal Gedackt 4'."[48] Both Trost and Johann Georg Finke built the Flute douce as a doubled rank: one rank was open, slightly tapered, of wood; the other was stopped, cylindrical, and metal. We have no idea how Scheibe built the Flute douce in the St. Paul's organ, but in Zschortau the Flute douce is one rank of stopped wooden pipes, essentially a wooden Gedackt, with a sound that is elegant and refined.

Compared with organs by Hildebrandt and Silbermann, the Pedal division in Zschortau—Subbass 16', Posaunen Bass 16', and Violon 8', all from wood—appears unusual, too. Silbermann generally placed just two stops, Subbass 16' and Posaune 16', in the Pedal of one-manual organs; if he added a third stop, which he did in only 3 of 11 organs of this size, he built a Trompete 8', and by the 1740s he was building one-manual organs with only Subbass 16' in the Pedal.[49] Hildebrandt's one-manual organs in Störmthal and Liebertwolkwitz, which may have been built according to a disposition previously submitted by Silbermann, also had only Subbass 16' and Posaune 16' in the Pedal. After that, though, Hildebrandt's one-manual organs had Pedal divisions with Subbass 16' and Octav 8' of wood.

The third Pedal stop—Violon 8'—is perhaps the most noteworthy. Built at either 16- or 8-foot, often of wood, the Violon imitates the bow stroke of a bass viol. It can be difficult to voice, especially if it has the narrow scaling the stop requires to achieve its effect. As Adlung put it, "It serves well in the pedal, purring just like a violone or bass viol when it is properly built."[50] In Thuringia, Violon 16' was the more common, appearing for the most part in larger organs—in the organs of Trost and Franciscus Volckland, for example. Violon 8' appears only three times in Adlung's large collection of dispositions, and each time it was together with Violon 16'.[51] Hildebrandt placed both Violon 16' and Violon 8' (from metal) in his organ for St. Wenceslas's in Naumburg, finished in 1746,[52] and Scheibe placed Violon 8' (but not Violon 16') in his two-manual organ for St. John's in Leipzig, built 1741–43.

It is noteworthy, then, to see a Pedal division in a small one-manual organ in Saxony with Violon 8' (which functions as a baroque cello) but not Violon 16' (which functions as a violone). An early example is in Pomßen, where a Violon 8' from wood was added in 1727 to the charming organ built in 1671 by Gottfried Richter, a circumstance that has been linked—albeit without hard evidence—to Bach's performance in Pomßen on 6 February 1727 of the cantata *Ich lasse dich nicht, du segnest mich denn* BWV 157.[53] Apitzsch added Violon 8' over and above the contract when he built the organ in Leutzsch in 1729.[54] And Violon 8' was also included in the organ built in 1743–47 for the village church in Klinga by Christian Schmidt (of Taucha).[55] Indeed, the Pedal disposition is exactly the same as in Zschortau: Subbass 16', Violon Bass 8', Posaunen Bass 16'. Also, Johann Ernst Hähnel (of Meissen) built Violon 8': in the two-manual, 14-stop organ for the church in Steinbach, about 35 kilometers/22 miles south of Leipzig, in 1736,[56] and in his largest organ, the two-manual, 31-stop instrument built in 1744–46 for St. Ägidien in Oschatz, for example.[57]

Zschortau's Posaunen Bass 16' has wooden resonators, wooden boots, wooden blocks, and leathered wooden shallots with brass tongues.[58] It was common in this period to build Posaunen Bass resonators of wood, of course, but shallots were most often cast in metal, not turned from wood. Casparini built full-length resonators from wood and shallots and blocks from cast metal.[59] Silbermann built wooden resonators and lead shallots.[60] In Naumburg, Hildebrandt built wooden resonators, lead shallots, and blocks and boots of pear wood.[61] Trost usually built "Clicquot" shallots, which he leathered, and resonators from wood.[62]

Examples of wooden shallots can be found in organs by Trost and Volckland in Thuringia. Organ builder and restorer Helmut Werner described the Posaunen Bass 16' in Großengottern, built in 1716, as having "original softwood

8. Wooden Posaunen Bass 16' pipes in the organ in Zschortau. Photograph by Lynn Edwards Butler.

resonators, blocks and boot tips from beech, boots from metal, shallots from hardwood covered with leather, tuning wires from hammered iron."[63] Adlung informs us that "some builders are in the habit of making wooden shallots, as is the case with the Posaune at St. Thomas's in Erfurt [Volckland, year unknown] and likewise at Zimmernsupra [Volckland, 1728]."[64]

Returning to organ building in Saxony, wooden shallots were built by Finke for the organ in St. John's in Gera in 1725, an organ examined by Bach. Finke's Trompeten Bass 8′ had resonators of metal and shallots "of chequer wood soaked in linseed oil."[65] Chequer (*Elsebeere* or *Sorbus torminalis*), a wood once highly valued by wood carvers and cabinetmakers, "has a fine, even structure, is hard and strong, can achieve a high polish, and has little warping."[66] (Trost used the same wood for the shallots of a Fagott 16′ in Waltershausen.)[67] Wooden shallots also were built for the organ constructed in 1729 by Johann Gottlieb Döltzsch in Grünlichtenberg.[68]

The Posaunen Bass in Zschortau has extremely wide scaling. Dänhardt described it as "loud without being sharp." Channel dividers separate the wind for the Posaunen Bass from that for the flues, a practice that Johann Lorenz Albrecht recommended: "Because [the bass pipes sometimes can overpower the treble] it is a good thing to direct a portion of the wind to the pallets for the reeds."[69]

Another unusual feature of the Zschortau organ is the presence of two divided stops: Viol di Gamba 8′ and Hohlflöte or Nasat 3′. (Throughout this book, I retain the commonly used baroque abbreviation: 3′ stands for 2–2/3′.) Each of these stops has divided sliders and two stop knobs, one controlling the lower two octaves, the other controlling the upper two octaves. (The division is between c^1 and $c^1_\sharp$.) Scheibe promised that the divided stops would provide "even more registration possibilities," and any organist can easily imagine the flexibility such stops offer—for playing a solo melody with accompaniment, duos, or a continuo part with different registrations in the left and right hands, among other possibilities. It is not known whether Scheibe was acquainted with the organ built in 1705 by Johann Christoph Oehme in Lucka (approximately 20 kilometers/12 miles from Altenburg). Oehme built a one-manual and pedal, 12-stop organ that had five divided stops—Klein Gedackt 4′, Octav 2′, Quint 3′, Superoctav 1′, and Sesquialtera—so that "one can play as if there were two manuals."[70] Two of Silbermann's small organs have divided stops: in Ringethal, where he built a 7-stop organ around 1725, five of the six manual stops are divided between c^1 and $c^1_\sharp$; in Schweikershain, he built a 6-stop organ before 1734 that has three of five manual stops divided between c^1 and $c\sharp^1$. Also, in his two small organs in Etzdorf (1745) and Frankenstein (1748–53), he built Nasat 3' and Sesquialtera 1–3/5' as treble stops.[71]

That the Zschortau organ has a wide-scaled Nasat 3', and not a narrow-scaled Quint 3', also is notable. Building Nasat 3' in a one-manual organ was not common practice for Hildebrandt, for instance. Silbermann regularly built Nasat 3' and rarely built Quint 3' in small organs, but Hildebrandt built Nasat 3' only once in his one-manual organs—in Störmthal, in a disposition apparently designed by Silbermann. Trost never placed Nasat 3' in small organs, but for his 22-stop organ for Großengottern he recommended it be included in the Hauptwerk, where it could be used, he wrote, "with the Quintatön 16' and Viol di Gamba 8', and likewise with the Gemshorn 4' and Bordun 8', and goes well with all registers."[72] The preference for Nasat 3' can be seen in Bach's recommendations for Mühlhausen, where, among other changes "useful for all kinds of new ideas," he wanted Quint 3' replaced with Nasat 3', and in his proposed disposition for a new organ in Berka, where he placed both Nasat 3' and Quint 3' in the Hauptwerk. (Discussing the change in Mühlhausen, Ernest Zavarsky noted that the wide-scaled Nasat darkens tone, while the narrow-scaled Quint brightens and strengthens it and as such is an important member of the principal chorus.)[73] Nasat was present in all of Leipzig's organs: at St. Paul's, St. Nicholas's, St. Thomas's (in both the large and small organs), the New Church, and St. John's.

There is also the "rare and costly" Viol di Gamba to be considered. Again, the presence in a one-manual organ of a Viol di Gamba—especially one divided into bass and treble registers—is unusual and never found in the small organs of Trost, Hildebrandt, or Silbermann. When Scheibe built a Viol di Gamba for the Brustwerk of the St. Paul's organ, he claimed no organ builder could have built it for "less than 100 taler"—a reference to how painstakingly the stop must be constructed and voiced—and a contemporary cited the Viol di Gamba as one of the organ's "rarest" or most unique stops.[74] It was desirable for the organ's Viol di Gamba to come as close as possible to the quality of the gamba itself, including its attack. Scheibe went so far as to call the register "Viol di Gamb[a] naturell," perhaps in an attempt to differentiate his version from earlier stops, which, being more widely scaled and differently voiced, did not achieve the quality of a stringed instrument.

Like Hildebrandt, Scheibe built the Viol di Gamba as a conical stop (it is funnel-shaped, wider at the top than at the bottom). In the bass (C–b) he used open wood pipes—the four lowest pipes are shared by the Principal 8'—and in the treble (c¹–c³) he used conical pipes of *Metall* (an alloy of tin and lead). (In the restored organ, all 23 of the wooden pipes are original, and 12 of the metal pipes, the C♯ side, are original.) Zschortau's Viol di Gamba is a charming register that combines well with flutes, but also with Octav 4' or Quintatön 16'. It adds gravity to the full organ. Also, because it is divided, it is possible to play a soprano solo on the Viol di Gamba—Johann Mattheson tells us it can be used this way "with good effect"[75]—to improvise a duo or a trio, or to accompany a solo treble registration.

Scheibe's (and Hildebrandt's) method of construction differed from Silbermann's, Casparini's, and Trost's. Silbermann built tapered Viols di Gamba of tin, and they have a flute-like quality. Similarly, Casparini's cylindrical, metal Viol di Gamba in Görlitz sounded "almost the same as a Hohlflöte in sound, as if it were made of wood," and Boxberg found it very useful for playing continuo and for adding gravity to the full organ.[76] Trost built cylindrical Viols di Gamba of tin, with extreme scaling, narrower even than what Friedrich Ladegast used in his romantic organs. He added box beards, sometimes with harmonic bridges (*Streichbärte*) in the treble, and acknowledged that the stop "required very special voicing if it was going to sound like the actual instrument."[77] In Trost's concept, the Viol di Gamba 8' belonged together with the Violon 16'. (As Gottfried Heinrich Stölzel, one of the examiners of Trost's Altenburg organ in October 1739, observed, "The Viol di Gamba, along with the Violon Bass, makes a tone that comes very close to the sound of a gamba. One would think strings were being played by a bow.")[78] Trost built Viol di Gamba 8' in the Hauptwerk of four organs, all of them two- or three-manual instruments, and in each he also placed Violon Bass 16' in the Pedal. (In Waltershausen, Trost also made the Viol di Gamba 8' available in the Pedal, by transmission.) Describing what he had proposed in Großengottern, Trost remarked, "A Viol di Gamba 8' will be placed in the Hauptmanual, which goes together with the Viol di Gamba 16' in the Pedal. Where there is one, there also must be the other, and the two Viols di Gamba together produce an excellent, beautiful harmony."[79] By contrast, in the one-manual organ in Zschortau, Scheibe placed Viol di Gamba 8' in the Manual but a wooden Violon 8' in the Pedal, where it combines extremely well with the Subbass 16'.

Notably, the string quality of the stop did not depend on whether it was constructed as a cylindrical, conical, or tapered stop. At the New Church, for example, Scheibe apparently kept the existing pipes, but with revoicing and rescaling he succeeded in making the stop sound like a "real" gamba.[80] (He probably moved the pipes down on the chest. Pipes are scaled to be wider in the bass than in the soprano; moving a pipe down from its original position places a narrower-scaled pipe in the new location.)

The principal chorus in Zschortau is composed of Principals at 8', 4', 2', and 1' as well as Mixtur III–IV. As restored, the mixture has the following composition:[81]

C			1–1/3'	1	2/3'
c		2	1–1/3'	1	
c#¹	2–2/3'	2	1–3/5'	1–1/3'	

The third-sounding rank (1–3/5') in the treble and the rising plafond are characteristic of mixtures with a strong polyphonic character.[82] The plenum could be expanded to 16-foot with the addition of the Quintatön, and in the Pedal, to which all of the Hauptwerk (except Quintatön 16' and Viol di Gamba 8') can be coupled, there is not only the broad foundation of the Subbass 16', but the cutting and gravity-providing Posaunen Bass 16'. For a "small" organ, the sound is full, complex, brilliant without being harsh, and remarkably satisfying.

Materials and Accessories

Scheibe specified "good pure *Bergzinn*" for the Principal 8'; well-boiled oak barrel staves for the manual wind chests; pine (*Kiefer*) and oak for the pedal wind chests; iron and brass for the manual rollers; wood for the pedal rollers; "good, dry, new wood, partly spruce [*Fichte*], partly oak" for the inner components (*Eingebäude*);[83] brass wire in the trackers; boxwood (naturals) and ebony (sharps) in the manual keyboard; and oak for the pedal keys. One notes the extensive use of wood: for all three Pedal stops, for the bass half of the Viola di Gamba 8', and for the Quintatön 16', Gedackt 8', and Flute douce 4'.[84]

In addition to the *Windkoppel*, already discussed, the Zschortau organ has the usual accessories found in small organs of the time: bellows-pumper signal (a stc ɔ knob connected to a bell, which lets the bellows pumper know when to begin to fill the bellows) and tremulant. In Zschortau, Scheibe built a Bocktremulant—that is, Dom Bedos's *tremblant fort*, an external tremulant in the main wind channel, a construction recommended by Praetorius and Esaias Compenius I, who also described its qualities: "The best way [to avoid problems] is for there to be 8 beats in a 4/4 measure, and it should beat quietly

9. Interior of St. Nicholas's, Zschortau, with the Scheibe organ in the west balcony. Photograph by Daniel Senf.

[*fein sanffte beben*], and dependably keep a regular beat. If the tremulant will be used with reeds, as is likely to be done, it is best to use a special kind, called Bocktremulant, which is the best and finest for this purpose."[85] Andreas Werckmeister described the same attributes: "The tremulant must beat very gently [*fein sanffte beben*] and must steadily maintain the speed to which it is set, even with big registrations."[86]

Pitch and Temperament

Typical of contracts from the time, there is no mention of the organ's temperament, nor is the organ's pitch ever identified. During the restoration in 2000, the organ's pitch was set at Chorton (464.4 Hz at 18° C), most certainly the organ's original pitch. It was not possible to determine the organ's original temperament. The temperament was set according to instructions included in Werckmeister's continuo treatise, a modified meantone temperament that allows modulation into all tonalities. (Werckmeister's *Kurzer Unterricht wie man ein Clavier stimmen und wohl temperiren könne* [Short instruction as to how a keyboard instrument may be tuned and tempered] was published in 1698 and 1715 as an appendix to his basso continuo treatise, *Die nothwendigsten*

Anmerckungen und Regeln, Wie der Bassus continuus oder General-Bass wol könne tractiret werden [The most necessary notes and rules as to how a *Bassus continuus* or Thorough-bass may be treated].) [87]

As with so many organ projects in this period, matters did not end with the organ's successful examination: Scheibe requested a supplement of 80 taler because the organ was larger than contracted, and without additional funds he would suffer a loss.[88] An additional payment of 60 taler was offered, and agreed to, and Scheibe was reminded that during the one year of the warranty period he was expected to visit the organ now and again and to make repairs, if any were necessary, without further compensation.[89] Scheibe was paid the supplemental fee several months later. The receipt, which Scheibe signed on 5 December 1746, includes an explanation that makes no reference to the additional stops: "Contrary to expectations, prices for leather and tin, as well as the cost of feeding his workmen, rose unexpectedly during the project."[90] Altogether, Scheibe was paid 560 taler—exactly the amount he had first requested.

Bach's favorable report certainly was a factor in the decision to pay a supplement—indeed, the report may have been drafted precisely as it was in order to provide justification for Scheibe's additional claims. As musicologist and organist Winfried Schrammek put it, "Certainly one can see Bach as the instigator of these additions [to the disposition], especially since he skillfully composed a report that could serve as justification for defraying the resulting cost overrun."[91] Drawing a similar conclusion, Dänhardt wrote, "At the examination, evidently, Scheibe portrayed his additions above the contract rather generously, probably in order to be in a better position to argue for an additional payment. Bach accommodatingly passed this on in his report."[92]

As the above comments make clear, Bach's "skillfully composed" report raises questions. In his initial proposal, Scheibe included the Viol di Gamba among the Manual's eight stops but insisted his fee did not include the cost for this rare stop, for which he was renowned, because it was to be provided gratis as "an everlasting memorial." However, Bach listed the Viol di Gamba 8′ among the five stops for which Scheibe should be paid extra. It may be that Scheibe agreed to build the Viol di Gamba at his own cost because the church insisted upon it during contract negotiations, but it seems more likely that he made such a generous offer to the church because he wanted to honor his birthplace. Scheibe had deep connections with Zschortau. He had restored the previous organ, his wife was godmother to the organist's son, and it is assumed that he was born there. In the official contract, the Viol di Gamba is mentioned almost offhandedly and not directly named: "Moreover, also a register already discussed as a gift in memory." No matter the circumstances, it is clear that Scheibe provided the Viol di Gamba at his own expense. Even if the Viol di Gamba was a stop requested by the congregation, Scheibe, while obligated to accede to the request, may also have felt within his rights to demand payment for it. Nevertheless, it strikes an odd chord that a stop promised as a "gift in memory" was later charged to the church.

Another of the extra stops listed by Bach—a "Fleute-Travers 4′ of wood"—also raises questions. The contract included a four-foot flute, but it was a wooden Fleute doux (Flute douce or recorder) 4′, not a Fleute-Travers (Flûte traversière or Querpfeife). Did Scheibe build a Fleute-Travers in addition to a Flute douce?[93] (This is the conclusion reached by Schrammek and organologist Ulrich Dähnert.) Was a Fleute-Travers 4′ built instead of a Flute douce 4′? There is no evidence of this. On the contrary, as noted by Hans Wolfgang Theobald, the 47 extant wood pipes from the Flute douce 4′ date to 1746. They are in all respects similar to the organ's other original wood stops (Quintatön 16′ and Grob Gedackt 8′), their rectangular feet exactly fit the holes on the chest, and they are stopped throughout the compass—that is, they are not open in the treble as they most likely would have been if they had been a later addition to the organ.[94] When organ builder Eduard Offenhauer examined the organ in 1870, he found only one four-foot flute, which he listed in his inventory simply as "Gedackt." Further, as the restorers noted in 2000, if there had been two four-foot flutes, there would have been one more slider on the chest. They concluded that "the Fleute-Travers 4′ [listed in the examination report], then, seems to be identical to the stop planned for and listed in the contract as Fleute doux 4′."[95] Is it possible that Scheibe built a Flute douce but provided a label that said Fleute-Travers, which made it look like there was a stop not in the contract? (This is the conclusion drawn by Theobald.) Unable to determine what the stop label might originally have said, in 2000 the restorers opted to give the stop its name according to the contract—that is, Fleute doux 4′. Either Bach thought the label accurately represented what Scheibe had constructed—which means that he never actually examined the pipework or that he examined it but did not recognize that it was a different stop from the label—or, as Theobald and Dänhardt have concluded, he knew the stop was a Flute douce, per the contract, but nevertheless claimed it was a Fleute-Travers, per the label. Although almost unimaginable, it appears Bach was willing to go this far—to do everything possible—so that the organ builder, probably both a good friend and an esteemed colleague, would not lose money on account of the project.

Were the additions to the disposition recommended by Bach? Schrammek thought so, as noted above, and so did Rubardt, who made reference to "the Bach-influenced Zschortau disposition."[96] Peter Williams wrote that the four additions—Quintatön 16', a string stop, an imitative flute (he believed the four-foot flute was a traverso), and the *Windkoppel* (which he assumed to be a pull-down construction)—were "unusually important and may suggest collaboration between Scheibe and Bach."[97] While we assume that Bach would have been consulted about organ projects taking place in his environs, evidence of such collaboration is scarce. It exists for an organ proposed by Scheibe for the church in Stötteritz (now part of Leipzig), where Scheibe provided a drawing and two disposition proposals, which were then given to Bach for his review (see chapter 10); however, there is no direct evidence that Bach influenced the Zschortau disposition.

Worth noting is that several of Scheibe's additions were stops that required special diligence and a lot of extra work. The Quintatön 16' of wood, the Viol di Gamba 8' of wood and metal, and the *Windkoppel* with its divided channels for all the pitches in the bottom two octaves of the compass (no matter whether it could be pulled on and off)—all required great expertise. The Superoctav 1', on the other hand, is not a difficult stop to construct, nor do its small pipes require much material. It seems possible that Scheibe had planned from the beginning to include it. Building one or more, often higher-pitched, stops over and above the contract was a widespread practice that put the builder in a good position to demand a supplemental payment. For this reason, Silbermann scholar Frank-Harald Greß has observed, it is rather common to see organ proposals, such as Silbermann's proposal for the Freiberg Cathedral organ or his proposal for a new organ at St. Paul's in Leipzig, where the 1' register is missing.[98]

Scheibe's organ apparently remained relatively untouched for some 120 years, although there were minor repairs and at least one overhaul, in 1843, for which organ builder Johann Gottlieb Müller, of Delitzsch, was paid 84 taler.[99] In 1870, though, the organ underwent major changes when it was moved to the upper of two newly built west-end galleries, altered, and enlarged with a second manual, a 4-stop Hinterwerk, by Offenhauer, of Delitzsch.[100] In 1954 the organ was moved by Hermann Eule Orgelbau to the lower gallery (its original location), and the upper gallery was destroyed. Changes were made not only to the secondary division but also to the two divided stops.[101] The case, which had been altered to fit the space and overpainted to imitate the wood of the balconies, was left unchanged. In 1984, at the same time the church was undergoing a major renovation, Hermann Eule Orgelbau cleaned the organ, made necessary repairs, and then reinstalled the organ and tuned it. The pipework and keyboard for the second manual, which did not belong to the original organ, were removed. Plans were made for a thorough restoration that would return the organ to its original disposition, which was carried out by Hermann Eule Orgelbau in 2000. The case was restored in 2009 (see above).

Scheibe built an innovative and versatile organ for the small church in Zschortau, an instrument whose sound continues to captivate its grateful listeners some 270 years later. Dänhardt expressed his high opinion of the organ's Principals in particular: "Special mention must be made of the fresh sound of the Principals . . . [which, together with] registration possibilities that tend toward the romantic, the strong bass, and a high number of eight- and sixteen-foot stops[,] make this organ unique among Baroque organs in the Leipzig area. Also noteworthy is a mixture that still has a third in the treble, which imparts pleasant color to high tones."[102] As its famous examiner remarked, it is an organ "skillfully, diligently, and well built," an instrument that is innovative, remarkably lively, surprisingly adaptable.

4 Building the Organ for St. Paul's

None of this [rebuilding] requires extraordinary expertise,
and besides, the organ builder [Scheibe] is honest, cheap, and
hardworking.
—Johann Kuhnau and Daniel Vetter, 1710

He so much wanted the instrument to be as perfect as possible. . . .
I am certain that to date he has not earned one taler of profit on
this entire project, the equal of which is not often seen, but likely
has been forced into debt on account of it.
—Johann Burchard Mencke, 1716

A Rebuild or a New Instrument for Leipzig University?

According to most accounts, two organ builders competed in 1710 to win the
contract to build a large new organ for St. Paul's, the University Church in
Leipzig. One was Gottfried Silbermann, 27 years old, recently returned to his
home state of Saxony after an apprenticeship in Alsace, eager to take on new
projects and already well respected. The other was Johann Scheibe, 30 years old,
a builder only recently active in Leipzig. Silbermann biographer Ernst Flade
described what he considered to be the disappointing result:

> The sum of 3,000 taler [that Silbermann requested for a three-manual, 44-stop
> organ] seems to have been too high for the university. Also, it was feared that
> Silbermann might not dedicate the necessary care to the Leipzig organ because
> he had by that time already concluded negotiations with Freiberg's city coun-

cil regarding building the cathedral organ there. Further, the second contestant, Johann Scheibe, was a Leipzig citizen. He promised to deliver a three-manual organ with 56 stops for 2,926 taler. After receiving his solemn oath, on 11 May 1711 an agreement was reached for [Scheibe] to build "a good instrument for the glory of God." As we learn from Sebastian Bach's examination of the organ completed in 1716, the university got a mediocre instrument for its church, which, compared with the organ proposed by Silbermann, took twice as long to complete and cost substantially more.[1]

Flade's account is neither accurate nor fair according to the archival sources now available. It is true that Silbermann offered to build a new organ for 3,000 taler. There is no evidence, however, that Scheibe submitted a proposal to build "a three-manual organ with 56 stops for 2,926 taler" or that he signed a solemn oath and agreement in May 1711 to build such an instrument.[2] Rather, the record

10. St. Paul's and the attached medicinal garden. Detail from J. E. Scheffler's *Scenographiae Lipsiacae*, 1749. Sammlung Bach-Archiv, Leipzig, Graph. Slg. 16/38.

shows that Leipzig University's decisions regarding the organ project at St. Paul's were made piecemeal, one step at a time, in a process fraught with political intrigue, disagreement, and a remarkable lack of long-range planning.

The organ project at St. Paul's started inadvertently. Leipzig University began offering worship services at St. Paul's in 1710 on a weekly basis—not just quarterly, as formerly. To accommodate the large number of students and faculty who would be attending, balconies were hastily erected, and a major renovation of the church was undertaken. Among other things, the pulpit was moved from its position on the south side to a pillar on the opposite side of the church, and the large organ was moved to the west gallery, the so-called *Schülerchor*, where student musicians and other instrumentalists had performed since its construction in 1678.

The organ's dismantling was sudden. Within days of the first academic worship service, which took place on 31 August 1710, August Quirinus Rivinus, a professor of botany and medicine who had just served as rector for the winter semester and was now overseeing the church's renovation, ordered the dismantling not only of the temporary balconies that had been quickly built for the first worship service but also of the organ that since the 16th century had stood in a gallery above and behind the pulpit.

Rivinus's order incensed some members of the academic community. They had approved a modest expenditure for relocating the organ but were surprised by the swiftness of Rivinus's actions, and they forced him to avow that he had acted without Council's consent.[3] (Among other duties, the Concilium Decemvirorum—Council, as it is called throughout this book—had oversight over St. Paul's and Leipzig University's main academic building, St. Paul's College [Collegium]. It was composed of 10 members: the rector and provost [dean of the philosophy faculty], who were elected to these posts each spring and winter semester, and 8 permanent members, who were the two longest-serving professors in each of the four faculties of theology, philosophy, law, and medicine.) Stung by Council's reproof, Rivinus solicited the support of Johann Kuhnau and Daniel Vetter and submitted a memorandum citing the reasons for his decision.[4] He reported that the organ had been in danger of falling into the church because the beams on which it stood were rotten. The organ's winding was inadequate and the badly corroded pipework, especially in the Rückpositiv, was in need of a complete and thorough repair. Further, the organ's location was poor. It projected across the nave rather than directly down the nave's length, and its great distance from the musicians in the west gallery "caused thousands of errors." Rats were eating the bellows, which were located immediately below the granary. And the organ took up space that could better be used for private chapels and additional balconies. (During the church's two-year renovation, 24 chapels were built for wealthy individuals—mostly professors—who were willing to pay, or contribute, up to 600 taler for the privilege of being assigned them.)

In support of Rivinus's decision, Kuhnau and Vetter provided additional reasons for moving the organ in a jointly signed memorandum, in Kuhnau's hand, dated 25 September 1710.[5] They reminded the university that just such a move had been recommended 30 years earlier by no less an authority than Werner Fabricius, organist at St. Nicholas from 1658 to 1679 and also music director to Leipzig University. (Fabricius is the author of *Unterricht, wie man ein neu Orgelwerk, obs gut und beständig sey, nach allen Stücken, in- und auswendig examiniren, und so viel wie möglich probiren soll* [Instruction as to how a new organ should be examined, inside and outside, as to whether it is good and durable, and tested as thoroughly as possible], a guide published posthumously in 1756.) Moving the organ would make it possible to build a new, more impressive facade, and the organ could be set up in its new location without blocking light. They agreed that "with the organ and the musicians together in one place," the organist would "better be able to observe the beat, or *Takt*, and therefore the disorder that has always been in the music can be corrected that much easier."[6]

They also made recommendations for the organ's improvement. A new, large, architecturally designed case would allow removal of the Rückpositiv, a division that did not belong "in the current *galant* style" organs.[7] They wanted more direct communication between the continuo organist and the director and to create more space for singers and instrumentalists. The organ's short-octave compass needed to be expanded by adding D♯, F♯, and G♯ to the bass octave in all stops. They considered the pipework, in general, to be "well constructed of good *Metall*" and "still good and useful."[8] Nevertheless, they identified a number of stops, including all the organ's reeds, they wanted replaced: Fistula humana, Posaunen Bass 16′ (which sounded like "beetles buzzing in a box"), Nasat 3′ and Trompete 8′ (in the Rückpositiv), Principal 2′ and Regal (in the Brustwerk), and the rest of the stops in the Seiten-Pedal (Dulcian Bass, Cornet Bass, and Bauerflöten Bass). Metal from the discarded pipework would be used to build several new stops, including three Pedal reeds (Trompeten Bass 8′, Schalmey Bass 4′, and Cornet Bass 2′). They wanted the new Posaunen Bass 16′ built with wooden rather than metal resonators, which would save money while at the same time producing the right effect: "A stop of this size, with its

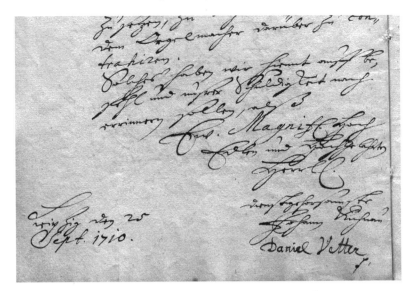

11. Signatures of kantor Johann Kuhnau and organist Daniel Vetter, memorandum dated 25 September 1710. UAL, Rep. II/III/B II 6, fol. 4v.

gravity and strength, must above all else be able to penetrate, just as one can hear in the organ at St. Nicholas's during congregational singing"[9]—a reference to the Posaunen Bass 16′ built by Zacharias Thayssner during the renovation carried out in 1691–94.

The experts advised that it would be necessary to make a contract with Scheibe and to emphasize that he must faithfully deliver the disposition that had been stipulated. They underscored how straightforward they regarded the project and described the builder's task as "not exactly equivalent to the Augean stables, which needed to be cleaned with Herculean effort." Most of the stops and their related parts already existed, and only minor repairs would need to be made. All the builder needed to do was construct a few new stops and the pipes necessary to expand the bass compass throughout. "None of this demands extraordinary expertise," they insisted, "and besides, the organ builder is honest, cheap, and hardworking."[10]

The memorandum included two dispositions. Kuhnau documented the 36-stop disposition of the existing organ.[11] The second disposition, in the hand of Vetter, specified the recommended changes: removal and addition of stops, improving the wind system, building three new keyboards, and adding a "Tremulant that affects the entire organ."[12] Vetter's proposed 37-stop disposition was only one stop larger than the existing organ. Both dispositions, it must be noted, vary slightly from the three-manual, 36-stop disposition published by Vogel around 1700.[13] (See appendix D-6 for a comparison of the three dispositions.)

Council members eventually accepted Rivinus's explanation and appear to have been persuaded by the arguments put forward by Kuhnau and Vetter. Insisting, however, that Rivinus take responsibility for his preemptive actions, Council resolved that henceforth "construction of the organ . . . shall remain the sole responsibility of Herr Doctor Rivinus."[14] Scheibe began receiving weekly payments in September 1710.

Even while Scheibe was dismantling and moving the organ, proposals were being solicited, and received, from other organ builders. A. H. Casparini appears to have made a proposal; Christoph Donat II, of Leipzig, offered to take on the project; and there may have been a proposal from a builder named Ritter.[15] The most prominent contender, however, was Gottfried Silbermann.

Just two days after he signed the memorandum in support of having the old organ repaired and improved, Kuhnau wrote to Immanuel Lehmann, a medical doctor and organ aficionado in Freiberg, requesting him to inform Silbermann that he was wanted in Leipzig immediately so that he could "take over [building] the new organ at St. Paul's."[16] Silbermann had made contact with Kuhnau on his way from Alsace to his hometown of Frauenstein, about 20 kilometers/12 miles southeast of Freiberg, where he was now building, at his own expense, his first organ in Saxony. As Kuhnau later described it to Mattheson, "[Silbermann] came some years ago from Strasbourg with good testimonials for superb organs and harpsichords that he had built not only in Strasbourg but also in various other places in France. Therefore at the time I also gave him a recommendation to take with him to Freiberg, where he was immediately entrusted with building a large organ, which he completed with great acclaim, delivering an unusually immaculate and accurately built work."[17] Kuhnau had told Lehmann that Silbermann had no equal when it came to knowledge of the fundamental mathematical and mechanical principles of organ building.[18]

Kuhnau's request was not immediately passed on. Silbermann's three-month-old proposal to build a new organ for Freiberg Cathedral had not yet been acted upon, and Lehmann feared that Freiberg was in danger of letting Silbermann "slip through its fingers." He warned that Silbermann was being sought after in a number of places. Not only had Kuhnau written, but Silbermann had been mentioned in a letter from Adam Rechenberg, professor of theology at Leipzig University, and, further, a letter of Vetter's could be produced in which he talked

of Silbermann having been recommended to build yet another organ. These letters were being "suppressed"—that is, not immediately shown to Silbermann—in
the hope of a quick, favorable decision by Freiberg's city council.[19] The authorities acted, and on 8 October 1710 Silbermann signed a contract to build a new,
three-manual, 41-stop organ for the cathedral in Freiberg by Christmas 1712.[20]
He would be paid 1,500 taler and provided all materials, as well as lodging and
meals for himself and his workers.

It was November before Silbermann came to Leipzig to see about building
the organ at St. Paul's. The joiner had already started to build the new organ
case, and Scheibe had been at work for more than 10 weeks. Council minutes
dated 20 November report that Silbermann "had a recommendation to make
concerning the organ project and had said he wished to look at the instrument."[21]
Silbermann's withering evaluation of the organ and the university's plan to repair
and improve it, and his self-confident proposal to build an entirely new organ
instead, is dated one week later, 27 November 1710.[22]

He regretted "from the bottom of my heart," Silbermann wrote, that he had
not found "a situation in which continuation of the renovation would conclude
satisfactorily." The organ's disposition and voicing were old-fashioned; the case
design and interior layout made it impossible to achieve a good playing action;
the stops were worthless, some not capable of producing "any loveliness or pleas-
antness at all"; the lead pipes had not been hammered and were very corroded,
especially the feet, and it was more work to repair them than to build new ones;
the facade Principal, like all of the stops, was patched together, and not only
did it not contribute to the organ's appearance, but it could never be brought
into proper harmony; to expand the compass and to support congregational
singing, he would need to add some stops and build additional chests, and he
could not imagine relinquishing the charm and sharpness of new pipework in
order to match "the dull, unpleasant and flute-like intonation of the existing
pipework." In short, "nothing anywhere in the organ relates to current fashion
and refinement."[23]

Silbermann anticipated the argument, sure to be raised by the university,
that the existing organ had served well and no doubt could continue to do so.
"It will of course be said that the organ has always been in use," he asserted,
"except, [the truth is] it was seldom used and only briefly, and never other than
with a large ensemble and with all the stops pulled. The major problems hidden
within it were not so easily noticed in the so-called *tutti* or full choruses of the
concerted music." Even though it had long been necessary, the director of music
had not thought it necessary to demand the organ's complete dismantling. But

circumstances had changed. "Now, partially to keep order in the congregational singing of chorales, partially also for the special pleasure of both locals and the increasing number of visitors, the new church services demand a more powerful, more pleasant, more perfect instrument, one more in keeping with the glory of such a world-famous university." Rebuilds and repairs of the old organ had been botched by inexperienced people who had not the slightest skill, Silbermann claimed. All one could do was rue the "tremendous costs expended so uselessly."[24]

Observing that "one could as easily build a new organ as sheathe the old one in patched-up new clothes," Silbermann offered to build a completely new organ. He proposed a three-manual, 44-stop organ to be delivered within two or two-and-a-half years. In payment he requested that he be given the tin and metal from the existing organ, that he receive a fee of 3,000 taler—he would provide the materials—and that the university would pay for the case and its carvings as well as for costs associated with cartage. He also voiced his intention to become the Leipzig University organ builder: "Out of love for this famous place, and since I wish to apply to you, most honored sirs, for academic citizenship in addition to the usual outright appointment as organ builder, and especially since Leipzig is so close to my city of birth, I will do my best to deliver a perfect new instrument according to the attached disposition, with 43 [*recte* 44] charming stops, some of which are not yet known in this country, although they are greatly admired in France."[25]

Even though he had just signed a contract to build a large organ for the cathedral in Freiberg, Silbermann was willing to move to Leipzig to become organ builder to the university and enjoy the privileges of academic citizenship. Biographer Werner Müller assumed this meant that Silbermann wanted to attend university lectures,[26] but the reference is to a class of academic citizens who, since the Middle Ages, were related to the university by being providers of services. Among other rights, those with academic citizenship were exempt from taxes and other duties and were allowed to purchase goods at favorable rates—an obvious advantage for an organ builder.

Silbermann's visit and his proposal came as a shock to Vetter. As he later recalled, his advice had been sought when the university decided to move the organ, and he had been asked to draw up a disposition that showed how the organ could be improved and to draft a contract with Scheibe. And he had been promised that he would be given responsibility for overseeing the project. Imagine his astonishment, then, when he learned that "a certain person's advice"—there is no doubt that the reference is to Kuhnau—was being followed by the university and that negotiations were being carried out with Silbermann, "whom this person had highly recommended."[27]

Vetter had no use for Silbermann's proposal. "Now, when I learned, as I lay on my sickbed, that [Silbermann] had recommended melting down the old 16-foot organ [with pipework] from very nice *Metall* . . . and building an 8-foot organ in its stead," he wrote some years later, "I could not refrain, as faint and weak as I was, from writing to the then rector, Herr Doctor [Johann] Schmid, to persuasively present the matter and to request that the Honorable University not be induced to undertake such a decision."[28] Vetter's impassioned letter, written hastily on Monday, 24 November 1710, made three main points: the old pipework was worthy of preservation, an organ should have a Hauptwerk based on a 16-foot Principal, and it was unlikely that Silbermann could build an organ for the price he had quoted.[29]

Vetter clearly was a preservationist. He acknowledged that the pipework in the existing organ was old but viewed it as rare and very much worth keeping. "It would be a shame if the admittedly old but rare registers were to be melted down, since the old instrument will give a good sound when it is moved to the choir [gallery]," he wrote.[30] The St. Paul's organ still had old pipework—pipework that had been repaired, voiced, and tuned many, many times but that nevertheless was highly valued by Vetter. He was determined to see it reused when the organ was relocated.

Vetter was no more accepting of Silbermann's plan to build a Hauptwerk based on Principal 8', and he was scathing in his rejection:

> If an entirely new organ is to be built, then it would be wholly unjustifiable if there were no manual Principal 16' in the facade, for it provides a strong and very splendid tone to the organ. It would be absurd to build an instrument with two manuals, each with a Principal at 8'. No difference would be heard when one plays back and forth between the manuals. This is a simple-minded suggestion for a disposition, the likes of which one would not find anywhere in Germany. In addition, this is a very large church, with a long reverberation time. If a Principal 8' were built for the Hauptwerk, many would find it laughable that a 16' instrument had been changed into an 8' instrument. Also, an 8' organ would not only sound too thin, it would not properly fill the church, just as at St. Nicholas's there is nothing lacking in the instrument except a Principal 16', and nevertheless people complain for this very reason.[31]

For Vetter, preserving a Hauptwerk based on Principal 16' was just as important as preserving the old and rare pipework generally. Not only did the 16-foot plenum provide the gravity[32] and massiveness required for playing hymns and chorales, as well as the praeludia and large-scale chorale preludes commonly improvised at the time, but it facilitated making echoes, the moving back and forth between larger and smaller registrations, as can frequently be found in chorale fantasias, for example.

The view that the 16-foot plenum was the organ's foundation slowly changed in the first half of the 18th century. Some large organs built around the turn of the century still included Principal 16' in the Hauptwerk (see table 5), but already by 1698, when Andreas Werckmeister published his revised and enlarged *Orgel-Probe*, it was considered no longer necessary. Werckmeister's "disposition for a large organ" included Principal 16', but it was "not imperative," and he suggested that "a Principal 8' might well take its place, since such a large stop has little appeal in a manual division."[33] Writing in the 1720s—Vetter died in 1721—Jacob Adlung observed, "Principal 16' is rarer in the manual [than in the pedal], but it adds excellent gravity as long as one does not play too many bass notes at the same time."[34] Much later, in the treatise published in 1758, Adlung noted that because it was expensive and also took up a lot of room, a manual Principal 16' of tin was rarely to be found in organ facades.[35]

Silbermann's concept achieved variety and contrast by differentiating the scaling and character of each division rather than by differentiating the basic pitch of the principal choruses in each division.[36] Werckmeister had proposed such an approach when he recommended that "in a large organ the builder might avail himself of different scaling [between divisions]. For example, [relatively] wide-scaled pipework might be used in the Oberwerk and Pedal, intermediate scaling in the second manual and quite narrow scaling in the third."[37] Silbermann proposed basing the Hauptwerk and Oberwerk divisions on Principal 8', the Brustwerk on Principal 4', and the Pedal on Principal 16'; the scaling would be "grave and imposing" (*gravitætisch und groß*) in the Hauptwerk, "sharp and penetrating" (*scharff und penetrant*) in the Oberwerk, "delicate and sweet" (*delicat und lieblich*) in the Brustwerk, and "strong and penetrating" (*starcken und durchdringenden*) in the Pedal. These formulations, as Greß has pointed out, were remarkably similar to the descriptions published by Christian Ludwig Boxberg in 1704 in his monograph on the organ completed in 1703 by the Casparinis for the Church of St. Peter and Paul in Görlitz, where "the Hauptwerk sounds stately [*prächtig*], the Oberwerk piquant and sharp [*spitzig und scharff*], the Brustwerk sharp and delicate [*scharff und delicat*]."[38] Greß suggests that Silbermann may have borrowed the terminology from the Casparinis.[39]

Finally, Vetter did not believe Silbermann could build a new organ for the price he had quoted. He thought Silbermann was trying to take advantage of the university. In short, he wanted to preserve old pipework that was still usable, and he found it ludicrous to build an organ with two manuals based on Principal 8′. He was certain Silbermann's concept would be ridiculed by connoisseurs. And further, he asked indignantly, was it not odd that the master builder submitted a drawing that he himself had not made?

Silbermann's proposal and Vetter's response were considered by Council at its meeting on 27 November 1710. Minutes noted that a new organ by Silbermann would cost 3,000 taler (1,000 immediately, 1,000 over time, and 1,000 when the organ was finished), that it would take at least two and a half years to complete, and that Silbermann wanted nothing to do with supervising the guild craftsmen such as tinsmiths or carpenters.[40] (Separate contracts were necessary with guild members such as carpenters and tinsmiths, and these costs were not paid by the organ builder, although sometimes the builder took responsibility for overseeing their work.) Vetter's memorandum "in which he disagreed with Silbermann" was read aloud. Council members' responses indicate how difficult it was to decide whether to accept Silbermann's proposal to build a new organ. A number of professors preferred to leave the decision to Rivinus, who had been assigned oversight of the organ project at their meeting a few weeks earlier:[41]

DR. [GOTTFRIED] OLEARIUS JUNIOR: Considers the situation quite worrying, and just doesn't know what to say.

DR. [JOHANNES] OLEARIUS SENIOR: Has nothing to say.

DR. [ADAM] RECHENBERG: If there were enough money, Silbermann should be allowed to build the organ.

DR. JOHANNES CYPRIAN: Doesn't know what to say.

DR. [CHRISTOPH] SCHREITER: Has no idea how he should decide. The decision should be left to Dr. Rivinus.

DR. [GOTTLIEB GERHARD] TITIUS: Agrees with Dr. Rechenberg.

DR. [POLYCARP GOTTLIEB] SCHACHER: Has just one reservation. What if, after one had contracted with him, Silbermann were to die? This would be a serious situation, and he wants no part of it, and it should be registered that he said this.

DR. [AUGUST QUIRINUS] RIVINUS: They should let him look after it; he would be responsible for bringing the instrument into better condition than it had been previously.

DR. [JOHANN WILHELM] PAULI: Doubts whether one should trust Silbermann with building the organ.

DR. SCHACHER (A SECOND TIME): Agrees with Dr. Pauli.

PROF. [JOHANN HEINRICH] ERNESTI: Shares Dr. Rechenberg's view.

DR. [JOHANN GOTTLIEB] HARDT: Abstains.

DR. MENCKE: If one had the money, one should have the [new] organ built.

DR. [JOHANN GEORG] ABICHT: One should entrust the organ to Silbermann.

DRS. [CHRISTIAN FRIEDRICH] BÖRNER, [JOHANN CHRISTIAN] S[CH]ELLE, AND [JOHANN CHRISTIAN] LEHMANN were unable to form an opinion.

That is, six professors were in favor of Silbermann building the new organ he had proposed, three did not think Silbermann should be hired, seven were uncertain how they should proceed, and one abstained from voting altogether. No decision is recorded, and there is no record of further discussion concerning Silbermann's proposal.[42]

Some weeks later, Silbermann was provided a gratuity. According to the record of expenses incurred during the week of 2–7 February 1711, Rector Johann Schmid paid 20 taler to "the organ builder from Freiberg for his journey here and his trouble."[43] A week later, Donat II offered to build the organ himself and severely criticized Scheibe, but on 4 December 1710 Council also refused this offer.[44]

Vetter was the city's most venerable and esteemed organist, held in high regard not only because of his seniority but for his knowledge of organ building. His thorough rejection of Silbermann's proposal and his plea to preserve and renovate the old organ were persuasive enough that Council could not form a majority in favor of accepting Silbermann's offer to build a completely new organ. "These ideas were judged to have such merit," Vetter claimed concerning the critique he had provided, "that what had been planned with Herr Silbermann was altered, and instead Herr Scheibe was contracted."[45]

To repeat: the process for deciding what should happen to the large organ at St. Paul's was chaotic and political. At the same time that the university was paying Scheibe to dismantle, move, repair, and enlarge the organ, it also was considering the proposal from Silbermann to build a new organ. Kuhnau very much wanted Silbermann to come to Leipzig, and Vetter might have been willing to have Silbermann take on the organ project—except that Silbermann refused to consider rebuilding or renovating the more than 200-year-old organ with its venerable pipework and instead made a proposal for a new organ that Vetter could not see his way to accepting. By early December the university had decided against building a new organ. Meanwhile, Scheibe and his associates, as well as the cabinetmaker constructing the new case, continued repairing and rebuilding the old one.

"That in this way Leipzig did not get a Silbermann organ can be regretted," Arnold Schering would write. "On the other hand, Scheibe eventually created a masterpiece . . . one of the newest and most beautiful organs in Germany."[46] Silbermann scholars have generally agreed with Schering's first sentiment but not his second. Flade concluded that Silbermann's 3,000-taler proposal was too high for the tightfisted university authorities who may also have feared that Silbermann would not be able to give the appropriate attention to the Leipzig project while also building the Freiberg Cathedral organ.[47] Flade also believed the university preferred Scheibe because he was a citizen of Leipzig. Müller was disappointed with the university's decision as well. He claimed that Scheibe's organ cost more than Silbermmann's would have and took seven [*sic*] years to build, while Silbermann had promised to build a new organ in just two and a half years. He, too, believed the university unfairly gave precedence to the local builder.[48]

Scheibe and Vetter must have been aware that the organ Scheibe renovated for Leipzig University would always be judged according to the new organ Silbermann had promised. Just before the organ's examination by Bach in December 1717, more than a year after the organ was finished, Vetter compared Scheibe's

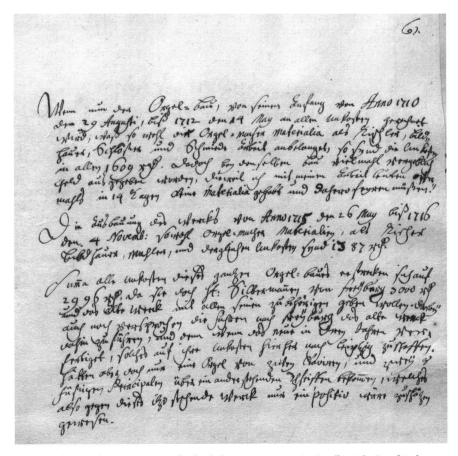

12. Daniel Vetter's comparison of Scheibe's renovation at St. Paul's with Gottfried Silbermann's proposal to build a new organ. Unsigned autograph. UAL, Rep. II/III/B II 5, fol. 61.

costs and concept to Silbermann's, and Scheibe included Vetter's comparison in his memorandum to the university:

> Now, if the organ project's expenses are calculated from its inception on 29 August 1710 until 14 May 1712, everything included—the organ builder, the materials, the carpenter, the carver, as well as locksmith and metal work—the expenses total 1,609 T. . . .
>
> The enlargement of the organ, from 26 May 1715 to 4 November 1716, for organ builder materials, as well as carpenter, carver, painter, and similar expenses, cost 1,387 T.
>
> In sum, total expenses for the entire organ project come to 2,996 T.[49]
>
> Now, Herr Silbermann of Freiberg would have charged 3,000 T. and also would have taken the old organ and everything belonging to it. In addition, he was promised transport of the old organ to Freiberg, and then, when the new organ was finished in three years, that it would be brought here to Leipzig at your [the university's] expense. But it would only have been an organ with 2 keyboards and 2 8-foot Principals, one in each division, which, no matter how you look at it, can only be considered a positive [a small organ] compared to the instrument that now exists.[50]

Scheibe Builds His Magnum Opus

Renovating the St. Paul's organ turned out to be a long and trying process. The project began in September 1710, when Scheibe dismantled the old organ, but regular payments were suspended in March 1712, even though the organ was nowhere near finished. Scheibe rebuilt the bellows over a four-week period from mid-April to mid-May 1712, but it was more than two years before the project was taken up again by the university. A contract to complete the pipework in the facade was drawn up in May 1715, a supplemental agreement for building the remaining pipework was recorded in November 1715, and Scheibe finished the three-manual, 54-stop organ in November 1716. Bach's examination took place in December 1717, but Scheibe did not receive the last installment of the monies owed him until March 1720, at the conclusion of a fairly acrimonious dispute with the university.

Phase One, 1710 to 1712

The organ Scheibe was to renovate had been in the old Dominican church dedicated to St. Paul since at least the early 16th century. According to sources relying on the description of the two-manual, 15-stop organ published by Michael Praetorius in 1619, the organ dated to around 1528.[51] However, according to

Werner Fabricius, who was appointed university music director in 1656, the organ had come into the church in 1537.[52] The organ was renovated twice in the 17th century: Josias Ibach attempted improvements in 1626–27;[53] his work was corrected, and the renovation completed, by Heinrich Compenius II and his son Esaias II in 1627–30;[54] and a renovation was carried out in 1685–87 by an unnamed builder but no doubt Christoph Donat I.[55] The church's positive organ was taken out during the Donat renovation, its pipe metal melted down and used for expanding the large organ.[56] By 1710, when it was dismantled and moved, the organ was a three-manual, 36-stop instrument.

According to Scheibe, the first phase of the organ's renovation started when he provided a cost estimate of 200 florins, excluding the wages and materials required by a carpenter and a laborer, to move, repair, and rebuild the organ in its new location.[57] Scheibe noted that while some items could be repaired, others would need to be newly built, and the organ's lack of wind had to be corrected. He warned that further problems were likely to be discovered once the organ was fully taken apart. The expenditure was approved on 6 September 1710, and Scheibe started receiving weekly payments from the university the following Saturday.[58]

What started as a project not worthy of "Herculean effort" rapidly grew more challenging and complex. Sometime that fall—the exact circumstances remain

13. Excerpt from record of wages paid to Johann Scheibe during the first phase of the St. Paul's organ project. UAL, Rep. II/III/B I 6, fol. 37.

unknown—it was agreed that the number of stops would be increased by 20, an increase of more than 50 percent, from 36 to 56 stops. Council minutes report that Scheibe offered to prepare an estimate for what "the new stops, separately, could cost,"[59] and memoranda from both Scheibe and Johann Burchard Mencke, who was rector during the second phase of the project, attest to the decision having been made in 1710 and to the organ having been prepared for the expansion "from the very beginning."[60] However, no estimate from Scheibe for additional stops survives, nor does any disposition proposal or contract for a 56-stop organ, and, other than the above, there is no correspondence relating to this decision.

Surprisingly, the only contract that survives from the early phase of the project also makes no mention of a major enlargement. A week before Christmas, three and a half months after the project had begun, Scheibe and the university apparently agreed to the project's parameters.[61] According to the contract, which was drafted by Vetter but never signed by the university, the organ's existing stops were to be retained and repaired as necessary. New stops, mostly replacements, included these: in the Pedal, Posaunen Bass 16′ with wooden resonators, Trompeten Bass 8′ (replacing Dulcian Bass 8′), and Principal Bass 16′ of *Metall*; in the Hauptwerk, Vox humana (replacing Fistula humana). The Rückpositiv division was to be moved into the main case, and Scheibe was to build new wind chests for the Brustwerk and the Pedal. New rollerboards would be necessary, and the bellows and wind trunks would be repaired and brought into perfect condition. Scheibe was to expand the short-octave compass by adding D♯ F♯ and G♯ to the lowest octave, a process that would involve building three new pipes for each stop as well as building supplementary chests, and to provide a new pedalboard and three newly built manual keyboards—the materials specified were ebony and ivory. In addition, Scheibe promised to build a "roller board" that would allow "the entire organ" to be played *manualiter* or *pedaliter*. It is clear that Vetter did not understand what Scheibe intended, because this enigmatic provision (#10 in the contract) must refer to the wind coupler (*Windkoppel*), a wind-chest construction that allowed Hauptwerk stops to be playable not only in the manual but also in the Pedal. For its part, the university promised to pay Scheibe 9 taler a week for 28 weeks, to provide or reimburse Scheibe for materials estimated at 200 taler (including six hundredweights of tin), and, in a provision that later became controversial, to pay 400 taler upon the organ's "proper delivery"—that is, on the organ's completion. Also, the university would be responsible for paying and providing materials to guild members such as joiners, carpenters, tinsmiths, or ironworkers.[62]

Over a period of some 18 months, from 13 September 1710 until 25 March 1712, the university paid Scheibe 793 taler in wages, usually at the rate of 9 taler per week (see p. 63).[63] Scheibe paid wages to his assistants and provided them food and lodging, but at what rate and to how many is unknown. In Altenburg, where Heinrich Gottfried Trost worked with three assistants, Trost was paid approximately 7 taler per week. His most experienced journeyman earned 1 taler 4 groschen, while the other two were paid 1 taler 2 groschen per week. Trost himself would have retained approximately 3 taler 15 groschen.[64] As we know from the payment record for the week ended 24 October 1711, Scheibe's journeymen each received 2 taler a week. That week, Scheibe received 7 taler rather than the usual 9, because, it was noted, "this week he had only one journeyman." In the same 18-month period, the university paid out 398 taler 15 groschen 6 pfennig for organ-building materials and made payments as well to guild workers who were building the case and decorating the facade—the sculptors who carved the figures and the pipe shades, the painter, the glazier who provided the glass in the gloriole at the top of the organ, the turner who provided the 62 stop knobs, the joiner who built the case, among others.[65]

In March 1712, even though the organ was not yet finished, regular purchases of materials and weekly payments to the organ builder were suspended, and Scheibe was told that no further funds would be assigned to the organ.[66] As Council minutes make clear, the university wanted the organ project finished as quickly as possible. To a request from Scheibe that he be allowed to examine and, if necessary, repair the bellows, Council resolved, "The organ builder should do the bellows, and he should be dealt with generally, but otherwise the organ project should be concluded."[67] When the last weekly wage was disbursed on 25 March 1712, Scheibe also received "2 taler, as a reward at the conclusion of the organ-building project."[68] The organ project that started without an official contract came to a halt without an official act.

On 16 April 1712, Scheibe signed a contract to completely rebuild the organ's six bellows, for which he was paid 30 taler and provided 60 pieces of leather and 120 horse veins or straps.[69] He completed the repair—essentially new bellows—on 14 May. A few days earlier, in the presence of university officials, he had turned over stops and materials that remained unused. (These were stored and returned to Scheibe in July 1715, during the second phase of the project.) In June, with the project on hold, Scheibe requested an advance on the agreed-upon 400-taler honorarium so that he could pay some debts; he received 50 taler on 2 August 1712.[70] With the church renovation complete and having spent most of the money that had been raised by selling private chapels, pews, and seats, the university closed the books. Including expenditures for the organ, according to the university's accounting, the renovation cost 9,918 taler 7 groschen; income totaled 10,906 taler 16 groschen; 988 taler 9 groschen remained unspent.[71] (For a detailed record of organ expenses, see appendix B-1.)

The first phase of the organ project cannot have been easy for Scheibe. First, there was the unusual circumstance that the university had not signed his contract. At the meeting held 18 December 1710, Rivinus had presented for approval the contract he and Scheibe had agreed to, but Council wanted it reviewed and refused to give Scheibe a discretionary payment he had requested until it had been determined that the contract was "good and airtight."[72] The university never did sign the contract but instead, time and again, requested that Scheibe swear an oath in which he agreed to work under the university's jurisdiction and to faithfully and honestly fulfill what he had promised. Scheibe considered this request an insult, saying that no organ builder had ever been asked to do such a thing, and refused to sign.[73]

Also, there was the situation with Professors Abicht and Schelle, who wanted Scheibe to prove that he was actually capable of getting the organ into playing condition.[74] Their intervention caused a lot of trouble. Scheibe's warning that setting up the organ too soon could cause severe damage was ignored, and the newly repaired bellows were damaged when the organ was played before they had fully dried. Also, Scheibe was forced to get the organ playing before he had had time either to modify the wind chests (for expansion of the short octave) or build new keyboards. "As I was told to my face," wrote Scheibe in May 1711, "all of this was for no other reason than that I was mistrusted and it was not believed that I could bring the instrument into [good] condition."[75]

There also was the problem with the pipes that had been removed from the old organ and stored for safekeeping in a large hall in the university library. When examined later, the pipework was found to be very damaged—"much of it, as if it had been done purposely—trampled by feet, and flipped over, and twisted." According to Vetter, who related this episode, he and Scheibe repaired the pipework with painstaking care and precaution, and by the end of 1711 organ rebuilding could resume.[76]

Finally, there was the frustration and annoyance that resulted from having the case and the organ built at the same time. The carpenters building the case were careless and allowed wood shavings, and even their planing tools, to fall into the pipes and chests. Everything filled with dust, and Scheibe had to remove pipes, clean, and set everything up "like new" again. As he wrote in May 1711, he anticipated the same vexation when the statues were installed on the case and when the mason broke into the wall for the new window near the organ, and he urged the university to have this work done as soon as possible, before more of the organ was put in place. After delaying commissioning the sculptor and ordering the window on several occasions, both orders were placed soon after Council received Scheibe's memorandum.[77] The pressure to finish things quickly must have been enormous.

By contrast, in Freiberg, where he had signed a contract on 6 October 1710 to build a new three-manual organ for the cathedral, Silbermann delayed setting up the organ, especially the pipework, until the case and its spectacular decoration were completely finished. The contract for the case was signed 13 June 1711, and like in Leipzig, it was to cost 200 taler and be finished in six months. In April 1712, however, the joiner was awarded an additional 50 taler and given three additional weeks to finish his work. Once the case was finally finished, on 27 May 1712 the sculptor was commissioned to decorate the case for a fee of 230 taler. His work included pipe shades, Corinthian capitals, and various figures, including four 8½′ angels (one of which holds a portative organ). This work took until the beginning of February 1713, significantly delaying Silbermann's installation past the promised completion date of December 1712. Silbermann had the Hauptwerk playing by mid-December 1713 and finished the organ in July 1714.[78]

A Two-and-a-Half-Year Pause

The St. Paul's organ was far from finished when payments stopped in 1712. As Scheibe explained in the memorandum dated 8 February 1713,[79] except for the two largest pipes (C, D), which he had already built, the new tin facade pipes were yet to be constructed. He still needed to construct the three pipes (D♯, F♯, G♯) that would complete the lowest octave in each register and to construct and install about 20 non-facade stops. He estimated that he would need 1,100 taler in wages and materials and about 9 months just to finish the facade; if he were to finish the organ entirely, he required approximately 1,600 taler and 21 months. There is no record of any response from the university.

With construction of the St. Paul's organ on hold, Scheibe took on other projects—an overhaul at St. Thomas's, repairs at St. John's and at St. Nicholas's, and building a 12-stop organ for the village church in Gundorf. This caused some members of the university to claim that Scheibe was living "rent-free" at St. Paul's while he took on outside work and a Council subcommittee to resolve that Scheibe "should be turned out of [his rooms at] St. Paul's College."[80] (In return for providing organ maintenance and tuning, housing was provided for Scheibe and his family as well as a space for tools and materials at St. Paul's.) Council now seemed reluctant for any further work to be done on the organ. Scheibe's unwillingness to give up his key to the organ—he was obviously still working on the instrument—was discussed on several occasions. Minutes from May 1714 report that Scheibe still held the key to the choir gallery and the organ, which he was unwilling to hand over, and that because he was always allowing students to play the organ, there was concern that the instrument would be damaged. The hope was expressed that the organ could be successfully examined by an organ builder and that the university would take over responsibility for the organ.[81] (During a renovation, the organ builder is fully responsible for the instrument.) Council unanimously agreed that "the key should be demanded from the organ builder." Rechenberg noted as well that the workshop in the Lampe had been ruined by the organ builders. Schacher went so far as to propose that a lock be put on the organ to keep Scheibe out.[82]

The uneasiness—even hostility—that persisted on the part of the university cannot have been helped by the criticism levied by Trost. Minutes dated 15 June 1713 report that "an organ builder who calls himself Trost came to His Magnificence [the rector] and told him that the organ at St. Paul's was no good, that it was badly voiced, that sheep's leather had been used in the wind chests, and much more of the same."[83] (Whether using sheep's leather is a fault is questionable, as some builders considered sheep's leather preferable. For example, during his negotiations with the church council in Mühlhausen, Johann Friedrich Wender cited the fact that he was using "the more durable sheep's leather" for the bellows as one reason why he could not reduce his fee.)[84] Noting that Kuhnau was responsible for the organ and that this was a thorny situation—or as the minutes put it, "a serious matter"—Council resolved "that organ builder Trost speak with Cantor Kuhnau and point out the defects to him."[85] Nothing further regarding the matter is recorded in Council's minutes; it is not known whether Trost ever spoke with Kuhnau or how Kuhnau might have responded. Nor is it known which Trost visited Leipzig and the St. Paul's organ. Heinrich Gottfried Trost, who is now best known for the organs he built in Altenburg and Waltershausen, had only just become a master builder; it would be some five years before he would establish his shop in Altenburg. His father, Tobias Gottfried Trost, who built the organ at St. John's in 1694–95, did not die until 1721. Either of them—or both of them—could have examined the work-in-progress at St. Paul's in 1713.

The situation changed, it appears, when Scheibe informed the university that he had fulfilled his contractual obligations and wished to be paid. In a memorandum dated 21 August 1714,[86] he described the history of the project, how a contract had been agreed to four years earlier in which he had promised "to reinstall the organ at St. Paul's, build new wind chests and wind trunks, and take the old bellows apart and replace them with entirely new ones, as well as increase by 20 stops the old pipework consisting of 35 [*sic*] registers and install them on the wind chests," and how the university had promised to pay 9 taler 6 groschen weekly to cover his assistants' wages and 400 taler to him "for my effort and work." He described some of the difficulties he had faced: how Professors Abicht and Schelle had tried to have the contract canceled, how work had slowed down when Professor Rivinus was no longer in charge and sometimes he could not work for weeks at a time for lack of materials, and how, finally, in the middle of his best work, he had had to drop everything when he was told there was no longer any money available. Nevertheless, he had completely repaired the old pipework (with new feet as well as pieces to the tops of the pipes), added a lot of new pipework, built new pedal stops, and corrected whatever needed correcting. Everything had been brought into good condition, and he asked that he now be paid 320 taler (the 400 taler he was due less what he had already received) and that the university not withhold from him what he had earned, either by never paying or by paying at some later date when the organ was completely finished.

The university took no action for a long time. The project that had started inadvertently and initially seemed so straightforward had dragged on for four years, twice as long as it had taken to renovate the church itself. Somehow the decision had been made to add 18 or 20 stops to the organ, considerably enlarging the project. From the university's point of view, the project probably seemed troublesome, complicated, unending, and, above all, expensive.

But then the unexpected happened. Gottlieb Gerhard Titius, distinguished professor of Roman law and rector for the winter semester 1713–14, died in office on 10 April 1714. In his last will and testament, signed just two days before his death, Titius bequeathed to "St. Paul's 1500—that is, fifteen hundred—taler, which are to be used as they are needed, especially for completing [enlarging] the organ."[87] It would be hard to overestimate the impact this generous gift would have.

It took 10 months for the university to respond. In February 1715 Council asked Vetter—in the company of an officer of the university—to investigate and report on the status of the organ,[88] and in March, when the matter of "the organ project, and that it should be brought to a conclusion," was considered, Council resolved that "the organ builder should be spoken with, and, to the

14. Gottlieb Gerhard Titius
(1660–1714). Engraving by Martin
Bernigeroth, 1713. Herzog August
Bibliothek Wolfenbüttel,
Portr. 1 13524 (A 22026).

greatest degree of accuracy possible, it should be determined what he would require to finish the organ, beginning with the facade," and emphasized that Scheibe "must submit to the university's authority."[89]

The university's distrust of Scheibe and its impatience with what was going on are demonstrated vividly by a discussion that took place later in the same meeting. It was reported that sometimes Scheibe or his assistants worked by candlelight at night in the church, a practice the professors deemed quite dangerous. (Working by candlelight was common, of course, but always carried the risk of fire from carelessness.) Council resolved that Scheibe "must relinquish the keys to the small door, the church, and the organ, and if he continues to work in the church without permission, he will be considered a delinquent."[90]

There is no evidence that Scheibe relinquished the key to the organ or that he ever was forced to pay for whatever damage occurred in the workshop space assigned to him in November 1710. He certainly was never forced to leave his rooms at St. Paul's College.

Phase Two, 1715 to 1716

The organ project was restarted when Mencke signed the contract on behalf of "the Most Worshipful University of the City of Leipzig" on 26 May 1715.[91] Mencke was appointed professor of history at Leipzig University in 1699, succeeded his father as editor in chief of *Acta Eruditorum* in 1707, and became official historiographer to the Royal Polish and Electoral Saxon Court and King's Counsel in 1708. He was a mentor to Johann Christoph Gottsched and had married Katharina Margaretha Gleditsch, whose father was the greatest German publisher of his age. Mencke served six terms as rector—including, crucially, the summer semesters of 1715 and 1717. Without his leadership and support, without his

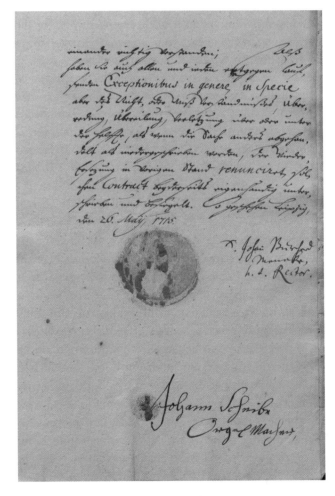

15. Signatures of Johann Burchard Mencke and Johann Scheibe on contract signed 26 May 1715. UAL, Rep. II/III/B II 5, fol. 82r.

diplomatic but fearless coercion of the university's Concilium Decemvirorum, it is unlikely the organ project ever would have been completed.

Scheibe promised "to completely finish the organ already begun," but as the contract terms and Scheibe's estimate for wages and materials make clear, the 950 taler being spent from Titius's bequest would be used primarily to finish the pipework missing from the organ's facade. For almost five years, ever since the organ had been dismantled, there had been no finished organ at St. Paul's. The organ had been moved to its new location, the new case had been finished by May 1711, and statues and pipe decoration had been added by the end of the year. Until 1715, however, the facade remained incomplete. Only the two largest pipes had been newly constructed from tin. The rest of the facade pipes, dull with age, were *Metall* pipes that had been retained from the old organ. Now, according to the contract, Scheibe would build new 16' pipes from tin for the remaining eight pipes in the outside flats, new 6' pipes from tin for the upper flats on either side of the Brust and the window, new feet from tin for existing Principal 16' pipes, and an octave of 8' pipes in order to turn the existing Principal 4' into a Principal 8'. All the old pipes would be polished, and every new pipe would be made from "good, pure, polished tin" (*guten reinen und hellen Zinn*). In addition, he would build the pipes needed for expanding the short-octave compass by three notes in each register, he would revoice the Posaunen Bass 16' and the Trompeten Bass 8', and he would build the necessary two new wind chests for the Quint 6'. Everything would be revoiced and tuned. Scheibe promised to complete the work in 20 weeks—even though he had estimated that, with four assistants, he would need 24 weeks—and agreed that the finished work should be examined by "one or more experienced organists" to be chosen by the university. If any shortcomings were discovered at the examination, he would correct them at his cost, and he would provide the usual one-year warranty.[92]

The university set very strict financial terms. Scheibe would be paid 15 taler a week for 20 weeks and would receive 150 taler after the organ was successfully examined. Another 450 taler were reserved for materials, which Scheibe was responsible for selecting and purchasing. If he were to spend more than the allocated amount, the difference would be deducted from the 150 taler he had been promised at the project's conclusion; on the other hand, the university would keep any money left unspent from the allocated amount. The contract specifically required that Scheibe "submit entirely to the Most Worshipful University's authority," and Scheibe signed an oath on 16 July 1715 to faithfully fulfill the contract, to not waste or use for his own benefit any of the materials, and to operate entirely under the jurisdiction of the university.[93] There was one further condition: Scheibe agreed to give up all claims against the university for any fees remaining unpaid; in return, he would be paid a gratuity of 50 taler at the end of the project and was given the promise that the university would make no further claims against what it perceived he owed.[94] (This is a reference to Scheibe living and working rent-free in return for maintaining and tuning the organ; see below.)

Scheibe completed the pipework for the facade on schedule. Shortly thereafter, at Council's meeting held 21 November 1715, Mencke, whose term as rector had expired in the third week of October, presented Council a plan for completing the organ, which was "finished except for 18 registers the organ builder wants to add."[95] He read aloud a draft of a contract that provided for Scheibe building the 18 registers by Easter 1716 for a fee of just 200 taler (covering wages and materials), and he explained to his colleagues where the funds could come from: 77 taler remained unspent from the amount previously allocated, 50 taler had been promised by Titius's brother (from the sale of Titius's library), and 73 taler could be taken from what remained of the Titius bequest.[96]

But Council could not muster the will. Rechenberg, who admitted knowing little about organ building and had heard that "it had not been necessary to build such a large instrument in such a small church," said he found no reason to continue building. Professor Lüder Mencke (Johann Burchard's uncle) thought they should abide by what had been accomplished in the previous contract and give no further thought to anything new, especially since the organ's maintenance would be a considerable burden in the future. Schacher, who had once proposed that a lock be put on the organ to keep Scheibe away from it, agreed that nothing further should be done. Lehmann said that a lot of money had already been spent, but nevertheless, "because it is a beautiful instrument [*ein schön Werk*] it would be a shame if it were not completely finished," especially since it would cost so little to do so. He offered to give 12 taler toward the organ's completion. Council resolved to "remain [content] with [what had been accomplished by] the previous contract."[97]

Stunned, Mencke wrote a trenchant memorandum dated 3 December 1715.[98] He expressed amazement that on account of "a paltry 70 or 80 taler" the university really wanted to be blamed for being unable to complete the organ. The Titius bequest stated "clearly and certainly" that the funds were to be used—here he was quoting directly from Titius's will—"*especially for completing [enlarging] the organ at St. Paul's*" (emphasis Mencke's). Council had accepted the bequest and now was obligated to carry out the bequest's terms. He knew some would argue that the recent contract with Scheibe had in fact been for the completion of the organ, but the very terms of the contract testified otherwise. Only the most absolutely necessary items had been included in the agreement, because, in spite of Titius specifying the amount of 1,500 taler in his will, an amount recommended to Titius by Mencke himself, Council accepted only 1,200 taler from the heirs. "Given that it was planned from the very beginning that the organ have 66 registers [including accessories]," he continued, "and the wind chests and the like all were prepared accordingly, clearly one cannot say that the organ is *complete* as long as eighteen of the 66 registers are still missing" (again, emphasis Mencke's).[99]

It was also wrong, Mencke asserted, to think that the bequest was solely for maintenance of the organ or that by building additional stops maintenance expenses would increase so much that the financial well-being of St. Paul's would be endangered. The tin and lead pipes to be added would require no regular maintenance "because, as all organ experts report, such pipes last for several hundred years before they become infected with *Salpeter* [corrode]."[100]

16. Johann Burchard Mencke (1674–1732). Engraving by Johann Georg Mentzel, 1715. City History Museum Leipzig, M 244.

Items that might require maintenance, such as the wind chests and bellows, had already been built and would require neither more nor less maintenance if the 18 stops were added. Further, he recommended paying for such maintenance with the interest earned by investing the 100 taler that would remain in the Titius bequest and informed Council that "the organ builder, in the burdensome oath already agreed to with the university, offered to maintain the organ in working order for life for the annual interest of 5 taler."[101]

Finally, Mencke made an offer that Council could not bring itself to refuse: he would guarantee that, including what had already been spent, the organ would be completely finished at a cost of no more than 1,100 taler altogether. If it cost more than that, he would pay the difference himself. Council's agreement is recorded succinctly in the minutes of the meeting held 5 December 1715: "It was agreed that the king's counsel, Mencke, should be assigned the requested 67 taler, in that he promises to handle everything, and whatever exceeds this amount, he obligates himself thereto."[102] Clearly, Mencke had brought pressure to bear on the university. With the apparent interference of the king himself, the "18 registers still missing"[103] now could be built.

Scheibe agreed to finish the organ by Easter—an unsigned draft of a contract survives[104]—but it was 29 October 1716 when Scheibe informed the university that the organ would be finished in two weeks. He asked to be informed when and how the organ would be examined and presented an accounting of income and expenses for all he had done since May 1715. By his reckoning, he was owed 347 (*recte* 346) taler 13 groschen in both wages and unreimbursed cash expenditures for materials.[105]

The last phase of the project took much longer than anyone anticipated: the especially cold winter had made it hard to work, the particularly large number of academic sermons and orations had interrupted voicing of the pipework, and—it must be admitted—Scheibe took on more than he had promised in the contract(s). He had built a new wind chest for the Rückpositiv (that was moved into the main case), because the old one "which had the short octave, could not be used." He had built an entirely new Principal 8′, rather than simply adding a bass octave of new pipes to the existing Principal 4′ in the Brustwerk facade, because, he said, it would have resulted in "an unequal harmony [blending]." He had paid a joiner to build "another case for the Brust[werk], not only because the previous one had an ugly appearance and ruined the look of the facade, but because it lacked height and there would not have been room for the 8-foot pipes agreed to in the contract." He replaced the mouths of the manual Principal 16′ pipes so that they would have the same Roman mouth shape as the new pedal

Principal 16′ pipes. He had added a Cymbelstern and sounding pipes to the gloriole at the top of the organ, because it was "necessary for the improvement of the facade and the organ's proper arrangement." He had replaced some 600 pipes "here and there throughout the organ"—pipes that were corroded, or no longer could hold their pitch, or could not even form a tone. He had had the ironmonger build 150 "iron arms for moving the registers and sliders" and had provided a coupler between the Brust and the Manual (Hauptwerk) keyboards. And he had set the organ's pitch at "proper Chorton, because it was much requested and demanded by the musicians . . . and was also necessary so that the organ could be used with the usual instruments accompanying the [concerted] church music." Scheibe also had built the additional new registers that he had been contracted to build—although three stops were excluded, "because installing any stop that in future will from time to time require either tuning or close attention was specifically prohibited [by the university]." (Scheibe is referring to reed stops that were not built, including Schalmey 4′ and Cornet 2′ in the Pedal.)[106]

With the organ complete, the university also heard from Mencke, who expressed both the certainty that Scheibe had fulfilled the terms of the contract—and much more besides—and the hope that the organ would be diligently examined by skillful experts at the earliest opportunity, that Scheibe would be found to be "free of all further claims," and that the university would provide Scheibe a discretionary "reward . . . for all that he has supplied over and above the contract."[107] In an attachment, he provided a detailed accounting (see appendix B-2). Mencke admitted that Scheibe sometimes did more than was required. "Partly his own ambition spurred him on," he wrote. "He so much wanted the instrument to be as perfect as possible, so that he would garner honor from both foreigners and locals, as in fact has been the case." Also, Scheibe had known about promises of additional funding—about the additional 50 taler from Titius's estate and about the 400 taler that Carl Gottfried Engelschall, court chaplain in Dresden, had offered to raise for the project. Scheibe was so encouraged by these promises, Mencke reported, that if he had not been restrained, he would have made the organ even larger (*weit stärcker*). Mencke believed that paying Scheibe something more for his extraordinary efforts was really a question of honor:

> I am certain that to date he has not earned one taler of profit on this entire project, the equal of which is not often seen, but likely has been forced into debt on account of it. The university is probably not legally required to give him anything more, but I nevertheless find it necessary to once again intercede on his behalf—a wretchedly

poor man who has grown very bitter and who has suffered many undeserved ac-
cusations—so that, when it is found at the instrument's examination that the organ
is even better than required by the contract, you will present him with a gratuity.[108]

Mencke also reminded the university that it had imposed, without his agreement, the additional demand that Mencke pay the outstanding rent the university deemed that Scheibe owed; however, paying the outstanding rent was
totally against what had been agreed to in the contract dated 26 May 1715, when
Scheibe had agreed to forfeit his claim to what remained of the 400 taler still
owed him from the first phase of the project and in return was promised, even
though it was well known at the time that he owed several years' worth of rent,
that no further financial claims would be made against him. In Mencke's view,
although the forgiveness of the rent debt was not explicitly stated, it was nevertheless implicit in the agreement that no further demands of any kind would
be made, and he had explained it this way to Scheibe at the time.

The rent charged for the rooms Scheibe had at St. Paul's College was a serious and lingering bone of contention. In years past, 4 taler annually had been
paid out, as if it were a salary, for the organ builder's rent—that is, the organ
builder earned an annual fee for maintaining the organ, but rather than paying
him directly, the amount was credited to the rental charge for his rooms at St.
Paul's College (a separate entity from St. Paul's Church). Beginning in 1710, the
annual rent, or maintenance fee, was increased to 12 taler, and the amount was
charged, but not credited, during the years the organ was being built. The unpaid
rent was discussed on three occasions in late 1715, and each time, in spite of
the terms of the 26 May agreement, Council confirmed its intention to collect
Scheibe's rental arrears by deducting the amount from any future gratuity or
cash payment.

At its meeting on 7 November, Council resolved that the 50-taler gratuity that had been promised to Scheibe upon completion of the facade should
instead become payable only after the organ was completely finished and successfully examined and only after deducting Scheibe's outstanding rent as of
Michaelmas, which amounted to 54 guilders 18 groschen—that is, 48 taler.[109] Two
weeks later, when Mencke proposed that Council commit the funds necessary
to completely finish the organ, he also asked Council to forgive Scheibe's rent
debt: "Scheibe has had many items made at his own expense and has debts.
Should they be taken care of, and the rent forgiven?" Again Council refused,
stipulating that anything due Scheibe would be paid only after his rent debt had
been cleared.[110] Finally, at its meeting on 5 December 1715, at the same time that
Council agreed to allow Mencke to oversee completion of the organ, it resolved,

without Mencke's approval, that he would be obligated to pay the room rent owed by Scheibe from the monies allocated to him to complete the project.[111]

When Scheibe learned of the university's renewed demands for payment of his rent, he pleaded for reconsideration. In a letter dated 24 February 1716, he said he never would have relinquished his claim for compensation relating to the first phase of the contract except with the understanding that the university, likewise, would relinquish its claim to be reimbursed for cash advances and for the rent that was accruing while he lived at St. Paul's. It had been his understanding when he signed the May 1715 contract that all his debts had been forgiven. He was incensed that he was being charged rent for such miserable accommodation, and he painted a heart-wrenching picture of the rooms where he and his family lived—rooms so "badly built, unhealthy, moldy, airless and poorly protected" that his family's health had suffered—indeed, two of his children had died there. Scheibe's anger at the injustice is palpable. "Surely for the large amount of rent that has already been charged to me one could provide more comfort," he protested.[112] Furthermore, the university was acting against accepted custom, according to which an organ builder who took on the building or major repair of an instrument would be provided, for the duration of the project, at no cost to the builder, both appropriate workspace and living quarters.

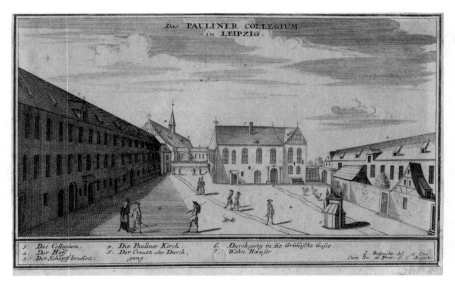

17. St. Paul's courtyard with the Collegium and residences. Engraving by Gabriel Bodenehr, first half of the 18th century. City History Museum Leipzig, 1759.

The university's position regarding Scheibe's rent remained firm, even though Council must have known it was in the wrong. Because the university had imposed a stipulation he had not agreed to and had not dared put the agreement in writing, Mencke declared the agreement null and void. He had the right to demand reimbursement for everything he had spent, he declared, but would be satisfied with 94 taler 22 groschen 1 pfennig—that is, the amount that remained unspent from the 1,100 taler assigned to the supplemental project. Mencke was paid on 4 February 1717.[113]

Christoph Ernst Sicul later described some of what Mencke had done on the organ's behalf:

> That the [organ] inscription should refer to Herr Counsel Mencke and that it should have been initiated when he was rector, is because in the summer of 1715, when he was *Rector Magnificus,* he zealously promoted the instrument, and the contract with the organ builder for the necessary completion of the instrument was concluded at that time, and, also, the work done under the first [supplemental] contract was completed during the time he was rector, even though later it was found useful to add some registers, and moreover, Herr Counsel Mencke was entrusted the sole direction of the project to its now successful conclusion.[114]

Mencke saw to it that the Titius bequest "for completing [enlarging] the organ" was honored after all. In the end, 100 taler remained unspent, monies that could be invested to cover annual maintenance and care of the organ. The problem of Scheibe's unpaid rent, however, remained unresolved.

Wages and Fees

Rather than being paid in three or four larger installments, Johann Scheibe was paid on a weekly basis, usually at the rate of 9 taler 6 groschen—9 taler to cover wages, lodging, and food for himself and his assistants and 6 groschen for candles (*Lichte*), and he was given a workspace. Irregular payments were made while the old organ was being dismantled and moved. Regular weekly payments began Saturday, 8 November 1710, and stopped on 25 March 1712, even though the renovation was incomplete. In early April 1712 pipes from a number of stops were placed in storage,[115] and on 16 April Scheibe signed a contract to rebuild the organ's six bellows, which he finished a month later, on 14 May. In what turned out to be the first phase of the project, Scheibe was paid 793 taler in wages and received 77 taler in advances on the 400-taler fee he had been promised at the project's conclusion—870 taler altogether. Tellingly, university records refer to one of these advances as being paid "in anticipation, as an advance on his *hoped-for* compensation" (emphasis added).[116]

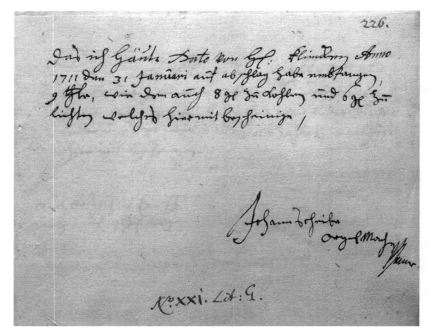

18. "That today, the 31st January in the year of 1711, I received from Herr Klimpke 9 taler as well as 8 gr. for coal and 6 gr. for lights [candles], is herewith acknowledged [by] Johann Scheibe, organ builder." Receipt for weekly wages. UAL, Rep. II/III/B I 5, fol. 226.

Scheibe also received weekly payments during the second building phase, which began on 26 May 1715 with the decision to build the remaining missing pipework and ended when Scheibe completed the organ on 4 November 1716. During this phase, Scheibe received altogether 591 taler: weekly rates varied from as little as 2 taler to as much as 21 taler; the average for the 75 weeks of the second phase was just under 8 taler per week. In addition, according to the settlement agreement reached in February 1718, Scheibe was paid 200 taler against expenses he incurred over and above the contract. In total, then, Scheibe was paid 1,661 taler for completely renovating the three-manual organ and expanding it to 54 stops.

A helpful comparison can be made with Silbermann and the payments he received while building the cathedral organ in Freiberg. When the contract was signed on 7 October 1710, Silbermann received an initial payment of 100 taler. In 1711 he received 450 taler in six installments; in 1712 he received 600 taler in seven installments; in 1713 he received 410 taler in five installments; and in 1714

TABLE 3   Comparison of building costs: Silbermann's new organ for Freiberg Cathedral (III/44, 1710–14) and Scheibe's rebuild of the organ at St. Paul's Church, Leipzig (III/54, 1710–16)

Silbermann		Scheibe
1,850	To the organ builder	1,661
	To artisans:	
251	Joiner	200
242	Sculptor(s)	180
204	Woodworker	
108	Smithy (*Schmiede*)	
100	Locksmith (*Schlösser*)	35
65	Painter	45
38	For screws and nails	14
37	Mason	
25	Turner (*Drechsler*)	7
10	Rope maker (*Seiler*)	
8	Tinsmith (*Klempner*)	
	Glazier	5
2	Brazier (*Rotgießer*)	
2	Belt maker (*Gürtler*)	
1,092 taler	Total to artisans	486 taler
	For materials:	
722	Tin and lead	365
151	Boards, posts, oak staves	146
57	Leather	75
32	Glue	28
21	Brass wire and sheets	19
10	Ebony and ivory	11
7	Writing paper, tallow, and wax	
7	Parchment	4
	Coal and firewood	33
	Bismuth	12
	Light (candles)	19
3	Other materials and expenses	147
1,010 taler	Total for materials	859 taler
3,952 taler	Grand total	3,006 taler

Source (for the Silbermann organ costs): Müller 1982, 124–25.

he received the remaining 290 taler in four installments. In total, Silbermann
was paid 1,850 taler for a new three-manual, 44-stop organ.[117]

There is no record of Scheibe and his assistants having been rewarded with
gratuities. Two taler were paid to Scheibe in March 1712 on "the conclusion of
building the organ," it is true, and his journeyman received a 16-groschen gratuity for the work involved in transporting the large wooden Pedal pipes.[118] When
the organ renovation was taken up again on 26 May 1715 and Scheibe signed a
contract to build the missing tin facade pipes, he was promised a 50-taler gratuity when he finished, but the only such disbursement was a 40-taler "general
advance" made on 13 December 1715,[119] and Mencke later claimed that Scheibe
had in fact spent his "50-taler compensation" on the organ, because he so much
wanted to finish it to his satisfaction and honor—indeed, had provided far more
than promised.[120]

Nor is there any record of Scheibe—and the organ—being honored with the
traditional celebratory meal at the conclusion of a project. The contrast with
Freiberg is stark. In addition to having their travel, food, and lodging covered,
Kuhnau and Gottfried Ernst Pestel, court organist in Altenburg, each were
paid a handsome fee of 24 species-taler—a species-taler is worth 32 groschen
or one-third more than a regular taler—for their examination of Silbermann's
cathedral organ in August 1714. In addition, Freiberg's city councillors believed
that "honor required that they not omit giving a ceremonial dinner," which took
place at the home of the mayor.[121] In Leipzig, Johann Sebastian Bach was paid
20 taler for examining Scheibe's organ at St. Paul's in December 1717.

Scheibe Seeks Fair Payment and an Appointment

It is a shameful chapter in the history of this project that in spite of the organ
having passed Bach's diligent examination in December 1717 (see chapter 5), the
university paid Scheibe neither promptly nor fully. Scheibe had first submitted
his bill for expenses on 29 October 1716, along with his request that the organ
be examined as soon as possible. In March 1717 it was decided to have the
organ examined but to put off the decision regarding any additional payment
to Scheibe. After the successful examination, Bach warned in December 1717
that Scheibe would continue to care for the organ only if he were promptly paid
what he was owed. But when Scheibe wrote again to the university on 17 January
1718, he still had received no payment. He repeated his request for an additional
payment, reminding the university that at the examination the items built over
and above the contract had been acknowledged by Bach as "indispensable."[122]

Although Scheibe agreed to settle for 200 taler on 11 February 1718, it was 1720 before he received a final payment.

In preparation for the organ's examination, Scheibe had sent a memorandum to the university. He documented his demand for some 337 taler—236 taler he had spent in cash for items not included in the contract and another 101 taler that had been charged to the builder's account when the university paid for case carvings, painting and gilding the case, and Vetter's gratuity, items not commonly paid by the builder. He reminded the university that the pipework damaged by a summer hailstorm needed to be repaired before the examination

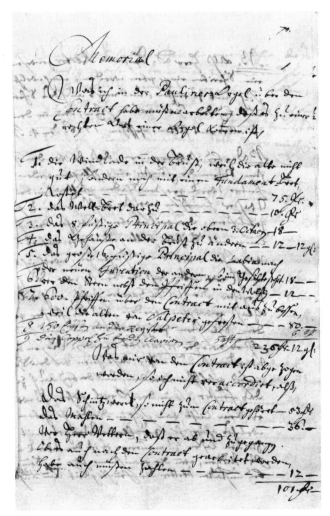

19. "Memorial." Page 1 of Scheibe's undated memorandum regarding costs incurred over and above the contract. UAL, Rep. II/III/B II 5, fol. 70r.

and that the window needed to be partially bricked in to protect the organ. He compared what he had accomplished with what the university would have gotten had they allowed Silbermann to build the organ, and he pleaded for a steady, reliable, well-qualified organist: "I ask you not to forget that a reliable [*beständig*] organist should always be at the organ, for otherwise, if this does not happen, and one [organist plays] today, another the time after, and the Herr Cantor the time after that, the instrument will soon be ruined. If the one [Gottlieb Zetzsch] who is now at the instrument remains, however, one would have nothing to fear." He begged the university to reimburse him no less than 250 taler—his cash outlay—because "the losses and damages have been hard on me," and he concluded by asking that the university appoint him at a fee of 12 taler annually and that he be extended a gratuity.[123]

The successful organ examination and what should be done about the organ builder's claim for additional payment were discussed by Council on 28 January 1718:

> THE *RECTOR MAGNIFICUS* PROPOSES: That inasmuch as the organ has been ex-amined by Johann Sebastian Bach, and he also has written the required report, and there is no major defect to be found in the organ . . . the question is, what to do about payment, and who will satisfy the organ builder in his remaining claims, and how much should it be? His demands could run to 280 taler [*sic*].
>
> DR. CYPRIAN: Noticed a number of items [in the report] that should be looked into first—for example, that the space was too small and everything was stuck in together, among others. In the end, one should offer 100 taler against [Scheibe's] demand, and see if he would be satisfied with that, and go on from there.
>
> DR. SCHACHER: Above all, one must see to it that the right [amount for a] payment is negotiated, and one could waive some part of the rent. Also, [one should] pursue whether Herr Rath Mencke can do something, whether he could con-tribute something.
>
> DR. RIVINUS: One should not let it come to that. After all, the organ builder has built a good instrument; he should be given what he is due and not have to debase himself. It should be made certain that there is a good result.
>
> DR. SCHMID AND PROF. ERNESTI: Both are of the opinion that one should find a good outcome to the situation with the organ builder.
>
> Herewith resolved: Above all, a proper final accounting must be agreed to with the builder, and he should be questioned about it, after which, on the basis of the negotiated amount, the room rent should be compensated, and the amount remain-ing [should be paid to him] either by St. Paul's or by king's counsel Mencke.[124]

Rechenberg bargained stiffly with Scheibe and, less than a week later, on 3 February 1718, was able to report that he had already gotten Scheibe to agree to a payment of 250 taler and that he believed he could get him to settle for 200. For its part, Council would have to forgive Scheibe the amounts owed for rent—which for the years 1710–15 had been dismissed by the terms of the previous contract and for the three years since then amounted to 12 taler a year. Council agreed: "The organ builder shall be paid 200 taler for his full claim. . . . As for the rent, it shall be forgiven him."[125] The sum of 100 taler was to be paid immediately, the remainder at Michaelmas, when the organ's one-year warranty period would expire. (Schmid abstained from voting on the rent issue, and Ernesti abstained from voting on all matters.) There was never any mention of Scheibe or his assistants receiving a gratuity.

Scheibe signed a settlement agreement on 11 February 1718 in which he relinquished any and all claims against the university and agreed to bear sole responsibility for any amounts that might be claimed in the future by any suppliers of materials or services relating to the organ project.

> Whereas the undersigned accepted and was appointed by the Worshipful University of Leipzig to finish its organ at St. Paul's, now, after I brought the instrument into good condition and it was examined at the request of said university by Herr Johann Sebastian Bach, Kapellmeister in Köthen, and found to be proper, I have [agreed] with said university concerning my outstanding and specified demands, both in wages and materials, which amounts to a total of 346 taler 18 groschen remaining from my total expenditures, in such manner that for the requested amount I will be paid only two hundred taler, one hundred taler immediately, another hundred taler at the next Michaelmas fair in 1718, [until which time] I have obligated myself to maintain the organ. As well, rent due for the room at St. Paul's that I have occupied from the beginning [of the contract period] will be waived through Easter 1718.[126]

On the day he signed the settlement, Scheibe was paid just 50 taler. A second payment of 50 taler was made on 22 April 1718. Scheibe received 18 taler on 3 June 1718 and a further 3 taler 12 groschen on 4 June 1718. By the end of 1718, Scheibe had received 121 taler 12 groschen.[127]

The university should have made prompt payment of the installments it had promised, but as Scheibe's desperate letter dated 28 December 1718 makes clear, this did not happen.[128] For the "labor, effort, and the cash" he had expended on behalf of the organ, Council had resolved to pay him, "lock, stock and barrel," altogether only another 200 taler. "I finally . . . allowed myself to be persuaded to be satisfied with the offer," he rued, "in spite of the large and, to me, a poor man, almost unbearable losses that I suffered in so many ways on account of this project, so that I have been totally ruined." Since there were still 78½ taler owed him at the end of the year, the university was in default, and he no longer needed to consider himself bound by their agreement but could demand full reimbursement for everything he had "justifiably demanded at the examination, as was clearly stated in Point VI of the examination report." (Bach wrote, "Even without any reminder from me, the organ builder is to be reimbursed for the parts newly built over and above the contract, and therefore not lose because of them."[129]) By Scheibe's calculation, from the entire amount of 347 taler 13 groschen, there remained 269½ taler plus interest to be paid. If the university refused, he would be forced to remove pipework and other items from the organ and sell them in an attempt to recover his losses. Further, if he did not receive full payment by the first of January, the university would surely not be astonished nor blame him for seeking his fortune elsewhere. And, if he was forced to bring suit in order to be paid, he would not neglect to list the following in his account: (a) the three years and 21 weeks when he was in "quiet exile," so to speak, waiting for the university's resolution to continue work; (b) the organ(s) that he could have built during this waiting period; (c) the 270 taler by which his account was reduced without cause in April 1715; (d) his waiting time between the date when he requested the final examination on 29 October 1716 and when it finally took place in December 1717; and (e) the 200 taler he had spent from his own cash—in sum, everything that he had suffered and lost from the beginning of the organ project, including the injury to his reputation when during the unnecessary delay he was talked about behind his back and when at the beginning of the project he was deemed not capable of bringing the organ to perfection. He hoped the matter could be resolved. He hoped he could forgive and forget all of this and continue working for the university.

Some fifteen months later, on 19 March 1720, Scheibe received 20 taler, the final installment of the 78½ taler still owed to him, and on 26 March he signed a full release:

> Inasmuch as the undersigned still had certain demands against the Worshipful University of Leipzig regarding the organ project at St. Paul's, and on that account the Highly Esteemed Worshipful University conferred on me 200 taler, in addition to completely waiving, up to Michaelmas 1718, the rent for the room I have occupied at St. Paul's College. Now, therefore, I accept this not only with obedient thanks, but also acknowledge receipt from the Highly Esteemed Worshipful University of 200 taler paid to me in cash, with waiver of any pretext regarding monies not received, and renounce herewith each and every demand made with respect to the organ project from the beginning until now, and specifically avow not to make or seek even the slightest further demand from the Worshipful University, herewith

forever relinquishing such right. In witness whereof and for its keeping this receipt is signed and sealed in Leipzig, 26 March 1720.[130]

Meanwhile, Scheibe had also been negotiating with the university regarding his appointment to maintain the organ. Rechenberg reported on 3 February 1718 that Scheibe had requested to be put under the protection of the university and be paid at the rate of 12 guilders a year.[131] The matter was discussed at the meeting held 21 April 1718. Now that the organ was finished and responsibility for it had been taken over by the university, was it not time for Scheibe to be hired and paid to maintain it? Previously the organ builder had been paid 4 guilders annually, but because the organ was now much larger, would it not be possible to add something more to that? Council resolved that "the organ builder shall be responsible for the oversight and tuning of the organ and receive 6 florins annually" and stipulated that Scheibe must swear to faithfully serve the university and agree not to "alter, construct, or take on even the smallest thing relating to the organ without foreknowledge and agreement of the Concilium Decemvirorum." Also, he was exhorted to give no one the key to the organ.[132] According to the payment records, no fee was paid at all for two years. When the arrears were finally paid in 1720, his salary was paid at the rate of 12 taler annually.[133] Scheibe was paid the amount he had requested after all.

5 Bach's Examination of the St. Paul's Organ

This organ finally was examined—admittedly already a few weeks ago, to be sure, in the worst possible weather—and found to be free of even the smallest major defect.

—Johann Scheibe, 17 January 1718

[Bach] could not praise and laud it enough, especially its rare stops, recently invented, and not to be found in very many organs.

—Daniel Vetter, 28 January 1718

Scheibe finished work on the St. Paul's organ on 4 November 1716, but it was more than a year later before the organ was finally examined.[1] Scheibe gave the university advance notice that he would be done, asked that he be told the date of the examination so that he could have the organ in tune, and requested payment for a number of items he had completed over and above the contract. In March 1717, four months later, the university finally resolved to have the organ examined, as soon as possible, by two experienced organists: Johann Kuhnau and Georg Friedrich Kauffmann, court organist in Merseburg. Kuhnau agreed to be present and to help with the examination, but although in July 1716 he, Kauffmann, and Jacob Christian Hertel, Kapellmeister in Merseburg, had examined Merseburg's 66-stop cathedral organ, an instrument renovated and enlarged by Johann Friedrich Wender, Kauffmann and Kuhnau never undertook an examination of Scheibe's organ at St. Paul's.

It was some months before Council again considered who, in addition to Kuhnau, should carry out the examination in Leipzig. At its meeting held 22

October 1717, at the beginning of Carl Otto Rechenberg's term as rector, Council decided to invite Elias Lindner, of Freiberg, "a famous and experienced organ builder [*sic*] and mathematician," and to pay him 18 taler for his "fee, travel, and other costs."[2] But this invitation, too, came to naught. Nothing indicates why, but it is certainly possible the university could have had second thoughts about inviting someone so closely allied with Gottfried Silbermann. Lindner, who had studied with Kuhnau in Leipzig, was organist of Freiberg Cathedral, where he played the organ Silbermann had built in 1710–14; its disposition is almost identical to the one proposed by Silbermann for St. Paul's. Surprisingly, there is no mention in Council minutes of the decision to have the organ examined by Bach. Bach had joined Kuhnau and Christian Friedrich Rolle, then cantor at the Market Church of St. Benedict in Quedlinburg, in examining the new three-manual, 65-stop Contius organ in the Market Church of Our Lady in Halle in April 1716.[3] It is probable that Bach—like Kauffmann and Lindner—was recommended by Kuhnau.

Bach undertook the St. Paul's examination at the request of Rechenberg, and it was Rechenberg who paid Bach a fee of 20 taler.[4] Rechenberg's receipt of reimbursement for the payment, dated 18 December, shows that he was repaid only 18 taler, the amount Council had authorized on 22 October 1717, when it had agreed to invite Lindner to examine the organ.[5] (This fact confirms that there was no further resolution when it was decided to invite Bach. One can only assume that Rechenberg himself made up the 2-taler difference between what the university had authorized and what Bach requested or Rechenberg offered.)

Before Bach could examine the organ, however, it had to be repaired. Pipework in both the Hinterwerk and Brustwerk divisions had been badly damaged when panes in the window near the organ shattered during a fierce hailstorm in the summer of 1717. In an undated memorandum written that fall, after the hailstorm but before Bach's examination in mid-December, Scheibe described the damage to the pipework and appealed to the university—not for the first time—to protect the organ from the sun's heat and the damage that could be inflicted by bad weather:

> It must also be said that the windows should long ago have been protected at the top with gutters; the Hinterwerk suffered great damage in the recent storm that broke the window and allowed a flood of hailstones to pour in. Also, as I have said many times, the Brust, where *the beautiful Viol di Gamba register* [emphasis original] is, was full of broken glass [and suffered damage not only] when the window was broken by hail, but also afterwards when it [the window] was repaired. Now, before the examination, it is necessary to work on these two divisions. At the same

time, the window at the organ needs to be bricked in as far as it does not let any light into the church anyway, which is approximately seven feet. It is worth at least 100[?][6] T. if the organ can be protected from the terrible summer heat and from moisture during inclement weather.[7]

Scheibe requested 16 taler 12 groschen to repair (or replace) the pipework but agreed to do the work for 12 taler. He was paid 6 taler on 24 November 1717 and another 6 taler on 9 December 1717,[8] while the glazier was paid 6 pennies a pane (altogether 4 taler 20 groschen 6 pfennig) on 4 September 1717, as well as 8 groschen for the trouble of getting up to the window (see figure 20).

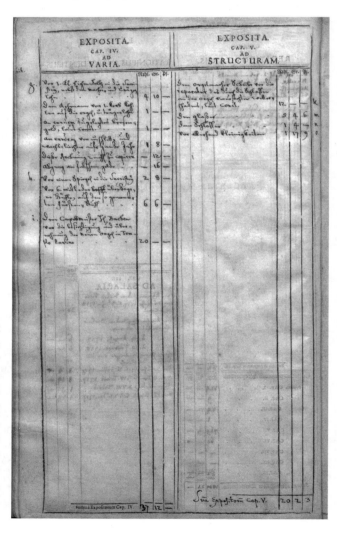

20. Payment of 20 taler to "Kapellmeister H[err] Bach for the examination and acceptance of the new organ at St. Paul's" and payment of 12 taler to Scheibe for organ repairs after a hailstorm. UAL, Rep. II/III/B I 3b, fol. 47r.

Why it took so long to repair the organ after the storm damage is unknown. After all, the glazier had been paid in early September for installing 233 panes of glass in "the new window by the organ."[9] That it took until November for Scheibe to receive permission to carry out the repair to damaged pipework may have had to do with the strong views of antagonistic members serving on Council. When Council approved the repair—at its meeting on 7 December 1717, only days before Bach would examine the organ—Dr. Polycarp Gottlieb Schacher made it known that he would give his approval only if "the organ builder resigned" but eventually agreed to go along.[10]

A number of officials witnessed Bach's diligent examination on 16 December. Representing the university were the then-current rector Carl Otto Rechenberg, former rector Johann Burchard Mencke, and Professors Johannes Cyprian and Johann Wolfgang Trier. Also present, at Scheibe's request, were Lorentz Lieberoth, an organ builder from Mansfeld, and Johann Michael Steinert, organist at St. John's in Leipzig, a man who had, "more than many others, special experience in organ building," but also "was not the least bit involved with this organ project."[11] Neither Kuhnau nor Daniel Vetter, who had overseen the six-year project, is mentioned as taking part in the examination. Bach's well-known written report—the most detailed of Bach's seven organ-testing reports that have survived—is preserved in the Leipzig University Archives.[12] On Saturday, 18 December 1717, Bach acknowledged receipt of 20 taler for testing and "taking over" of the organ, as well as his pointing out "the problems that might occasionally present themselves."[13] There is no indication that Bach performed a dedication concert, although it is inconceivable that he did not improvise at the organ and demonstrate its stops, as was his custom.[14]

We do not know when Bach arrived in Leipzig. According to Vetter, Bach examined the organ on Thursday, 16 December.[15] In Halle, where Kuhnau, Rolle, and Bach had tested a 65-stop organ, the examination was scheduled for 29 April 1716 (Wednesday) and the report was written, or dated, 1 May 1716 (Friday).[16] Kuhnau had carried out the three-day examination even though he was very pressed for time: he was responsible for composing and conducting a solemn music for the university's celebration of the birth of the emperor's daughter and also was preparing "several large-scale sacred works" for an Easter Fair Sunday. He asked the authorities in Halle to consider postponing the examination by four days, until after his obligations were concluded. If he arrived Thursday, after having performed the solemn music, and had to leave again on Saturday, only one full day would be available for the examination. In Kuhnau's opinion, "Just a Friday for the careful examination of such a large instrument and the delivery of the customary report would without doubt not suffice."[17] Surely, in Leipzig, Bach continued the examination on Friday and wrote his report the same day; he received payment and departed on Saturday.

Bach's evaluation addressed a number of items—some for which there was no solution, some that were immediately fixable by the builder, and some he believed likely to be encountered in the future. In the first and fifth points, Bach dealt with problems resulting from the "very tightly confined" case: that some parts would be difficult to reach when repairs were needed and that there had not been adequate space for laying out a sensitive playing action. Expectations regarding "roominess" changed in the eighteenth century. Andreas Werckmeister's well-known guide to testing an organ never explicitly mentions the need for a roomy case, although he does say the key action should not be too crowded, that pallets need to be easily accessible, and that problems may arise if pipes are mounted too close together.[18] In a later guide to testing, compiled by Jacob Adlung, a case so crowded that repairs were difficult to make was considered a

---

Bach's report on examining the St. Paul's organ

Since at the desire of Your Most Noble Magnificence Dr. Rechenberg, currently rector of the Most Worshipful University of Leipzig, I have undertaken the examination of the partly newly built and partly repaired organ in St. Paul's Church, I have done this to the best of my ability, noting any faults, and in general as regards the entire organ project, would like to put in writing the following:

1.) As concerns the case, it clearly cannot be denied that it is very tightly confined, and it is thus difficult to reach each part in the event that, with time, something needs repair. Herr Scheibe, builder of said organ, offers as excuse that, first, he did not build [design?] the case himself and he has had to accommodate the internal layout to it as best he could, and second, he was not granted the additional space he had desired in order to arrange the layout more capaciously.

2.) The usual main parts of an organ—wind chests, bellows, pipes, roller boards and other parts—have been well and carefully built, and there is nothing to call to the university's attention, other than that the wind must be made more uniformly steady, so that the occasional wind surges might be avoided. The rollers should indeed have been secured in frames, in order to avoid ciphering in bad weather, but since Herr Scheibe built roller boards [without frames], as is his custom, and guarantees that this is as good as using frames, this was allowed to pass.

3.) The stops listed in the disposition, as well as everything included in the contract, have been provided, in both quality and quantity, except that 2 reeds—namely, Schallmey 4' and Cornet 2' —had to be left out at the order of the Worshipful University, and in their place an Octava 2' in the Brustwerck and a Hohlflöte 2' in the Hinterwerck were added.

4.) The various faults revealed in the uneven voicing must and can be improved immediately by the organ builder—that is, that the lowest pipes in the Posaunen- and the Trompeten-Bass do not speak so roughly and with such a rattle, but with a pure and firm tone; and then the remaining pipework that is uneven must be diligently corrected and made even, which can be conveniently done when the entire instrument is once again tuned—and indeed, this should happen when the weather is better than it has been recently.

5.) To be sure, the organ's playing action should be somewhat lighter and the key dip should not be so deep. The very narrowly confined case made it impossible to build the action in any other way, so one must let it go this time, and in any case, it is still possible to play in a manner that one need not fear a key will stick while playing.

6.) The organ builder had to build a new wind chest for the Brust over and above the contract—because the old wind chest that was to have been used instead of building a new one was, firstly, made with a table, and thus twisted and warped, and secondly, was also built in the old manner, with a short-octave bass, missing the remaining notes, which could not be added to it in order for all 3 keyboards to be the same, and using the old chest would have created inequality [*deformité*], so it was highly necessary that a new one be built, both to avoid the problems that would soon become troublesome and to keep a fine uniformity [*conformité*] among the manuals. Even without any reminder from me, the organ builder is to be reimbursed for the parts newly built over and above the contract, and therefore not lose because of them.

The organ builder also requested that I lodge a complaint with the Most Praiseworthy University regarding various items charged to his account that were not agreed to—namely, among other things, the carvings, gilding, and the fees received by Herr Vetter for his oversight—for which he is not responsible, nor has it ever been customary for the builder to assume these expenses (otherwise he would have calculated his estimate differently). He very respectfully requests likewise not to incur any expense because of them.

Finally, it cannot go unmentioned that (1) at least as far as the window rises up behind it, the organ should be protected from further threats of weather damage by means of a small brick wall or a strong piece of sheet iron placed inside the window; and (2) it is customary and most necessary that the organ builder provide a one-year warranty in order to fully take care of any problems that may occur, which he is willing to do, as long as he is promptly and fully reimbursed for the costs he has incurred over and above the contract.

This is what I have found it necessary to make note of as regards the examination of the organ. Placing myself entirely at the disposal of Your Most Noble Magnificence, Dr. Rechenberg, and the entire Worshipful University, I remain

Your most obedient and humble

Joh. Seb. Bach.

Capellmeister to the Prince of Anhalt-Cöthen

Leipzig, 17 December 1717

Sources: Wolff and Zepf 2012, 145–47 (slightly modified), citing *NBR*, 83–85 (no. 72), and Bach-Dokumente I, 163–65 (no. 87). The original document is held by the Universitätsarchiv Leipzig (Rep. II/III/B II 5, fols. 63r–64r).

major fault,[19] and in testing guidelines attributed to Silbermann one reads the same admonition.[20] At St. Paul's, Bach accepted Scheibe's explanation that "he did not build the case himself," and, further, that the university had refused his request for additional space that would have allowed him to build more capaciously.

Scheibe's comment that he had not built the case himself appears nonsensical at first glance. "Verfertiget," the term used by Bach, means "built" but also "drawn up" or "designed." It is unlikely Scheibe meant he had not physically built the case himself—a disingenuous response at best—because organ builders rarely built the cases themselves but assigned the work to a joiner, to whom they supplied a drawing or design. Did Scheibe mean, then, that he had not *designed* the case himself? This was not unusual. The case for Silbermann's organ in Freiberg Cathedral, for example, was built by a joiner according to Lindner's design and Silbermann's instructions.[21] But it is unlikely that in Leipzig the builder did not design the case himself; after all, Vetter had criticized Silbermann for not making his own design drawing,[22] and Scheibe himself, in his earliest estimate, referred to instructing the joiner as to how "one thing or another should be made according to my stipulated design and specifications."[23] And because he probably provided a case design himself, it is unlikely Scheibe was referring to a facade design from A. H. Casparini, a possibility discussed in chapter 6.[24] Perhaps Scheibe simply meant that he had not designed the case for *this* organ, so dramatically enlarged beyond the original concept. The case design was determined early in the project. The joiner began building at the beginning of November 1710, when Vetter's plan to rebuild the organ as a 37-stop instrument (see chapter 4) was still in place, and finished his work six months later, at the end of April 1711. As Scheibe explained to Bach, the university had not allowed him the additional space he had requested; he ended up being confined to a case that was too small, resulting in an internal layout that was crowded. As Bach reminded the university, Scheibe's hands were tied; he had had to accommodate the internal layout to the restrictions of the allowable space as best he could.

That the confined case would result in a difficult playing action was something Silbermann had already noticed when he visited Leipzig in November 1710. He warned that, "if built according to the proposed *Structur* [interior layout], the keyboards will be unplayable."[25] As Bach indicated in point five of his report, "The organ's playing action should be somewhat lighter and the key dip should not be so deep. The very narrowly confined case made it impossible to build the action in any other way, so one must let it go."

In the report's second point, Bach confirmed that all essential parts of the organ had been "well and carefully built" (*mit gutem Fleiße verfertiget*). There was nothing the university needed to be made aware of, except that there were occasional surges in the wind that needed to be minimized and that Scheibe had affixed the rollers to roller boards, as was his practice, rather than mounting them on a frame. Vetter had described the old organ as lacking "strong wind," and he wanted the renovation to provide larger bellows valves and wind trunks with "adequate dimensions."[26] In fact, Scheibe built a completely new wind system at St. Paul's: new bellows, new wind trunks, and new wind chests.

That the occasional wind surges were not considered a major fault is a point that needs emphasis, especially since Scheibe is often criticized for having built an organ with wind problems.[27] Subsequent bellows repairs—outlined in the next paragraph—suggest normal wear and tear rather than any major defect. In addition, changing registration practices over time would have demanded ever stronger and steadier wind.

Bellows repairs were required only twice during the 30 years Scheibe took care of the organ: in 1718 and 1731, the first after a severe summer drought. In 1730, in a repair that was examined by Bach, Scheibe employed an "invention" to repair ciphering in the wind chest(s).[28] Wind-system repairs were likely made during the 20 years (circa 1750 to 1770) the organ was cared for by Johann Christian Immanuel Schweinefleisch, but no details are available. Nor do we know anything about Schweinefleisch's major repair in 1751 or the renovation in 1767. The bellows were replaced in 1774–75 by Johann Gottlieb Mauer, Schweinefleisch's successor; the wind chests were re-leathered around 1780 by Gottlob Göttlich; the "very worm-eaten" bellows were repaired by Christian Heinrich Wolf in 1790–92; and Johann Gottlob Trampeli built six new bellows and replaced the wind trunks as part of a major renovation in 1802.[29] In other words, the wind system regularly required repairs, and a major overhaul was necessary every 25–30 years. According to university organist Johann Gottfried Möller, in a memorandum dated 21 October 1802, Trampeli's work finally fixed "the extremely strong and to the instrument highly detrimental wind surges [*nachtheilige Windstossen*]". With all stops pulled, he reported, the instrument now had "reliably adequate, proper, and even wind, and thus also there is no more wind deficiency."[30]

By comparison, it is worth noting that the large organ built by Christoph Contius for the Market Church of Our Lady in Halle is today considered a success, and Contius's reputation remains good, even though the wind pressure was too low for an organ of its size and the shaky wind in the Oberwerk was so severe that the examiners (including Bach) cited it as a major fault—that is, a fault that had to be corrected at the builder's expense before the organ could be accepted. Interestingly, the term used in Bach's Leipzig report—*stossen*, or surging, pushing—is somewhat unusual in passages concerning an organ's winding and is found in Werckmeister's treatise only in his discussion of the tuning problems that can occur when an organ has borrowed stops, or transmissions.[31] Adlung was not against transmissions. He cited Werckmeister's passage in its entirety but added that problems could be avoided if a builder used the necessary intelligence and built with precision.[32]

That Bach's obvious preference for a frame rather than a roller board has rarely drawn attention from modern writers is surprising. Here Bach and Adlung seem to be in agreement. According to Adlung, it was sometimes "more convenient or satisfactory" to mount rollers in oak frames, a practice that apparently had become customary by the 1750s.[33] Werckmeister, by contrast, had decided against the practice. While a "strong oak frame" could provide a more dependable key alignment, he observed, nevertheless it was "best to retain conventional roller board construction" and to equip the keyboards with adjusting screws.[34]

Bach's positive evaluation—the main parts of the organ had been "well and carefully built"—must have been very welcome to Scheibe. As we have seen, early in the project Scheibe's skill had been disparaged by Vetter and Kuhnau, who told the university that the task of moving and repairing the large organ required no special ability and that they could recommend Scheibe as "honest, cheap, and hardworking."[35] Some Council members distrusted Scheibe's ability so much that they insisted on hearing the organ played in the midst of its repair and renovation, apparently while it was still dismantled. The newly repaired bellows, which were not fully dry, ripped apart during the demonstration, and new skins had to be procured. The same Council members then blamed Scheibe for the damage to the organ.[36] These and other slights rankled. Seeking redress from the university, Scheibe wrote that his "honor and the possibility of being further recommended" had "suffered painful and irrevocable damage."[37]

In point three of his examination, Bach confirmed that Scheibe had provided the stops listed in the disposition as well as everything included in the contracts. Unfortunately, whatever disposition Bach consulted does not seem to have survived—none of the surviving contracts with Scheibe includes the organ's disposition—and it is impossible to know exactly what Bach had in hand during the examination. Bach mentioned *two* Pedal reeds not built by Scheibe, but in a 1713 memorandum urging the project's completion, among the stops yet to be built Scheibe listed *four* reeds: Schalmey 4′ and Cornet 2′ in the Pedal, and

Vox humana 8′ and Schalmey 4′ in the Hinterwerk.[38] And in a memorandum written in 1716, Scheibe noted that the university had "specifically prohibited" him from building *three* stops in case they would—as reeds do—"from time to time require either tuning or close attention,"[39] a circumstance Bach confirmed in his report. It is impossible to explain this discrepancy; however, it is easy to pick out the positions reserved for two Pedal reed stops in the engraving of the organ's stop-knob arrangement (see fig. 25, p. 137).[40] On the right-hand side, in the second column in from the extreme right, among the Pedal stops are two stop knobs without names. One, below the Hohlflöten Bass 1′, would have been for the Cornet 2′; the other, below the Trompeten Bass 8′, for the Schalmey 4′.[41]

Bach makes the point that because Scheibe had been prohibited from building more reed stops, he had built other stops—stops not included in the proposed disposition—in their place. Scheibe himself reminded the university that one stop he built was extremely valuable, a stop that "no organ builder could build for less than 100 taler."[42] This was clearly a reference to the Brustwerk's "beautiful Viol di Gamba,"[43] a stop that garnered considerable acclaim. Bach does not mention the Viol di Gamba, perhaps because it had been included in the original specification and he is here only making the point that Scheibe built the exact number of stops he had been contracted to build.

Bach also discussed the voicing, which had various faults that were to be "improved immediately." He specifically mentioned the lowest pipes of the Posaunen Bass 16′ and the Trompeten Bass 8′, which spoke "roughly" and with "a rattle" rather than with a pure and firm tone. These Pedal reeds had been newly built in the first phase of the project, the Posaunen Bass with wooden rather than metal resonators. During the second phase of the project, when he was building the tin pipes for the facade, Scheibe was asked also to make the new Pedal reeds sweeter (*lieblicher*), or more elegant. In testing guidelines attributed to Silbermann, one finds a similar goal: "The speech of the reeds . . . should not be primitive [*grausam*], but nicely elegant [*fein lieblich*]—especially the Posaunen Bass, which should speak promptly."[44] Again here, though, it is worth comparing the assessment in Leipzig with the assessment of Contius's organ in Halle, where the examiners requested additional voicing of the Subbass 16′ and the Posaunen Bass 32′ and of other reeds. It was not uncommon at examinations for builders to be asked to make improvements in voicing, especially of reeds.

At both St. Paul's and in Halle, it was noted that the organs would need to be tuned more accurately after the examinations. It was a sore point with Scheibe that the examination, which had been delayed for more than a year, then took place, as he put it, "in the worst possible weather."[45] Bach acknowledged this when he recommended that Scheibe perfect the voicing and retune the organ when "the weather is better than it has been recently." Bach said nothing about either the pitch or the temperament, which suggests they were acceptable to him. The pitch at St. Paul's had been lowered at least a half tone, to Chorton, an item not included in the contract and also not billed separately by Scheibe, even though there was considerable work involved. Scheibe's son, Johann Adolph, wrote that the temperament was "exceedingly comfortable and harmonious" (*überaus bequeme und wohlklingende*).[46] (In Halle, by contrast, after discussion at the examination, Contius agreed to reset the temperament.)

As already noted, Bach's report also dealt with some of the extra work Scheibe had done and included the recommendation that he be reimbursed for the parts newly built over the contract—in particular, the "new wind chest for the Brust." Ernst Flade erroneously claimed that Bach had found the Brustwerk chest so old-fashioned at the examination that he had insisted Scheibe build a new one and be paid a supplement for the additional work.[47] In fact, Scheibe had already built two new wind chests for the Brustwerk; had he been required to rebuild them, this surely would have been considered a major fault in an instrument that suffered no major faults. The archival record suggests otherwise as well. Because the newly built organ would not have a Rückpositiv, the plan from the beginning had been to move the old Rückpositiv chest to "the Brust"—that is, into the interior, or breast, of the organ case. This new division, which became known as the Hinterwerk, was playable from the lowest keyboard, just as the Rückpositiv had been.[48] The Hinterwerk was in addition to the already existing Brustwerk, playable from the top keyboard, which was retained and enlarged. When Bach talks about a new chest for "the Brust," then, he is referring to the new chest Scheibe built for the Hinterwerk "in the Brust." Long before Bach had written his report, Scheibe had already explained to the university why it had been necessary to build a new chest for the Hinterwerk rather than reuse the old Rückpositiv chest.[49] He gave the same reasons later cited by Bach: that a new chest had been necessary because the old chest had a table (rather than sponselled channels) and only enough channels to accommodate a short-octave bass. It not only had been impossible to build a supplemental chest—perhaps because of the tightly confined case—but also would have been very time-consuming and difficult to repair the old chest's warped table (one large piece of wood that covered the entire chest), a method of construction that in any event had gone out of favor. Bach noted one further reason why the new chest was necessary: it was important that all three keyboards have the same compass (with a "complete" rather than a "short" bottom octave), something that was neither required nor particularly desired in earlier organs but that clearly the Leipzig organists—and Bach—now considered essential.

At the examination Bach must have had a copy of Scheibe's bill in hand, for Scheibe had specifically requested that his description of the extra work be available. One can be sure that if the university itself did not provide it to Bach, Scheibe would have. Other than the new wind chest, Bach made no mention of other items on Scheibe's list—such as the costs for building four octaves of tin pipes for the Principal 8′ in the Brustwerk and altering the facade so it would better accommodate it, for replacing the mouths in the old Principal 16′ remaining in the facade, or for building the Cymbelstern and the pipes for the gloriole at the top of the organ. Perhaps the university had already indicated its willingness to pay for these items, all of which relate to the organ's facade and appearance, but the record is clear that Rechenberg bargained stiffly with Scheibe. Bach also addressed, at Scheibe's request, the issue of amounts deducted from Scheibe's agreed-upon fee without his permission. The total was considerable—101 taler, according to one of Scheibe's calculations[50]—for fees advanced to the sculptor, the painter, and the project's overseer. Bach agreed it was not customary for such items to be charged to the organ builder and asked that Scheibe "not lose because of them." Here Bach's concern for Scheibe's financial welfare mirrored that of Mencke, who was rector during the important second phase of the organ's construction. As described earlier, Mencke urged the university to treat Scheibe fairly, noting that Scheibe had with certainty "not earned one taler of profit on this entire project, . . . but likely has been forced into debt on account of it"—a project, he emphasized, "the equal of which is not often seen."[51]

Bach commented on two other issues: the unprotected window near the organ and the usual one-year warranty offered by a builder. As already mentioned, the university was concerned that the organ not block light from the west window any more than necessary, and the earliest contract included this restriction among its provisions. A month before the joiner finished building the case, the university decided to improve the lighting by installing new windowpanes,[52] and at the Easter fair in 1711, 720 *Doppelscheiben* (large panes) and 720 *Spiegelscheiben* (small panes) were purchased for the "window in the organ."[53] Installing a window to the side of the organ was also considered. Scheibe agreed that providing more light was important but complained in a memorandum written on 1 May 1711 that sawdust and tools dropped carelessly by the joiner had already been a great burden and annoyance during construction of the case. He was not sure how he could protect the organ from the damage certain to occur if the wall were broken into for a side window, but if it were going to happen, he recommended it be done before even more of the organ was set up.[54] The university's decision, taken shortly after receipt of Scheibe's memorandum, was to make "the window at the organ, as well as the new one behind the pulpit,"[55] although it remains unclear whether reference was being made to a new window at the side or to installing the new windowpanes in the existing window in the middle of the organ.

The summer before Bach came to examine it, the newly completed organ was severely damaged, as noted above, when panes in the west window were shattered in a fierce summer hailstorm and Scheibe had to repair damaged pipework. He urged the university to do whatever was necessary to protect the organ from inclement weather as well as summer heat, suggesting that the window at the organ be bricked up at least as far as it was covered by the organ and did not allow any light into the church anyway—that is, about seven feet.[56] But even though the university agreed on 28 September 1717 to do this if it could be accomplished without inconveniencing the church or damaging the organ,[57] nothing was done either before the organ's examination or after Bach had affirmed Scheibe's request by reiterating it in the examination report. Nor was action taken after Scheibe reminded the university the following January that it was necessary not only to fix the window but also to cover the back and top of the organ.[58] Rather, the following spring it was decided simply to install a window jamb on the inside and provide a covering.[59] We do not know how large the covering was or what it was made of, but in any event it did not stop sun from hitting the pipework. Silbermann's nephew Johann Andreas Silbermann noted this, saying that because "the sun shone on part of the organ, this part was higher in pitch, and never in tune [with the rest]. Naturally."[60]

Finally, there is Bach's not-so-subtle point regarding the one-year warranty to consider. He reminded the university that it was normal practice for the builder to provide a warranty for at least one year. Scheibe was willing to do this, he said, as long as "he is promptly and fully reimbursed for the costs he has incurred over and above the contract." In fact, the contracts signed by Scheibe on 26 May and 5 December 1715 both included a one-year warranty provision. Bach was basically saying, then, that Scheibe would be willing to meet the terms of his contracts *only if* the university "promptly and fully" reimbursed him for his out-of-pocket costs. As was discussed earlier, the university paid neither promptly nor fully. Scheibe had first submitted his bill for expenses on 29 October 1716, along with his request that the organ be examined as soon as possible. Despite Bach's warning, Scheibe had still received no payment when he wrote again to the university on 17 January 1718. He repeated his request for payment of some 347 taler, reminding the university that at the examination the items built over the contract had been acknowledged as "indispensable." In February 1718 the university forced Scheibe to accept only 200 taler, with 100 taler payable immediately and the remaining 100 taler due in September. At the end of the year, when Scheibe still had not been paid in full, he threatened to satisfy his claim by, among other things, removing pipes from the organ. Finally, on 19 March 1720, almost three and a half years after he had made his initial request, and fifteen months since Bach's examination, Scheibe received a last payment.[61]

The 200-taler settlement and its grudging payment of it are only two examples of the university's tightfistedness and lack of support for the organ. The project was delayed for months and months, during which time Scheibe was criticized for taking on work elsewhere. When the project was finally resumed, it was only to build what was necessary to complete the facade; only under pressure from Mencke, who also served as counselor to the king in Dresden, did the university finally agree to use the balance of the funds in the organ bequest to build the remaining 18 stops that had been prepared for from the beginning. Mencke not only promised not to exceed the amount the university reluctantly agreed to—and if he did so, to pay the expenses himself—he also solicited private contributions from colleagues in both Leipzig and Dresden. The St. Paul's professors in charge wanted the project to be done with, but along the way Scheibe was often forced to suspend work because materials were not available. He and his family suffered hardship and loss in the unhealthy living quarters the university provided, and he even worked for a time without a contract because the university could not decide how to proceed. The university ordered Scheibe not to work at night and threatened to take the keys to the church from him. Against his will he was forced to sign a bond. Mistrusted by some of the professors, he apparently suffered slander in addition to financial loss.

In spite of this, Scheibe fought for recognition and fair treatment from the university, not only with respect to pay but also with respect to receiving the usual in-kind benefits, such as free housing during a major rebuilding project. Indeed, the need for patronage from the university may be one reason Scheibe felt forced, or was willing, to endure such unfavorable and unsupportive treatment. Veit Heller recently observed that because organ builders were not members of a guild, the protection the university finally offered Scheibe when it made him an employee was very important, shielding him from attacks from competing artisans who were members of guilds and allowing him, for example, to take on apprentices.[62] As organ builder for Leipzig University—his official appointment on 21 April 1718 was retroactive to Michaelmas 1717—Scheibe enjoyed throughout his career the privileges the university's protection afforded.

In this context, then, Bach's examination report must be seen as a measured but forceful reproach of the university's actions. To repeat what I hope is now obvious: Bach enumerated the organ's immediately fixable problems as well as problems about which nothing could be done and problems likely to be encountered in the future. But the report is also a spirited defense of Scheibe: a document explaining why the organ builder should not be held responsible for anything he could not fix and why he should be paid, as he had requested more than a year before, for the work done over the contract. The record thus confirms reports that Bach's intervention on behalf of organ builders "went so far that, when he found the work really good and the sum agreed upon too small, so that the builder would evidently have been a loser by his work, he endeavored to induce those who had contracted for it to make a suitable addition—which he in fact obtained in several cases."[63] There is no doubt that Bach's reputation for doing all he could to ensure organ builders received fair remuneration was in part established here at St. Paul's. According to the builder (Scheibe), the buyer (the university), and the project's overseer (Vetter), Bach's examination revealed no major fault. Indeed, whereas Silbermann's organs were criticized for "the all-too-uniform stoplists, which arise merely from an excessive caution in not risking stops of which he was not completely certain, so that nothing in them would miscarry for him,"[64] according to Vetter, Bach had praised the unusual stops in Scheibe's organ.

Contemporary sources are unanimous in declaring the examination as successful. Scheibe himself said the organ was "found to be free of even the smallest major defect."[65] The university agreed. Council minutes reported, "The organ has been examined by Johann Sebastian Bach, and he also has written the required report, and there is no major defect to be found in the organ, but only a few inconsequential items—for example, that the pipework was not yet properly in tune[66] and that the space for the organ somewhat too cramped, about which there was nothing the organ builder could do."[67] Vetter reported that there were no major defects and that Bach had praised the organ: "At the request of the honorable University the instrument was examined on 16 December 1717 by the Capellmeister from Köthen, Herr N. [no first name provided] Bach, with not one major defect, and judged in such a way that he could not praise and laud it enough, especially its rare stops, recently invented, and not to be found in very many organs."[68] According to Christoph Ernst Sicul, nothing about the organ required any concern on the part of the university; everything had been properly made: "Now Herr Capellmeister Bach investigated everything with diligence and found little that needed to be reported, in that he attested that the major parts of an organ, such as wind chests, bellows, pipes, roller boards, and the rest, had been well made, and therefore there was nothing that needed to be pointed out [to the university]. Those things though that could be improved were in part adequately excused, and in part can easily be corrected by the organ builder."[69]

In the 300 years since Scheibe's St. Paul's organ was completed, descriptions, evaluations, and points of view have varied considerably. As noted above, Vetter, the first to describe the organ, emphasized the organ's unusual stops. Sicul, the Leipzig historian who first published the disposition, highlighted the organ's size, declaring that, according to Bach's estimation and acclaim, the organ had to be counted "among the greatest achievements in all of Germany."[70] Leipzig chronicler Anton Weiz described how "an incomparable instrument" was created anew when the organ was moved from the south side to the west end of the church, its pipes melted down and reused.[71] Music critic Johann Adolph Scheibe said

21. Bach's opinion of the St. Paul's organ as reported by Daniel Vetter, memorandum dated 28 January 1718. UAL, Rep. II/III/B II 5, fol. 75r.

that his father's extraordinary skill was demonstrated in the organ's "splendor, energy, and exceedingly comfortable and harmonious temperament."[72] Johann Lorenz Albrecht, cantor and music director at St. Mary's in Mühlhausen and the first editor of Adlung's *Musica mechanica organoedi,* called Scheibe's organ magnificent (*prächtig*).[73] Carl Ferdinand Becker said that in Leipzig the best organists chose to display their skill on Scheibe's organ, which had "a profusion of sweet, strong, very unusually timbered registers."[74]

While positive judgments continued for many years, a negative tone was set when Flade—perhaps not the most objective voice as concerns Scheibe—claimed the university had received a decidedly mediocre instrument when Silbermann would have built "a masterpiece." Flade's views marked a turning point, and they seem to have influenced subsequent writers who, without commenting on the positive aspects of Bach's report, instead emphasized what Flade labeled "Bach's serious concerns": the available space was used poorly, the wind was unsteady, the voicing uneven, the action heavy, and the wind chest design out-of-date.[75] Werner David called Bach's report "lukewarm and critical,"[76] a sentiment echoed by musicologist Hermann Busch, who concluded that because Bach had expressed reservations without giving any compliments, "the organ appears not to have impressed him very much."[77] In 1994 scholars became aware of the comments of Silbermann's nephew Johann Andreas, who visited the organ in 1741. (Johann Andreas was born in Strasbourg; learned organ building with his father, Andreas Silbermann; and at the age of 22, in 1734, took over his father's organ-building shop. He later learned from and was influenced by his uncle Gottfried and built some 57 organs, primarily in Alsace. His travel notebooks and his documentation of organs in Alsace, including his father's and his own, were edited by Marc Schaefer and published as *Das Silbermann-Archiv: Der hand-schriftliche Nachlaß des Orgelmachers Johann Andreas Silbermann [1712–1783]* in 1994.)[78] Johann Andreas tells us he visited the St. Paul's organ "incognito," and that Schacher—who, as we have seen, was no friend of Scheibe's—made arrangements for the organist Gottfried August Homilius, "who played very well," to demonstrate the organ. According to Johann Andreas—in what may be the only voice of dissent in the 18th century—"the tone and workmanship" of the 25-year-old organ "do not accord with the report of Herr Capellmeister Bach." The playing and stop actions were difficult, the Pedal reeds "not worth a damn," the internal layout confusing.[79] J. A. Silbermann's viewpoint seemed to confirm Flade's assessment, and this became the standard reading of the episode. In his recent study of repairs made to the organ after Scheibe's death, Bach scholar Andreas Glöckner thus emphasizes what he called the organ's "substantial construction problems,"[80] while Christian Ahrens describes the university's decision not to commission Silbermann as one that, "considering the shortcomings of the new organ, would soon have been regretted."[81]

Further, with the publication in the late 19th century of Philipp Spitta's Bach biography, the St. Paul's organ began to be judged solely in relation to Bach. Spitta believed the organ "fulfilled the highest expectations" and that Bach would have chosen it when he wanted to play for his own pleasure or before other people.[82] Flade suggested that Bach's Leipzig organ works would have been conceived and heard for the first time on the St. Paul's organ,[83] but he also believed the organ had not been a success. In his monograph on Silbermann, first published in 1926, Flade concluded that if Silbermann had built the organ for Leipzig University, he would have created a masterpiece, but because the university cast its lot with Scheibe, it ended up with "a very mediocre instrument."[84] Arnold Schering considered the organ a masterpiece. "Scheibe's success, confirmed by no less a figure than Sebastian Bach," he wrote, demonstrated that the citizens of Leipzig "had not erred in their estimation of the local builder. . . . The University Church in Leipzig now owned one of the newest and most beautiful organs in Germany."[85] For musicologist and organist Hans Klotz, the organs played by Bach in Arnstadt and at St. Paul's—instruments that exhibited a move away from early baroque ideals—were symptomatic of "the decline in organ building."[86] In his book on Bach's organ works, Hermann Keller insisted that even though the Scheibe organ only had four reeds, it nevertheless far surpassed the organs in Leipzig's principal churches.[87] Organist Karl Matthaei, in an essay on Bach organs published during the Bach bicentenary in 1950, also criticized the organ's paucity of reeds; such a disposition had nothing to do with the baroque, he claimed. Bach had praised the many reeds in the Hamburg St. Catherine's organ and had also explicitly noted the absence of two reeds at St. Paul's, reeds that had been planned for but not built.[88] Paul Rubardt put it succinctly: "Such a disposition [with only four reeds] would never have entered Bach's mind."[89] Ulrich Dähnert mildly observed that the presence of only four reeds, and the absence as well of a 32′ register in the pedal, seemed not to be "consistent with Bach's sound ideal."[90]

Such criticisms were accepted. In his influential book *Johann Sebastian Bach's Orgeln,* published in 1951, David said it was no longer possible to say which Leipzig organ Bach might have preferred but that, in accordance with Rubardt's views, it might very well have been the organ at St. Nicholas's. This organ, which had been renovated by Zacharias Thayssner in 1691–94, had not only an almost completely new disposition but also a structure that apparently corresponded to

Bach's wishes.[91] A few years later, Flade again characterized the St. Paul's organ as mediocre, citing Bach's examination report and what he interpreted as "Bach's grave reservations."[92]

From this point forward, there was no agreement about Scheibe's organ. Scholars based their assessments on Bach's examination report, which had not yet been contextualized; on the record of repairs to the organ, which was misunderstood; and on whether or not the organ met what they understood to be Bach's requirements in an organ. Assessments moved away from describing the instrument itself to describing its relationship to standards developed in the 20th century. Schering's view, as expressed in 1941, remained a lone voice. He described the organ as "one of the most beautiful, most modern organs in Germany, a masterpiece of the skillful Scheibe," but noted how poorly the St. Paul's organist was paid and the meager demands made of him and expressed disappointment that Leipzig University's pride in the organ seems to have been satisfied merely by possessing it.[93]

Fortunately, however, in assessing the success of the St. Paul's organ project, we are not limited to the opinions of Scheibe's contemporaries, to the views of later writers, to sentiments ascribed to Bach, or even solely to Bach's report itself. Archival documents examined for this study, many of them written by Scheibe, have made it possible to expand considerably on and to reassess the bird's-eye view that Bach's report gives us of the project and allow us to view it in a new context. They reveal the university's ambivalent and tightfisted attitude toward the organ and its builder as well as Scheibe's heroic efforts to complete the project in a manner of which he could be proud. They allow us to understand more fully the problems enumerated in Bach's report, both those immediately fixable and those he believed likely to be encountered in the future, and they provide background for Bach's insistence that Scheibe be judged fairly and compensated fully.

6 Disposition and Tonal Character of the St. Paul's Organ

Certainly this instrument can be counted among the greatest
achievements in all of Germany. . . . The most extraordinary stop in
this organ is the Viol di Gamba, and the pipes in the facade, which
are all from pure *Bergzinn,* are large and beautiful beyond measure.
—Christoph Ernst Sicul, 1718

One of the more surprising aspects of the St. Paul's project is that the
earliest records of the organ's disposition do not originate in a builder's proposal
or signed contract. Rather, the first complete record of the three-manual, 54-stop
disposition is found in the *Leipziger Jahrbuch* (Leipzig Yearbook), an account
published by Christoph Ernst Sicul in 1718, two years after the organ's completion
(referred to hereafter either as the "Sicul disposition" or simply "Sicul"; see fig.
22 and also table 4).[1] As well, the disposition can be inferred from a drawing
of the organ's stop knobs and labels, obviously made at the same time as the
organ, that was originally part of the first volume of Johann Salomon Riemer's
handwritten account (in three volumes) of Leipzig's history from 1714 to 1777
(hereafter, the Riemer Chronicle).[2]

Sicul reported both that the new organ at St. Paul's had 70 stop registers—that
is, stop knobs—and that it had 61 registers, a disparity that can be explained. His
disposition lists 54 sounding registers or stops: 14 in the Hauptwerk, 12 each in
the Brustwerk and Hinterwerk, 4 in the Brust-Pedal, 6 in the Seiten-Pedal (the
large pedal wind chests on each side), 6 Pedal transmissions, and 7 accessory
stops (5 ventils, Cymbelstern, and bellows signal bell)—"in all, 61 registers."
Because the Brust-Pedal had 2 chests, one on each side, there also were 2 sets

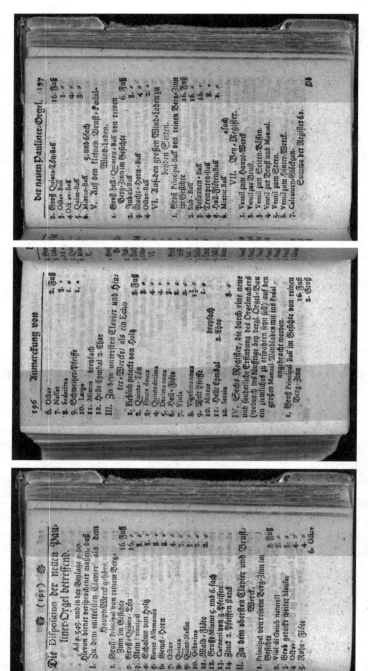

22. Disposition of the St. Paul's organ as recorded by Christoph Ernst Sicul in a supplement to the *Leipziger Jahrbuch*, 1718. Sammlung Bach-Archiv, Leipzig, Rara II, 43/1-A.

of 4 stops, drawn by the left hand or the right hand. And 5 stop knobs remained unlabeled, partially because the university refused to have more reeds added to the organ. In all, then, the organ had 70 stop knobs. The pictorial source found in the Riemer Chronicle (see fig. 25, p. 137), "Specification of the Registers in the St. Paul's Organ in Leipzig," reflects the Sicul disposition almost exactly—or, vice versa. In the drawing, 5 stop-knob labels are blank, but 65 of the 70 stop knobs are labeled. The drawing has two obvious orthographic errors: on the left side of the stop knobs, the uppermost stop, "Principal zur brust 16. Fus.," should read "Principal zur brust 8 Fus.," and directly below it, the stop knob that reads "Groß. Principal Bass 8. Fus." should read "Groß. Principal Bass 16. Fus."

Also dating to the 18th century is the disposition as it was written down by Paul Christoph Wolf, of Dresden, when he visited the organ on the Feast of St. Michael in 1736. It was included in what is now called the Dresden Manuscript, a collection of dispositions partly compiled by Wolf between circa 1729 and 1740 and first published in 1931.[3] A fourth 18th-century source for the disposition is *Sammlung einiger Nachrichten von berühmten Orgel-Werken in Teutschland* (A collection of information regarding renowned organs in Germany), a compilation of organ dispositions published by Carl Gottfried Meyer in 1757 (referred to hereafter as *SeN*). The compiler relied on Sicul for the St. Paul's disposition, adding no original information. A fifth 18th-century source, which did not become available until it was published in 1994, is the material on St. Paul's in the notebooks of Johann Andreas Silbermann, who copied the disposition from Sicul's report in the *Leipziger Jahrbuch* loaned to him for the purpose when he visited Leipzig during his European organ tour.[4] He also wrote down his impressions of the organ and, importantly, acquired what turns out to be the only surviving drawing of the organ's facade (see chapter 7). The only other 18th-century source for the organ's disposition dates to 1780, almost 40 years after J. A. Silbermann's visit. Gottlob Göttlich recorded the disposition when he took over the organ's maintenance and repair in a contract dated 5 December 1780.[5]

The disposition recorded in the Dresden Manuscript has what appears to be a number of anomalies or errors. In the Hinterwerk, which Wolf calls a Seitenwerk, he lists Flute douce 8' and Mixtur IV (rather than the Flute douce 4' and Mixtur III found in all other accounts) and includes both Principal 4' and Quinta decima 4'—which are, however, the same stop (see the discussion of the Hinterwerk, below). There are also two errors among the Pedal stops, where he lists Mixtur VI (rather than Mixtur IV) and omits Mixtur V–VI from the transmissions. Although Wolf observed that there were two sets of stop knobs for some stops and speculated (correctly) that it probably was necessary "to pull the stop on with both the left and right hands on either side," he was not able to differentiate between stops in the Brust-Pedal, which were divided between two chests, and the stops that, by transmission, were available in both the Hauptwerk and Pedal. Also, Wolf included a tremulant, an accessory stop not found in any other contemporary account of the organ's disposition. (That the organ clearly had one is confirmed in 1801 by organ builder Johann Gottlob Trampeli; see below.) In spite of the errors, Wolf's account is valuable for details only he provides, such as his helpful descriptions of the organ's unusual stops and the manual coupling system and his observation that the divisions were color-coded.

J. A. Silbermann, too, provided details not mentioned in the disposition he copied from Sicul: that the organ had shove couplers, six single-fold bellows (each 8' × 4 1/2'), keyboards with bone naturals and ebonized accidentals, a compass that did not include the lowest C$_\sharp$, and a pedal keyboard with two octaves and that the pipes in the gloriole were "from the mixture."[6]

Scholars who have written about the St. Paul's organ have relied on various of these contemporary dispositions, sometimes conflating two or more sources. Adlung's *Musica mechanica organoedi* refers readers to *SeN* for the disposition of "the magnificent organ at St. Paul's in Leipzig."[7] Philipp Spitta, as well, relied on *SeN* for the disposition he published in 1880 in the second volume of his monumental Bach study.[8] (As noted above, *SeN* used Sicul as the source for the St. Paul's disposition.) Werner David apparently believed the Dresden Manuscript to be more reliable than either the Sicul disposition or *SeN*, which he does not mention in his overview of Bach organs. Perhaps Wolf's detailed descriptions of some of the stops or his firsthand experience lent, in David's eyes, more credibility to his recorded disposition.[9] Some later authors followed David's example or relied on his expertise. Ulrich Dähnert, for example, in his catalog of historical organs in Saxony, published in 1980, drew upon the disposition from the Dresden Manuscript as the basis for a sort of conflation of all the sources available to him.[10] Thomas Harmon, for his book on registration of Bach's organ works, published in 1981, relied on David.[11] Peter Williams, in 1984, relied on the Sicul disposition as published in Bach-Dokumente I and noted the differences in other versions.[12] The first edition of the handbook on Bach organs written by Christoph Wolff and Markus Zepf, published in German in 2006, relied on the Dresden Manuscript while also including specific details from J. A. Silbermann's description.[13] For the English edition of the Wolff and Zepf guide, *The Organs of J. S. Bach,* published in 2012, the source is the Sicul disposition.[14]

TABLE 4   Disposition of the Scheibe organ (III/P/54) at St. Paul's Church, Leipzig University

I. Belonging to the middle keyboard, the HAUPTWERK

1. Groß Principal 16' in the facade, pure *Bergzinn*
2. Groß Quintatön 16'
3. Klein Principal 8'
4. Schalmo [Chalumeau] 8', wood
5. Flaute allemande 8'
6. Gemshorn 8'
7. Octav 4'
8. Quinta 3'
9. Quint-Nasat 3'
10. Octav 2'
11. Waldflöte 2'
12. Große Mixtur V–VI
13. Cornetti III
14. Zinck [Sesquialtera] II

II. Belonging to the top keyboard, the BRUSTWERK

1. Principal 8' in the facade, pure *Bergzinn*
2. Viol di Gamba naturell 8'
3. Grob Gedackt 8', wide-scaled
4. Octav 4'
5. Rohrflöte 4'
6. Octav 2'
7. Nasat 3'
8. Sedecima 1'
9. Schweizerpfeife 1'
10. Larigot [1–1/3']
11. Mixtur III
12. Helle Cymbel II

III. Belonging to the lowest keyboard, the HINTERWERK, as an ECHO

1. Lieblich Gedackt 8', wood
2. Quintatön 8'
3. Flute douce 4'
4. Quinta decima 4'
5. Decima nona 3'
6. Hohlflöte 2'
7. Viola 2'
8. Vigesima nona 1–1/3'
9. Weitpfeife 1'
10. Mixtur III
11. Helle Cymbel II
12. Sertin [Sordino] 8'

IV. Six [Transmissions:] Registers on the large Manual [Hauptwerk] wind chest that by means of a new and special invention of the organ builder . . . are made available in the Pedal

1. Groß Principal Bass 16' in the facade, pure *Bergzinn*
2. Groß Quintatön Bass 16'
3. Octav Bass 8'
4. Octav Bass 4'
5. Quint Bass 3'
6. Mixtur Bass V–VI

V. On the small BRUST-PEDAL wind chests

1. Groß Hell-Quinten Bass 6' in the facade, pure *Bergzinn*
2. Jubal Bass 8'
3. Nachthorn Bass 4'
4. Octav Bass 2'

VI. On the large wind chests to either side [the SEITEN-PEDAL]

1. Groß Principal Bass 16' in the facade, *Bergzinn*
2. Subbass 16'
3. Posaunen Bass 16'
4. Trompeten Bass 8'
5. Hohlflöten Bass 1'
6. Mixtur Bass IV

VII. AUXILIARY STOPS

1. Hauptwerk ventil
2. Brust[-Pedal] ventil
3. Seiten-Pedal ventil
4. Brust[werk] ventil
5. Cymbelstern ventil
6. Hinterwerk ventil
7. Bellows signal bell

Tremulant
6 single-fold bellows (8' × 4½')
Manual compass: CD–c³
Pedal compass : CD–c¹
Pitch: Chorton

Sources: Sicul 1718, 195–97 (appendix A-20), also cited in Bach-Dokumente I, 167 (no. 87); Dresden Ms. 1736 (appendix A-32, 43); *Silbermann-Archiv,* 157–58.

While the organ's disposition itself is well documented, the person who drew it up initially has been called into question. Unusually, most modern scholars do not give credit to Scheibe, the organ's builder, for having devised the organ's disposition. The 37-stop disposition proposed by Daniel Vetter in 1710 was ultimately expanded to 54 stops, but was it Vetter or Scheibe who determined which stops to add? Did Vetter formulate the disposition that was finally built? Was the disposition a collaboration between Vetter and Scheibe? According to Paul Rubardt, the disposition originated with neither Scheibe nor Vetter but with A. H. Casparini. "It has been clear since 1938," Rubardt wrote in 1961, "that [the St. Paul's disposition] was supplied, at the request of Leipzig University, by organ builder Adam Horatio Casparini, of Breslau," and in his entry on Scheibe for *Die Musik in Geschichte und Gegenwart,* he wrote in 1963 that "the [St. Paul's] disposition . . . originated with Horatio Casparini."[15] Rubardt based his conclusion on economic historian Wilhelm Stieda's report that "organ builder Casparini, of Breslau, received a species ducat 'as gratuity for the *Orgel-Riß* he had sent'" and that "he was not personally in Leipzig, but probably gave his advice as an experienced professional from afar."[16]

The archival record does not decisively support Rubardt's conclusion. The surviving documents contain no disposition proposal from Casparini, nor is he mentioned anywhere in the memoranda relating to the project or in Council minutes. His name also does not appear in the text on the plaque mounted on the finished organ acknowledging those responsible, or in the description of the project—which includes the organ's disposition—published by Sicul. Casparini's name appears only once: in the receipt signed 28 January 1711 by university instructor Johann Christoph Lotsch acknowledging reimbursement of the ducat he had paid Casparini "for the *Orgel-Riß* he had sent." (The term *Orgel-Riß* can refer to a proposal that includes a disposition and a facade drawing, or it can refer simply to a drawing.) The receipt also includes "one guilder for the postal expenses involved in writing back and forth various times."[17] In other words, we know for certain only that Casparini sent an *Orgel-Riß* and corresponded with the university. For this he was paid a one-ducat gratuity.

Both Vetter and Johann Kuhnau had personal connections in Breslau, where A. H. Casparini worked. Vetter was born in Breslau and maintained relationships there. Around 1695 he composed a four-part vocal setting with organ accompaniment of Caspar Neumann's hymn "Liebster Gott, wenn werd ich sterben?" (Dearest God, when will I die?) for the funeral of Jacob Wilisius, cantor at St. Bernhardin's in Breslau, where Casparini later built a new organ. (Bach used Vetter's setting, slightly modifying it, for the opening and closing movements of his chorale cantata *Liebster Gott, wenn werd ich sterben?* BWV 8, composed in 1724.) Vetter and Kuhnau knew the organist of the Casparini organ in Görlitz, Christian Ludwig Boxberg. Boxberg had been appointed in 1702 and for 10 years before that had been organist in Großenhain, but from 1682 until 1692 he had been in Leipzig, studying at the St. Thomas School, at Leipzig University, and with Adam Strungk, for whom he wrote a number of opera libretti. A. H. Casparini was probably the most successful organ builder active in Silesia at the time. Even now, the name Casparini is associated first and foremost with the three-manual, 57-stop organ he and his father, Eugenio, built at the Church of St. Peter and Paul in Görlitz, one of the largest and most important organs built in Silesia, then part of Saxony. Dedicated in 1703, the organ was well known not only on account of its famous builder (Eugenio Casparini had served as organ builder to the Holy Roman Emperor Leopold I), its size, and its amazing facade (it was called the "sun organ" on account of the arrangement of pipes within circles) but also because of Boxberg's very detailed description of the instrument in a monograph that was widely disseminated.[18] Either Vetter or Kuhnau, or both of them, could have owned a copy.

A. H. Casparini never traveled to Leipzig. In 1710, when the university was trying to decide what to do about its organ, Casparini had been working in Breslau for some three years and was in the middle of building the 31-stop organ at St. Bernhardin's.[19] The *Orgel-Riß* he provided Leipzig was sent by mail. Perhaps he provided a facade drawing and proposed disposition. Perhaps he commented—as Silbermann did—on the university's plan to rebuild and expand the existing organ. Although the surviving archival materials hold no proposal from Casparini for an organ at St. Paul's, among the records from St. Thomas's preserved in the City Archive of Leipzig is a handwritten copy of the Görlitz disposition.[20] Perhaps he provided nothing more than a copy of the disposition of the Casparini organ in Görlitz. Or perhaps he provided a proposal that was not accepted and then was paid a gratuity for his trouble. This seems to be the most likely scenario. Builders often were paid for submitting proposals that were not accepted—indeed, the university made such a payment to Silbermann. Similarly, Johann Heinrich Gräbner, Royal Polish and Electoral Saxon Court Organ Builder and organist at Our Lady's Church (Frauenkirche) in Dresden, was paid 16 florins for his costs in 1702 when he was "invited to Leipzig and consulted regarding building a new organ" at the New Church.[21] There are also examples of the reverse situation. When, without being asked, Scheibe submitted a drawing and two dispositions to the church in Gollma and requested that his materials be returned and his expenses reimbursed when he discovered that someone else would be building the organ, he was told that the church was under no obligation to reimburse his expenses because he had not been invited to make a proposal (see chapter 10).

Given that Leipzig University authorities decided not to build the new organ proposed by Silbermann, that they seem also not to have accepted a proposal sent by A. H. Casparini, and that they either discarded, amended, or replaced Vetter's proposed disposition, one might reasonably expect that another, competing plan was under consideration. Given that Scheibe was the builder of the organ, one would expect there to be a proposal from him for a three-manual instrument with at least 57 stops—Scheibe was restrained from building 3 stops that had been proposed—perhaps including a facade drawing. Scheibe's authorship of the disposition, after all, was not called into question until Rubardt did so in 1961. But no proposal of any kind is contained among the surviving archival documents. Indeed, Scheibe's 1713 estimate for completing the organ lists stops yet to be built that are not found in the published disposition[22]—a circumstance that suggests that the disposition was developed little by little, over a period of time. Whether it was the work of organist Vetter or builder Scheibe, or both, cannot be determined.

Modern scholars and performers have been somewhat puzzled by the disposition and character of the Scheibe organ at St. Paul's. Hermann Busch described the disposition as "a 'modern,' albeit very personal, organ concept."[23] Williams described the 54-stop organ as not rivaling the "completeness" of the 52-stop organ at St. Mary's in Lübeck. He wondered about the purpose of the organ's Echo or Hinterwerk division and observed that neither manual reeds nor strings figured prominently, while at the same time there was "an array of small flutes," not dissimilar to the Casparini organ in Görlitz, with which the St. Paul's disposition had much in common.[24] Scheibe's organ conforms to no known building style; it is unlike organs built by North Germans or by Heinrich Gottfried Trost, Johann Georg Finke, Zacharias Hildebrandt, or Silbermann, Scheibe's central German contemporaries, and while there are similarities with the Casparini organ in Görlitz, there are also major differences, especially in construction methods. Regrettably, the St. Paul's organ does not survive, and although one contemporary record—the Dresden Manuscript—describes stops that were considered unusual, we have no description as detailed as, say, Boxberg's essay on the Casparini organ in Görlitz. Nevertheless, by looking carefully at the ways the organ was altered during its renovation and major rebuilding, by comparing the disposition with dispositions created by contemporaries, and by keeping in mind what we know about Scheibe from his only surviving organ, the 13-stop instrument in Zschortau, it is possible to draw a fairly detailed picture of the organ—an organ with "so much that is special," Scheibe's son tells us, that it astonished foreigners and locals alike.[25]

Hauptwerk and Pedal

As Vetter had insisted, the newly built organ retained Hauptwerk and Pedal divisions based on Principal 16'. Indeed, the foundation of the Hauptwerk principal chorus—consisting of Principal 16', Principal 8', Octav 4', Quint 3', and Octav 2'—appears to have remained unchanged,[26] but the mixture was now composed of five and six ranks, and the compound stops were replaced. Fistula humana was replaced—as Vetter had proposed—by Nasat 3', and Zinck II was added. Scarpe appears to have been replaced by Cornetti III. (According to the Vogel Chronicle, Fistula humana was a two-rank stop "over 1 1/2'," while Scarpe was a three-rank stop.)[27] Quintatön 16' and Gemshorn 8' were retained, but Gemshorn 4' and Gemshorn 2' were removed. Six stops—all of them solo stops—were newly built: Zinck [Sesquialtera] II, Cornetti III, Flaute allemande 8', Nasat 3', Waldflöte 2', and Schalmo [Chalumeau] 8'. The division thus possessed not only the gravity and pomp of a 16-foot principal chorus—the sound so precious to Vetter—but also a variety of solo stops and combinations.

Without naming them, Vetter reported that Bach could not give too much praise to the organ's rare, newly invented stops.[28] Two such stops—the Flaute allemande and Schalmo, both very new stops at the time—were in the Hauptwerk. The Flaute allemande, or Flauto traverso, was just becoming known in Germany around the second decade of the 18th century, its most famous and influential players including the virtuosos Pierre-Gabriel Buffardin, who became flutist in Dresden in 1715, and Johann Joachim Quantz, who began his study of the flute in 1718. It is all the more astonishing, then, that already in 1708–10 Johann Heinrich and Christian Gräbner added Flaute allemande (Flûte d'Allemagne) to their organ for the Church of the Three Kings (Dreikönigskirche) in Dresden.[29] The Gräbners described the stop as "narrow, sweet, of wood." Similarly, the Dresden Manuscript describes the Flaute allemande at St. Paul's as "a narrow-scaled, open flute made of wood, somewhat sharply voiced, imitating the sound of a Flauto traverso."[30]

The appearance of Schalmo, or Chalumeau, is just as remarkable. As already noted, even outside the organ the chalumeau was a relatively new instrument at the time, and most of the following examples are from later in the century. "Schallomo" is included in the disposition (published in 1757) of Ignatius

Mentzel's organ built in 1712 for St. Mary's in Breslau.[31] Chalumeau was proposed for the Brustwerk of two dispositions that were designed by Boxberg around 1715 for Peter the Great of Russia, but neither of the immense dispositions—one has 92 stops, the other 114—was ever built.[32] Beginning in the 1730s, however, Silbermann successfully included Chalumeau in the Brustwerk of his large three-manual organs in Dresden (Our Lady's Church, Hofkirche), Zittau, and Greiz.[33] In 1743 a Chalumeau "throughout half the keyboard" appeared in Christian Ernst Friderici's proposal to rebuild the Thayssner organ in Naumburg.[34] In the 1760s a Chalumeau 8', from English tin, was built by Johann Gottfried Hildebrandt for the organ—donated by Johann Mattheson as a memorial to himself—in St. Michael's, Hamburg,[35] and, in the 1780s, Trampeli included a Chalumeau in the new organ he built for St. Nicholas's.

It is difficult to know exactly how the wooden Schalmo in the St. Paul's organ was used, although it is clear it was a soft and sweet solo stop. A characteristic Fuxian orchestral texture—Johann Joseph Fux has been called the most prolific and poetic composer of chalumeau obbligati—was the combination of obbligato soprano chalumeau with viola da gamba and continuo.[36] Colin Lawson, an expert on the instrument, reports that in Vienna there was a preference for pairs of soprano chalumeaux or for the combination of soprano chalumeau and flute.[37] (Thus, perhaps the Hauptwerk's Schalmo 8' and the Flaute allemande 8' were registered together for a novel tone color; or the Schalmo 8' was accompanied by the Brustwerk's Viol di Gamba 8'.) Lawson relates that Georg Philipp Telemann often reserved the chalumeau "for poignant dramatic moments, for example in the passion-oratorio *Seliges Erwägen,* where [alto and tenor chalumeaux] are combined with muted horns, bassoons and muted strings at the beginning of the eighth meditation 'Es ist vollbracht.'"[38] In the introduction to his cantata collection *Harmonischer Gottes-Dienst* (1725), Telemann suggested that the chalumeau (or violin, recorder, or bassoon) could replace a singer if necessary.[39] According to Silbermann, the register he built was so natural sounding "that one could scarcely tell whether one was listening to Mr. Wilhelmi, the virtuoso on this instrument in Dresden, or to the organ itself." Silbermann found the effect "impossible to describe when one heard a trio [played] with the Chalumeau in the Oberwerk and the Trompete in the Hauptwerk."[40] Certainly this very registration—Chalumeau 8' and Sertin 8'—was possible at St. Paul's.

As noted, the Hauptwerk had two compound solo stops, Zinck II and Cornetti III. Both terms may have been borrowed from Casparini. In Görlitz, Zinck II was composed of Quint 2–2/3' and Tierce 1–3/5'—essentially, it was a Sesquialtera II by another name—while Cornetti III was composed of three ranks in the 16-foot series, 5–1/3′, 4′, and 3–1/5′. Boxberg said this "unfamiliar and unusual" stop in the Oberwerk worked well "for use in the right hand with [the left hand playing] the Bombard 16′ and other stops in the Hauptwerk."[41] Perhaps Scheibe's Cornetti III also was built as a 16-foot stop. If so, an organist looking for a powerful solo registration in the Hauptwerk at St. Paul's would have been able to choose either an 8-foot solo using the Zinck II or a 16-foot solo, based on Quintatön 16′, using the Cornetti III.

Both Zinck II and Cornetti III could be employed to enhance a plenum registration. Such a practice can be inferred from Arp Schnitger's comment that the Mixtur VI–VIII he was proposing for the three-manual, 62-stop organ at St. John's in Magdeburg, built 1690–95, would be divided into two registers; one register would be a Sesquialtera II, but pulling both registers would result in the full mixture of VI–VIII ranks.[42] Similarly, Johann Friedrich Walther, organist at the Garrison Church (Garnisonkirche) in Berlin, where Joachim Wagner built a three-manual, 50-stop organ in 1724–26, described the organ's Hauptwerk Cornett V as fine not only for playing a chorale melody but also for giving power to the full-organ registration.[43] Also, Boxberg claimed that the Cornetti III "blends well with the plenum" in the small Oberwerk division at Görlitz.[44]

The Pedal division was completely rebuilt and vastly enlarged by Scheibe. Previously, five stops were located on two small Seiten-Pedal chests, and three stops were located on the Hauptwerk chest. Scheibe removed the Rohrflöte 16′—probably a stop built by Heinrich Compenius II[45]—but kept the Principal 16′ and Quintatön 16′, which remained available, by transmission, in both the Hauptwerk and Pedal divisions. He built new Seiten-Pedal chests, on which he placed a new Subbass 16′, a new Posaunen Bass 16′ (with wooden resonators), and a new Trompeten Bass 8′ (with tinplate resonators), as well as Hohlflöten Bass 1′, Mixtur Bass IV, and the Principal Bass 16′. The Dulcian 8′ and the Bau-erflöten Bass 2′ were removed. Plans to also build a new Schalmey 4′ and a new Cornet 2′ were thwarted by the university. Scheibe made six Hauptwerk stops available in the Pedal by means of double pallets or transmissions: Principal 16′ and Quintatön 16′ (already mentioned), as well as Octav 8′, Octav 4′, Quint 3′, and Mixtur V–VI—that is, stops necessary for a plenum registration. (Essentially, then, he created a Hauptwerk/Pedal coupler, but only for six Hauptwerk stops.) These six stops had individual stop knobs in both the Hauptwerk and Pedal. Finally, Scheibe built small wind chests, which he placed on either side of the Brustwerk and on which he placed four stops: Jubal Bass 8′, Groß Hell-Quinten Bass 6′, Nachthorn Bass 4′, and Octav Bass 2′.[46]

In all, 16 stops were available in the Pedal, which makes Scheibe's Pedal division comparable to Pedals in organs by Heinrich Herbst, Casparini, and Contius. Scheibe distributed independent Pedal stops among four chests in two locations—6 stops on the "large wind chests on each side" and 4 stops on the "small Brust-Pedal wind chests." Herbst distributed the 17 Pedal stops in the Halberstadt organ (three manuals, 74 stops, completed 1718) among "two upper wind chests" and "two lower wind chests," with 10 stops on the upper chests and 7 stops on the lower chests.[47] In the Görlitz organ (three manuals, 57 stops, completed 1703), Casparini distributed 21 Pedal stops among four locations. Remarkably, except for the absence of 32-foot stops and the presence of Quintatön 16′, Scheibe's Pedal disposition is almost identical to the 18-stop Pedal in Contius's organ for the Market Church in Halle (three manuals, 65 stops, completed 1716), an instrument built contemporaneously with Scheibe's. Even though there is no indication that Contius did so, it is not out of the question that he, too, distributed the Pedal stops among numerous wind chests in various locations.

Although Vetter had insisted on preserving the manual Principal 16′, which he considered essential, by the early 18th century this stop was being built only in the largest organs. The organs built in Görlitz, Magdeburg, and Halle, by Casparini, Schnitger, and Contius, respectively, all had Principal 16′ in the Hauptwerk. More striking, however, is that these other large organs had multiple 16-foot stops (see table 5). Scheibe and Casparini placed two 16′ stops in the Hauptwerk, but Contius built three, and Schnitger built four. Only Scheibe's organ had no 16′ in a secondary division. Only Casparini's organ had no Quintatön 16′ in the Hauptwerk. (Quintatön 16′ has many uses, but in a plenum registration, as Johann Friedrich Agricola made clear,[48] it provides an alternative to the Principal 16′.) Only Scheibe's organ had no 16′ reed in the Hauptwerk. Registering a plenum based on Trompete 16′, which was possible in either Magdeburg or Halle, was out of the question at St. Paul's. Further, only Scheibe's organ had no 32′ stop in the Pedal, whereas the organs by Contius and Schnitger had two 32′ stops (Subbass and Posaune). (Subbass and Untersatz are different names for the same stop.) Scheibe planned to provide a Groß Untersatz 32′ at St. Paul's—it is listed among the stops yet to be added in his February 1713 memorandum—but he never built it.[49]

Two stops in the small Brust-Pedal division, Jubal Bass 8′ and Groß Hell-Quinten Bass 6′, are described in the Dresden Manuscript (see appendix A-32). Again, their names appear to derive from Casparini and the Görlitz organ. Groß Hell-Quinten Bass 6′ was a wide-scaled 5–1/3′ stop that reinforced the 16-foot. In organs of Schnitger, Georg Christoph Stertzing, and Contius, the

TABLE 5   16-foot and 32-foot stops in four organs built ca. 1695–1715

Casparini St. Peter and Paul, Görlitz III/57, 1697–1703	Schnitger St. John's, Magdeburg III/62, 1690–95	Contius Market Church, Halle III/65, 1712–16	Scheibe St. Paul's, Leipzig III/54, 1710–16
Hauptwerk	**Hauptwerk**	**Hauptwerk**	**Hauptwerk**
Principal 16′	Principal 16′	Principal 16′	Groß Principal 16′
	Quintatön 16′	Quintatön 16′	Quintatön 16′
	Rohrflöte 16′		
Bombarde 16′	Trompete 16′	Trompete 16′	
Oberwerk	**Oberwerk**	**Oberwerk**	**Brustwerk**
Quintatön 16′	Bordun 16′	Bordun 16′	
		Fagott 16′	
Brustwerk	**Brustwerk**	**Brustwerk**	**Hinterwerk**
	Dulcian 16′		
Pedal	**Pedal**	**Pedal**	**Pedal**
Groß Principal 32′ (from F)	Subbass 32′	Untersatz [Subbass] 32′	
Octave 16′	Principal 16′	Principal 16′	Groß Principal 16′ (by transmission)
			Groß Principal 16′
Bordun Subbass 16′	Subbass 16′	Subbass 16′	Subbass 16′
Open Contrabass 16′			Quintatön 16′ (by transmission)
	Posaune 32′	Posaune 32′	
Posaunen Bass 16′	Posaune 16′	Posaune 16′	Posaunen Bass 16′
Fagott 16′	Dulcian 16′		

principal-scaled Quint 6′ was placed in the Hauptwerk, whereas Scheibe and Casparini placed it in the Pedal division.[50] The Jubal Bass 8′ was a mild Principal. Played together with the Subbass 16′ on the Seiten-Pedal, it would have reinforced the fundamental. When registered together, the Quint 6′ and Jubal 8′ would have suggested or simulated a soft 16-foot pitch, which the small Brust-Pedal division otherwise did not have.

Hinterwerk

Scheibe once referred to the Hinterwerk as "the small Hinter Werck," while Sicul labeled it "Hinter-Wercke" or "Echo."[51] Later builders, such as Göttlich, who carried out major repairs of the organ between 1780 and 1788, called it the

Oberwerk.[52] Like the Rückpositiv it replaced, the Hinterwerk played from the lowest keyboard, while the Hauptwerk and Brustwerk played from the middle and upper keyboards, respectively.

The Hinterwerk division had 12 stops after the renovation, four more than the previous Rückpositiv. In general, it held a large number of soft and suave stops, stops ideal for accompanying soloists or a small ensemble and for playing continuo. There is Lieblich Gedackt 8′ of wood, the soft stop so essential for continuo playing and that can be drawn together with Quintatön 8′ to provide a good foundation for the division's plenum. There is a Flute douce 4′ made of wood, imitating the mild, sweet sound of the recorder,[53] a stop Scheibe also built in Zschortau. The Viola 2′, a somewhat narrow-scaled stop, is quite unusual—although there was such a stop in the St. Thomas's organ. And there is a mild reed, the Sertin, which sounded like a muted trumpet.[54] Scheibe built a Sertin once again when he renovated the New Church organ in 1721–22,[55] but the Sertin (also Sordino or "muted trumpet") was not his invention. Heinrich Compenius II had placed "Trommeten gedempft 8′" (muted trumpet 8′) in his organ for Riddagshausen in 1619,[56] and a "gedämpfft Trompeta 8′ aus Metall" (muted Trompete 8′ of *Metall*), which was described as "very pleasant and not too quiet," had been built for the City Church (Stadtkirche) organ in Wittenberg during a renovation in 1713.[57]

C. H. Wolf compared Scheibe's Sertin to a Vox humana when he repaired the St. Paul's organ in 1791–94. Wolf reported that he had replaced "the old register [Sertin], a kind of Vox humana," with a completely new Vox humana with a range of c^1 to c^3.[58] During the 1716–17 renovation of the cathedral organ in Merseburg, Johann Friedrich Wender built a "Sordino 8′, with resonators of tinplate and tin 'hats', which sounds like a Vox humana."[59] Kuhnau, who was one of the Merseburg organ's examiners, wrote Mattheson that the organ had "pleased everyone with the beautiful registration possibilities, especially of its quiet [*doucen*] stops."[60] A Sordino 8′ could also be found in the city church of St. Maximi in Merseburg, an instrument Wender renovated in 1722,[61] and in St. Mary's in Mühlhausen, after the complete renovation carried out by Christian Friedrich Wender (the son of Johann Friedrich) in 1734–38, the organ had "Sordino oder gedämpfte Trompete durch das ganze Clavier 8′."[62] The comment that this stop was built throughout the compass (*durch das ganze Clavier*) suggests that other examples may have been treble stops.

The Weitpfeife 1′ was "a metal, open, very wide-scaled and sharply voiced register also known as Glöcklein-Thon."[63] Casparini built Glöcklein-Thon 2′ in Görlitz, and the Gräbners built Glöcklein-Thon 1′—perhaps in imitation of

Casparini—for the organ in the Church of the Three Kings in Dresden. The stop had a bell-like quality—hence its name. Organist Boxberg found that Glöcklein-Thon 2′ worked well combined with a Quintadena 16′ in running passages with a soft accompaniment on another manual.[64] It is possible this same effect was achieved at St. Paul's by combining Quintatön 8′ and Weitpfeife 1′.

In the Hinterwerk there were three stops with Italian names—Quinta decima 4′, Decima nona 3′, and Vigesima nona 1–1/3′, suggesting that Scheibe was influenced by Casparini and the organ in Görlitz. The Görlitz disposition—both in the contract and as recorded by Boxberg[65]—had Decima nona and Vigesima nona in the Hauptwerk. At St. Paul's the Vigesima nona is at 1–1/3′—pitch, and in Boxberg's version as well, the Vigesima nona (the 29th) is at 1–1/3′. According to Mary Murrell Faulkner, Boxberg's indication that the stop was at 1–1/3′ was clearly an error; a 29th is an octave-sounding rank, not a quint, and the stop is correctly identified as a 1′ in the Görlitz contract disposition (as well as in the Leipzig copy of the disposition). In German organ building, however, according to musicologist Christhard Mahrenholz, the term Vigesima nona often referred to a 1–1/3′,[66] and this is how the stop was built by Scheibe. Scheibe built a 1–1/3′ and gave it the name Vigesima nona, whereas in Görlitz, the Vigesima nona, although labeled 1–1/3′ by Boxberg, was in fact a 1′. Quinta decima 4′, on the other hand, appears neither in Boxberg's account nor in the contract disposition but only in the handwritten copy of the disposition that is now preserved in the Leipzig city archives (perhaps provided by A. H. Casparini).[67] Scheibe built a 4′ stop that he called Quinta decima, even though the Quinta decima (the 15th) refers to the pitch two octaves above the division's fundamental pitch—that is, a Quinta decima 4′ suggests the presence of a 16′, such as a Quintadena 16′ or Bordun 16′. Apparently, even though there was no 16′ in the Hinterwerk, and perhaps as the logical continuation of the Hauptwerk with Principal 16′ and the Brustwerk with Principal 8′, for the Principal 4′ in the Hinterwerk Scheibe adapted the term found in the Leipzig copy of the Görlitz disposition: Quinta decima lieblich 4′.

Brustwerk

Originally an 8-stop division based on Principal 4′, after Scheibe's renovation the Brustwerk became a 12-stop division based on Principal 8′. There was no 16-foot stop—although it would have been possible to couple the Brustwerk to the Quintatön 16′ in the Hauptwerk. The base of the principal chorus consisted of stops at 8′, 4′, and 2′, to which could be added either Mixtur III or, building the plenum with individual registers, Larigot 1–1/3′ and Sedecima 1′. The flute chorus consisted of Grob Gedackt 8′, Rohrflöte 4′, Nasat 3′, and Larigot 1–1/3′. (Because the Larigot's scaling sits between principal- and flute-scaling, it is usable both in plenum and solo flute registrations.) The Larigot 1–1/3′ is described in the Dresden Manuscript as "a wide-scaled, open, metal stop that sounds similar to the Glöcklein-Thon," but in dispositions recorded later, by builders repairing or renovating Scheibe's organ, the stop is referred to simply as Quint 1–1/3′.[68] That Scheibe (or the author of the organ's disposition) referred to this stop as "Largo" suggests knowledge of Silbermann's proposal to Leipzig University, which included "Largo 1–1/2′," also in the Brustwerk division. The makeup and character of Scheibe's Mixtur III and Helle Cymbel II are unknown.[69]

The Brustwerk contained two narrow-scaled, string-like registers: Viol di Gamba naturell 8′ and, unusually, Schweizerpfeife 1′. The Schweizerpfeife 1′ had a "gentle, sharp and viol-like sound."[70] It spoke slowly, and Adlung said it had to be used with "slow tempi and simple chords, without runs," which makes it similar to a Viol di Gamba.

The Viol di Gamba—the organ's most extraordinary stop[71]—was difficult to build and required painstaking care to get it to speak with the slightly reticent and veiled tone that is so characteristic of the viol. Scheibe proudly pointed out, in what was obviously a reference to the difficulty of building a Viol di Gamba naturell, that he had provided a stop that "no organ builder could build for less than 100 taler."[72] According to Mahrenholz, Scheibe was probably the first to discover how to build a Viol di Gamba that sounded as natural as the stringed instrument it was named after.[73]

The Viol di Gamba was not a newly invented stop when Scheibe built it for St. Paul's, however. In Leipzig there already was the Viol di Gamba 4′ in the organ at St. Nicholas's, added by Zacharias Thayssner when he renovated the organ in 1691–94,[74] and a Viol di Gamba 8′ in the New Church organ the Donats had built in 1703–4. Everyone knew, however, that creating an organ stop that properly imitated the elegant sound of the instrument was an art that demanded "a good master."[75] That Scheibe gave his register a new name—Viol di Gamba naturell—was perhaps in order to emphasize that his stop got very close to the quality of the gamba itself, including the attack. The presence of an artful, beautiful Viol di Gamba in the St. Paul's organ was special, and it is no surprise that when he renovated the Donat organ at the New Church, Scheibe used his expertise to wring a "proper gamba-like tone" from the Donats' register. Indeed, Scheibe's reputation as a builder of this stop remained with him throughout his career. Not surprisingly, it was a Viol di Gamba that he chose to donate as a memorial gift when he built the organ in Zschortau a few years before his death.

Various designs were employed for the Viol di Gamba, and it is not known how it was constructed at St. Paul's—only that its construction was painstaking. In Zschortau, Scheibe built Viol di Gamba 8′ as a divided stop; the 23 lowest pipes, up to b, are made of wood (the four lowest notes are shared with the Principal), while the upper two octaves, from c^1 to c^3, are metal, conical pipes. Trost built cylindrical Viols di Gamba of tin, with extreme scaling, narrower even than that which Friedrich Ladegast used in his romantic organs. He built the Viol di Gamba with box beards, sometimes with harmonic bridges (*Streichbärte*) in the treble, and acknowledged that the stop "required very special voicing if it was going to sound like the actual instrument."[76] Like Scheibe's, his stop was praised for its craftsmanship and tonal quality. Agricola claimed that Trost's Viol di Gamba in Altenburg was "an exceptional register, much more beautifully executed than others,"[77] a stop that "exceed[ed] in beauty that of many other so-called Violas da Gamba in organs."[78] Silbermann, on the other hand, who trained in the French tradition and did not favor string stops,[79] built his Viols di Gamba as open, tapered Spitzflötes, which he then voiced to be reticent and somewhat veiled.[80] Similarly, Boxberg said Casparini's metal "Viol di Gamba neu" sounded like a Hohlflöte, as if it were made of wood, and that it was particularly useful for playing continuo. As is evident, the Viol di Gamba was a particularly versatile stop; depending on its character, it could serve as a solo register,[81] as an overtone-rich stop for accompanying solos,[82] for playing continuo, or for adding gravity to the full organ.[83]

As organist at Arnstadt's New Church from 1703 to 1707, Bach had played a new Wender organ with a Viol di Gamba 8′ in the Hauptwerk. In Mühlhausen, where Bach oversaw Wender's renovation of the organ at St. Blasius's, Bach recommended replacing the Gemshorn in the Hauptwerk with a Viol di Gamba.[84] The renovation took place in 1708–9, after Bach had already left Mühlhausen for Weimar. Also, in 1708 Johann Christian and Georg Christoph Stertzing renovated the organ in Arnstadt's Upper Church in ways that improved the organ's continuo-playing capabilities: they added a Viol di Gamba, expanded the short-octave compass with C♯, D♯, F♯ and G♯ and improved the Subbass 16′.[85]

It must be emphasized that the Viol di Gamba from the time of J. S. Bach and the "Gamba" stop as it was built after 1860 had only their name in common; scalings and other characteristics, as well as tonal function, were very different.[86] As already noted, at first not all Viols di Gamba actually sounded like the string instruments they were meant to imitate. How successful builders became at evoking the instrument's character can be seen in the following description, written by organist Georg C. F. Schlimbach, in 1801—note, however, that the stop was no longer considered agile enough for quickly moving lines:

> Viola di Gamba. Violdigambe. One of the finest and most delicate of organ stops when made by a master builder. In slow passages of strict counterpoint, especially in the range from f or g up to c^2 or e^2, it gives a melting, alluring tone, but requires a manner of playing that suits it, and tolerates anything other than quick, colorful settings. It is a flute found at 8′ and 4′, but 8′ is its natural pitch, if it is to reach perfection. It would be a shame to build such a beautiful register from wood or poor metal, for it deserves good tin.—Many organ builders make the gamba in cylindrical form, many build it like a Gemshorn, narrower at the top than at the bottom [i.e., tapered]. I prefer the latter. And I should mention that it is narrow scaled.—The gamba that I am most fond of is in the organ in St. Michael's in Ohrdruf.[87] And, oh, how beautifully my never-to-be-forgotten teacher, the late [Johann Andreas] Bach, handled it![88]

Mixtures

The composition of the organ's six mixtures is unknown. In 1713 Scheibe had described three mixtures yet to be built: "Scharffe Mixtur III (C, g, and c)" and "Zimbel II (C and c)" in the Hinterwerk and "Mixtur IV (C, G, g, and c")" in the Brust, but we have no idea whether this is how he composed the Mixtur III and Helle Cymbel II, both of which appear in each secondary division. In the Zschortau organ, built some 30 years later, the Mixtur III has ranks at 1-1/3′, 1′, and 2/3′, with a fourth rank, a 1-3/5′, added when the mixture breaks back at c^1. To complicate matters, without providing any explanation, dispositions written down by builders making repairs in 1780 and 1790 refer to both the Hauptwerk Zinck II and the Brustwerk Cymbel II as Tertian II (which is usually 1-3/5′ + 1-1/3′).[89] That the Hauptwerk Mixtur V–VI was at 2′ we know from the article Scheibe published in 1732.[90] Although nothing else indicates that the organ had a tierce rank in a mixture or as an independent stop, it would be unusual for the time if no tierce rank were available for a plenum registration. Perhaps the tierce was provided by including either the Zinck II or the Cornetti III in the Hauptwerk plenum, or perhaps the tierce was included in the Mixtur V–VI, whose ranks remain unknown.

Scheibe's son, Johann Adolph, defended the use of mixtures, quints, and tierces when they came under attack in the late 18th century. From his example of which pitches and overtones are heard in a C major chord when a plenum registration is drawn, we see that his four-rank mixture included a tierce—producing, on C, the pitches c^2, e^2, g^2, c^3—that is, 1′, 4/5′, 2/3′, 1/2′. Scheibe argued that when a plenum included mixtures, quints, and tierces, "the whole instrument gains more power and sharpness and becomes adequate for a large congregation."[91] Silbermann added an independent 1–3/5' to his later dispositions so that a plenum could be registered using a tierce, and Contius's organ at the Market Church in Halle also had a 1–3/5' in each of its three manuals, but there is no independent 1–3/5' in the Scheibe organ.

Reeds

Because the university insisted during the second construction phase that no more reeds be added to the organ, the Schalmey 4' and Cornet 2' were left out of the Pedal, as Bach noted in his report. Reeds were also eliminated from the manual divisions; we know from his 1713 memorandum that Scheibe had proposed including Vox humana 8' and Schalmey 4' in the Hinterwerk. In the entire organ, then, there were only four reed stops.

Now it is well known that Bach greatly admired reeds. Concerning Bach's 1721 performance on the organ at St. Catherine's in Hamburg, which had 16 reeds, Agricola reported, "The late Capellmeister, Mr. J. S. Bach in Leipzig, who once made himself heard for two hours on this instrument, which he called excellent in all its parts, could not praise the beauty and variety of tone of these reeds highly enough. It is known, too, that the famous former Organist of this church, Mr. Johann Adam Reinken, always kept them in the best tune."[92] Earlier in his career, Bach had not avoided making changes and additions to the reed stops in the organ at St. Blasius's in Mühlhausen. In the rebuilding proposal of 1708, he recommended three changes: improving the gravity of the Posaune 16' by giving it new wooden resonators and modifying the shallots; exchanging a manual Trompete 16' for Fagott 16', a beautiful and delicate stop he considered very useful for active bass lines; and including Schalmey 8' among the stops in the new Brustwerk. On the other hand, as also is well known, Adlung was no friend of organ reeds (called *Schnarrwerke* in German). In his *Musica mechanica organoedi,* the 18th century's most detailed and wide-ranging guide to the art of building organs and other keyboard instruments, he called them *Narrwerke,* or "fool's pipes," because they go out of tune easily and "cause a lot of fuss and bother for the organist." He advised against putting too many of them in an organ because of "the dreadful task of tuning them."[93] Perhaps Adlung's view was the prevailing one. Disposition collections reveal that throughout the 18th century, the number of reed stops in organs steadily declined.

Though few in number, the reeds at St. Paul's were of note. The unusual Schalmo and Sertin have already been described, but Scheibe's Posaunen Bass 16'

also was unusual in being built with wooden shallots (as well as with wooden resonators, wooden boots, wooden blocks, and brass tongues). In Leipzig, Scheibe
built or rebuilt four Posaunen Bass stops, the first of which was at St. Paul's. In
1721–22 he built new resonators, new shallots, and new tongues for the Posaune
in the Donat organ in the New Church; in 1741–43 he built a Posaune for the
new organ at St. John's; and in 1744–46 he built a Posaune with wooden shallots
and brass tongues for the new organ in Zschortau. Examination reports suggest
that Scheibe's results varied. The examiners of the New Church renovation were
disappointed that the Posaune 16' was "very *cantabile*" rather than strong and
penetrating. At St. Paul's, on the other hand, Scheibe was asked to revoice the
Posaunen Bass 16' and Trompeten Bass 8', stops he had built during the first
phase of the project, so that they would have a "sweeter" (more *lieblich*) tone.
(The term *lieblich* suggests narrow scaling in the pipes.)[94]

The surviving Posaune 16', in Zschortau, is very wide-scaled and surprisingly strong. The quality of the wooden Posaune at St. Paul's, however, remains
unknown. One rather intriguing description of a Posaune with wooden shallots
comes from the compiler of the Dresden Manuscript. (Paul Christoph Wolf, who
owned the Rittergut Lichtenberg, funded the organ built in 1729 and contracted
separately, at a cost of 20 taler, for the Posaunen Bass.) According to Wolf, "The
Posaunen Bass resonators are quite long, with appropriately proportioned wide
scaling. The blocks and shallots are from good, hard, very smooth wood, and
the brass tongues have their proper strength, so that the stop sounds quite good
and grandiose. Nevertheless, because of the wooden shallots, it is not too loud
but is similar to a sharply bowed violone in quality."[95]

Also, it is not known whether the Posaunen Bass 16' at St. Paul's was used in
concerted music. At Freiberg Cathedral, however, its use in concerted music is
documented. Silbermann, who built the cathedral organ in 1710–14, was asked
in 1719 to alter the Pedal reeds. The Posaunen Bass rattled too much (the shallots were not lined with leather) and the shallots were too small, so it lacked
proper gravity, "a most important quality." Further, the Posaunen Bass did not
work properly in concerted music. It was too loud when it was accompanying
just a few stops in the manual(s), and at the same time, it was not as powerful
as it should have been when used with a full chorus.[96]

A West-Gallery Organ

The organ's new location and appearance reflected its change in character. The
most visible alteration was the organ's location. From a position on the south

side, up and behind the pulpit in the nave, the organ was moved to the student gallery at the church's west end, where it now sounded directly down the length of the nave. The large new case, built according to the laws of architecture, was designed to promote the blending of sound. Rather than the divisions being separated visually, architecturally, and aurally, all were now housed within one large case, its facade filled with polished Principal pipes.

The makeup of the instrument can no longer be determined solely by looking at its facade. The Rückpositiv, a division with its own case located at the organist's back, usually on the railing that separates the gallery from the nave, has been replaced by a Hinterwerk, a division placed inside the case, behind another manual division. This reorientation, where a third manual division

23. Nave and interior of St. Paul's, with Scheibe organ (photoshopped) in the west gallery. Original photograph by Hermann Walter, ca. 1895. City History Museum Leipzig, F/1116/2007. Photoshopped version by James Wyly, 2020.

is neither a Rückpositiv nor a Brustwerk—a small division normally placed below the Hauptwerk, often with doors that opened just above the organist's head—occurred in Central Germany around 1700. Wolf Bergelt has described Schnitger's organ for St. John's in Magdeburg (1695) as an early example of this reorientation, and he traced the trend in organs of Joachim Wagner. In his first organ, for St. Mary's in Berlin (1720–23), Wagner positioned the third manual division as a Hinterwerk.[97] Schnitger's organ at St. John's had four divisions: Hauptwerk, Oberpositiv, Brustpositiv, and Pedal divisions. Because there was no Rückpositiv, Schnitger built the Brustpositiv in the form of a large, forwardly placed Unterwerk. Another example is Christoph Treutmann's monumental organ in Grauhof (1734–37), which has Hauptwerk, Oberwerk, Hinterwerk, and Pedal divisions.[98] At St. Paul's, the organ had Hauptwerk, Brustwerk, Hinterwerk, and Pedal divisions—all housed within one large case.

Further, the organ's location in the west gallery and the facade's slightly concave shape facilitated the gathering of musicians and instruments in one place, and the organ's position in the middle of the singers and instrumentalists reflected its integral role within the instrumental ensemble. The organist provided not only the prelude that introduced the concerted music, and to which the other instrumentalists tuned, but also realized figured bass as one member of the continuo group. The organ's pitch—Chorton—was convenient for the other instruments: it was identical to the pitch of the brass instruments, such as trumpets, but a full step higher than the pitch employed by the baroque string band, which played at Cammerton. Thus, so that they would be at the same pitch as the ensemble, organ continuo parts were transposed down by a whole tone (or a minor third). The organist would have improvised the prelude in a key a whole note lower than the key in which the concerted piece was written.

Contemporary comments confirm the organ's role as a member of the instrumental ensemble. As was noted, one reason Kuhnau and Vetter supported moving the St. Paul's organ to the west gallery was that having the organ and the musicians in the same place would make it easier for them to perform together, with fewer errors and less disorder. At St. George's, Eisenach, Johann Christoph Bach initiated and oversaw a major renovation by Georg Christoph Stertzing in which the organ was moved to the west gallery and completely rebuilt and expanded, a project that lasted from 1696 to 1707 (the renovation was all but complete when Bach died in 1703). The organ was pushed back as far as possible and given a concave shape so that other musicians in the instrumental ensemble would also find room in the gallery. As can be seen in a drawing that was published in Eisenach's hymnal, under a banner that exhorts "sing[ing] and play[ing] to the Lord your God," members of the vocal and instrumental ensemble are found on either side of the organist's seat at the key desk, while the student choir that sang the chorales in unison found its place in the lower balcony.[99]

In Freiberg Cathedral, too, the consultants argued in favor of a west-gallery location for the new organ because the side gallery, where the old organ had stood, was "not at all convenient for concerted music."[100] In Lindner's engraving of the organ that Silbermann built in 1710–14,[101] we see the musicians gathered together in the half-moon-shaped balcony. To the right of the director, who faces us, paper roll in hand, are some singers, string players, the lutenist, and what looks like a cornetto player. To the director's left are more singers, the trumpeters, the timpanist, and what appear to be four young sopranos behind a music stand. A text placed above the organ exhorts praising God with all manner of instruments and dance (Psalm 150:3–6), and on the organ itself carved figures play trumpets, a portative organ, and drums. In a cartouche below the organ one sees trumpets and timpani, cornetti, a lute, a violin, a harp—instruments that form part of the ensemble of which the "new organ in the Cathedral of Freiberg" is part. Can there be a more eloquent portrayal of the organ and its role in church music at the time?

Similarly, when a new organ was required in Altenburg's Court Church (Schlosskirche) in 1733, Trost proposed building a three-manual organ that included a Rückpositiv, but Kapellmeister Gottfried Heinrich Stölzel rejected the Rückpositiv, saying that "in order to gain more room in the gallery, and to make it more comfortable for performance of large works [with many performers], the old Rückpositiv should be moved into the main organ case."[102] "The Rückpositiv is to be removed," Stölzel wrote in another document. "In this way space is won so that the ducal orchestra can play in the gallery."[103]

During Scheibe's time in Leipzig, the director of music at St. Paul's was Johann Gottlieb Görner, a former Kuhnau student, St. Thomas School alumnus, organist first at St. Paul's, then at St. Nicholas's, and finally at St. Thomas's (see table 10, p. 185), and director of one of the two collegia musica in town.[104] Görner's role at St. Paul's was fairly substantial; he later stated that he provided instrumental and vocal music there on 22 occasions annually—for feast days and during the three trade fairs at New Year's, Easter, and Michaelmas.[105] For the festive services at Easter, Pentecost, Christmas, and Reformation (the so-called old services), however, concerted music was the responsibility of the Thomaskantor. Likewise, the Thomaskantor remained responsible for the music at the quarterly academic orations, when motets were performed by the St. Thomas School choir.[106] "Bach conscientiously attended to the Old Services," Wolff notes, "taking his ensembles four times a year across the city to St. Paul's, just a three-minute walk from St. Nicholas's and no more than seven minutes away from St. Thomas's, for a repeat performance of the cantata."[107]

Initial performances of some Bach works took place at St. Paul's. On 17 October 1727, Bach's *Laß Fürstin, laß noch einen Strahl* BWV 198, also known as the Trauer Ode, was performed at the memorial service for Christiane Eberhardine, Electress of Saxony. On 20 October 1729, for the funeral of Johann Heinrich Ernesti, rector of St. Thomas's, headmaster of the Thomas School, and professor of poetry at Leipzig University, Bach's motet *Der Geist hilft unsrer Schwachheit auf* BWV 226 was performed. It is possible that *Die Freude reget sich* BWV 36b, the congratulatory music performed 16 October 1735 on Johann Florens Rivinus's appointment as university rector, took place at St. Paul's.

Secular concerted music was performed at St. Paul's, too, sometimes arranged for independently by individuals or a particular university faculty. One such special occasion was the just-mentioned memorial service for the recently deceased Christiane Eberhardine. Bach wrote and directed the first performance of the Trauer Ode, a piece "in the Italian style" and for which, we are told, Bach himself played the harpsichord. (The service was arranged by a student nobleman, Hans Carl von Kirchbach.) On that occasion, the pealing of church bells accompanied a formal academic procession of university officials and town councillors as it moved from St. Nicholas's to St. Paul's. While attendees found their places in the church, there was preluding on the organ and beadles distributed the oration text written by Johann Christoph Gottsched, professor of poetry and philosophy at Leipzig University. The first part of Bach's Trauer Ode was performed, the oration was presented by a university student, and then the second part of Bach's composition was performed. At the conclusion of the service, members of the formal procession left the church to the playing of the organ.[108] On another occasion, in 1717, just a year after the Scheibe organ was finished, Kuhnau led performances at St. Paul's that celebrated the 200th anniversary of the Reformation. Again, those attending the service processed from St. Nicholas's to St. Paul's accompanied by the pealing of bells in all the city's churches. Once everyone had gathered, and no doubt after an organ prelude, Kuhnau led a work for three choirs. A second work, an *Ode Seculari* (*psaLLIte DoMIno In Choro Vt et tIbIIs et tVbIs*—the chronogram Roman numerals add up to 1717), was performed between the *Oration* and the *Carmine Seculari*, and the service concluded with the German *Te Deum laudamus* performed with trumpets and timpani. For the three-choir pieces, two choirs were placed directly across from the large organ, in the Schmidt and Olearius chapels in the east gallery, each with its own positive. The third choir of voices and instruments was placed in front of Scheibe's newly finished organ.[109]

Even though Bach's report made no mention of the innovative features of Scheibe's organ, Vetter reported to the university that Bach could not have praised the organ's "rare and unusual" stops more highly.[110] As observed previously,[111] Vetter's comment surely was meant to emphasize the organ's forward-looking concept and the builder's success at incorporating the newest and most fashionable elements of central German organ building—elements such as the organ's location in the west gallery, its architectural case with no Rückpositiv, the presence of stops specifically for continuo playing, its "extremely comfortable and harmonious temperament,"[112] the extended compass, the rare and unusual stops, and the presence of stops providing gravity as well as those that allowed an astonishing diversity of registrations. Thus, by preserving the old pipework so much admired by Vetter and by incorporating so much that was innovative and new, Scheibe's organ at St. Paul's possessed a balance rarely achieved.

7 Construction Details of the St. Paul's Organ

The splendor, effect, and the extremely comfortable and harmonious temperament of this large instrument [at St. Paul's] demonstrate [Scheibe's] extensive experience and extraordinary skill.
—Johann Adolph Scheibe, 1738

Given that the organ no longer exists, the richness of detail in what follows is perhaps surprising. Leipzig University's archives are remarkably complete, however, and records that are now more than 300 years old not only reveal the disputatious nature of the project but also evoke an era in which everything was handmade. We learn what types of metal, wood, wire, and leather were used and for what purposes, how materials were measured, from whom items were procured, the names of various artisans, and much more. For a fulsome account of the materials used and the expenses incurred week by week, the reader may consult appendixes B-1 and B-2 on the companion website.

The description of the organ that follows is based on those accounts, but information also has been gleaned from the documentation of Scheibe's Zschortau organ, which survives, and from descriptions of instruments built by Scheibe's contemporaries Heinrich Gottfried Trost, Zacharias Hildebrandt, and Gottfried Silbermann.

Case and Facade

The only image of the St. Paul's organ to survive is the engraving preserved in the notebooks of J. A. Silbermann, Gottfried Silbermann's nephew.[1] Nothing is known about the engraver except for his name, "Süsse," but his engraving reveals much about the organ. The case takes up all the available space in the gallery, obscuring the pillars on either side and pushing right up against the Gothic vaulting. It is as wide at the bottom (15 Elle 8 Zoll) as it is at the top.[2] (An Elle was about two feet; a Zoll is an inch.) From the choir floor to the arches of the vault was 20 Elle. The organ's shape reflects the shape of the vault—higher in the middle and sloping to the Pedal towers on the sides. The front is convex; its depth is 4 Elle in the middle and 3 Elle on the sides. While the new facade is not completely flat, neither does it have the baroque's usual rounded or pointed projecting towers. The 10 flats that hold the polished tin pipes are now concave, now convex, suggesting motion, and the decorative lines of the pipe mouths, moldings, and the acanthus-leaf carvings emphasize this fluidity. (See fig. 24 and also fig. 23, p. 127, where this engraving has been photoshopped into a photograph of the interior at St. Paul's.)

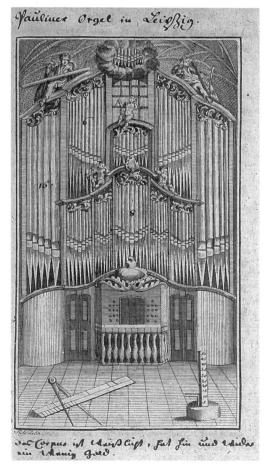

24. Facade of the Scheibe organ at St. Paul's, Leipzig University. Copper engraving, ca. 1720, with notes in the hand of Johann Andreas Silbermann. Sächsische Landesbibliothek—Staats- und Universitätsbibliothek, Dresden. Mscr.Dresd.App.3165, p. 38, digital.slub-dresden.de /id280760329 (Public Domain Mark 1.0).

The window behind the organ is partly visible and the facade is crowned with a gloriole and two sculpted reclining figures, David and Solomon, inventors of musical instruments whom Michael Praetorius credited with funding and building the "famous, well paid, and well attended chapels in Jerusalem."[3] David, the figure on the right, is shown holding a harp, finger to forehead. Wise Solomon, on the left, also holds a finger to his forehead and in one hand is a pair of dividers or a compass. Across his knees is what looks to be a monochord, an instrument associated with setting temperament. There are also three putti. The first, a musical director, holds a rolled-up score and has cupped his ear with his hand; the second holds (plays) a trumpetlike instrument; the third simply gestures toward the organ's facade, perhaps suggesting that one use one's eyes to "read" what is there or perhaps referring to the organ as one member of the ensemble composed of director, instruments, and organ. In the foreground of the engraving are the two most notable symbols of the organ builder's art: on the left, the compass and ruler used to set pipe scales; on the right, the wind gauge used to measure and set wind pressure.

Just over the key desk (the engraving does not realistically portray the organ's three keyboards and 70 stop knobs) is a medallion on which a text was inscribed giving lasting recognition to Johann Burchard Mencke, the professor of history, king's counsel, and rector who saw the organ to completion; Johann Bohn, physician and professor of medicine as well as provost of the university; Gottlieb Gerhard Titius, legator, legal counsel to the elector of Saxony, and professor of botany; and organ builder Scheibe:

D.O.M.S.
ORGANVM HOC MVSICVM
ANNO REP. SAL. M D C C X V.
RECTORE
D. JO. BVRCARDO MENCKENIO
CONSILIARIO ET HISTORIO REG.
HIST. P.P.
ET
PRAEPOSITO TEMPLI HVIVS
D. JOH. BOHNIO, THERAPEVT. P.P.
FAC. MED. DEC.
E LEGATO
D. GOTTLIEB GERH. TITII, JCTI
REGI ET ELECTORI SAX. A CONSILIIS
APPELL. COD. P.P.
MDCCXIV. D. X. APR. IN IPSO
RECTORATV

PIE DEFVNCTI
FELICITER RESTAVRATVM, EXORNATVM
AC MIRE LOCVPLETATVM
OPERA
JOHANNIS SCHEIBII.

The facade contains brilliantly polished large Principal pipes. Christoph Ernst Sicul reported that they were "all from pure *Bergzinn*"and "large and beautiful beyond measure,"[4] and Paul Christoph Wolf described a facade filled with "large 16-foot Principal pipes."[5] Although the case was too small for the organ—Bach characterized it as "tightly confined"—its large facade pipes gave the impression of a grand scale, a quality Sicul emphasized by providing measurements; he claimed the largest pipe was almost 9 Elle in length and had a diameter of almost 13 Zoll.

J. A. Silbermann described the case as "whitish, a little gold leaf here and there."[6] According to the payment records, in late 1711 a painter was paid 6 taler for gilding "the rays on the organ"[7]—by which may have been meant the clouds of the gloriole—while Heindrich Hüffner was paid 12 taler for painting the organ (no further installments are itemized) and reimbursed 2 pfennig for metal he had purchased for organ gilding.[8]

Joiner Johannes Gerlach constructed the new organ case "according to the drawing" in the six-month period from November 1710 to the end of April 1711.[9] He was paid 200 taler, which he received in five installments between 1 November 1710 and 15 June 1712.[10] In May 1711 sculptures for the case were commissioned from Christian Crother, an artisan in Merseburg who agreed to make two eight-foot statues, a gloriole, and five "small children," or putti, one of which was to be a four-foot statue of a musician, for a fee of 100 taler.[11] Three large statues were brought from Merseburg in August, and the rest of the commission was picked up in September. Apparently, the initial plan was amended; according to the engraving that survives, the organ had two large statues and three—not five—putti. In September 1711, 150 pieces of wool ticking were purchased, which were to be painted and used for curtains at the organ.[12] A woman was paid 8 groschen for sewing together the cloth and two paintbrushes were purchased for 2 groschen,[13] but the work done by artist David Näther, of Leipzig, did not meet specifications, and the hangings or draperies were not used (see below). In June 1711 Näther was paid 15 taler for painting faux cloth pipe shades,[14] but four years later, in September 1715, Council agreed that "in place of the cloth that has been there up until now, carvings need to be made," and wooden pipe shades were commissioned for 50 taler from a "sculptor in Taucha," about 10 kilometers/6 miles northeast of Leipzig.[15] A bill from Hüffner—apparently a student of Näther—lists the items that were painted or gilded (or both): the gloriole, the two large statues and everything belonging to them, two large pilasters, three putti, two pilasters in the Brust, two pilasters over the Brust, two pilasters on each side, five ornamental coverings, 124 tassels. His invoice dated 24 December 1711 for 23 taler 2 groschen included eight days of labor, wages for a handyman (or assistant), and gesso.[16] Scheibe claimed that he had added the pipes and cymbelstern to the gloriole to improve the organ's appearance. Placed behind the mixture pipes, the glass provided for the gloriole is likely to have been blue, creating the effect of sky behind the clouds.[17]

Several modifications to the case took place during the second building phase. The Brustwerk's Principal 4' was replaced with Principal 8', and Scheibe paid a joiner 12 taler 12 groschen to build "another case for the Brust, not only because the previous one had an ugly appearance and ruined the look of the facade, but because it lacked height, and there would not have been enough room for the 8-foot pipes."[18] Mencke wrote the inscription for the organ when Scheibe was building and installing the tin pipes in the facade; the inscription plaque itself had been affixed by sculptor Näther in December 1711.[19]

Although the case design accommodated the church's west window, more light was needed. In March 1711 Council decided to put new panes in the organ window, and August Quirinus Rivinus purchased 1,440 panes of glass—720 *Doppelscheiben* (large panes) at approximately 6 pfennig apiece and 720 *Spiegelscheiben* (small panes) at approximately 1 pfennig apiece.[20] In May 1711 Council decided to have a new window built.[21] Scheibe had noted how necessary it was to have a new window at the side of the organ and had urged that the construction happen sooner rather than later—and that the organ be properly protected.[22] In July the window in the middle of the organ was covered with canvas[23]—perhaps as protection once the old panes were removed—and in September the glazier was paid 14 taler for installing the new windowpanes.[24] A tombstone had to be moved before the window could be cut into the wall; the mason, his handyman, and a smithy worked six days and were paid 4 taler 14 groschen 3 pfennig in mid-September.[25]

Keyboards and Key Desk

The three manual keyboards had ivory naturals and ebonized accidentals and a compass of four octaves, CD–c³.[26] The three veneered key frames were made by a joiner.[27] The new pedalboard had a compass of two octaves, CD–c¹. For the keyboards and pedal, Scheibe purchased an unspecified amount of oak and ebony in the first week of November 1710 and another 7 pounds of ebony and 2½ pounds of ivory in February 1711. In March 1711 Scheibe commissioned key fronts from the engraver, and cloth was purchased to put under the keys. In April 1711 the turner made 62 stop knobs. Another 8 stop knobs were turned during the second building phase.

Scheibe color-coded the divisions. The front of the Brustwerk keyboard and the initial letter of the Brustwerk stop names were painted red; likewise, in the Hinterwerk both the front of the keyboard and the initial letters of the stop names were painted blue.[28] The Hauptwerk and Pedal divisions were left uncolored, the Pedal stops easily identifiable by their "*Bass*" endings. The Casparinis color-coded the stop knobs in Görlitz, although Christian Ludwig Boxberg does not identify which colors were used.[29] Color-coding also was employed by Trost—for example, in the organ in Waltershausen. According to Ernst Flade, Casparini invented the practice.

The three manual keyboards were framed by six vertical rows of stops (see fig. 25). In a more or less orderly arrangement, they started with the Brustwerk stops on the inside, closest to the player, followed by the Hinterwerk, Hauptwerk,

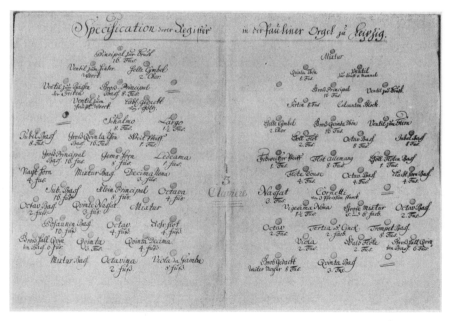

25. "Specification of the Registers in the St. Paul's Organ in Leipzig," a drawing showing the organ's stop-knob arrangement on the left- and right-hand sides of the key desk. Photograph by Markus Zepf of the Leipzig Bach Archive.

Seiten-Pedal, and then the Brust-Pedal (outside, farthest from the player), with the Pedal transmissions wedged in among the Hauptwerk and Pedal stops. There are two sets of stop knobs for the Brust-Pedal—8 altogether, because each of the four registers was divided between two wind chests, one on each side of the Hauptwerk chest. And, of course, there are also separate stop knobs for the six Hauptwerk transmissions to the Pedal. In the drawing, 65 of the 70 stop knobs are labeled (7 are for accessories), while 5 stop-knob labels remain blank.

The key desk likely was protected by lockable doors, as was common at the time. This appears to be confirmed by Council minutes. When Scheibe continued to work on the organ even though he was no longer being paid, Council considered forcing him to give up the keys to "the choir gallery and the organ."[30]

Stop and Key Actions

Scheibe completely rebuilt the stop action. The stop knobs were ebonized and had ivory buttons in the middle,[31] and the stop names were inscribed on white parchment labels that were affixed below them. The stop knobs cost 2 groschen apiece and were turned by Andreas Syfang Burger, who was paid for 62 of them on 30 April 1711. Additional stop knobs were turned in early October 1716, and in November 1716 white parchment was purchased for 70 stop labels and an unnamed person was paid 1 groschen apiece for inscribing them. Scheibe had an ironmonger make 150 iron arms for the stop action, parts he deemed "necessary and useful for the durability of the organ."[32]

Apparently, the stop action was stiff. During a demonstration of the organ in 1741, J. A. Silbermann tells us, Scheibe "pulled the stops himself, and although he was a strong man, he nevertheless really had to struggle to pull them out; they moved with far too much difficulty." In Johann Andreas's view "the action was not made in the most proper way; it ran somewhat confusedly in a jumble."[33] A description of the action written in 1834 also paints a picture of some disarray: "All the registers are badly laid out, the rollers equally cumbersome, and the trackers lack the necessary neatness and lightness; also, their ends are not protected with parchment, but are simply bound with string."[34]

The key action was another casualty of the narrowly confined case. Bach's criticism that "the organ's playing action should be somewhat lighter and the key dip should not be so deep" was fairly mild—no doubt because, as he wrote in his report, "the very narrowly confined case made it impossible to build the action in any other way, so one must let it go this time, and in any case, it is still possible to play in a manner that one need not fear a key will stick while playing."

(As Flade remarked, "Organists of the old school preferred playing on an organ with a somewhat stiff action over one in which the keys went down easily but often got hung up [produced a cipher].")[35] J. A. Silbermann, whose bias in any event was toward French organs and their magnificently light actions, was far less forgiving. The key action at St. Paul's was "horribly difficult" (*entsetzlich hart*), he wrote in 1741. The organist demonstrating the organ had to use all his power and had said privately to him, "I can hardly keep on, help me press [the keys]."[36]

The difference of opinion between Bach and J. A. Silbermann was surely a matter of degree. While clearly unhappy with the action, Bach nevertheless accepted the result of the organ's limitations; Johann Andreas, a builder steeped in a completely different tradition, found the result unacceptable. Also, how organs were built, and what organists demanded of them, changed dramatically over time. Not only did registration combinations that used multiple low-pitched stops require more wind, but manual and pedal couplers began to be used with greater and greater frequency throughout the 18th century. This alone could account for the difference of opinion between Bach (in 1717) and J. A. Silbermann (in 1741).

Interestingly, we find a similar difference of opinion in the reports regarding Casparini's large organ in Görlitz, an organ completed roughly 12 years before the St. Paul's organ. The manual keyboards were described by Boxberg as "comfortable to play,"[37] whereas J. A. Silbermann experienced the keys as "so hard and stiff" and with "such a deep key dip" that he "could not have played anything on them." "The old, famous Mr. Bach of Leipzig did not judge this instrument unfairly when, in discussing it with my uncle [Gottfried], he called it a 'plough horse organ,' because one has to be strong as a horse to play it," he wrote.[38] Here, then, Bach and J. A. Silbermann seem to have shared the same opinion, and Johann Friedrich Agricola, who apparently knew the same story about Bach and the organ in Görlitz, reported that "eminent organ experts" complained about the hard action of the Casparini organ in Görlitz.[39] The same complaint was voiced by David Nicolai, the Bach student who became organist in Görlitz when Boxberg died in 1729 and who showed the organ to J. A. Silbermann when he visited in 1741. Nicolai requested and was awarded an annual supplement to his salary because the organ's key action was so very heavy.[40] Nicolai's son, David Traugott, wrote that if one used the couplers, the action became so heavy that it was not possible to play for more than a few minutes. Anyone who wanted to play quickly and with mastery, so that every tone spoke fully, and not tire himself, would have to accustom himself to the action from his earliest years.[41]

Of course, we do not know whether the key actions in Leipzig and Görlitz were similar. All we know for certain is that for both organs, opinions expressed at the beginning of the century differed from opinions expressed later.

Nevertheless, caution is recommended. How Johann Christoph Altnickol, Bach's pupil and son-in-law and organist at St. Wenceslas in Naumburg from 1748 until his death in 1759, described the playing action of the Hildebrandt organ in 1758 is instructive:

> The action of this large instrument is playable [*tractable*], and I can assure you that I have encountered instruments much less playable that are nowhere near as large and do not have the 16-foot stops that mine does. In a word, it is playable. I will provide just one embellishment: For example, when I pull on several 8-foot stops alone in the Haupt Manual, I am able to play a good mordant [*guten Prall-Triller*], but this is not possible when all stops are drawn. On the other hand, if I couple all three keyboards together, [creating] the biggest possible force [*in völliger angezogenen* Force], I am able to play a trill [*Trillo*], in spite of the couplers, which says a lot. It must be mentioned that (1) among the Hauptwerk's 15 stops there are three 16-foot stops; (2) there is one 16-foot stop among the 14 stops in the OberClavier; and (3) the Rückpositiv has 12 stops, among which is a Fagott 16'—I mention this so that you will see that it is a large instrument that is also capaciously built. And as regards the 16-foot stops, their pallets are wider, so that when playing with full organ it is probably not possible to play as one can with only a few stops drawn. Moreover, Herr Hildebrandt has also built small instruments that play very well. I have no complaints and have been [playing] here in Naumburg for five years.[42]

Bellows

In the disposition proposal dated 25 September 1710, Daniel Vetter stipulated that "the bellows, which are in terrible condition, must be thoroughly repaired,"[43] and in November 1710 he observed that the wind supply, which previously had not been strong enough, now "can be improved by [putting in] larger valves [in the bellows], and, in future, also the wind trunks can be improved by giving them adequate dimensions."[44] The contract made just before Christmas 1710 specified that the bellows and wind trunks be fully "taken in hand," and in February 1711 new horse veins were purchased for the counterweights at 3 groschen apiece.[45] But eventually the bellows required a special effort. On 16 April 1712, at the end of the first building phase, a contract was made to completely rebuild the bellows, which had been damaged from dampness.[46] Scheibe later reported that he had "take[n] the old bellows apart and replace[d] them with entirely new ones."[47] Whether Scheibe built frame bellows (as opposed to board bellows), as he did later in Zschortau, is not known. According to J. A. Silbermann, the organ's six single-fold bellows measured 4 Elle × 2¼ Elle, or approximately 8′ × 4½′.[48]

The bellows had previously been close to where grain was stored in the church's attic, but with the organ in its new location in the west gallery, the bellows room apparently was built next to a narrow street or lane. In March 1711 a carpenter billed 4 taler—3 taler for "a door to the bellows room at the organ" and 1 taler for "a window frame" in the same.[49] The glazier Johann Jeremias Groschner charged 2 taler for providing glass panes in the oval window in the bellows room "which goes into the alleyway."[50]

There is no indication what wind pressure the organ may have had.

Wind Chests and Wind Supply

Improving the wind supply had been a major goal from the beginning of the project. Scheibe noted that it would be necessary to build new wind trunks "so that the full organ does not lack for wind," and Vetter, too, mentioned the need for wind trunks with "adequate dimensions."[51] As well, partially for greater wind capacity, the organ needed new wind chests. It had been stipulated in 1710 that Scheibe would build two new chests for independent pedal stops in the Seiten-Pedal and that the Brustwerk chest would be replaced with two new ones placed on either side of the Hauptwerk, but Scheibe also ended up building new chests for the Hauptwerk and Hinterwerk divisions, as well as two small chests for the Brust-Pedal stops—in other words, all the organ's wind chests were newly built. It can be assumed that Scheibe built sponselled wind chests at St. Paul's, just as he did in Zschortau—that is, rather than providing a board (one large glued-up wooden panel covering the channels), individual wood pieces (sponsels) were glued into the tops of the channels. The payment records show that Scheibe used oak, oak barrel staves, alum-tanned leather (*Weißgar Leder*), and parchment.

Improving—that is, increasing—an organ's wind supply was part of many renovations carried out at this time. The approach taken in Gröningen (near Halberstadt) was more conservative but had the same goal. During the well-known renovation by Christoph Contius in 1704, which was supervised and documented by Andreas Werckmeister,[52] the eight multifold wedge bellows were retained but repaired and re-leathered. So that the Rückpositiv received more wind, the wind trunk was rearranged and enlarged, and the wind-chest channels were made larger. As a result, Werckmeister noted, the reeds spoke with greater liveliness. The Oberwerk wind chest also was altered so that it received more wind: pallet openings were enlarged and new pallets installed so that "the full organ has its proper volume of wind."[53]

Transmissions

The organ's transmissions were considered newsworthy. Sicul emphasized the "Six registers on the large Manual [Hauptwerk] wind chest which, by means of a new and special invention of the organ builder (which in future organ building should be quite a saving), are made available in the Pedal."[54] The transmissions' particular characteristics are described in an article written by Scheibe that he published in a Leipzig scientific journal in 1732:

> In the University Church of St. Paul's here, in the large organ completed by him [Scheibe] in 1715 [sic], six individual stops at 16', 8', 4', 3' and 2' were installed in such a way that even though they all stand on the Haupt-Manual wind chests, nevertheless they also can be used separately in the Pedal—not in the usual manner by means of a coupler or pull-downs, but in such a way that if one holds down a key in either the manual or the pedal and at the same time plays the same note in the pedal or manual, one hears a new and distinct attack, making one think that another pipe has spoken—that is, each pipe allows one to hear two distinct and accurate unison pitches at the same time, just as if there were in fact two separate pipes even though there is only one. Therefore, the aforementioned six stops are as good as twelve. The benefit of this invention is that for many stops that one otherwise builds separately for the manual and the pedal, whether 16' or smaller, one can save building the pedal stops, and, as a result, large and powerful instruments can be built with a small[er] number of stops, so that churches, depending on the size of the organ, can save from 100 to 1,000 taler.[55]

For Scheibe to build the Hauptwerk wind chests as transmission wind chests involved building double channels, double pallets, double springs, double sliders, and double stop knobs (six for the manual and six for the pedal). Each transmission register had two sliders. When the register was used in the manual, the wind opened the manual's pallet to the pipe and at the same time closed the pedal's pallet to the pipe. Using the register in the pedal worked in the opposite manner, so that the wind automatically closed the pallet to the manual channel. But when both manual and pedal transmission registers were used, the pipe received double the wind, but with only a very small impact on the overall loudness and pitch.[56] Scheibe pointed out one of the great advantages of this system: "If one holds down a key in either the manual or the pedal and at the same time plays the same note in the pedal or manual, *one hears a new and distinct attack* [emphasis added], making one think that another pipe has

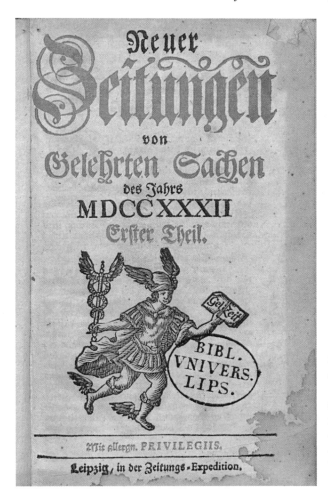

26. Title page, *Neue Zeitungen von Gelehrten Sachen*, 1732. Scheibe's article on his inventions appears on pages 833–34. Courtesy Bibliothek, Universität Leipzig. Public Domain.

spoken—that is, each pipe allows one to hear two distinct and accurate unison pitches at the same time, just as if there were in fact two separate pipes." This meant—and this point is extremely important for all organists who have had to deal with this problem—that when a note played in the hand crossed a note being held in the pedal, for example, one would hear a new attack. The counterpoint retained independence and clarity.

One can only speculate as to whether Scheibe discovered transmissions by "notable industriousness and his own ingenuity,"[57] as he reported, or whether he learned to build them from his teacher or another organ builder. There is no evidence that transmissions were ever built by either Christoph Donat I or

Eugenio Casparini—both of whom have been proposed as Scheibe's teachers. However, transmissions were built by the Trosts (father Tobias Gottfried and son Heinrich Gottfried), Johann Georg Finke, and probably Christian Förner. Also, transmissions were regularly built by members of the Compenius family of organ builders—including Heinrich Compenius II and his son Esaias II, who worked on the St. Paul's organ in 1627–30.[58] We have no knowledge of what Compenius did at St. Paul's exactly, but the record shows that he built new "wind chests, bellows, and a substantial amount of pipework"[59]—in other words, it was a major rebuild that very well might have included building transmissions. Before it was rebuilt by Scheibe, the St. Paul's organ had two stops on the Hauptwerk chest—Principal 16′ and Quintatön 16′ —that were playable in both the Hauptwerk and the Pedal. While clearly not entirely an innovation, then, the building of transmissions by Scheibe was, to quote Felix Friedrich describing the work of Trost, "special, noteworthy, and extraordinary."[60]

Couplers

The manual couplers are described in the Dresden Manuscript: "The manual keyboards are coupled by shoving one over the other; the middle keyboard pulls the upper, and, in an opposite manner, pushes down the lower."[61] Scheibe built shove couplers, then, just as Silbermann and Hildebrandt did. The upper manual coupled to the Hauptwerk keyboard by means of a fork coupler (*Gabel Koppel*); the lower manual coupled to the Hauptwerk by means of a cleat coupler (*Klötzchen Koppel*).

There was no Hauptwerk/Pedal coupler in the new organ. Johann Gotthold Jehmlich noted its absence, and the presence of transmissions, in 1834: "Further, the manual couplers are no good, and the pedal coupler for all manual stops is missing altogether and is only available for six Hauptwerk stops: Principal 16′, Octav 8′, Octav 4′, Quintatön 16′, Quinta 3′ and Mixtur VI."[62]

Pipework

Altogether, approximately 90 pounds of tin were purchased during the first building phase (September 1710 to March 1712), including 8 pounds of "good English" tin purchased 17 January 1711. According to the receipt, the tin was for "the organ Posaune."[63] Perhaps Scheibe intended to repair Posaune resonators. The old Posaune stop put into storage in April 1712—apparently having been replaced by Scheibe's new wooden Posaunen Bass—consisted of "21 pipes of good tin, among which are 3 from Blech [Weissblech, sheet iron plated with tin] and 3 mangled pipes from tin."[64] The stored pipes were returned to Scheibe in 1715 but must have been melted down for new pipework since, according to the unsigned contract from December 1710, Scheibe was to build a new Posaunen Bass 16′ with wooden resonators.

A rare description of work in progress dates to March 1712 when Scheibe purchased one-quarter hundredweight of tin, approximately 28 pounds, and 2 pounds of bismuth (which is added to soldering metal).[65] In the "small Hinter Werck," his note explained, he needed to replace the lowest octave of the Quintatön 8′ and the two upper octaves of the Octav (or Viola) 2′. In the Oberwerk, or Hauptwerk, he needed to lengthen the following stops because they had been cut or bent out of shape and could not be brought to the proper pitch or tuned: Octav 4′, Octav 2′, Groß Gemshorn 8′, Klein Waldflöte 2′, Mixtur VI, and Mixtur III.[66] (Mixtur III, however, was in the Brustwerk division.)

Most of the new pipework was made during the second building phase (May 1715 to November 1716). For the facade pipework, which the contract specified should be made of "good, pure, polished tin,"[67] Scheibe purchased 10 hundredweight (1,100 pounds) of tin. (His estimate had been for 12 hundredweight [1,320 pounds].)[68] We do not know from whom Scheibe purchased the tin. For Silbermann's organ project in Freiberg, the burgomaster negotiated in 1711 with Daniel and Hartmann Winckler, in Leipzig, to purchase 18½ hundredweight at 24½ taler each, and he purchased an additional 4 hundredweight of tin from merchants in Goslar.[69]

For the remaining, interior pipework—the "18 registers still missing" contracted in December 1715—Scheibe had estimated needing 3 hundredweight of tin and an equal amount of lead.[70] However, he purchased only 2 hundredweight (220 pounds) of tin and a little more than 3 hundredweight of lead.[71] If these were the only materials used, it would suggest an alloy for the interior pipework of approximately one part tin to two parts lead, or 33 percent tin. But Scheibe expected to use the metal recovered from melting down unused registers and pipes, so the percentage of tin probably was higher. For example, to build the three low pipes missing in each of the existing registers, he calculated needing to purchase only 1½ hundredweight of tin and 3 hundredweight of lead, because he would also be able to use the hundredweight of tin leftover from casting the facade pipes.[72]

The facade pipes at St. Paul's were made of pure *Bergzinn*, a material considered only slightly inferior to English tin. Mined in the Ore Mountains (Erzgebirge) near Altenburg, *Bergzinn* had iron bits in it that tended to rust over time, which made it more difficult to work and less durable than English tin.[73] English tin always was very expensive, but was especially so during the War of Spanish Succession (1710–13).[74] Tin for the St. Paul's organ cost about 26 taler a hundredweight, whereas, according to Adlung, writing in the 1720s, tin could be had for 10 taler a hundredweight.[75]

While all contemporary sources agreed that tin produced especially good pipes—pipes that were not only more durable but also produced a better sound—having pipes with a high percentage of polished tin in the facade also seems to have been a matter of prestige. The organ at St. Paul's joined organs recently built in Magdeburg, Eisenach, and, most famously, Görlitz in having tin facade pipes.[76] For the rebuild of the organ at St. Blasius's, Mühlhausen, undertaken just a few years earlier, Bach requested in 1708 that the three stops being added in the facade of the new Brustpositiv be made of "good 14-worthy tin"[77]—that is, an alloy of 87.5 percent tin.

According to Johann Philipp Bendeler, the most authoritative source on pipe building from the period, the higher the percentage of tin the better, not only on account of durability but also for the sound.[78] Bendeler was not satisfied with an alloy of less than 25 percent tin for pipe bodies and at least 50 percent tin for pipe feet.[79] For Werckmeister, pipe metal with a minimum of 33 percent tin was "a good metal alloy," especially for village organs, but a better alloy was 50 percent tin, and even better was when the alloy was two parts tin to one part lead, or 66 percent tin.[80] We do not know what the percentage of tin was in the "good pure *Bergzinn*"[81] facade pipes at St. Paul's—only that Jehmlich was not satisfied when he evaluated the organ in the 19th century: "The Principal pipes in the facade, given their mix or alloy, cannot at all be considered *Principalia*, and must be replaced by completely new ones made from pure English tin."[82]

Scheibe cast his pipes on sand,[83] a technique that was well known and used throughout Europe in the 17th and early 18th centuries.[84] Trost generally cast on sand, although there is also reference to him using a "linen-covered casting table."[85] Silbermann poured his metal on dimity (*Barchent*), a hard-wearing cotton fabric.[86] Casparini cast on linen.[87]

Pitch and Temperament

Scheibe reported that "the organ . . . was brought into proper Chorton." This had been "requested and demanded by the musicians, not only those who held positions but others as well, and was also necessary so that the organ could be used with the usual instruments accompanying the church music and because the old organ was not at the proper pitch [*inegal*] but at least a half tone too high throughout almost the entire organ."[88] In other words, Scheibe lowered the pitch to Chorton so that it could be played with the instrumental ensemble. In an earlier memorandum, Scheibe had described adding "pieces to the tops [of the pipes]"[89] as part of his complete repair during the first phase of the project. Now, however, he was required to set all the pipework to Chorton. This suggests that the previous pitch of the organ was High Chorton. Similarly, in his instructions for the major renovation of the organ in St. George's, Eisenach, which took place in 1696–1707, J. C. Bach specified that "the entire instrument, which is now a semitone too high and therefore cannot be used either with cornetto, sackbut, or flutes, is to be lowered to Chorton."[90] According to Scheibe, setting the organ at Chorton "took effort, time and expense, and soldering, altering, and building some things from scratch before the pitch could be attained, [an effort] which those who understand organ building will easily be able to judge."[91]

There is nothing about the organ's temperament in the archival documents relating to Scheibe's rebuild, and Bach did not mention it in his examination report. However, Johann Adolph Scheibe noted "the splendor, the energy, and the extremely comfortable and harmonious temperament of this large instrument," which reflected the extensive experience and extraordinary skill of the builder.[92] The terms "comfortable and harmonious" are vague, but that J. A. Scheibe was a proponent neither of equal temperament nor of an unsuccessful circulating temperament is obvious from a letter he published in *Der Critische Musicus*. He describes an organist in an unnamed location—obviously the court chapel in Altenburg—who is ridiculed for the bad temperament that resulted when he insisted that the organ be tuned in equal temperament. After much discussion, a compromise temperament was agreed to that resulted in two very harsh triads.[93] Just how "comfortable and harmonious" the St. Paul's temperament was is perhaps indicated by Bach's *Der Geist hilft unsrer Schwachheit auf* BWV 226, a funeral motet that was performed at St. Paul's in October 1729. The organ part, in the hand of Bach, is in A♭ major.[94]

Later repairs indicate that pitch standards continued to change. In repairs carried out by Wolf in 1792–94, "the entire organ, which before falsely had been tuned in Cammerton, now was laboriously re-tuned to proper Chorton, therefore quite a bit higher, and more comfortable for the church music and the wind instruments alike."[95] Wolf set the temperament "so that it is possible to play in all 24 keys."[96] Not many years later, Johann Gottlob Trampeli found "the entire organ [to be] too high for Cammerton and too low for Chorton," and in 1801–3, he set a new temperament and put the organ "in proper Chorton, so that the wind instruments will be in harmony with the organ."[97]

Materials

Materials were paid for by the university, but Scheibe was given the right to purchase them and was reimbursed upon request. As an organ builder purchasing for himself, he could negotiate better prices than could an institution such as the university:

> I would like to remind Your Magnificence and Most Worthy Sirs—without intending to prejudice your judgment—that would you rather procure the materials yourselves, they will without doubt cost more than what I have set out, since any merchant takes into account that whoever is having something built must pick up and pay for items, and can pay sooner than when [acquiring materials] is assigned to the [university's] builder [*Werck Meister*], and he must seek his profit therein as well. As became clear already a year ago, often a thing is much more expensive [for the university] to buy than it is when I am allowed to buy in my own name.[98]

Another time, Scheibe mentioned that the materials required for new Hauptwerk wind chests would be more expensive because the trade fair at which he could buy at particularly good prices had already taken place.[99]

During the organ's first building phase, the university disbursed 398 taler for materials. Expenditures to various guild artisans—the ironworker, painter, glazier, joiner, turner, sculptors, and the screw and nail maker—were billed separately and totaled 392 taler. And there were also expenses related to installing windows and decorating the organ's facade, almost none of which were billed to the organ project itself. Materials for the second building phase cost 461 taler, and in addition there were payments to the carver, turner, and gilder totaling 94 taler.

Cash was not always available when it was needed. Scheibe and his workers sometimes had to stop working because the university had no money to purchase materials.[100] Also, wages were sometimes paid late. In December 1711 Scheibe's wages for the first week were paid by Rivinus (there is no record that he was ever reimbursed), the second week's wages were not paid until two weeks later, and another week's wages were at first paid only partially and the remainder received later.

Accessories

Accounts differ as to which accessories the organ had. According to Sicul, the seven accessories were cymbelstern, bellows-pumper bell, and five ventils for the Hauptwerk, Brust[werk], Hinterwerk, Seiten-Pedal and Brust[-Pedal] divisions. According to the entry in the Dresden Manuscript, the accessories were tremulant, cymbelstern, bellows-pumper bell, and four ventils for the Haupt-werk, Hinterwerk (called a Seiten-Werk in this source), Brust, and Pedal.

Scheibe appears to have built the traditional Bocktremulant—a tremulant mounted on the outside of the wind trunk. Although the tremulant was included among the organ's stops in the Dresden Manuscript, a tremulant is not mentioned in the archival records associated with the organ until 1801, when Trampeli agreed to replace "the old tremulant, which is on the outside of the wind channel and therefore has ruined the bellows, with a new one, which will be placed inside the main wind trunk."[101]

The Cymbelstern was an extra added by Scheibe. In the bill submitted in October 1716, he requested 12 taler "for the [mixture] pipes and Cymbelstern in the 'cloudburst' [gloriole], because it was considered necessary for the improvement of the facade and the organ's proper arrangement."[102]

8 Renovations and Maintenance

> To renovate an organ made by another master requires greater art
> than building a new one.
> —Organists George Balthasar Schott, Christian Gräbner, and
>   Johann Gottlieb Görner, 1722

> My father, a very well-known organ builder [in Saxony], brought
> all the organs in Leipzig into their present condition, partially by
> building new organs, partially by carrying out important major
> improvements.
> —Johann Adolph Scheibe, 1748

Renovating an existing organ—"carrying out important major improvements," as J. A. Scheibe put it—was far more common in the 18th century than
building an entirely new instrument.[1] Materials were expensive, and pipework
made by renowned builders was highly valued. An instrument could be so
substantially rebuilt that it was referred to as a "new organ" and yet contain
materials and pipework that had been reused from an existing organ.

Evidence of this practice can be seen throughout the history of Leipzig's
organs. Johann Lange reused material from a 15th-century organ when he built
a "new organ" for St. Thomas's at the turn of the 16th century. At St. Nicholas's,
at the end of the 17th century, Zacharias Thayssner rebuilt the organ already
rebuilt by Christoph Donat I and reused material from the organ built by Lange a
hundred years earlier; he newly built 70 percent of the pipework. When Scheibe
built a "new organ" for St. John's in the 1740s, he reused material from an organ

that had been at St. Thomas's for more than 200 years. At St. Paul's, Scheibe reused material from the existing organ when he provided the university with a "new organ." An aficionado who visited the organ in 1736 wrote, "Although in certain respects this could be called a very old instrument . . . it also in certain ways is to be considered a new instrument, since nothing from the old organ can be found in it other than the beautiful large Principals and other pipework of the same scale. Everything else, even including the case, was newly built."[2] Donat's "almost completely ruined and unusable" organ[3] at the New Church was so substantially rebuilt by Scheibe in 1721–22 that the result was essentially a new organ. At a cost of 500 taler, he newly built 75 percent, and revoiced 100 percent, of its pipework and made important changes to the wind supply and action. Even when the result was not "an essentially new organ," a renovation could be extensive. At St. Thomas's, in 1720–21, Scheibe's "complete and full renovation of the large organ, along with [construction of] four new bellows and 400 new pipes belonging to the mixture," cost 390 taler.[4] At St. Nicholas's, the renovation of "the entirely unreliable and faulty organ" in 1724–25 cost 600 taler (see table 6).[5]

Most renovations were less invasive than those just described—and cost far less. Organs were overhauled or reconditioned when regular maintenance could no longer keep up with everything that was not functioning properly—there were too many leaks in the wind supply, there were frequent ciphers, the actions needed adjusting, not all the pipes were speaking, pipework and chests were filthy dirty, the organ was out of tune. The "urgently needed" overhaul of the New Church organ in 1713 is an excellent example. After examining the organ with organist Melchior Hoffmann, Christoph Donat II reported on 4 March that so much dirt had accumulated at the pipe mouths that many pipes were not speaking at all, and he was afraid that, because they were so near the damp church wall, the pipes would "be attacked by *Salpeter*"—that is, they would corrode.[6] He recommended that all the stops be removed, cleaned, revoiced, and tuned. Dampness also was affecting the pull-down pedal, which would have been sticking and causing ciphers had he not seen to problems while he was doing regular maintenance. Nevertheless, the pull-down mechanism needed to be cleaned, and the keyboards needed to be removed, adjusted, and put in good condition and brass screws installed in place of the iron ones, which had rusted. The stop registers were very hard to pull out, and to correct the problem he needed to remove (and correct) both the wind-chest sliders and the rollers. Leaks in the bellows and wind trunks needed to be repaired. Donat said that it

TABLE 6   Organ renovations in Leipzig, ca. 1720 to ca. 1750

	1720s	1730s	Late 1740s–1750
St. Paul's	1710–16: new and rebuilt organ, 2,996 T (Scheibe; examined by Bach in 1717)	1736: major overhaul, 160 T (Scheibe; overseen by Klausing)	1751: renovation, 350 T (Schweinefleisch)
St. Thomas's, large organ	1720–21: complete renovation, 390 T (Scheibe)	1730, evaluation by Scheibe and Görner; cleaning, resetting of temperament, tuning, adjusting Posaune, 50 T (Scheibe; examined by Görner)	1747 (26 June–24 Nov.): complete overhaul, cleaning, tuning, 200 T (Scheibe; examined by Görner and Bach)
St. Thomas's, small organ	1720–21: overhaul, 8 T (Scheibe) 1727–28: overhaul of 8 stops, 15 T (Hildebrandt)		1740: dismantling of small organ, 15 T (Scheibe)
New Church	19 Dec. 1721–8 Nov. 1722: renovation, 500 T (Scheibe; examined by Steinert, Schott, Gräbner, and Görner)	1732: overhaul: cleaning, resetting of temperament, tuning, 32 T (Scheibe)	4 Nov. 1746: evaluation by Scheibe and Gerlach; cleaning and repairs, 50 T (Scheibe) 1753: evaluation by Schweinefleisch and Gerlach; repairs, 47 T 12 gr. (Schweinefleisch; oversight by Görner)
St. Nicholas's	1718–19: cleaning, tuning, and repair, 30 T (Ficker) 1724–25: renovation, 600 T (Scheibe)	23 Dec. 1732 to sometime in 1733: complete repair, 45 T (Scheibe; examined by Schneider)	1750–51: renovation, 300 T (Hildebrandt)

would take him four or five weeks to get the organ back into good condition, that he could undertake the work during Lent (when the organ was silent), and that his fee, including materials, would be 60 taler. (He would not be responsible for the cost of erecting a scaffold.)[7] When Donat signed a contract two weeks later, he agreed to do the work for 35 taler and promised his work would not interfere with services on the Feast of the Annunciation (25 March), Palm Sunday, and Easter.[8] From a 21st-century point of view, Donat's description of the condition of an organ that was not yet 10 years old and that had been regularly maintained by its builder is hardly believable. But as this document preserved in the account books of the New Church reveals, the environment for organs was harsh. Thus, though regularly serviced and maintained, every so often organs had to be completely overhauled and brought back into perfect playing condition.

Overhauls and renovations in Leipzig occurred in clusters, and the material in this chapter is organized in the same way. After Scheibe's rebuild and expansion of the organ at St. Paul's, the organs in Leipzig's other main churches underwent major renovations in the 1720s, were brought into perfect playing condition again in the 1730s, and were renovated once again in the late 1740s and early 1750s. Throughout, the organs were regularly repaired, cleaned, and tuned. Three conclusions are inescapable: Leipzig's organs were regularly updated to meet changing musical requirements, older material was valued both economically and musically, and Leipzig's organs were well maintained.

Major Renovations in the 1720s

The New Church, 1721–22

When the New Church opened after refurbishment in September 1699, it became the third church within Leipzig's city walls where Lutherans could attend worship services. At first a newly appointed organist played a positive organ, but on 7 July 1703 a contract was made with Christoph Donat and his son of the same name for a new two-manual organ.[9] The organ was dedicated on 7 September 1704 by Georg Philipp Telemann, who had been appointed organist and director of music at the New Church just a week earlier. Telemann served at the New Church for only one year, however, and did not himself play the organ. As he wrote to Johann Mattheson, "I only played the organ for the dedication. Afterward I passed it over to various students, who squabbled over it among themselves."[10] His successors included Hoffmann, Johann Gottfried Vogler, Georg Balthasar Schott, and then, in an appointment that lasted some 30 years, Carl Gotthelf Gerlach. During Schott's tenure as organist and music director, it was decided to completely update the Donat organ. In the rebuild that took place in 1721–22, the barely 17-year-old Donat organ was changed dramatically, both structurally and tonally. Scheibe increased the wind supply; built new, wider-channeled chests for the Hauptwerk and Pedal; improved the playing action; made the Pedal division independent; rescaled, revoiced, and retuned the pipework; and made numerous tonal changes. The result was essentially a new organ.

27. The New Church, Leipzig. Detail from J. E. Scheffler's *Scenographiae Lipsiacae*, 1749. Sammlung Bach-Archiv, Leipzig, Graph. Slg. 16/38.

The Donat organ had been regularly maintained since its dedication in 1704—its overhaul in 1713 is described above—but an inspection in 1721 revealed that it was "almost completely ruined and unusable" and in need of a "major renovation" (*Haupt-Reparatur*). A contract to bring "the entire organ into good condition again" was signed with Scheibe on 19 December 1721.[11] For a fee of 500 taler, Scheibe agreed to pay the wages of any assistants, whether organ builders or otherwise, and to secure and pay for all materials, including tin. The contract specified that action squares be lined with brass, that brass wire be used to connect the new trackers to the keys, and that the new wind chests be constructed of oak. No organ building was allowed during church services, when everything was to be cleared away, and Scheibe also promised to be careful with fire and not to let any of his workers carelessly drop their pipe ashes. As for supervision, Scheibe was answerable not only to Johann

28. The organ in Leipzig's New Church, built 1703–4 by Christoph Donat and his son, rebuilt 1721–22 by Johann Scheibe. Engraving by Johann Christoph Oberdörffer, ca. 1720, based on a drawing by Johannes Christian Seyler. City History Museum Leipzig, 2441 (detail).

Kuhnau, to Wolfgang Jöcher (the church's trustee), and to the president of the city council but also to organists Schott (New Church) and Johann Gottlieb Görner (St. Nicholas's).[12]

The agreed-upon fee was 100 taler less than Scheibe had requested but only half the 1,000-taler estimate received from "an organ builder from Merseburg"—probably Johann Friedrich Wender, who worked on projects in Merseburg during the 10 years from 1714 to around 1724. It was not a foregone conclusion, then, that the local builder would carry out this renovation. Scheibe got the contract because his estimate was more attractive and because Kuhnau recommended him: "An organ builder from Merseburg who has looked at the New Church organ wants over 1,000 taler, whereas Scheibe, from here, requests only 600 taler, and also has been given a good testimonial by the cantor."[13] The work was to have been completed by St. Bartholomew's Day (24 August) 1722, but it was early November when the renovation was examined. Organists Schott, Christian Gräbner, and Görner wrote the detailed and very complimentary report, which is dated 8 November 1722.[14] (Kuhnau had died on 5 June 1722, and Bach had not yet been appointed to replace him.)

Donat's organ for the New Church was quite conservative—indeed, the disposition differs hardly at all from the 21-stop organ Donat built some 20 years earlier for the castle church in Eisenberg, Thuringia, and both organs were later renovated. In Eisenberg the organ was rebuilt and modernized in 1731–33 by Heinrich G. Trost. Trost lowered the organ's pitch from Cornetton to Chorton (by lengthening all the pipes) and rescaled and revoiced all the pipework. He also repaired leaks in the bellows and wind chests, corrected the "falsely proportioned" channels in the wind chests, and replaced materials. Tonal changes were relatively minor. In the Oberwerk, he replaced Trompete 8′ with Flaute Travers 8′, expanded the mixture by adding of a rank of Tierce pipes, and changed Gemshorn 2′ to Hohlflöte 2′. In the Pedal, he replaced Subbass 16′ of metal with Subbass 16′ of wood, and Schalmey 4′ with Octav Bass 8′. The renovation was nevertheless so extensive that Trost asked for, and eventually received, 126 taler in addition to the agreed-upon 350-taler fee.[15]

Scheibe made similar changes to the Donat organ in the New Church. To increase the wind supply, he strengthened and replaced valves in the bellows and built new wind trunks, new counterweights, and new, better proportioned wind chests for the Hauptwerk and Pedal. The bellows operated quietly after Scheibe's adjustments, and his improvements not only eliminated the "gulping and shaking"[16] that had plagued the Donat organ but also created greater wind capacity, one sufficient for any registration. He also replaced two of the organ's three wind chests. In lieu of Donat's "badly proportioned" Hauptwerk wind chest, Scheibe built a new chest that the contract specified would be "the same as the old one but somewhat larger," so that it could hold more wind and the organ would acquire "gravity and strength."[17] The Hinterwerk chest was trued up and re-leathered, and new brass springs were installed.

Donat had built the New Church organ with what he called Förder- and Hinterwerk wind chests. The terms for the two divisions—"Förderwerck zum untersten Clavier" and "Hinterwerck zum Ober Clavier"—make the construction clear: A "Vorderwerk" or Hauptwerk division at the front was played by the lower keyboard; a Hinterwerk division placed behind the Hauptwerk was played by the upper keyboard. By 1721, when Scheibe undertook the renovation, the divisions were simply referred to by the positions of their keyboards: Unterwerk or Hauptwerk and Oberwerk or Hinterwerk (also Kleinwerk). The setup was similar to—perhaps the same as—what Donat had constructed in 1662 in Neuenkirchen (Lower Saxony), where there also was limited height for an organ case. Donat's ingenious solution was to build a "double wind chest": in the middle, a partition across all the channels separated the wind chest into a front pallet box and a rear pallet box. (Arp Schnitger imitated Donat's plan in the organ he built in Dedesdorf in 1698.)[18]

Like the organ in Eisenberg, Donat's New Church organ had a pull-down pedal: whatever stops were pulled in the Hauptwerk also played in the Pedal. Scheibe made the Pedal division independent, so that the Subbass 16′ was playable not just with the Hauptwerk but also with "soft stops" in the Hinterwerk.[19] (Like the reworking of the Viol di Gamba, described below, this change was made over and above the contract.) The report makes no mention of a new coupler being installed, but given the Pedal disposition, a coupler would have been essential.

Scheibe also vastly improved the playing action. The Donat organ had such a deep key dip and the action was so hard that simple chords were hard to play for "even the strongest fellow."[20] After Scheibe's improvements, the organ played easily; according to the examiners, an artist could accomplish anything required as long as the nature of each stop was respected.

Scheibe completely changed the organ's pipe scales. The Donat organ was considered "too narrow [*Jung*], too weak, and not in proper harmony"[21]—that is, the balance between a soprano range that was "lovely and bright" and a bass range that was "splendid and solemn," as Andreas Werckmeister described it, no longer matched the ideal.[22] To improve the organ's balance and harmony, and to widen the scaling throughout, Scheibe either rebuilt the pipes with new, wider scales, moved pipes up on the chest, or replaced the stop altogether. In the Hauptwerk, all stops in the 16′ to 2′ range were newly scaled. In the lowest octaves of the Principal 8′ and Quintatön 16′—and in any other stops where this seemed preferable—this was accomplished by building new, wider-scaled bodies and new languids; in the remaining octaves, pipes were moved up on the chest. In the Hinterwerk, lower-pitched stops in the 8′ to 2′ range were changed by having their bodies cut apart and the languids replaced, and then they were resoldered and revoiced.

In the end, Scheibe "thoroughly corrected all the pipework—with no exception—building new feet and languids and seeing to it that everything was well and equally voiced, so that on inspection it would be taken for entirely new pipework." The examiners were especially pleased with the Gedackt stops, which they described as "very graceful and useful for [playing continuo in] concerted music," but Scheibe exceeded both the contract's specifications and the organists' expectations in his reworking of the Viol di Gamba. Using "his unique art," the organists wrote, Scheibe gave the stop "its proper gamba-like tone," so that, "when played in a way that is not contrary to its nature, [the Viol di Gamba] has a sweet sound."[23] How Scheibe achieved this is not described; musicologist Christhard Mahrenholz suggested that he may have changed the scaling by moving the pipes on the wind chest.[24] What the Leipzig organists meant by playing the stop "in a way that is not contrary to its nature" is not entirely clear. An open flue register, the Viol di Gamba is very narrowly scaled so that it can imitate the bow stroke and the nasal quality of stringed instruments, particularly the viol. Mattheson recommended the Viol di Gamba for playing a solo melody,[25] while Johann Friedrich Agricola described using it for rapid runs and arpeggios. In the organ of the castle church in Altenburg, he wrote, the Querflöte 16′ and the "exceedingly beautiful" Viol di Gamba 8′ had the same scale. When registered together and used to play rapid runs and arpeggios—not slow chords, which is the inclination of most organists—the effect is very beautiful, and the "pleasant keenness" that is present in both these stops "comes as close to the attack of a bow stroke on a [stringed] bass as is possible to achieve with pipes."[26]

Scheibe also rebuilt the Posaunen Bass 16′, giving it new resonators of tin-plate,[27] wooden shallots, and brass tongues, and he also replaced the shallots and adjusted the tongues in the Trompeten Bass 8′ and Schalmey Bass 4′. Because of the new wind chest and the more ample wind supply, the reeds spoke "more promptly and with greater gravity" after the renovation. Nevertheless, as the report makes clear, Scheibe appears not to have fully succeeded with the Posaune: "The Posaunen Bass 16′ is voiced very cantabile, to be sure, but it would be nice if it were somewhat stronger and more penetrating—although, given the height of the ceiling and the fact that this can only be an 8-foot instrument, one can well let this pass, especially since his work on this renovation will find full approval from those who are impartial and knowledgeable."[28]

The Posaunen Bass served a dual function. Its first, and most prominent, role was as part of the organ's plenum or full-organ registration. But it also was used in smaller registrations, such as in tutti movements of concerted works, as we know from Elias Lindner's request that Gottfried Silbermann alter the Posaunen Bass in Freiberg because it "could only be used with the full organ, and not with individual stops, which is nevertheless necessary in concerted music, where it would sound especially well in a tutti [section or movement]."[29]

In creating a new tonal palette for the New Church organ, Scheibe also replaced all the organ's mixtures using 14-worthy tin (metal comprised of 87.5 percent tin). Without naming them, the examiners reported that Scheibe installed "4 entirely new mixtures . . . two in the Hauptwerk, one of which has 6 ranks, the other two in the Kleinwerk [Hinterwerk]."[30] (It seems they were referring to Mixtur IV and Zinck II in the Hauptwerk and Rausch Zimbel II and Mixtur III in the Hinterwerk; see appendix D-4.) He also built Sesquialtera II in the Hinterwerk, and, in place of the Vox humana 8' that had been built by Donat (an addition to the contract), he put in Sordino 8', a mild, muted, trumpetlike reed also sometimes called Sertin. (Scheibe also had built a Sertin 8' for the St. Paul's organ.) Mixtures built from tin produce overtone-rich pipework that is pungent in character but is at the same time refined and silvery. By changing the Hauptwerk mixture from one mixture with four ranks of metal pipes to two mixtures with six ranks of tin pipes and reforming an existing stop into Tierce 1–3/5', it became possible to compose the crown of the Hauptwerk principal chorus in various ways, with or without the Tierce. Likewise, a variety of plenums could be registered using the Sesquialtera II and the mixtures in the Hinterwerk.

Not all the changes outlined in the contract actually took place. Indeed, the disposition changes mentioned in the contract appear to have been suggestions, the start of a conversation about what might be done rather than a definitive plan. For example, it was suggested that the Nasat 3' could be replaced with a Gedackt 4' for continuo playing. But the Nasat remained. Likewise, the contract stated that the Schalmey 4' in the Pedal would be replaced with Cornet 2', but in fact the Schalmey 4' was kept (and given new shallots and brass tongues).

Just as we do not know for certain what the Donat disposition was when the organ was completed in 1704—based on Scheibe's renovation contract, it looks like Donat provided 24 stops, 3 stops more than the contract called for—so, too, we cannot be certain of the disposition after Scheibe's major rebuild in 1721–22. According to an anonymous report, preserved as a draft among New Church records, Scheibe's "good and skillful" work, which took place over the "39 weeks and 6 days" between 15 January and 21 October 1722, resulted in a "majestic, well sounding organ" that had altogether 1,372 pipes, of which 1,034 had been newly built—although Scheibe later remarked, with typical hyperbole, that the organ had "almost 2,000 pipes."[31] The disposition that appears in table 7 is conjectural, based on the 1703 contract with Donat, the 1721 contract with Scheibe, and the 1722 examination report and on references to stops made by organ builders who worked on the instrument later. (A table comparing these

TABLE 7 Disposition of the organ (II/P/24) in the New Church, Leipzig, after the renovation by Johann Scheibe in 1721–22

Hauptwerk (11) (Förderwerk, Unterwerk; lower manual)	Hinterwerk (9) (Oberwerk, also Kleinwerk; upper manual)	Pedal (4)
Quintatön 16′	Lieblich Gedackt 8′ zur Musik	Subbass 16′
Principal 8′	Viol di Gamba 8′	Posaunen Bass 16′
Grob Gedackt 8′	Rohrflöte 4′	Trompeten Bass 8′
Spitzflöte 8′	*Nasat 3′*	Schalmey Bass 4′
Octav 4′	Octav 2′	
Klingend Gedackt 4′ zur Musik [for continuo]	*Sesquialtera II*	
	Rausch Zimbel II	
Quint 3′	*Mixtur III 1′*	Auxiliary stops:
Superoctav 2′	*Sordino [8′]*	Tremulant
Gemshorn 2′		Cymbelstern
Mixtur IV		Bellows pumper bell
Zinck II		

Sources: Donat disposition (New Church Accounts, 1703–4, fols. 96–97); Contract 1721 (appendix A-26); Report 1722 (appendix A-27); contract with Johann Gottlieb Mauer dated 20 December 1773 (New Church Accounts, 1773–74, fols. 6r–10r); Johann Gottlob Mende, proposal dated 23 September 1833 (Stadtarchiv Leipzig, Cap. 41 C. Nr. 4, fols. 1v–2). For a comparison of the source information, see appendix D-3.

Note: Italics indicate a new stop.

dispositions can be found in appendix D-3.) To emphasize a point made earlier: Scheibe's renovation was a major intervention. Just as we refer to the organs built at St. Paul's and St. John's as Scheibe organs, we can refer to the New Church organ as a Scheibe organ.

The importance of our knowledge of Scheibe's New Church renovation cannot be overemphasized. Whether from necessity or by design, the renovation provided the opportunity for both mechanical and tonal improvements, and the result was a more up-to-date, more versatile disposition, a disposition entirely appropriate for the modern music regularly performed in the New Church. Scheibe had just done a similar "complete and full renovation"[32] of St. Thomas's organ and would just a few years later carry out a renovation of the "entirely unreliable and faulty"[33] organ at St. Nicholas's, but for neither of these projects do the contracts or examination reports survive. Thus, the New Church renovation sheds much-needed light on the kinds of repairs and changes carried out in Leipzig's two principal churches shortly before and shortly after Bach took up his post as music director and Thomaskantor in 1723.

The Leipzig organists who examined Scheibe's renovation were very pleased.[34] "As we noted above when we gave witness that he had fulfilled the contract and had brought the organ into better condition than anyone in the beginning could have hoped," they wrote, "once again we would like to emphasize that to renovate an organ made by another master requires greater art than building a new one, and because [Herr Scheibe] carried out his work to great satisfaction, not only here, but also last year in the renovation at St. Thomas's, in our estimation in days to come he will advance far in his profession."[35]

St. Thomas's, 1720–21

The large and small organs at St. Thomas's were repaired and renovated in 1720–21. At the same time, and at considerable cost, to provide more light in the student gallery, nine windows, including one "beside the organ," were enlarged. The entire project cost 1,056 taler 15 groschen 6 pfennig, the organ window alone costing just over 149 taler.[36] As well, an elaborate, beautiful new baroque altar was commissioned that cost more than 4,000 taler.[37] Considerably less was spent on the organs. In 1720–21 Scheibe received 200 taler—against an agreed-upon fee of 300 taler—for "4 new bellows and a thorough renovation of the large organ."[38] The project was expanded, and Scheibe's fee increased to 390 taler when it was agreed he would also provide "400 new pipes belonging to the mixture,"[39] and he finished the renovation and received the remaining 190 taler in 1721–22. In that same fiscal year (which ran from Candlemas to Candlemas), the mason was paid 3 florins 15 groschen for securing the new bellows; the master carpenter received 40 florins for building supports for the new bellows and the scaffolding, which provided access to the organ as well as a place to store pipes being removed for cleaning and repair; the blacksmith was paid 7 florins 12 groschen for "various items"; and the locksmith was paid 7 florins 7 groschen "for 32 wood screws, 24 squares, and other work on the organ." In addition, two bellows pumpers received 17 florins 13 groschen for "treading bellows and doing odd jobs" during a period of 15 weeks, 2½ days.[40] Neither the contract with Scheibe nor an examination report survives.

St. Thomas's large organ was already old in 1525 when it was acquired, along with "the large table and the books," from the Antonine religious house in Eicha,[41] and by the time Scheibe undertook its renovation in 1720, it had already been fully rebuilt at least twice. Lange, Saxony's preeminent 16th-century builder,

rebuilt it in around 1600. Josias Ibach was paid to renovate the organ in 1619–
20,[42] and Donat renovated it several times in the second half of the 17th century.
In 1657 he built four new reed stops for the Pedal and expanded the short-octave
compass; in 1670 he added seven stops to the Brustwerk and Subbass 16′ to the
Pedal, and major modifications were made to the case, including constructing
three columns "under the organ"; and in 1702 Donat made repairs to the organ's
bellows and to pipework in the Oberwerk and Rückpositiv.[43] As published by
Johann Jacob Vogel around 1700, the organ's disposition was for a three-manual
organ with 35 stops as well as Tremulant, Vogelgesang, Cymbelstern, and 10
bellows.[44] Scheibe undertook an overhaul of the organ in 1713, for which he was
paid 50 taler.

Scheibe's renovation of the organ at St. Thomas's was praised, retroactively, by
the city's three principal organists. As noted above, in a report dated 8 November

29. St. Thomas's, Leipzig. Detail from J. E. Scheffler's *Scenographiae Lipsiacae*,
1749. Sammlung Bach-Archiv, Leipzig, Graph. Slg. 16/38.

1722, approving Scheibe's renovation of the New Church organ, they emphasized that "to renovate an organ made by another master requires greater art than building a new one." Scheibe had carried out the renovation to great satisfaction, not only at the New Church "but also last year in the renovation at St. Thomas's."[45]

The magnitude of Scheibe's renovation at St. Thomas's must be emphasized. The work included removing, cleaning, revoicing, and tuning existing pipework, as well as building and installing some 400 new pipes. The organ's multiple bellows were replaced with four new wedge bellows, obviously with larger dimensions and greater wind capacity. In addition, key and stop actions would have been adjusted, any leaks in the bellows and wind trunks would have been repaired, and wind chests would have been cleaned and springs regulated, perhaps replaced.

The ambiguous phrase "400 new pipes belonging to the mixture"[46] has led to various hypotheses. Noting that the organ part for the opening chorus in Bach's *St. Matthew Passion* BWV 244 directs that the solo melody be played using the Rückpositiv's Sesquialtera and that the disposition published by Vogel around 1700 lists no such stop in that division, Wilhelm Rust, one of the editors of the Bach-Gesellschaft edition of Bach's complete works, proposed that a Sesquialtera must have been added to the Rückpositiv during Scheibe's renovation.[47] Philipp Spitta accepted this thesis, and when he published the organ's disposition in the second volume of his Bach biography, he added Sesquialtera to the stoplist he acquired from the Vogel Chronicle.[48] Ulrich Dähnert, too, placed a Sesquialtera in the Rückpositiv of the St. Thomas disposition, to which he assigned the date 1722—after Scheibe's renovation and one year before Bach arrived to take up his position in Leipzig.[49]

Only two contemporary records of the organ's disposition survive, and neither has its origin during the time that Scheibe was active in Leipzig. Vogel included the St. Thomas disposition in his chronicle of Leipzig's history, which was published without date around 1700.[50] Johann Salomon Riemer, Vogel's successor, recorded the disposition in 1757, after a major renovation by Johann Christian Immanuel Schweinefleisch, and clearly identified the stops newly built by Schweinefleisch. Because the Vogel disposition differs in several respects from the Riemer disposition, and Scheibe's 1720–21 renovation seems to have been the only time when pipework was added (or replaced), it seems reasonable to assume that Scheibe made changes to the disposition, especially when one sees similar changes—primarily to mixtures and mutations—in other Leipzig organs.[51]

Changes in the disposition occurred primarily in the upperwork (see table 8). (The term "upperwork" refers to the principal-scaled higher-pitched stops, usually 2′ and higher, including mutations and mixtures.) In the Hauptwerk, Mixtur VI–VIII–X has been changed to Mixtur VIII 2′, a mixture with eight ranks throughout the compass, while in the Rückpositiv the mixture has been changed from four ranks to three. The Hauptwerk's Sesquialtera II has been changed to Tertian III (2′ + 1-3/5′ + 1-1/3′). In the Rückpositiv, Rauschquinte II has become Sesquialtera II (1-1/3′ + 4/5′), and Schallflöt [Hohlflöte] 1′[52] has become Tierce 1–3/5′. (Together, the Tierce and Sesquialtera II produce a high-pitched Tertian III.) Also, Grob Gedackt 8′ has replaced Lieblich Gedackt 8′, and Super Octav 2′ has replaced Violin 2′. Further, the Vogel disposition lists several stops in the Rückpositiv—Klein Gedackt 4′, Traversa [Querflöte] 4′, and Krummhorn 16′—that do not appear in the Riemer disposition. As the Krummhorn 16′ is specifically mentioned in the 1747 renovation contract, it

TABLE 8   Disposition of the large organ (III/P/35) at St. Thomas's, Leipzig, after renovation by Johann Scheibe in 1720–21

Oberwerk (9) (middle keyboard)	Rückpositiv (12) (lowest keyboard)	Brustwerk (9) (top keyboard)	Pedal (5)
Principal 16′	Principal 8′	Grob Gedackt 8′	Subbass 16′
Quintadena 16′	Quintadena 8′	Principal 4′	Posaunen Bass 16′
Principal 8′	*Grob* Gedackt 8′	Nachthorn 4′	Trompeten Bass 8′
Gemshorn 8′*	Traversa [Querflöte] 4′	Nasat 3′	Schalmey Bass 4′
Octav 4′	Spitzflöte 4′	Gemshorn 2′	Cornet 2′
Quint 3′	Klein Gedackt 4′	Sesquialtera [1–3/5′]	
Super Octav 2′	*Super Octav 2′*	Zimbel II	
Tertian III 1–3/5′	*Tierce 1–3/5′*	Regal 8′	Tremulant
Mixtur VIII 2′	*Sesquialtera II 1–1/3′*	Geigen Regal 4′	Vogelgesang
	Mixtur III 1′		Cymbelstern
	Krummhorn 16′		3 ventils
	Trompete 8′		4 bellows

Sources: Vogel Chronicle, 111–12; Riemer Chronicle, vol. 3, 1048.

Note: Italics indicate change observed by comparing dispositions from the two sources mentioned above; see appendix D-2 on the companion website.

* According to Adlung ([1768] 2011, § 195), Spitzflötes are conical in shape, like Gemshorns, but wider at the lip and come to more of a point on top.

cannot have been removed until the Schweinefleisch renovation in 1755–57. The same is perhaps true of the other two stops, which appear to have been replaced by Schweinefleisch's new Octav 4' and Quint 3'. If this is so, the Rückpositiv would have remained a division with 12 stops after the renovation of 1720–21. (See appendix D-2 for a comparison of the Vogel and Riemer dispositions.) These differences might simply be scribal errors, but because the changes produce a more colorful and versatile disposition, one with many more options for variation in registration, it is worth considering that they were intentional.

What was the organ like after Scheibe's renovation? First, the plenum was different. In the Oberwerk (or Hauptwerk), the principal chorus that began with Principal 16' and included principal ranks at 8', 4', 3', and 2' now could include Tertian III and/or Mixtur VIII. This facilitated variation in registering the "crown" of the plenum, which could be composed of (a) simply the Mixtur VIII (its lowest rank, a 2', doubles the highest rank of the individual ranks); or (b) simply the Tertian III, which continues the overtone series up to the sixth harmonic (this registration would likely have been based on the Principal 8'); or (c) Tertian III and Mixtur VIII, a plenum with a Tierce. The plenum combination in the organ's Rückpositiv had one unusual characteristic: it was missing the second harmonic in the series. The Rückpositiv had Principals at 8', 2', 1–3/5', II, and III (1'), and the plenum would have been constructed with the Spitzflöte 4' substituting for the missing Octav 4', together with (a) the Sesquialtera II and Mixtur III, (b) the Tierce and Mixtur III, or (c) just the Mixtur III (and thus no third). In the Brustwerk, there seems to have been no principal chorus as such—that is, its Cymbel II may have been used exclusively in solo registrations. Combined with the flute chorus (8' + 4' + 3' + 2'), it creates what organist Harald Vogel has described as "a colorful, ever-changing sound effect that is both intense and shimmering."[53] For yet another variation of color, the independent Tierce could have been added to this registration.

Replacing a Sesquialtera with a Tertian is an especially interesting choice. Tertian II (1–3/5' + 1–1/3', sounding the third + the fifth) differentiates itself from the Sesquialtera II (2–2/3' + 1–3/5') by having the third, rather than the fifth, as its lowest pitch. The result is a sound that provides brilliance in both the bass and soprano ranges, whereas the Sesquialtera is too raw to be used below the tenor range. A registration such as 16' + 8' + 4' + Tertian III (2' + 1–3/5' + 1–1/3')[54] would be very colorful and powerful, a useful solo registration for a cantus firmus, for lines that cross each other, or for lines that extend low into the tenor or bass ranges (see Bach's Schübler chorales "Wachet auf, ruft uns die Stimme" BWV 645 and "Ach bleib bei uns, Herr Jesu Christ" BWV 649, "Ein feste Burg ist unser Gott" BWV 720, or the Sinfonia BWV 146/1, for example). In the Rückpositiv, where a higher-pitched Sesquialtera II (1–1/3′ + 4/5′) was installed, it can be assumed that, like the Tertian III, it extended, without breaks, throughout the compass, making it available for use in the plenum.[55] Further, by combining the Tierce 1–3/5′ with Sesquialtera II, one could create in this division another version of a Tertian. Assuming that the Sesquialtera in the Brustwerk was always a single rank at 1–3/5′, that division, too, had a Tertian registration available. Indeed, the combination of Gedackt 8′, Nachthorn 4′, Nasat 3′, Gemshorn 2′, and Tierce 1–3/5′ is very close to Gottfried Silbermann's "Tertian combination."[56] Having different mutation colors in each division produces a nuanced, tiered effect: in the Hauptwerk, an intense Tertian combination; in the Rückpositiv, a strong, high-pitched Sesquialtera combination; and in the Brustwerk, where the Sesquialtera is formed by combining the flute-scaled Nasat 3′ with the principal-scaled Tierce, a milder, darker, more lyrical Sesquialtera sound.

Whether independent or as part of a Sesquialtera or Tertian, Quints (stops that produce the fifth, at 2–2/3′ or 1–1/3′) and Tierces (stops that produce the third, at 3–1/5′, 1–3/5′, or 4/5′) were valued not only for their ability to fill in the harmonic pitches in constructing a principal chorus or plenum but also for their ability to provide variety in registrations. As Werckmeister noted, the compound Tertian is quite useful but would be even better if each of its ranks were available separately so that "one can have a greater variety of registrations."[57] (Jacob Adlung, too, valued variety, remarking, "Variety is the soul of music; for this reason, one has many stops built, both flues and reeds, so that one has many registration possibilities.")[58] In the renovation of the famous Gröningen castle church organ, overseen by Werckmeister and completed by Christoph Contius in 1705, four of the five tonal changes involved mutations: in both the Oberwerk and Rückpositiv divisions, Quint 2–2/3′ and Tierce 1–3/5′ replaced other stops "so that everything can be found in this organ that belongs to a complete ensemble and disposition."[59] (Or, as Werckmeister put it in the very next paragraph, "so that the overtone series is complete and the stops in the plenum are correct.")[60] Contius's own large new organ for the Market Church in Halle, examined by Kuhnau, Christian Friedrich Rolle, and Bach in April 1716, also contained independent Quints and Tierces in each of the three manual divisions, as did the organ he built for Glaucha in 1718.[61] In his examination report dated 10 November 1721 of Silbermann's new organ in Rötha, Kuhnau observed that Silbermann had added a Tierce 1–3/5′ over and above the contract because it is useful "for filling in the harmony and for providing variety in registration."[62]

Slightly more than a month later, on 19 December 1721, the contract was signed for the renovation of the New Church organ—a contract that included building an independent Tierce 1–3/5′. (Notably, on the other hand, Scheibe's organ for St. Paul's included no independent Tierce.)

How independent mutation stops were to be registered was a matter of some concern. Adlung warned that Quints, Tierces, and compound stops generally are never used alone but always need to be combined with as many octave-sounding stops as are necessary to cover their "ugly sound" (*Uebelklang*). Further, the octave-sounding stops are to be pitched lower than the Quint to disguise what would otherwise be progressions of fourths. Pitches in the upper octaves require less "cover" than pitches in the lower octaves, however. Adlung cited the mathematician and philosopher C. F. M. de Chales, who believed that Quints and Tierces always were to be combined with at least two octave-sounding stops, except where the melody remains in the upper octaves, when a single octave-sounding stop could suffice. As examples, de Chales suggested that Quintatön 8′ or Gedackt 8′ with Tierce 1–3/5′ could be tolerated quite well and that an Octav 4′ often was adequate to cover the Sesquialtera when one is playing in the treble.[63]

Every organ in Leipzig had independent mutation stops, and a perusal of the dispositions provided by Adlung in his *Musica mechanica organoedi* (1768) reveals that independent mutations were part of organs by Christian Förner, Christoph Junge, Thayssner, Contius, Johann Georg Finke, Gottfried Silbermann, Zacharias Hildebrandt, Heinrich Gottfried Trost, and Scheibe. By the 1740s, however, the presence of high-pitched stops began to be criticized. More than one writer recommended banning them from organs altogether, and, as Ernst Flade noted in his lexicon of organ builders,[64] J. A. Scheibe rushed to their defense: "An organ will always be weak and without force if all its stops consist in only principal ranks that are only one or more octaves apart from each other. To fill the churches and support the congregation, mixtures, quints, and tierce registers need to be included, yet with this precaution: the dissonances that result therefrom must be partially covered."[65]

St. Nicholas's, 1725

Carl Benjamin Schwarz's late 18th-century watercolor *The Former Organ at St. Nicholas's in Leipzig* documents the large, beautiful organ that was soon to be replaced during a major renovation of the church in 1784–97. Situated on a balcony on the west side of the southern aisle, the organ is painted by Schwarz with its smaller Rückpositiv doors closed but its Oberwerk doors open, the two Renaissance paintings clearly visible: on the left, King Pharaoh and his troops perishing in the Red Sea; on the right, Miriam leading the women in a song of triumph and thanksgiving. The Oberwerk's highly decorated flat Renaissance facade is divided into five sections, with seven pipes each in the center and side towers. The two smallest flats hold an indeterminate number of pipes, perhaps 11, perhaps 13; their closeness gives the impression that the pipes have been

30. Carl Benjamin Schwarz's watercolor *The Former Organ at St. Nicholas's in Leipzig*, ca. 1785. Stadtarchiv Leipzig, RRA (F) nr. 316.

squeezed into the space, as if there are more pipes in these narrow flats than may originally have been planned. Looking over the Rückpositiv to the main case, one discovers the pipes of the Brustpositiv.

At the time it was painted, the organ was about 190 years old. Lange had provided a two-manual, 28-stop organ in 1597–98, whose completion was celebrated in 1601, apparently after a three-year warranty period. Michael Praetorius, organist to Duke Heinrich Julius of Braunschweig-Wolfenbüttel, wrote a 12-voice composition for the occasion,[66] and published the organ's disposition in 1619.[67] After numerous changes in the 17th century, the organ underwent a major renovation by Thayssner in 1691–94. (Thayssner was based in Quedlinburg and Merseburg from around 1677 to 1713 or so.) He built four new bellows, new wind trunks, new wind chests and pipework for the Brustpositiv and Pedal divisions, new keyboards and a pedalboard, and three new couplers. He also repaired the old wind chests in the Oberwerk and Rückpositiv and rescaled and revoiced any pipework he did not newly build. New pipes accounted for 1,456 of the organ's 2,076 pipes. The result was an essentially new three-manual, 36-stop organ; altogether, 26 of the organ's 36 stops were newly built.[68] As is clearly visible in Schwarz's painting, Thayssner's new Pedal was placed discreetly to the side of the main case, which otherwise appears to be unaltered. The left side of the organ is not a mirror image of the right; the decorated hip has been altered, and the case extends down to the floor and all the way out to the edge of the balcony. Visiting in 1741, J. A. Silbermann noted the organ's old-fashioned appearance and succinctly described Thayssner's Pedal: "Stands on the left, on the floor, very hidden."[69]

Although the organ at St. Nicholas's was regularly repaired and had been overhauled in 1718–19 for a fee of 30 taler by Wahl Friedrich Ficker, 30 years after Thayssner finished his work the organ was judged to be "entirely unreliable and faulty" and a contract for its renovation was signed with Scheibe on 11 December 1724.[70] No report on the organ's condition in 1724 survives. Bach had been Thomaskantor and director of music for the city of Leipzig since 1723, but it may have been Görner, a student of Kuhnau's who had been appointed to succeed Daniel Vetter in April 1721, who initiated the work. Further, neither Scheibe's contract nor a report from the examiners has survived. Only a brief entry in the Riemer Chronicle suggests the extent of Scheibe's work: "On 14th of this month [July 1725] organ building began at St. Nicholas's, pipes were removed, and [the organ was] enlarged by 150 pipes. One continued to play the organ throughout [the renovation], however, making robust use of it, and the organ builder, Herr Scheibe, brought the organ into good condition."[71]

For the renovation at St. Nicholas's, the third major renovation Scheibe carried out in the 1720s, he earned the substantial fee of 600 taler,[72] considerably
more than the 390 and 500 taler he was paid for the renovations at St. Thomas's
and the New Church, respectively. Spitta characterized the renovation as "very
extensive,"[73] and Arnold Schering thought that the project's high cost "obviously
indicated a substantial alteration of the instrument."[74] Although neither scholar
speculated as to what Scheibe might have done, similar projects allow us to infer
the renovation's scope.

The proposal Scheibe provided in 1746–47 for renovating the organ at St.
Jacob's in Köthen is especially relevant.[75] St. Jacob's also had a Thayssner organ,
built by Zacharias and his brother Andreas in 1674–76. For a fee of 460 taler,
Scheibe said he would repair, strengthen, and re-leather the bellows; relocate
and lengthen the wind trunks; clean the wind chests and replace iron wire with

31. St. Nicholas, Leipzig. The 76-meter/249-foot tower was added in 1731. Detail
from J. E. Scheffler's *Scenographiae Lipsiacae*, 1749. Sammlung Bach-Archiv,
Leipzig, Graph. Slg. 16/38.

brass; correct the playing action; clean all the pipework; remove *Galmey* (cala-mine, a combination of zinc oxide and ferric oxide) from the shallots and adjust the tongues in the reeds; replace pipes, primarily in the upperwork, that had been attacked by *Salpeter* or had been "cut up too much"; and also set a "good temperament" and tune the entire instrument. For an additional 100 taler, he would also replace the "evil spring chests" with slider chests.[76] (Scheibe's Köthen proposal is discussed in detail in chapter 10.) Surely Scheibe carried out similar repairs when he renovated the organ at St. Nicholas's. He would have cleaned, repaired, adjusted, replaced as necessary, and tuned. In other words, he would have brought the organ into perfect playing condition, or something as close to that goal as was possible.

Also, though, Scheibe added or replaced 150 pipes. A comparison of the disposition after Thayssner's 1694 renovation with the disposition recorded in 1741 reveals that at least five tonal changes were made (see table 9): Viol di

TABLE 9   Disposition of the organ (III/P/36) at St. Nicholas's, Leipzig, after renovation by Johann Scheibe in 1724–25

Oberwerk (13)	Brustpositiv (7)	Rückpositiv (10)	Pedal (6)
Principal 8'	Principal 4'	Principal 4'	Subbass 16'
Gemshorn 8'	Octav 2'	Grob Gedackt 8'	Posaunen Bass 16'
Grob Gedackt 8'	Quint *1–1/3'*	*Nasat 3'*	Octav Bass 8'
Quintadena 16'	Sesquialtera 1–3/5'	Gemshorn 4'	Trompeten Bass 8'
Octav 4'	Mixtur III	Quintadena 4'	Schalmey Bass 4'
Super Octav 2'	Quintadena 8'	Octav 2'	Cornet Bass 2'
Sesquialtera 1–3/5'	Schalmey 4'	Quint *1–1/3'*	
Quint 3'		Sesquialtera 1–3/5'	Tremulant
Nasat 3'		Mixtur IV	Cymbelstern
Waldflöte *4'*		Bombarde 8'	Vogelgesang
Fagott 16'			4 wedge bellows
Trompete 8'			Couplers:* P/OW, RP/OW, BP/OW
Mixtur VI			
			Manual compass: CD–c³
			Pedal compass: CD–c¹

Sources: Vogel Chronicle, 97; *Silbermann-Archiv*, 171 and 173. For a comparison, see appendix D-4.

Note: *Italics* represent changes likely made during Scheibe's renovation; see appendix D-4.

* Z. Thayssner, memorandum dated 1 March 1694, StA Leipzig, Stift IX A 2, fol. 17v.

Gamba 4′ was replaced with Nasat 2–2/3′, and several stops were changed by an octave: Waldflöte 2′ became Waldflöte 4′, Quint 2–2/3′ became Quint 1–1/3′, and Octav Bass 4′ became Octav 8′ (see appendix D-4). Some changes required unusual adjustments. The Octav 8′ pipes "stood in front of the Cornet [2′], two feet above the wind chest, and were connected by square conductors, which were crammed between the reed pipes."[77] In other words, the new 8-foot pipes did not fit on the chest and had to be offset with wooden conductors.

As with other changes we have seen in the Leipzig organ dispositions, these changes appear haphazard at first, or perhaps seem like simple scribal errors, but it is clear that these alterations make possible an even greater variety of registrations, especially for solo lines. For example, as we know from Agricola, Bach's student in Leipzig from 1738 to 1741, the new Waldflöte 4′ could be nicely paired with Quintadena 16′:

> It is inadvisable to omit an octave in the middle [of a registration]. For example, an 8′ and 2′ registration without a 4′ would sound far too hollow, especially when playing full chords. But if one is playing a single melodic line on a manual—in a trio, for example—then one may indeed unite a 16′ and 4′. Thus, for example, Quintadena 16′ and Hohl- or Waldflöte 4′ produces, in this instance, a good effect. Even Bordun 16′ with Sifflet [Sifflöte] 1′ has a good effect if fast single-line passages are played on them. In choosing stops, a great deal depends in general on whether one is playing a single line or a full texture on a manual.[78]

Similarly, changing the Quint from 2–2/3′ to 1–1/3′ allows formation of a Tertian registration (by combining Tierce 1–3/5′ with Quint 1–1/3′). The advantage of having a prominent third as the lowest pitch in the registration, already noted above, is that a solo line can be played in all ranges of the keyboard, whereas the Sesquialtera II registration, which combines Quint 2–2/3′ with Tierce 1–3/5′, is usable primarily in the alto and soprano ranges. Also, with the Nasat 3′ having been added to the Rückpositiv, and the Octav 8′ having been supplied in the Pedal, it became possible at St. Nicholas's to register the combination called *Tierce en Taille*. Also used for solo lines when the melody extended into the low alto or tenor range, the *Tierce en Taille* was described by Agricola as a registration "often found in French organ books" that consists of "Bordun 8′, Octav 4′, Nasat 3′, Tierce 1–3/5′, and Octav 2′, to which one might also add a 16′ Gedackt. On the second manual, where the accompanying voices are performed, one draws a single 8′ Principal or a few flutes, and in the Pedal a 16′ Principal Subbass and an 8′ Octav."[79]

Again, it seems plausible that these changes were made during Scheibe's renovation. Again, the changes provide that increased "flexibility and variability in registration" so much valued by Werckmeister[80] and others. And again, this view is supported by the fact that one sees similar disposition changes during the renovations in the 1720s at St. Thomas's and the New Church.

The organ's disposition was recorded by J. A. Silbermann in 1741 when he visited Leipzig during his tour of organs in France and Germany. Silbermann described what for him were some of the more unusual stops in the St. Nicholas organ, stops not common in the French organ-building tradition in which he worked. The Waldflöte 4′ was "very full, very beautiful, and had a good effect"; the Quintadena 16′ "made a good effect"; the character of the Gemshorn was somewhere "between a Bourdon and a Principal." Reed resonators, he noted, were made of tinplate. In the Rückpositiv, Bombarde 8′ "sounded almost like a Cromorne in the soprano, except not quite so nazard-like," and "in the bass [it sounded] between Cromorne and Trompette." The Cornet 2′ was "very bright" and "very narrow, much narrower than our narrowest *Clairon*, especially in the soprano, but it made a tremendous effect. [It had] wooden boots and blocks." The Schalmey 4′ in the Brustpositiv had "very narrow scaling, like the Pedal Cornet." Fagott 16′ sounded "hollow, like one of our trumpets that has not yet been fully voiced; in the soprano it was similar to a Vox humana." He gave the organ's compass as CD–c³ in the manuals, CD–d¹ in the pedal.[81]

Silbermann noted the elegant, richly carved and gilded facade, and there were other old-fashioned elements as well. The Rückpositiv's iron stop knobs were shoved sideways within long notches, and the Brustpositiv, which was "above the organist," with the Schalmey 4′ at the front of the chest, had stop knobs that were "iron shafts with rings." Stop knobs like this are described and illustrated by Adlung. About the width of a thumb and about half an inch thick, they could be pulled outwards, but they also were moved along slots—upwards, downwards, or sideways.[82] He provides a diagram of stop knobs arranged in this manner in the organ in Naumburg, a three-manual instrument that Thayssner renovated in 1695–1705, after he finished his work in Leipzig. At the bottom of Adlung's diagram are two horizontal rows of stops, immediately next to the keyboards are what look to be stop knobs in the shape of rings, and next to the rings are rows of obviously metal knobs being moved in oblique notches.[83] Silbermann noted that the Brustpositiv stop knobs could no longer be moved but concluded, "Other than that, the instrument does quite well for an old organ."[84] This assessment stands in contrast to the opinion expressed by Gottfried August Homilius, who, while they were visiting the Scheibe organ at St. Paul's, told Silbermann that Scheibe also had renovated the organ at St. Nicholas's but had "more ruined than improved it."[85] (Homilius, in Leipzig from 1735 until 1742, was a student of

Johann Schneider, organist at St. Nicholas's, and he apparently substituted for Schneider from time to time.)[86]

The organ's four bellows were "pumped by foot," wrote Silbermann, and had "many folds." Whether this observation was accurate or whether, as both Thayssner and Vogel reported, the organ had "wedge bellows with a single fold"[87] is unknown. Silbermann's comment suggests that while Scheibe no doubt repaired Thayssner's bellows, he apparently did not change them. Single-fold bellows provided a larger volume of air and hence a stronger sound and were much desired at the time. If Thayssner built multifold wedge bellows and Scheibe kept them, it suggests that the organ's voicing, in keeping with an early baroque wind supply, must have been less powerful, but perhaps more elegant, than counterparts with expanded, powerful wind supplies.

The changes at St. Nicholas's were nowhere near as far-reaching as they were at the New Church. In many ways, Scheibe preserved the St. Nicholas organ much as he found it. He did not replace the old-fashioned stop action, for example, and he made fairly minor changes to the organ's disposition. That he built only 150 new pipes—Thayssner had built 1,456 new pipes—suggests that in 1724 the cantor and organists did not wish, or need, to make a large number of tonal changes.

Overhauls in the 1730s

St. Thomas's, 1730

Having been recently renovated, the large organ at St. Thomas's was in excellent condition when Bach took up his positions as music director and Thomaskantor in Leipzig in 1723. But seven years later, when Scheibe and Görner assessed its condition and Scheibe penned a report on the first Monday in Lent, 27 February 1730, the organ's pipes were so dirty and so out of tune that the organ's temperament could no longer be recognized. Scheibe recommended that the pipes be cleaned, that the temperament be set from scratch and everything tuned, and that he make improvements to the Posaunen Bass 16'.[88] Scheibe no doubt carried out the overhaul during the Lenten season, a time when the organ was silent and no concerted music was performed with the exception of Good Friday. (Lent in 1730 started on Ash Wednesday, 22 February, and ended on Easter Sunday, 9 April.) The renovation was examined and accepted by Görner.[89] No examination report survives.

For a long time, the work done by Scheibe in 1730 was misunderstood. Rust suggested that Scheibe's repairs in 1730 included adding a separate and independent keyboard attached to the Rückpositiv case—at the time it was thought the

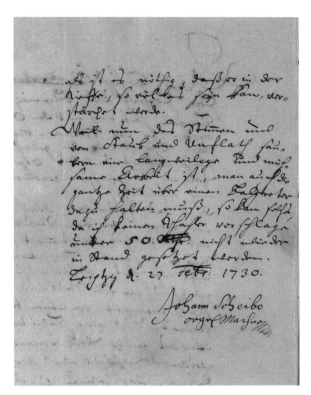

32. Scheibe's signature on his proposal to overhaul the St. Thomas organ dated 27 February 1730. Stadtarchiv Leipzig, Stift IX A 2, vol. 1, fol. 70v.

Rückpositiv was located on the railing of the musicians' gallery, some distance from the Hauptwerk case at the rear of the gallery—so that it could be played by a second organist (at the same time that the Hauptwerk was played by the first organist).[90] This conjecture was accepted by Spitta,[91] and not until 1908, when Bernhard Friedrich Richter published the text of Scheibe's report to Leipzig's city council, was this rather unusual theory disproven.[92]

Two items give particular significance to the overhaul in 1730: the revoicing of the Posaunen Bass 16', one of an organ's most important pedal stops, and the resetting of the organ's temperament. The Posaune 16' was considered "somewhat weak" and not able to "cut through well enough."[93] It was not providing the gravity and clarity that was expected of such a stop. To correct this, Scheibe strengthened its bass octaves.

That the temperament was reset at this time is also significant. As Bach scholar Don Franklin has demonstrated, after 1730 Bach no longer avoided certain keys but wrote in all the keys available in a circulating but irregular temperament.[94]

We do not know for certain that Scheibe set a completely new temperament. He might have reset an existing temperament or have made only minor adjustments to it, but, given that the organ at St. Paul's already had an "exceedingly comfortable and harmonious temperament" in 1716,[95] it is likely that the rest of Leipzig's organs would likewise have been tuned in circulating temperaments.

An organ's temperament was of crucial importance. Theorists from Werckmeister to Georg Andreas Sorge agreed that organs needed to be tempered so that it was possible to transpose and modulate into all keys, whether when improvising preludes or playing continuo in concerted music. The move away from meantone is described by Sorge, an organist and composer (and an acquaintance of Bach): "They believe they are perfectly justified in sacrificing one fifth out of 12, and four major thirds out of 12, so that the remaining—but this applies only to the thirds, not to the fifths—are that much better. However: [while] in former times this was fairly feasible because one both had to, and could, limit oneself to such a narrow range of keys, in today's practice it is not at all practical."[96]

While temperaments were set by organ builders, builders clearly were advised by organists and consultants. The earliest record of an organ being tuned in one of Werckmeister's temperaments dates from 1677, when Thayssner signed a contract for a new organ in Quedlinburg's Stiftskirche (Werckmeister had been organist there since 1675) that required him to set and tune an "accurate temperament, according to today's custom, in which the majority of musical works are composed using *ficta* [non-diatonic] notes, so that all keys, both common and uncommon, can be used harmonically."[97] Thayssner employed a similar temperament at St. Wenceslas's in Naumburg, where the 1705 attest noted that "the accurate musical temperament is very pleasant to hear."[98] Whether Thayssner tuned the St. Nicholas organ in an "accurate temperament" is not known, but it must be considered possible, as Kuhnau was a prominent spokesperson in favor of tunings that allowed one to transpose and modulate freely. In a 1717 letter, Kuhnau wrote that a temperament should be structured so that every key (pitch or note) had two uses—G♯ as well as A♭, for example.[99] He was quite persuaded by Johann Georg Neidhardt's temperament, he admitted, although he was not aware of it actually being used in any organs.[100] Silbermann and Wender did not tune according to Neidhardt, he noted, but used temperaments that gave preference to the keys most often used.[101]

Whatever temperament was set at St. Thomas's in 1730, its character surely would have been discussed among the organ builder (Scheibe), the organist (Görner), and the cantor (Bach). We know nothing of Görner's preferences. As for Bach's preferences, we rely primarily on information passed down by two of his students, Agricola and Johann Philipp Kirnberger. As reported by Friedrich Wilhelm Marpurg, Kirnberger said more than once that Bach "expressly required of him to tune all the thirds sharp."[102] Agricola reported that "real connoisseurs"—by which we assume he meant Bach—criticized Silbermann's meantone temperament as being "all-too-individual."[103] (From 1716 on, Silbermann started setting what now would be labeled a well-tempered tuning.)[104] The viewpoint that Silbermann's temperament was too limiting—and that a more flexible temperament was desirable—was stated forcefully by Sorge, who wrote, "In a word, Silbermann's kind of tempering is incompatible with modern practice. To testify that all this is the pure truth I call upon all unbiased and (in this matter) expert musicians, especially the world-famous Mr. Bach in Leipzig."[105] Sorge wrote extensively about the deficiencies of Silbermann's temperament, which he described after visits to Silbermann's organs in Greiz (1739) and Burgk (1743) as being a regular 1/6-comma temperament that narrowed 11 of the 12 fifths in order to produce eight fairly "good" thirds at the cost of having to put up with one unusable fifth (G♯–D♯), the wolf, and four "unbearably barbaric" major thirds (really diminished fourths). The result, Sorge explains, is that major triads built on A♭, D♭, G♭, and B are "totally intolerable," and even the closely related keys of E♭ and E "must suffer the same misery."[106] He wrote,

> In today's practice it is not at all practical [to limit oneself to a narrow range of keys], for a continuo part can be in A♭ Major just as easily as in G Major, as all of today's composers will confirm and as their compositions will attest. One must therefore understand that it is not necessary to turn one's back on major thirds that are sharp by a quarter, a third, or 5/12 of a [lesser] *Diesis*, because a third can tolerate much more [out-of-tuneness] than a fifth, as Werckmeister and Neidhardt have fully proven. . . . I therefore suggest a different solution: Because not one of the 12 major thirds can be dispensed with, even if one is not using it as the fundamental key, it is much better that they beat by 1/3 a *Diesis*, or some little less—1/4 or 7/24—or more—3/8 or 5/12—but all are usable, yes, properly seasoned, fresh and awake, than that a third [of the twelve]—just imagine it—are unusable, or at the least, much too raw and disagreeable—yes, quite oversalted—and beat 2/3 a *Diesis*, that is, much wider than a Comma.[107]

Here, then, is a description of one or more temperament(s) in which all the thirds are tuned sharp—exactly as Bach apparently instructed Kirnberger to do. Sorge describes in detail and provides charts for a number of unequal tuning systems with sharp thirds—notably by Werckmeister and Neidhardt—but when asked by his pupil what would be a short and simple instruction to give an inexperienced instrument tuner, he responded, "Thus: Do not let even one fifth, but on the other hand, let all major thirds, beat sharp, nevertheless so that the third never beats more than 5/12, or not quite half, of the *Diesis*. In this way the problem is solved. This [instruction] is sufficiently short and clear."[108] Werckmeister had stated the same principle: "If you want to tune so that you are not restricted in any key, you need only allow all major thirds to beat high."[109]

To state the obvious: we do not know what temperament Scheibe set at St. Thomas's—or, indeed, in any of Leipzig's churches—but it is a reasonable assumption that it allowed the organist to play in, and modulate to, remote keys.

The New Church, 1732

The New Church organ was in need of cleaning and a major tuning 10 years after its major renovation in 1721–22. Scheibe reported on 6 December 1731 that "a great amount of dust has fallen into the organ, and it has become entirely impure and out of tune, so that it cannot be brought into good condition again without a thorough cleaning and major tuning. In order to accomplish this, every pipe must be taken out separately and cleaned with special instruments, and then the organ must be tuned and a temperament set from scratch."[110] Because the organ had "almost 2,000 pipes" that were difficult to reach and he would need the help of an assistant throughout the overhaul, Scheibe requested a fee of 36 taler. As a note at the bottom of Scheibe's estimate informs us, a fee of 32 taler was agreed to on 1 February 1732. He must have received his fee immediately, because the payment is recorded in the New Church account books for the period Candlemas 1731 to Candlemas 1732. Whether Scheibe did the work during the several weeks in Advent when there was no concerted music, or whether he did not begin the work until Lent, which began on Ash Wednesday, 29 February 1732, is unclear. According to the payment record, Scheibe was paid for "dusting the entire organ, in that it was full of dust, for cleaning it, and for a major tuning [*Haupt-Stimmung*] of the whole instrument, as well as repairs."[111]

Bach had no official duties at the New Church, but he nevertheless had connections there. New Church organists Schott and Gerlach often substituted for Bach when he had to be out of town or was otherwise unable to perform his duties at St. Thomas's and St. Nicholas's.[112] More importantly, in March 1729 Bach took over the collegium musicum that regularly performed concerted church music there[113] and gave weekly performances of secular music at Zimmermann's coffeehouse (twice weekly during the three annual trade fairs). As well, several of Bach's cantatas were performed at the New Church, including one for the third Sunday after Epiphany (*Herr, wie du willst, so schicks mit mir* BWV 73), a performance that Andreas Glöckner dates to around 1730.[114] This circumstance may provide a hint to the organ's temperament. The first movement has a part for *Corno da caccia,* which Gerlach rewrote in his copy as an organ obbligato part. Transposed down a tone to sound at Chorton pitch, the part includes a motive, a♭–a♭–f–a♭, which outlines a third that is quite unpleasant in anything but a well-tempered tuning.

St. Nicholas's, 1733

In late 1732, Scheibe and Johann Schneider assessed the condition of St. Nicholas's organ, and by city council's order dated 23 December 1732, Scheibe was paid an installment of 15 taler for the "necessary renovation" (*Reparatur*). Another 30 taler were paid in 1733 "in fulfillment of the agreed upon 45 taler for the fully completed renovation."[115] While no details are known, we can assume the maintenance work was similar to that carried out by Scheibe at St. Thomas's in 1730 and at the New Church in 1732—that is, cleaning, repairs, setting a temperament, and tuning. As it turned out, the time Scheibe had to accomplish this repair would have extended far beyond the season of Lent. Friedrich August I ("August the Strong"), elector of Saxony and king of Poland, died 1 February 1733, and the official mourning period, during which no concerted music took place in the churches, lasted until July. Concerted music resumed on 2 July, with the Marian Feast of the Visitation, possibly with a performance of Bach's Magnificat in D Major BWV 243.

St. Paul's, 1736

According to Council minutes, when Scheibe repaired "one thing and another" in the St. Paul's organ in 1730, he also informed the university that an overhaul was necessary: "The organ builder, Scheibe, reports that he repaired one thing and another on the St. Paul's organ and requests nothing more than his out-of-pocket expenses, which amount to 12 taler. Also, [he reports] that further repairs are necessary, which, if delayed, could cost the sum of 200 taler. Resolved: Herr Cantor Bach should look at what Scheibe has built and what it is that needs to be repaired."[116] Six months later, the organ and its maintenance were again discussed by Council. The somewhat garbled minutes dated 28 September reported,

> The organ builder, Scheibe, previously claimed that he had invented something for the St. Paul's organ that will help prevent the ciphering that occurs during changes of weather, and although such work would normally cost 200 taler, he requested only 12 taler. At Council's request, Cantor Bach looked at Scheibe's invention and

reported that it is good and that Scheibe's requested fee is not unreasonable. In
addition, however, Scheibe claims that a cleaning of the pipework is absolutely
necessary because the pipes are very dirty from smoke and dust, and if the pipework is not helped in a timely manner, major damage and high repair costs could
result. He requests 92 taler for such work and Herr Bach has approved it, although
he believes the amount could be somewhat reduced. . . .

   Resolved: The organ should be reexamined and Herr Dr. Klausing and Herr Dr.
Schacher are requested to be present at such examination.[117]

Council, or the recorder at this meeting, apparently misunderstood what was
happening with the organ. Scheibe had indeed requested only 12 taler, but, as
noted above, it was for repairing "one thing and another" in the organ and, at
the same time, Scheibe had said that an overhaul was necessary that might cost
as much as 200 taler. Amazingly, having received Bach's evaluation, Council
resolved that the organ should be reexamined in the presence of Professors
Schacher and Heinrich Klausing. (Members of the Klausing family were organ
builders based in Herford.)

The university's explicit lack of trust in Bach's opinion and recommendations
is hard to fathom. Glöckner concluded—and I agree—that the university distrusted Bach because, as he had shown during the organ's examination in 1717,
he had the concerns of the organ builder in mind and the university wanted
someone making recommendations who would, above all, have *its* interests
at heart.[118] Bach's expertise must have been well known and appreciated, however. It had been 13 years since he examined the St. Paul's organ and 7 years
since he became Thomaskantor. Just recently he had overseen the reshuffling
of the organist positions at the principal churches, and during Lent Scheibe had
undertaken a major overhaul of the organ at St. Thomas's when he cleaned the
pipework, set the temperament from scratch, and tuned the organ throughout.
The fact that similar overhauls would be undertaken in 1732 at the New Church,
in 1732–33 at St. Nicholas's, and finally, in 1736, at St. Paul's suggests that the
cleaning at St. Paul's was part of a general plan—certainly approved by Bach if
not actually initiated by him—to overhaul the organs in the principal churches.
As details of the work reveal, "cleaning the pipework" most often also included
revoicing, setting a temperament, and tuning. It is not clear why the university
would have reacted so strongly against such a renovation at St. Paul's, except,
of course, that it was expensive.

As the minutes dated 7 November 1730 reveal, Klausing and Schacher apparently did not agree that the overhaul was necessary:

Scheibe, the organ builder's son, owes rent to the college, to which the father has
objected, as though his invention for the organ, for which he requests 12 taler,

should take its place; further, he has submitted a memorandum concerning a renovation of the organ, [saying] that, because of dust, some pipes are, and some pipes are not, speaking, and he would like to clean them with instruments adapted for the purpose, for which he requests 50 taler and a bellows pumper for 6 weeks.

Resolved: The renovation [*Haupt Reparatur*] should be postponed. Scheibe should be paid the 12 taler for the invention, but the money will not be put in his hands but rather, on account of the rent owed, will be paid from the church's account to the college's account.[119]

Council resolved to pay Scheibe for his invention—the special instruments were not described by Scheibe in the article he wrote describing his innovations—but to postpone the renovation, even though Scheibe had reduced his fee. Rather than paying the 12 taler to him directly, however, Council used Scheibe's fee to pay a rental debt owed by his son. As Glöckner observed, Scheibe received not a penny.[120]

The issue of the organ's overhaul apparently was not raised again until 1735, and it was 1736 before the university agreed to undertake the work. Minutes from April 1735 once again note that a thorough cleaning had been recommended: "The organ builder Scheibe reminds us about the smoke and dust on the pipes and languids, and that, if a major repair is not undertaken, then at least the pipes should be repaired and cleaned, for which he demands the sum of 160 taler."[121] The 160-taler fee was considerably higher than the amounts Scheibe had requested four and five years earlier, and the university requested a detailed calculation of expenses.[122] A year later, minutes report again that Scheibe had written regarding the necessity of making repairs and doing a cleaning, had requested 170 taler for the "necessary repairing and cleaning of the St. Paul's organ," and warned that if the work were put off even longer, the resulting damage would be "even greater."[123] Again Scheibe was asked to provide details regarding the length and scope of the work. And yet again he provided an estimate, requesting 160 taler, and warned that further delay could result in a substantial increase (of up to 400 taler!) in costs.[124] Finally, on 5 April 1736, the work on the organ was approved. Klausing—not Bach—was designated to oversee the project on the university's behalf and also to specify what would be done and how. A contract for 160 taler was signed on 13 April 1736, and on 31 August Scheibe was paid the third, final installment "for the renovation of the organ."[125]

There is no evidence that any disposition changes were made, but there also can be no doubt that this was a complete overhaul of the organ. (Unfortunately, no copy of a proposal or contract has survived.) Scheibe had at one point requested a bellows pumper for six weeks, apparently during revoicing, setting (or resetting) the temperament, and tuning. In addition, the pipework had to be cleaned and everything brought into perfect working order. Scheibe described the process in some detail when he undertook a similar overhaul at the New Church: "All the pipework, in every register, must be removed from the wind chests, and each pipe, separately, cleaned of dust and filth . . . the chests must be cleaned . . . the actions need to be adjusted . . . leaks in the bellows and wind trunks are to be repaired . . . and the pipework throughout the entire organ must be voiced again and tuned."[126] A cost comparison also reveals how extensive the overhaul or renovation must have been. Overhauls cost 50 taler at St. Thomas's (1730), 32 taler at the New Church (1732), and 45 taler at St. Nicholas's (1732–33).

Renovations in the 1740s

The New Church organ was renovated once again in 1746. Scheibe and Gerlach examined the organ and "a major renovation"[127] was approved by the city council on 4 November. Scheibe's report on the organ's condition[128] seems to quote earlier reports—Donat's 1713 report on the New Church organ, his own 1730 report on the St. Thomas organ, and his 1731 report regarding the New Church organ—almost verbatim: The pipework was so "full of dust and filth" that many pipes could not speak and were in danger of being attacked by *Salpeter*. All the pipes needed to be cleaned individually and the reeds needed to be cleaned of *Galmey*. The wind chests needed cleaning, actions required adjustment, and leaks in the bellows and wind trunks needed repair. Finally, all the pipework would have to be revoiced and tuned. Scheibe was paid an installment of 16 taler on 14 November 1746 and the remaining 34 taler just after the work was finished, on 29 December 1746.[129]

In 1747 the large organ at St. Thomas's was renovated. According to the contract signed on 28 June, the organ was "almost unplayable" due to the large amount of dust and filth. It had suffered damage during the heat wave in the summer of 1746, and cleaning and repairs, long overdue, were necessary to prevent the organ from falling further into decay. The cost of the repair—200 taler as opposed to the 50 taler it cost to do the overhaul in 1730—indicates a more extensive overhaul or renovation. Scheibe agreed to repair everything, including the bellows that had been damaged during the heat wave; to bring the pipework into good condition (by removing all the pipes and repairing, cleaning, and polishing them, and cleaning *Salpeter* and *Galmey* from the shallots and tongues of the reeds—"the Posaunen Bass and Trompeten Bass, the Trompete and Krummhorn in the Rückpositiv, as well as the two reeds in the Brustwerk");

to clean and bring into good condition the pallets in the wind chests; to repair the action where the iron and brass had broken; to adjust the two manual couplers; to revoice and tune all the pipework—in short, to "tune the whole organ purely throughout, and to bring everything into good *Harmonie*, orderly *Disposition*, and even voicing." (*Harmonie* refers to balance between bass and soprano, for example, or seeing that one pipe is not louder or softer than its neighbor. An "orderly *Disposition*" would be one in which everything is in good and working condition.)[130]

Over a four-month period—rather than the four or five weeks necessary in 1730—Scheibe made all the necessary repairs, revoiced the pipework, and tuned, at the same time making sure that some of the "more necessary" organ stops were playable for services.[131] There is no evidence that any stops were altered or added. Scheibe was paid 30 taler on signing the contract; 30 taler on 15 July and again on 17 August and 9 September; 25 taler on 30 September; and 55 taler, the final installment, on 4 November 1747.[132] Bach and Görner examined Scheibe's work, which they found to be "skillful and good."[133] No written report survives.

The renovation at St. Thomas's was Scheibe's last significant project in Leipzig. He died the following year, and when a renovation of the organ at St. Nicholas's became necessary, in 1750, it was Hildebrandt, his son Johann Gottfried, and an apprentice who carried it out. Neither the contract nor the examination report survives, but payment of the 300-taler fee was made in fiscal year 1750–51—that is, between Candlemas 1750 and Candlemas 1751.[134] Unfortunately, nothing is known about what was done; the extent of the project is indicated only by the number of workers and the modest fee—half of what Scheibe had been paid in 1724–25 but 100 taler more than Scheibe was paid for the renovation at St. Thomas's in 1747. That Hildebrandt agreed on 10 August 1750 to supervise the construction of Silbermann's three-manual, 47-stop organ for Dresden's Hofkirche, the contract for which the ailing Silbermann signed on 27 July, suggests that the work in Leipzig was either complete or nearly complete before Bach died on 28 July 1750. It is not difficult to imagine that the death of Bach—Hildebrandt's colleague, supporter, perhaps friend—would have made it easier for Hildebrandt to contemplate leaving Leipzig. He may have departed for Silbermann's workshop in Freiberg in August.

One further renovation was carried out at this time. At St. Paul's, Schweinefleisch was paid 350 taler for a major repair and renovation in 1751.[135] (Also, for their "oversight and effort," in 1752–53 Görner, the university's music director, received 12 taler, and Schneider, organist at St. Nicholas's, received 2 taler 18 groschen.) According to Riemer—reporting in 1755 but apparently referring to the work done in 1751[136]—Schweinefleisch added (or replaced) three registers: Principal 8′ and Schalmey 4′ in the Pedal, and Principal 4′ in the Oberwerk.[137] Schweinefleisch carried out an even more extensive renovation in 1767, for which he was paid 742 taler.[138] Unfortunately, no proposals or contracts relating to this work appear to have survived.

Daily Work: Maintenance of Leipzig's Organs

"For decades, year in and year out," wrote Schering in 1926, "partially in the form of complete rebuilds, [Scheibe] kept up the city's organs."[139] Schering's observation is confirmed by the record of payments made to Scheibe from the city and university of Leipzig. Throughout his career, Scheibe made repairs as required and kept Leipzig's organs in playing condition. Years in which no fees for maintenance or repairs were paid occurred primarily after overhauls and renovations, which suggests that such work was carried out under warranty. Payments for maintenance—the regular "tuning, servicing, and dusting" (*stimmen, warten, und abkehren*) as it is called in the New Church records—became more regular after 1730, when Scheibe returned to Leipzig after an approximately three-year absence. Whether this resulted from negotiations between Scheibe and the Leipzig city council, or from the organists or the Thomaskantor insisting on more regular attention to the organs, or for some other reason is impossible to ascertain.

Maintenance and repairs were carried out by an organ builder, to be sure, but the church's organist also had responsibility for the organ; in a sense, organ builders and organists were interdependent. Organists were required to carry out minor repairs and tuning of organ reeds and to notify authorities when an organ builder's assistance was required. Organists and organ builders together assessed an organ's condition in preparation for repairs or renovations. Often organists were the experts who carried out official examinations and wrote reports after major renovations or when new organs were finished. As Scheibe's memoranda show, organ builders had a vested interest in seeing that competent organists were hired to play (and care for) the organs they built, renovated, and maintained. Speaking of the St. Paul's organ, in 1717 he wrote, "I ask you to remember that a reliable organist should always be at the organ, for otherwise, when this does not happen, and one [organist plays] today, another the time after, and the Herr Cantor the time after that, the instrument will soon be ruined."[140] The tight relationship between organists and builders was described by J. C. Bach, organist of St. George's in Eisenach and, from 1696 until his death

TABLE 10   Leipzig organists and Thomaskantors, ca. 1700–1750

Thomaskantors	
Johann Kuhnau	1701–22
Johann Sebastian Bach	1723–50
St. Nicholas organists	
Daniel Vetter	1679–1721
Johann Gottlieb Görner	1721–29
Johann Schneider	1730–66
St. Thomas organists	
Johann Kuhnau	1684–1701
Christian Gräbner	1701–29
Johann Gottlieb Görner	1730–78
St. John's organists	
Johann Michael Steinert	1694–1731
Johann Gottlob Reinicke	1731–47
Johann Georg Hille	1747–66
New Church organists (from 1704, also directors of music)	
Christian Augst	1699–1704
Georg Philipp Telemann	1704–5
Melchior Hoffmann	1705–15
Johann Gottfried Vogler	1716–20
Georg Balthasar Schott	1720–29
Carl Gotthelf Gerlach	1729–61
St. Paul's organists	
Johann Adam Stolle	1710–13
Johann Christian Pitzschel	1713–16
Gottlieb Zetzsch	1716–20
Johann Gottlieb Görner	1720–21
Johann Christoph Thiele	1721–74
Georgenhaus organists	
Johann Georg Hille	1744–47
Christian Colditz	1747–66

in 1703, overseer of the major renovation and rebuilding of the organ by Georg Christoph Stertzing:

> As the currently employed organist, and as far as my abilities allow . . . I am willing to do all that I can and to give advice to the organ builder on account of one stop or another when it is necessary so that everything is precisely and accurately

scaled, well voiced, and each stop, according to its nature, is elegantly equal and sounds good to the ear, and thus, first and foremost, that it technically will become an excellent organ. For where there is a well-designed, good organ, it generally also attracts good organists—indeed, such an instrument in certain ways makes good organists.[141]

According to the contract made with organists at the New Church, the organists were responsible for routine maintenance. Likewise, at St. Nicholas's, Görner was required to be "attentive to the organ and to see to it that anything wrong with it is corrected in a timely manner."[142] Bach signed similar contracts as organist. In Arnstadt he promised "to keep a watchful eye over [the new Wender organ] and take faithful care of it, to report in a timely fashion if any part of it becomes unreliable, and to give notice that necessary repairs need to be made . . . in general, to see that damage is avoided and everything is kept in good order and condition."[143] Likewise, in Halle, where he turned down the position of organist, the employment contract he was offered required that he "take good care that the former [the large and small organs, the regal, and other instruments belonging to the church] are kept in good condition as regards their bellows, pipes, stops, and other appurtenances, and in good tune, without dissonance; and if anything should become unreliable or broken, to report the same at once . . . so that it may be repaired and greater damage averted."[144] Werckmeister made this obligation very clear. He believed every organist should be willing and able to move an adjustment screw at the keyboard after a weather change, or hook back into place a loose tracker, or remove a speck of dust or dirt that may have gotten into a reed pipe, but he also warned that an organist might not have the proper tools and materials at hand and, if he were "too determined," that he "might in his zeal do more damage than good."[145] In a city such as Leipzig, where Scheibe was regularly paid fees for maintaining and repairing the organs, it is unlikely the organists were required to do more than tune the reeds and make very minor repairs. Nevertheless, the close relationship between organ builder and organist cannot be overemphasized.

Repairs and maintenance carried out in Leipzig (see table 11) are discussed briefly in the following paragraphs. For more detail, readers may consult appendix E, which is available on the companion website.

At Leipzig University, where records of payments for organ repairs, renovations, and the organ builder's lodgings were kept regularly from 1685 on (see appendix E-1), the builder is rarely identified. The two exceptions were the payments in 1697–98 and 1700–1701 of 4 guilders—the normal annual fee from 1685 to 1710—to "Christ[oph] Donat"; otherwise, most entries of the annual payment are simply to the "Orgelmacher" (organ builder), "Organoedo," or "Organopoeo." Scheibe's name, for example, is mentioned only in entries for repairs done outside of the annual maintenance. As is described elsewhere,[146] the university's organ builder was not paid in cash. Instead, St. Paul's Church paid St. Paul's College an amount each year equal to the rent the builder was assessed for his living quarters at the college. (In the discussion that follows, such payments are referred to as annual maintenance fees.)

During Scheibe's renovation of the St. Paul's organ and until the one-year warranty period was over and the organ had been successfully examined, there were no payments for either repairs or maintenance. Also, no maintenance fees were paid during the period that Scheibe's demand for an additional payment remained unresolved, whereas the bellows pumper began to be paid in 1717 at the rate of 12 taler annually. (The substantial increase over the 12 guilders paid previously no doubt was necessary because the organ was so much larger than it had been.) Scheibe's appointment, made official on 21 April 1718, was retroactive to Michaelmas 1717, and when payments resumed in 1719–20, the salary for annual maintenance and tuning was increased to 12 taler and a payment of 36 taler was made that included that year as well as the two years (1717–18 and 1718–19) in arrears. Twenty years later, Scheibe requested that his fee be raised to 16 taler annually "for steadfastly keeping the organ in usable condition,"[147] and in 1743 he requested that St. Paul's also pay the rent for his second room. Both requests were denied. Starting at Easter 1744, his salary was raised by 4 groschen per year;[148] he died just four years later. His apprentice Johann Hinrich Jentz requested to be his successor, and he apparently was interviewed,[149] but there is no indication that he took over the position, and in 1751 it was Schweinefleisch who carried out a major renovation.

In addition to the annual maintenance fee, Scheibe was paid in cash for specific repairs.[150] In 1717–18, he was paid 12 taler for repairing pipes damaged by glass shattered in a hailstorm and in 1718–19 was reimbursed 8 taler 18 groschen for materials (tin, lead, glue). In 1719 he was paid for repairing the bellows and wind chests after a summer heat wave. Three bellows cracked apart and the bungboards (*Spünde*) in almost all the wind chests contracted so much that there was about a quarter-inch gap. Scheibe needed 10 skins of leather and two pounds of glue for the repairs, which also included replacing two iron arms in the Principal Bass.[151] He requested 10 taler 20 groschen for the repairs—exactly when they were carried out is unclear—and was paid 10 taler on 7 October 1719.[152] Johann Burchard Mencke observed, in the discussion about whether the repairs should be done, that "in future it would be better if the organist did not attack the organ so heavily and the bellows pumper did not leave the window near the wind chests open, which allows heat to stream in."[153]

Scheibe was paid 12 taler for repairing "one thing and another" in 1729–30[154] and in 1730–31 was paid 16 taler for repairing the bellows.[155] (Also in 1730, a 12-taler payment for his invention went to rental arrears rather than directly to Scheibe.) In 1736 Scheibe carried out the major renovation discussed above and was paid 160 taler. Two further repairs were undertaken. In December 1739 Scheibe's recommendation that he build a "covering over the arms" (at a cost of 16 taler) was approved,[156] although there is no record of a payment, and in fiscal year 1741–42, a payment of 6 taler was made to Scheibe "for procuring and installing iron arms on the 21 torn-off organ registers."[157]

The substantial fees paid for annual maintenance—12 taler for an organ builder, 12 taler to the bellows pumper, and, occasionally, payments for greasing the bellows—suggests that Leipzig University was proud of its new instrument and wished to keep it in good playing condition. Despite assertions to the contrary,[158] the record of repairs shows that the organ suffered not from structural defects but from ordinary wear and tear.

TABLE 11   Fees received by Scheibe for maintenance, repairs and renovations in Leipzig, ca. 1705–1748

Year	St. Thomas's	St. Nicholas's	New Church	St. John's	St. Paul's
1706–7		4,-,-			
1707–8					
1708–9					
1709–10					7,8,-
1710–11					6,18,-
1711–12		2,12,-			870,-,-
1712–13	20,-,-	1,12,-		16,12,-	
1713–14	30,-,-				
1714–15					
1715–16		3,-,-			591,-,-
1716–17	3,-,-				
1717–18	1,-,-			15,-,-	24,-,-
1718–19					20,18,-
1719–20	2,-,-	12,-,-	4,-,-	-,10,-	222,-,-
1720–21	208,-,-		4,-,-		12,-,-
1721–22	190,-,-	4,-,-	154,-,-		12,-,-
1722–23			354,-,-	13,-,-	12,-,-
1723–24			4,-,-		12,-,-

Year	St. Thomas's	St. Nicholas's	New Church	St. John's	St. Paul's
1724–25		250,-,-	4,-,-		12,-,-
1725–26	40,-,-	394,-,-	24,-,-		12,-,-
1726–27			4,-,-		12,-,-
1727–28					12,-,-
1728–29					24,-,-
1729–30					28,-,-
1730–31	50,-,-	5,8,-	4,-,-	3,18,-	12,-,-
1731–32	1,16,-	4,-,-	36,-,-		12,-,-
1732–33	2,8,-	20,8,-	4,-,-		12,-,-
1733–34	2,8,-	31,8,-	4,-,-	2,-,-	12,-,-
1734–35	5,-,-	4,-,-	4,-,-		12,-,-
1735–36	2,8,-	4,8,-	17,-,-		172,-,-
1736–37	3,8,-	6,-,-	4,-,-		12,-,-
1737–38	1,16,-		4,-,-		12,-,-
1738–39	4,8,-		4,-,-		12,-,-
1739–40	12,16,-		15,-,-	1,8,-	12,-,-
1740–41	15,-,-		4,-,-	4,-,-	12,-,-
1741–42	10,-,-		5,12,-	350,-,-	18,-,-
1742–43	7,-,-		4,-,-	100,-,-	12,-,-
1743–44	7,-,-	1,8,-	6,12,-		12,4,-
1744–45	7,-,-		4,-,-		12,4,-
1745–46	7,-,-		4,-,-	252,-,-	12,4,-
1746–47	7,-,-		54,-,-	2,-,-	12,4,-
1747–48	204,-,-		4,-,-	3,-,-	12,4,-
1748–49	4,-,-	2,-,-		3,-,-	12,4,-

Sources: St. Thomas Accounts; St. Nicholas Accounts; New Church Accounts; St. John Accounts; St. Paul Accounts A, St. Paul Accounts B, St. Paul Accounts C.

Note: Amounts shown are in taler, groschen, pfennig. The amounts paid to an (unnamed) organ builder in 1709–11 probably were received by Scheibe; the 870 T. shown as being paid in 1711–12 was received over the period 1710–12, during the first phase of the organ project at St. Paul's.

At St. Thomas's, the organ was taken care of by Christoph Donat I and his son Christoph Donat II until 1713. Although Christoph Donat II was paid in 1712 for maintenance carried out in March and September, on 28 January 1713, during a lull in his work at St. Paul's, Scheibe agreed to repair "the Pedal stops in the organ, and other necessary items," for a fee of 50 taler. (The contract does not survive.) Much of the work appears to have been done during Lent, with payments made on 22 March (on signing of the contract), 17 April (the day after Easter), and 4 October.[159] Johann Christoph Gottlob Donat (a son of Christoph

Donat II who had studied with his uncle Johann Jacob Donati in Zwickau) repaired the bellows in 1715–16, but Scheibe carried out the major renovation in 1720–21, and, except for David Apitzsch making repairs while Scheibe was away from Leipzig in 1726–29, Scheibe cared for the large St. Thomas organ for the rest of his life. In 1747 he was responsible for another renovation, and in 1748, the year he died, Scheibe was paid for a half year of maintenance. Jentz took over at Christmas 1748 and maintained the organ in 1749, after which the organ was cared for by Schweinefleisch.

There is no record of regular maintenance of St. Thomas's second organ, the two-manual, 21-stop instrument located in an east-end gallery. Possibly it was tuned and repaired as often as the large organ, a task so well understood that it was not even mentioned in the payment records. Possibly the organ was not much used and was brought into repair only infrequently. In any event, after a major renovation by Donat in 1665 and a minor repair in 1678 (when Donat was paid 8 taler for making repairs to both organs at St. Thomas's as well as to the regal in the St. Thomas School),[160] there was a long period when—according to payment records—no further repairs were made to the small organ, even though numerous repairs were made to the large organ. In 1720–21, at the same time that the large organ was undergoing a major renovation, Scheibe was paid 8 taler—the same amount Donat had received in 1678—"for repairing the small organ, which had been completely unusable." In 1727–28, while Scheibe was away from Leipzig, Hildebrandt was paid 15 taler, including travel costs, "for bringing 8 registers in the small organ into playing condition." The organ was removed in 1740.[161]

The organ at St. Nicholas's was maintained and repaired by various builders. For 12 years after Thayssner's renovation, completed in 1694, there were no expenditures for maintenance at all, but in 1706–7 Scheibe and Christoph Donat II each were paid 4 florin 12 groschen for "repairs to the organ," and 3 years later, one David Müller was paid 1 florin 3 groschen "for repairs to the keyboard, roller board, and registers," circumstances that suggest it was not completely certain who would succeed Christoph Donat I, who had died on 17 August 1706. Scheibe made repairs in 1711, 1712, and 1715. In 1718 Ficker was paid 34 florin 6 groschen for "cleaning, tuning, and repairing the organ as well as the bellows."[162] (He had made repairs two years earlier on the organ at St. Wenceslas's in Naumburg,[163] an instrument that also had been rebuilt by Thayssner.) In 1719 Scheibe was paid for repairing the bellows, wind chests, and "other necessary items" in the organ, in 1721 he was paid for repairs and tuning, and he was responsible for the organ's major renovation in 1724–25. No one was paid for maintenance during the years Scheibe was away from Leipzig; payments to Scheibe resumed in 1730 and continued through 1736. Beginning in 1737, Hildebrandt took care of the organ, which he continued to do through Easter 1743, when he moved to Naumburg to renovate the large organ in St. Wenceslas's. That year, Scheibe again tuned the organ at Christmas. For a number of years (from 1744 to 1747), no payments were made for organ maintenance, but Scheibe tuned the organ again at Easter 1748, his assistant tuned the organ at Easter in 1749, and in 1750 Hildebrandt and his son undertook a major renovation.

The organ at the New Church was built by Christoph Donat I and his son Christoph Donat II in 1703–4, and as long as any family member was working in Leipzig, the organ was maintained by a Donat: Christoph Donat II took care of the organ from around 1706 until his death in 1713 and also carried out the organ's overhaul in that year, and Johann Christoph Gottlob Donat (Christoph Donat II's son) maintained the organ from 1713 to 1718. Except for the period when he was absent from Leipzig in 1726 to 1729, Scheibe took care of the New Church organ for 30 years, from 1718 to 1748, and also undertook a major renovation of the organ in 1721–22 and a complete overhaul, including retuning, in 1731–32. Entries for organ "tuning, servicing, and dusting" at the rate of 4 taler annually occur year after year in the New Church's payment records, but there are also entries for individual repairs. Apitzsch was paid 6 taler for repairing the bellows in 1727–28; Scheibe was paid 17 taler for building a new bellows (and repairing the other one) in 1735–36; and Scheibe was paid 15 taler for another bellows repair in 1739–40. In the same year, Hildebrandt provided a new spring for the Pedal wind chest. Scheibe was paid 5½ taler in 1741–42 for renovating two Pedal reeds (Trompeten Bass 8′ and Schalmey 4′) and for resoldering mouths in some 36 different pipes, and in 1743–44 he was paid 2½ taler for adjusting the trackers and the action. For four years after Scheibe's death in 1748, no maintenance payments were made. Schweinefleisch took over the organ's maintenance in 1752.

At St. John's, the organ built by Tobias Gottfried Trost in 1694–95 was repaired by Christoph Donat II in 1703 and 1704. There apparently was no agreement for regular annual maintenance, though, and repairs happened irregularly. After 1712, Scheibe usually made the necessary repairs, but when Scheibe was away from Leipzig in 1726 to 1729, Apitzsch made repairs, and Hildebrandt also made repairs on two occasions in the 1730s. The new Scheibe organ was paid for in 1741 and 1742, and thereafter Scheibe received regular annual payments for maintenance. Jentz made repairs in 1749 and 1750, after which the organ was taken care of by Johann Georg Hille, the church's organist.

As Werckmeister observed more than 300 years ago, "In a well ordered household one can often find a medicine cabinet. When this or that [member of the family] is indisposed, one uses a home remedy. In the same manner, an organist may become the physician attending to minor problems of the organ entrusted to his care. For more serious defects, however, an organ builder ought to be called. If he is dependable, particularly when under a maintenance contract, a church actually increases its capital, as the interest accruing [from such arrangements] is worth several times over the fee paid to the contracted organ builder."[164]

Leipzig's Scheibe Organs

As the above descriptions of renovations and repairs make obvious, the organ culture of Leipzig was anything but static. Leipzig's organs were not only regularly maintained—the constant complaints about the organs being unusable and completely filled with dust are exaggerations and understood as such both by those who wrote them and by those who acted on them—but also regularly altered and changed (see table 12). Renovations could be extensive. Frequently, they transformed an organ's character; at other times the reshaping was modest. They included altering the composition of mixtures, adding independent mutations, and altering compound mutation stops. They resulted in more robust wind supplies, in more gravity and depth of sound, in temperaments that allowed playing in a wider range of keys, in greater flexibility and nuance in registration of both solo and plenum combinations, in more solo possibilities—to name only some of the changes documented above.

Old pipework was often retained. The organs in the two principal churches had been built around 1600 by Lange, one of Germany's finest organ builders, and some of his pipework was retained throughout numerous renovations. In his proposal to rebuild the St. Thomas organ in 1773, Johann Gottlieb Mauer recommended replacing all the Hauptwerk pipework—except for six old (Lange) stops, which were "as good as new and really fine."[165] Even though revoiced many times, Lange's principal chorus was retained until a new organ was built in 1889. Also, Lange's Regal stops were kept long after they had gone out of fashion and were removed neither in 1720–21, during Scheibe's renovation, nor in 1757, during Schweinefleisch's renovation. Remarkably, the organs at St. Thomas's and St. Nicholas's retained their separate Rückpositiv divisions, even though in most 18th-century organ renovations Rückpositiv divisions were moved into the main organ case in order to facilitate performance of instrumental and vocal music

TABLE 12   Organ-building activity in Leipzig, ca. 1705 to ca. 1750

Leipzig church or school	Condition in 1717 (see chapter 1)	Type of work done
St. Paul's	built 1710–16 (S)	maintenance 1716–48 (S) maintenance 1748–50 (Je? Sch?) major overhaul 1736 (S) renovation 1751 (Sch)
St. Thomas's, large organ	renovated 1657 and 1670 (D) overhauled 1702 (D) and 1713 (S)	maintenance 1713–48 (S) renovation 1720–21 (S) overhaul 1730 (S) overhaul 1747 (S)
St. Thomas's, small organ	renovated 1665 (D)	maintenance 1713–40 (S) overhaul 1720–21 (S) partial overhaul 1727 (H) removed 1740 (S)
New Church	new organ 1704 (D)	maintenance 1704–18 (D) maintenance 1718–48 (S) renovation 1721–22 (S) overhaul 1731 (S) overhaul 1747 (S)
St. Nicholas's	renovated 1691–94 (Th)	maintenance 1706–16, 1719–25, 1730–36 (S) maintenance 1737–Easter 1743 (H) maintenance at Christmas 1743 (S), Easter 1748 (S), and Easter 1749 (Je) overhaul 1718–19 (Fi) renovation 1724–25 (S) overhaul 1732–33 (S) renovation 1750–51 (H)
St. John's	new organ 1695 (Tr) overhaul 1703 (D)	maintenance 1712–48 (S) maintenance 1748–50 (Je? Sch?) new organ 1741–43 (S)
Royal Catholic Chapel		new 6-stop organ with pulldown pedal 1720 (He) overhaul 1723 (S?)
Georgenhaus		8-stop positive installed 1744 (S) renovation (addition of Pedal) 1746 (Hi)
St. Thomas School	4-stop positive built 1685 (D)	3-stop *Trauungspositiv* built 1720 (Fi)

Note: Organ builders are identified with the following abbreviations: D = Christoph Donat (and family); Fi = Wahl Friedrich Ficker; H = Zacharias Hildebrandt; He = Johann Christoph Hennig; Hi = Johann Georg Hille; Je = Johann Hinrich Jentz; S = Johann Scheibe; Sch = J. C. Immanuel Schweinefleisch; Th = Zacharias Thayssner; Tr = Tobias Gottfried Trost.

together with organs located in west galleries. At St. Paul's, for example, the
Rückpositiv was relocated to the main organ, where it became the Hinterwerk.
At the same time, new organs built in the 18th century usually were built without
a Rückpositiv division. In Leipzig, the New Church organ built in 1703–4 and
rebuilt in 1721–22 never had a Rückpositiv; neither did the new organ built for
St. John's around 1743. At St. Thomas's, the Rückpositiv remained until Mauer's
rebuild in 1773; at St. Nicholas's, it remained until the Trampeli brothers rebuilt
the organ in 1787. This is not to say that these organs remained "Renaissance
instruments," artifacts to be studied and learned from, as Winfried Schrammek
argued regarding the St. Thomas organ.[166] Rather, the organs retained valuable
older parts—beautiful cases, wind chests constructed with seasoned ancient
wood, pipework made by past masters—even as the dispositions were modestly
updated.

Even a casual observer will have noticed two parallel considerations: on the
one hand, a deep respect for the old and valuable; on the other, a desire for the
new and innovative. At St. Paul's this initially created conflict. Vetter argued successfully in favor of retaining the organ's old Principal 16′ and for renovating the
existing organ; Kuhnau had hoped to replace it with a new organ by Silbermann,
who proposed building stops not well known in Germany although greatly
admired in France. At St. John's, the organ built in the 1740s was an innovative,
forward-looking instrument. In general, at the New Church and Leipzig University newly renovated, modernized organs supported modern church-music
programs.[167] At the principal churches of St. Thomas and St. Nicholas, however,
traditional organs supported traditional music programs. These organs, too,
were renovated and to a degree brought up to date, but, as was argued above,
they nevertheless retained much that was old and revered.

Spitta was well aware that Leipzig's organs had undergone renovations. He
noted that the large organ at St. Thomas had been renovated in 1721 and that
"principal improvements" were made in 1730 and 1747, and that the St. Nicholas
organ had been renovated twice after the rebuild in the early 1690s. Nevertheless,
for the organs in Leipzig's principal churches, he published the organ specifications as they had appeared around 1700, years before the renovations.[168] For
the disposition of the organ at the New Church, scholars have relied either on
the disposition recorded in the contract with the Donats or on the (unreliable)
disposition included in Mattheson's collection, neither one of which reflects
the organ after its major rebuild. Prior to this study, neither Scheibe's complete
rebuild of the Donat organ nor his renovations of the organs at St. Thomas's
and St. Nicholas's had been taken into consideration when dispositions were

cited. Thus, even though scholars and organists have been aware that Leipzig's organs underwent renovations, one nevertheless gains the false impression that the organs remained unchanged throughout half a century, that they were the same when Bach died in 1750 as they had been at the turn of the 18th century.

To put it more specifically, and to state briefly what is discussed above in great detail, Scheibe's renovations expanded wind supplies; replaced wind chests; improved playing actions; replaced iron parts with brass; repaired or replaced corroded pipes; made the Pedal division independent from the Hauptwerk; replaced shallots, tongues, and resonators of reed stops; made mutations, including the Tierce, available as independent ranks; revised mixture compositions; widened pipe scales; revoiced pipework, including, famously, the Viol di Gamba; set or reset the temperament; and provided new stops such as the Sordino, a solo reed. Not one Leipzig organ remained unaffected by such changes, and it is no exaggeration to speak of Leipzig's organs during Bach's tenure as "Scheibe organs."

9 An Innovative Organ for St. John's

[The facades of the organs by Scheibe] are composed of concave,
outwardly curved pipe fields to the left and right of a large central
field: a bold, unconventional design full of graceful movement.
—Winfried Schrammek, 1988

Scheibe's organ for St. John's is well known—not so much because of
its brilliant disposition for a medium-sized organ or its innovative forte/piano
device, or because the key desk and organ bench (but nothing else) have survived and are now on display at the Bach Museum Leipzig, but because it was
rigorously and thoroughly examined by Johann Sebastian Bach. Philipp Spitta
provided no information about this organ but remarked about the examination,
"Although Scheibe's son, the author of the 'Critischer Musicus,' had incurred
Bach's displeasure, the Cantor was thought impartial enough to try the organ,
and he pronounced it faultless; though Agricola frankly says that he put it to
the severest test that any organ had perhaps ever undergone."[1] Johann Friedrich
Agricola's comment is invoked almost every time mention is made of the St.
John's organ. Meanwhile, the instrument itself and the history surrounding its
creation have all but been forgotten.

One reason the St. John's organ has elicited so little interest is that Bach,
directly, had little to do with St. John's. No concerted music took place there.
The fourth, least expert chorus of the St. Thomas School, which was limited to
singing chorales in unison, appeared under the direction of the prefect only on
the three high feasts of the church year, at Easter, Pentecost, and Christmas.[2] The
simple services were attended by St. John's Hospital patients, some burghers,

laborers, and other poor people who lived in the area outside the city walls.[3] St. John's, mentioned first in 1305, stood at the Grimma Gate, in the middle of what was known as "God's Acre" (the city's churchyard or graveyard), not far from St. John's Hospital, founded in 1280. The church was rebuilt in the late 16th century, and in 1607 artist Valentin Silbermann provided a new pulpit (now on display in the City History Museum Leipzig). The church's walls were hung with epitaphs and portraits of pastors, and the ceiling was flat and covered with painted panels, the crest of the city of Leipzig in the middle. Until 1746, there was only a small tower that held two bells; the magnificent baroque tower seen in most paintings of St. John's was built in 1746–49, not long after Scheibe built the new organ.[4]

For 45 years, and throughout most of Bach's tenure in Leipzig, the organ at St. John's was the 10-stop instrument built in 1694–95 by Tobias Gottfried Trost. In 1741 Scheibe agreed to build a new, much larger organ and, in partial payment, was given both the Trost organ and the small old organ from St. Thomas's, the organ that stood on its own balcony on a high wall that separated the nave from the crossing. Built as a swallows-nest organ in 1489, the St. Thomas organ had undergone four renovations and been repaired and moved numerous times. No

33. St. John's with churchyard and God's Acre at the Grimma Gate, Leipzig, ca. 1700. A 57-meter/187-foot tower was added in 1746–49. Sammlung Bach-Archiv, Leipzig, Graph Slg. 17/27.

longer necessary to the church music of the time, the organ was dismantled and removed in 1740 but took on new life in Scheibe's organ for St. John's.

The Trost Organ at St. John's

For the first 17 years of Bach's tenure in Leipzig, the organ at St. John's was the small instrument built by Trost (see table 13).[5] Trost had learned organ building with Christian Förner, inventor of the wind gauge and one of Germany's most important 17th-century organ builders.[6] Trost lived and worked in the area of Grimma, near Leipzig, from 1690 to 1696 and was the father of Heinrich Gottfried, now known especially for the organs he built for the court church in Altenburg (1739) and in the town church in Waltershausen (1717).

The Trost organ was not the first instrument at St. John's. Positive organs had been purchased in 1533 and 1577, the latter from St. Nicholas's,[7] and in 1656 St. John's again acquired a positive from St. Nicholas's, paying 100 guilders for an 8-stop positive that Hermann Raphael Rodensteen had built in 1579 for 150 guilders. Christoph Donat I was hired for 60 taler to move, repair, and tune it to Chorton, and Caspar Albrecht was paid 37 taler to paint the organ and the

TABLE 13   Disposition of the Trost organ (I/P/10) at St. John's, built 1694–95

Manual (8)
Gedackt 8'
Quintatön 8'
Principal 4', polished tin, facade
Gedackt 4'
Quint 3'
Octav 2'
Sesquialtera [1–3/5']
Mixtur III 1'

Pedal (2)
Subbass 16', wood
Principal Bass 8', wood

Tremulant
2 single-fold bellows
Manual compass: CD–c³
Pedal compass: CD–c¹

Source: St. John Accounts, 1694, fol. 187.

gallery. Some 40 years later, the small Rodensteen positive, now 116 years old, was sold to Laußick for 60 taler,[8] and on 18 August 1694, Trost agreed to build a new organ for St. John's. Both Trost's drawing and the contract for 175 taler survive.[9]

Trost's drawing shows a well-proportioned facade with three projecting towers, the highest in the center. The facade's Principal 4′ pipes were made of polished tin, the two Pedal stops were made of wood, and the rest of the organ's pipes were made of *Metall*. The organ had two single-fold wedge bellows, a tremulant, and the usual compass of CD–c^3 and CD–c^1.[10]

From 1712 the Trost organ was cared for by Scheibe, although repairs also were made by David Apitzsch (when Scheibe was away from Leipzig in the late 1720s)

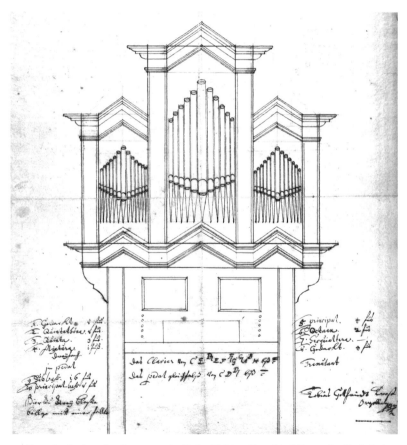

34. Facade design for the organ built by Tobias Gottfried Trost for St. John's, 1694. Stadtarchiv Leipzig, RRA (F) nr. 657.

and Zacharias Hildebrandt (in 1735 and 1739). By 1740 the organ had become unreliable, and probably too small for the congregation's needs, and Scheibe was paid 4 taler that year to keep the instrument "in playable condition." In May the Leipzig city council resolved to remove St. Thomas's small organ and make it available for purchase, and in December it agreed to pay St. Thomas's 200 taler, the organ's value according to Scheibe's assessment (see below), and to let St. John's purchase the organ for half its assessed value, or 100 taler—the exact amount that St. John's had paid for the Rodensteen positive it had acquired from St. Nicholas's a century earlier.[11]

The Small Old Organ at St. Thomas's

The organ removed from St. Thomas's in 1740 had been installed by an anonymous builder in 1489, some 250 years earlier. Referred to at first as the large organ, it underwent its first major rebuild in 1511, when Blasius Lehmann, of Bautzen, carried out a renovation for a fee of 500 florins.[12] In 1525, when St. Thomas's acquired the organ from the monastery in Eicha, the two organs were placed side by side in the west gallery and the organ from Eicha now became "the large organ," the organ rebuilt by Lehmann "the small organ." The small organ was renovated again in 1630, by Heinrich Compenius II, of Halle,[13] but a few years later the organ was moved again. During a renovation of the church interior in 1638–39, a balcony large enough for 13 *Stände* (seats or pews) was built at the axis of the middle aisle, above the choir arch, and the smaller organ was moved to this location and renovated by Andreas Werner and Erhardt Müller, who were paid 184 guilders. (The bellows pumper/handyman was paid for 43 days of work.)[14] Artist Hans Richter oversaw the entire renovation and also painted and gilded the organ and balcony, including the four panels, as well as the large angel that was placed below it.[15] A painting, the so-called large perspective, was applied high on the nave's east wall, and nave columns were painted reddish-gray, with spiraling black bands. On the organ's doors, or shutters, appeared the text "Sanctus Sanctus Sanctus/Dominus Deus Zebaoth" and the dates 1489, the year the organ was built, and 1639, the year of the renovation.[16] The organ was played in its new location for the first time on the 150th anniversary of its creation, at Easter 1639.

By the 1660s a sagging choir balcony had caused the small organ to become faulty and unreliable,[17] and on 20 August 1665 Donat agreed to renovate it. He was paid 280 taler for providing six new bellows and six new registers, work that he carried out in the eight months between 26 January and 5 October. The bellows pumper was paid for 28 days of labor (over a period of three and a half months).[18] Other costs included payments to the metal worker for long rods to go through the vaulting to support the organ; to the carpenters for stairs, a floor, and a new bench and roof for the bellows; and to painter Christoph Spetner for painting repairs and for "regilding the ornamented crown surrounding the small pipework."[19] Also, a four-glass sand clock (hourglass) was installed. (Each glass would have measured, respectively, 15, 30, 45, and 60 minutes.) Costs for the renovation, which included a 2-taler gratuity paid to Donat's assistants, totaled 438 florins 11 groschen 10 pfennig.[20] In 1678 Donat made repairs to both organs at St. Thomas's as well as to the regal at St. Thomas School, for which he received 9 florins 3 groschen.[21] Scheibe was paid the same fee in 1720–21 "for repairing the small organ, which had been completely unusable."[22] The last major repair took place in 1727–28. Hildebrandt—Scheibe was away from Leipzig at the time—was paid 15 taler "for bringing 8 registers in the small organ into playable condition, and for travel costs."[23] The small organ's fate was sealed on 21 May 1740, when the city council took the following resolution: "Privy war councilor [Gottfried] Lange, as director of St. Thomas's, proposed that since the old organ in said church already had threatened collapse 15 years ago and is, besides, being considered for purchase by both St. John's and [the church in] Stötteritz, a resolution be taken as to whether [the organ] should be evaluated and sold, the vacant space used for constructing Capellen, etc. etc. Resolved: That the organ be taken out [and sold]."[24] At the city council's request, Scheibe assessed the value of the old organ and removed it.[25]

The organ was valued at 200 taler: the pipework, 406 pounds of tin and 631 pounds of lead, was assessed at 125 taler; the remaining parts—stops not made of metal, the case, ironwork, bellows, wood, and the like—were worth 75 taler.[26] St. John's was able to acquire the small St. Thomas organ for 100 taler, half its assessed value. The church in Stötteritz, which also had been interested in the organ, did not get a new organ until 1754 (see chapter 10).

Scheibe's evaluation includes important details about St. Thomas's small organ. He identified 8 stops worth retaining or reusing and 10 stops that could be melted down and their metal recast for new pipes. Three stops (Dulcian 8' in the Rückpositiv and Subbass 16' and Fagott 16' in the Pedal) were excluded from his list for the simple reason that they were not built from tin or lead, the valuable materials he was assessing. The Subbass was made of wood, while the resonators of the Dulcian 8' and Fagott 16' were made of sheet metal, and it was not common practice to record the weight of sheet metal. (For example, Jacob Adlung reported the weight of a Vox humana II, a stop that had 96 pipes in all,

TABLE 14   Disposition of the small organ (II?/21/P) at St. Thomas's, 1740

Hauptwerk (7)	Rückpositiv (8)	Brustwerk (3)	Pedal (3)
Principal 8', in the facade	*Grob Gedackt 8'*	Rancket 8'	Subbass 16'
Grob Gedackt 8'	*Principal 4'*	Spitzflöte 2'	Fagott 16'
Quintatön 8'	*Hohlflöte 4'*	Octav 1'	Trompete 8'
Octav 4'	*Nasat 3'*		
Quint 3'	*Octav 2'*		
Mixtur III	Sesquialtera 1–3/5'		
Cymbel II	Dulcian 8'		
	Trompete 8'		

Tremulant

Cymbelstern

Bellows pumper signal

Manual coupler

Hauptwerk compass: CDEFGA–c³

Pedal compass: CDEFGA–c¹

Sources: Vogel Chronicle, 111; Stadtarchiv Leipzig, Stift IX A 2, fol. 105r–v.

Note: *Italics* indicate stops that Scheibe considered reusable.

48 of *Metall* and 48 of *Blech* [sheet metal] as "140 lbs. of *Metall*, not counting the *Blech*.")[27]

Scheibe's evaluation reveals that the Hauptwerk and Pedal divisions had short-octave compasses. The Hauptwerk was missing the low D♯, F♯, and G♯ and probably had a compass of CDEFGA–c³. The Pedal compass was 21 notes—that is, it also had the short-octave compass, CDEFGA–c¹. Scheibe says nothing about the compass of either the Brustwerk or the Rückpositiv and gives no indication whether the small organ had two or three keyboards—that is, whether the stops in the Brustwerk were played from their own keyboard or shared a keyboard with the Hauptwerk, which is far more likely.

Scheibe's list of stops is not identical with the disposition published some 35 or 40 years earlier in the Vogel Chronicle, but whether the differences indicate disposition changes made between circa 1700 and 1740 or are simply scribal errors is difficult to ascertain (see appendix D-5 for a comparison of the two dispositions). Octav 1' (Scheibe) and Sifflöte 1' (Vogel) are both narrow-scaled, 1-foot Principals—essentially the same stop by a different name. Vogel lists

Gedackt and Lieblich Gedackt, gedackts with wider and narrower scaling, respectively, whereas Scheibe identified both gedackts as Grob Gedackt. Other differences between the dispositions, though, seem to indicate that changes had been made. The weight of the Sesquialtera stop—24 pounds—corresponds almost exactly to the 25-pound weight given by Adlung for a single-rank Sesquialtera 1–3/5′[28]—which suggests that the stop had been altered to one rank, a third. The Rauschpfeife, too, apparently had been changed from two ranks to a single rank, a fifth (Quint 2–2/3′). Likewise, it appears that the old composition of the Mixtur (IV–X ranks) had been altered to Mixtur III. More difficult to make sense of is the listing of Rancket rather than Trichterregal, as these are very differently constructed short-resonator reeds.[29] Had the Trichterregal been replaced? Was Scheibe not able to differentiate among short-resonator reeds?

Identifying when such disposition changes could have been made, and by whom, is problematic. It is possible that Scheibe made disposition changes in 1720, at the same time that he was renovating the large organ, but the modest fee he was paid does not indicate a renovation. Hildebrandt could have made disposition changes when he brought eight stops into usable or playable condition in 1727, but again, the 15-taler fee is modest. Nothing in the records indicates which stops Hildebrandt worked on, but while it is tempting to imagine they were the same eight stops Scheibe later considered reusable—all of them lower-pitched stops that do not go out of style quickly—the disposition differences appear in the higher-pitched stops such as mutations and mixtures, stops that tended to be altered or replaced fairly often (see table 14).

By 1740, then, a second fixed organ at St. Thomas's was no longer deemed necessary. The decision to have the organ dismantled—surely with Bach's permission—is not surprising. At St. Paul's, the second organ had been sacrificed during a rebuild of the large organ in 1685–87; likewise, as Arnold Schering reported, the smaller organ at St. Nicholas's, which stood "next to the large organ on high," was broken apart in 1693 and the tin from its pipework was used by Zacharias Thayssner during his renovation of the large organ.[30] Johann Jacob Vogel's claim that the small organ at St. Thomas's was played on major feast days[31] surely reflected a past or dying practice. Large sums were expended in 1638–39, when the new gallery was built and the small organ moved into it, and in 1665, when the organ was thoroughly renovated and enlarged, its gilding refreshed or newly applied,[32] and an hourglass purchased and installed in the eastern gallery. Almost sold to the New Church in 1702,[33] at risk of collapsing along with the gallery in 1665 and again in 1725, and apparently no longer essential to the liturgical life of the church, and with wealthy citizens willing to pay for the privilege of constructing private chapels in the space made free by its removal, the small old organ at St. Thomas's was finally given up.

Scheibe's Organ for St. John's

Scheibe signed the contract on 10 March 1741, agreeing to build an organ at St. John's for 625 taler, his fee to be paid partially in cash and partially by his taking possession of the Trost organ being replaced, worth 75 taler, as well as the pipes, bellows, and wood from the organ he had removed from St. Thomas's, worth 100 taler. A cash payment of 350 taler was made on signing the contract[34]—no copy of the contract survives[35]—and 100 taler were paid in 1742.[36] In addition, in 1745 Johann Gottlieb Görner was paid an honorarium of 2 taler 18 groschen "for his many endeavors" during the organ project.[37] The dismantling of the Trost organ began on 1 June 1742.[38] One wind chest, at least, was finished by late summer, and, in what turns out to be the only surviving record of his date of birth, Scheibe provided an inscription: "Completed 22 August 1742 by Johann Scheibe, currently organ builder to the Honorable University of Leipzig, 62 years [of age] in May."[39]

Surprisingly, the organ's stops were tested sometime before the end of August as well, for which the bellows pumper from St. Paul's was paid 8 groschen.[40] In organologist Hubert Henkel's view, this highly unusual demonstration of the stops prior to an official examination was simply the city council and the church being overly cautious in their dealings with Scheibe, in spite of his good reputation.[41] More likely, in my view, is that an unofficial examination of the stops in advance of final voicing and tuning would have made it possible for Scheibe to request final payment, and in fact Scheibe was paid "the rest of what was promised him [in cash], according to the contract, *upon completely finishing the new organ* [emphasis added]" before the end of August 1742.[42] The organ clearly was taken into use: the organist, Johann Gottlob Reinicke, and the bellows pumper, whose name is unknown, were paid 6 taler and 1 taler, respectively, their salaries for the last two quarters of 1742.[43]

Final voicing and tuning, as well as facade decoration, took place over the next eight or nine months. The bellows pumper was paid 7 taler 10 groschen for working 89 days in the period December 1742 to September 1743, and Johann Salomon Riemer reported that the organ was played in public "for the first time, even though not yet entirely finished," on Pentecost, 2 June 1743.[44] Sculptor Caspar Friedrich Löbelt received 7 taler 18 groschen for making "2 large vases,

1 shield with palm leaves, and 4 [carvings in the form of] sword-belts over and on the organ,"[45] and the painter was paid 58 taler for "gilding the carvings on the new organ with fine, good gold" and "painting with oil the four lower columns, the choir gallery, organ and ceiling, as well as the panels and acanthus leaves."[46] Expenses that year also included 26 taler for a hundredweight of Marienberg tin (tin from the Erzgebirge or Ore Mountains) for organ pipes. (This may have been a late payment for material provided in 1742, or perhaps the tin was used for building pipework provided over and above the contract. Scheibe later claimed that he had built additional stops at the request of a church director.)

The organ's disposition is recorded in only one contemporary source, *Sammlung einiger Nachrichten* (or *SeN*), the compilation published by Carl Gottfried Meyer in 1757.[47] The organ had two manuals and 22 stops, 10 in the Hauptwerk, 8 in the Oberwerk, and 4 in the Pedal, as well as a coupler between the pedal and the manual, Tremulant, Hauptwerk and Oberwerk ventils, and a bell for the bellows pumper. The facade was decorated in rococo style, and there were three wedge bellows.[48] We know from measurements taken in 1897 that the case was 3 meters high, 3.5 meters wide, and 2.5 meters deep.[49] In its rather squat form,

35. Interior of St. John's, with the organ built in 1741–43 by Johann Scheibe in the middle of the west-side balcony. Photograph by Hermann Walter, prior to 1894. City History Museum Leipzig, F/2018/255.

36. Disposition of the Scheibe organ at St. John's, from
*Sammlung einiger Nachrichten von berühmten Orgel-Wercken in
Teutschland mit vieler Mühe aufgesetzt von einem Liebhaber der
Musik* (Breslau: Carl Gottfried Meyer, 1757). Public domain.

it resembles Scheibe's organ in Zschortau. At least one pipe was decorative.[50]
Scheibe's organ was 12 stops larger than the previous Trost organ, making it
comparable in size to the organ in the New Church.

The well-thought-out disposition is worthy of consideration (see table 15). In
the Hauptwerk, the principal ranks include 8′, 4′, 3′, 2′, and 1′ plus Mixtur IV.
Plenum registrations can also include Quintatön 16′. The presence of Quintatön
16′ rather than the Bordun 16′ frequently found in organs of the Silbermann
school, for example, should be noted. The Cornetto II, which probably was a
Sesquialtera and composed of 2–2/3′ and 1–3/5′ ranks, could be used either as
a solo stop or in the plenum (where it provides a third rank). The flute chorus
begins with the Quintatön 16′ and extends to the 4′ level.

TABLE 15   Disposition of the Scheibe organ (II/P/22) at St. John's, built 1741–43

Hauptwerk (10)	Oberwerk (8)	Pedal (4)
Quintatön 16′	Quintatön 8′	Posaunen Bass 16′
Principal 8′	Lieblich Gedackt 8′	Subbass 16′
Gedackt 8′	Spielpfeife 4′	Trompeten Bass 8′
Spielpfeife 4′	Principal 4′	Violon 8′
Octav 4′	Hohlflöte 3′	
Octav 2′	Weitpfeife 1′	Coupler (*Separatio*) between
Quint 3′	Octav 2′	Pedal and Manual
Octav 1′	Tertian II	Tremulant
Cornetto [Sesquialtera] II		Hauptwerk ventil
Mixtur IV		Oberwerk venil
		3 bellows

Sources: SeN, 56; *Oehme 1978, 115.*

Note: "Of special interest in this instrument is . . . that by engaging a stop it is possible to play piano and forte on one manual extraordinarily well." *SeN*, 56.

The Oberwerk has a small principal chorus (Quintatön 8′, Gedackt 8′, Principal 4′, Octav 2′) with no mixture. Gedackt 8′ and Quintatön 8′ together serve as the basis for plenum registrations, which can vary in color and strength. Flute stops are available at 8′, 4′, and 3′, which, when used together, provide a wide-scaled Nasat solo combination, and, of course, the Lieblich Gedackt 8′ is ideal as the basis for continuo registrations. The Tertian II, composed of principal-scaled ranks at 1-3/5′ and 1-1/3′, may have broken once. Registered in a solo combination, it would have been excellent for melodies that ranged throughout the compass. The Weitpfeife 1′, open, wide-scaled, very bright, could be combined with the Quintatön 8′ to create another solo combination. (Similarly, Christian Ludwig Boxberg recommended combining Quintatön 16′ with Weitpfeife 2′.)

One notes the absence of 8-foot solo stops such as transverse flute and Viol di Gamba; there are neither reeds nor string stops in the manual divisions. Full-organ registrations in either manual can be constructed with or without a third rank and with various combinations of higher-pitched ranks. In general, the disposition provides marvelous contrast between the two manual divisions, which are basically an octave apart, and great flexibility in registrational possibilities.

The Pedal, with stops at 16′ and 8′, provides a solid bass. In plenum registrations, the Pedal would have had to be coupled to a manual division; the coupler was probably to the Hauptwerk. The Violon 8′ together with the Subbass 16′ is an ideal combination for continuo or trio playing; Posaunen Bass 16′ and Trompeten Bass 8′—the most common Pedal reed stops and the only reeds in the entire organ—provide both gravity and clarity to the bass line. The Posaunen Bass 16′ also was used in continuo playing, as can be seen, for example, from Friedrich Erhardt Niedt's instructions to an organist realizing a figured bass: "If an entire choir consisting of 8 or 12 voices or more begins to sing . . . then in the Pedal an Octav 8′ can be added along with the Subbass 16′. If the composition calls for trumpets and timpani, then, in addition to the Octav 8′ in the Pedal, a Posaunen Bass 16′ is pulled. The notes played by this latter combination of stops should not be held out [sustained] for a half or entire measure, but rather allowed only to reach their full sound and then be released."[51] (Posaunen Bass was a stop also used in continuo playing on Silbermann's organ at Freiberg Cathedral; see chapter 6.)

As noted above, Scheibe was given for his use the old Trost organ as well as the pipes, bellows, and all of the wood, iron, and other parts from St. Thomas's small organ. He offered to sell Trost's organ to the church in Stötteritz several years later, which suggests that he preserved some—or all—of it. There is no doubt that he used stops, or materials, from the St. Thomas organ for the new organ at St. John's, but he also may have used material from the St. Thomas organ in another organ he built in the 1740s. The restorers of Scheibe's organ in Zschortau (built 1744–46) observed that a number of pipes in the Mixtur III definitely date to a time before 1870 and possibly even to a date before Scheibe's organ was built, which raises the possibility that in Zschortau Scheibe may have used some mixture pipes from St. Thomas's small organ.[52]

As he had at St. Paul's, Scheibe gave Italian names to two stops at St. John's—a practice that is often attributed to the influence of Casparini and the organ at Görlitz. "Cornetto" indicates a Sesquialtera; "Separatio" referred to the coupler between manual and pedal.

A device in the St. John organ is particularly intriguing: "By engaging a stop," the description provided along with the disposition tells us, "it is possible to play piano and forte on one manual extraordinarily well."[53] The feature may have been similar to something invented by Christoph Gottlieb Schröter, the organist and composer in Nordhausen who is credited as being one of the inventors of a hammer action for stringed keyboard instruments. According to Schröter, the challenge was "to make an organ at which one can play, at will and at various levels, first loud, then soft, and indeed, only on one keyboard, without pulling on or removing stops."[54] Schröter declined to reveal how this could be accomplished—like the egg of Columbus, it was apparently a simple solution to what would seem to be an impossible task—even though he had been offered 500 taler for the secret "by someone in a high place." Schröter wrote to Lorenz Mizler about the idea in 1735, presented the idea to Mizler's Society of the Musical Sciences in 1738, and provided a drawing to accompany the description of the invention that appeared in part three of the third volume of Mizler's *Musikalische Bibliothek*, published in 1747.[55] The discovery was also briefly mentioned by Adlung, in his *Anleitung zur musikalischen Gelahrtheit*, published 1758, where he writes of "a very nice invention" of Schröter of Nordhausen, by which "in certain registers on an organ it is possible to play forte and piano."[56] It may be relevant that Mizler was living and lecturing in Leipzig in the late 1730s and early 1740s. Mizler—or Schröter himself—could have passed on information about the invention before publication of the description in 1747. It is not known that Schröter ever actually built such an organ.[57]

The above is only speculation, of course. We have no specific information regarding the device in the St. John's organ, or whether the mechanism effected a sudden or gradual change between piano and forte. Whatever it was, though, it attests to Scheibe's ingenuity and inventiveness. Importantly, Scheibe's invention must be seen in the context of other keyboard inventions of the period—inventions such as Pantaleon Hebenstreit's pantaleon and Bartolomeo Cristofori's *Gravecembalo col piano e forte*, both from shortly before 1700; Schröter's hammer-action model, demonstrated before Friedrich August I, elector of Saxony and king of Poland in February 1721; Johann Nicolaus Bach's lute harpsichord, a gut-stringed, undamped instrument that had three keyboards to provide three dynamic levels, forte, piano, and *più piano*, apparently seen by Adlung during his student years in Jena, 1723–27, and perhaps the same design as one specified by Bach during his tenure in Köthen; Gottfried Silbermann's cembal d'amour, completed by 1720; Wahl Friedrich Ficker's cymbal-clavir, described in a Leipzig newspaper of 1731; and, of course, Silbermann's own fortepiano, invented by 1732 and publicly demonstrated in 1736.[58]

As John Koster has pointed out, "expressive" keyboards of the time can be differentiated by whether they create forte and piano all at once or gradually. For example, Adlung's account of Ficker's hammer-pantaleon describes its most beautiful attribute as "the alteration of forte and piano by a pedal [that operates] a mechanism that moves a piece of leather or cloth under the hammers, so that is not necessary to break off playing [in order to make a change]."[59] Cristofori and Silbermann fortepianos, on the other hand, allowed the player to create dynamic nuance within a registration. Whatever Scheibe's mechanism was, however, will remain a mystery.

No written report of the organ's official examination has ever been found, nor is there any record of expenditures for the customary celebratory meal. The identity of the organ's examiners is provided by Agricola, who reported that the organ "was declared faultless by Kapellmeister Johann Sebastian Bach and Herr Zacharias Hildebrandt in the most severe inspection that perhaps has ever been undertaken of an organ."[60] According to Henkel, the examination most likely took place in September or October 1743, immediately after the last voicing and tuning,[61] because Hildebrandt would have left Leipzig for Naumburg by mid-November 1743.[62] In any event, the *terminus ante quem* for the examination date is 13 December 1743, when city council minutes include the comment that "according to the report of the examiners, the organ was well built."[63]

In the obituary published four years after Bach's death, Bach's son C. P. E. Bach and Bach's former student Agricola claimed that Bach's complete approval of Scheibe's organ at St. John's "did no slight honor both to the organ builder and, because of certain circumstances, to Bach himself."[64] They did not explain what was meant by "certain circumstances," but most scholars assume the authors were referring to Bach's quarrel with Scheibe's son, Johann Adolph, a quarrel sparked by his criticism, published in 1737, of Bach's compositional style, which in turn, some say, was sparked by Johann Adolph's extreme disappointment at not being appointed organist at St. Nicholas's in 1729.[65] Bach was honorable because he judged impartially in spite of the rancorous dispute.

However, there is no evidence that Johann Adolph held a grudge against Bach.[66] Indeed, Scheibe's attack was characterized by musicologist George Buelow as "mild words of aesthetic disagreement."[67] After all, he noted, Scheibe's son blamed his lack of success at the St. Nicholas audition not on Bach but on Görner. And not two years later, in 1731, when Johann Adolph applied for another organist position (at Freiberg Cathedral), he submitted a strong recommendation from Bach.[68] As Buelow, in his spirited defense, put it, "It is inconceivable that Scheibe would have asked Bach for such a letter of recommendation at this time if (i) he thought he had been unfairly judged by Bach just two years earlier, [or] (ii) if he were known to Bach as the leader of public opinion against him."[69] Further, had they not been on good terms, it is unlikely that Johann Adolph and Bach would have visited the organ in Altenburg together in the summer of 1739—a visit described not only by court officials but by J. A.

Scheibe himself.[70] By the time Bach examined the organ at St. John's in 1743, the audition at St. Nicholas's was long past.

In 1986 Henkel offered an alternative theory: the very thorough examination at St. John's was necessary not because of the quarrel with Scheibe's son but because Bach (and Hildebrandt) wanted to support the organ builder's claim for a substantial additional payment.[71] Only a strict and impartial examination would be acceptable—and, in fact, during the dispute with the builder, the city council threatened to call in an out-of-town expert for a second opinion. Bach must have been annoyed that his considerable expertise was questioned. In relating the story, the writers of Bach's obituary chose to emphasize Bach's vast knowledge of organ building, the age and experience of the builder, and the strictness of the examination that resulted in Bach's "complete approval."

Bach and Hildebrandt surely were aware when they undertook the examination that Scheibe had built more than the initial contract required. After all, as Andreas Werckmeister pointed out, an examiner's first task is to carefully read the contract and compare what was specified with what has actually been provided by the organ builder.[72] In the report written after the organ's examination, Bach confirmed that he had "carefully compared [the organ] with the original contract" and that there were a number of stops built over and above the contract.[73] Knowing that Scheibe had built more than the contract required, Bach and Hildebrandt must have anticipated the dispute that lay ahead.

Bach's reputation as an organ examiner was addressed not just in his obituary but also in Johann Nikolaus Forkel's extended study on Bach, published in 1802. We are told that Bach acted "conscientiously and impartially" when he examined candidates for vacant organist positions or reported on new organs.

> He could as little prevail on himself to praise a bad instrument as to recommend a bad organist. He was, therefore, severe, though always fair, in the tests he applied, and as he was thoroughly acquainted with the construction of the instrument it was hopeless to attempt to deceive him. . . . His sense of fairness was so strong that, if he found the work really well done, and the builder's remuneration too small, so that he was likely to be a loser, Bach endeavoured, and often successfully, to procure for him an adequate addition to the purchase price.[74]

City council may have wanted an additional organ evaluation precisely because of Bach's reputation for taking the part of the organ builder, going so far as to pressure those who were trying to pay too little to make "an adequate addition." Would not the prospect of a dispute over payment, coupled with a desire to support Scheibe, an experienced and respected builder, have pushed Bach and Hildebrandt to make a painstaking, rigorous examination of the organ?

Matters did not end with the organ's successful examination, for Scheibe demanded a substantial additional payment. For well over a year, Scheibe and the authorities fought over how much he would be paid for work he claimed to have done over and above the contract.[75] As the minutes from the city council's meeting on 13 December 1743 report, Scheibe had requested an additional 156 taler for stops he had added at the verbal request of the church's director,[76] who promised to pay extra for them. The director had died in the meantime, however, and the new director knew nothing about such an arrangement. Council members were asked whether something should be given to Scheibe and reminded that "in similar cases a gratuity is always given," that according to the report of its examiners the organ was well built, and that the organ builder was "a poor man."[77] One member suggested 50 taler, two members recommended 100 taler, and six members wanted to pay 60 taler. The council resolved to pay Scheibe 60 taler.

Building more than had been contracted for and then requesting an additional fee was common practice in organ building at the time. In Eutritzsch, for example, where Hildebrandt added an additional rank of pipes to the mixture, the examiner, Johann Schneider, recommended he be paid an additional 12 taler. In Leutzsch, where Apitzsch added two stops and a tremulant above the contract, the examiner, Görner, recommended he be paid an additional 50 taler. Silbermann, too, was known to add one or more stops above what had been contracted for.[78] Here, Scheibe's initial request for an additional 156 taler indicates that he had done much more than had been originally agreed to. As a comparison, for the work done over and above the contract at St. Paul's, Scheibe had requested an additional payment of some 340 taler.

Not surprisingly, Scheibe refused the city council's offer of 60 taler, and further discussions took place. On 9 January 1744 the council offered 200 taler, almost a third again as much as Scheibe had originally requested. Again, Scheibe refused—indeed, emboldened, he now demanded "much more than 500 taler."[79] On 28 February the council resolved to have the contract carefully reviewed and, in any event, to have the organ examined and evaluated by an out-of-town expert. As far as we know, no outside evaluation took place, however, and the dispute remained unresolved for more than a year. On 17 December 1744, a receipt for payment of 250 taler to Scheibe was prepared, but it remained unsigned and appears to have been part of unsuccessful negotiations undertaken by St. John's without the city council's knowledge.[80] In a meeting on 26 March 1745, Scheibe's latest demand was reported: if he was not paid "528 taler 4 groschen as well as the 75 taler that remained unpaid from the contract,"[81] then the organ's real worth would need to be evaluated, in his presence, by a knowledgeable organ builder. Council refused to budge from its previous offer of 200 taler, and four days later Scheibe reduced his demand to 400 taler. Two councilmen were willing to give it to him, but another member, who may have been aware of the unsigned receipt prepared in December 1744, insisted that Scheibe deserved nothing more than 250 taler. Finally, on 17 April 1745, Scheibe agreed to a payment of 250 taler, signed a receipt, and promised to make no further claims. According to the release, city council paid "out of pure benevolence, as a gratuity, and because various items were added and constructed that were not part of the signed contract."[82] The size of the settlement—substantially more than Scheibe's original request and 50 taler more than the extra payment he had received from St. Paul's 25 years earlier—indicates that Scheibe was in the right. Together with the "gratuity" of 250 additional taler, for a two-manual, 22-stop organ Scheibe received cash and materials worth 875 taler.

Scheibe's organ survived, albeit with changes, until 1894, when it was dismantled so that a new church and plaza could be built, a project completed in 1897. Paul de Wit, of Leipzig, acquired Scheibe's organ for his music history museum, but the case and wooden pipes were so badly worm-eaten that the organ could not be displayed. Wit reconstructed a facade by putting together usable parts from the key desk and the old case. (Unfortunately, it is not known whether the stop knobs on the surviving St. John's key desk were made by Scheibe's wood-carver. Their style indicates they were added later, perhaps in 1833, at the same time as the manual and pedal keyboards were replaced by Johann Gottlob Mende, or perhaps in 1867, when the organ was worked on by Friedrich Ladegast.) Wit also preserved one facade pipe, a "74-cm pipe of polished tin and composed of separate pieces soldered together in a spiral shape," and the organ bench.[83] Wilhelm Heyer acquired these parts in 1905, and in 1926, together with his entire collection, they came to the University of Leipzig's Musical Instrument Museum, which still owns all that remains of the organ—the reconstructed key desk and the organ bench. (The facade pipe seems to have disappeared.) The keys that had been replaced were stolen in 1947 by someone who believed they had been touched by Bach.[84] After restoration to its circa 1900 condition by Marcus Stahl, of Dresden, in 2009, the key desk and organ bench are now on display in the Bach Museum Leipzig.

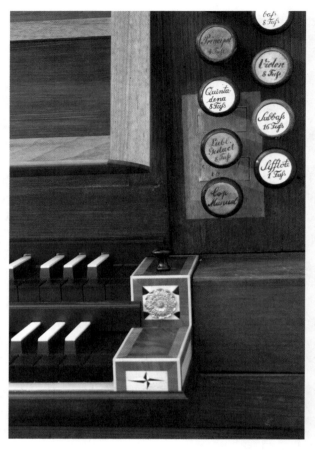

37. Detail, key desk of
the Scheibe organ at St.
John's, on permanent
loan to the Bach
Museum Leipzig.
Photograph by
Marcus Stahl.

Of the organ's sound, regrettably, only memories remain. In their diary, musicians Robert and Clara Schumann described playing the organ in the fall of 1841: "Once we also played the organ at St. John's. A dreadful memory, because we didn't handle it at all masterfully. Clara was never able to get past the second entry in the Bach fugues—as if she stood at the edge of a wide brook [*ein weitem Bach*]. We shall try again soon; the instrument, after all, is so glorious."[85]

10 Small Projects and Proposals

[Both dispositions] were passed on to Court Composer and Cantor H[err] Johann Sebastian Bach so that he could express his thoughts about them. He then chose the first disposition, but nevertheless suggested one thing or another for its improvement.
—patron Christiana Clara Glafey and superintendent Salomon Deyling, 1748

Scheibe's activities as organ builder included not only building new organs but also renovating and at times removing existing organs, maintaining organs in the city and environs of Leipzig, building stringed keyboard instruments, and writing about his ideas and inventions. Not all plans came to fruition. In this chapter, Scheibe's small projects and (unsuccessful) proposals will be discussed: his one-manual organ in Gundorf (examined twice, the second time by Georg Friedrich Kauffmann, of Merseburg), his proposal to build an organ in the village of Leutzsch (he was underbid by David Apitzsch), his attempt to build an organ in the village of Gollma (the church instead hired Johann Dietrich, from Merseburg), his proposal for a new organ for the recently opened chapel in Leipzig's Georgenhaus (which the city council refused to approve because at the time it did not want also to have to hire an organist), his proposal to renovate the Thayssner organ at St. Jacob's in Köthen (which apparently was just too great an undertaking for the Köthen authorities), and his proposal for a new organ in the nearby village of Stötteritz (Bach reviewed two dispositions and recommended one, but Scheibe died before the project could be carried out).

A Village Organ for Gundorf

The village of Gundorf is less than 10 kilometers/6 miles from the center of Leipzig. Its small church, which dates to the 12th century, has a wide west tower, an equally wide nave, an indented choir, and a rounded apse. Its altar is a late-Gothic sculpted representation of the Virgin and Child with St. Anne, and the pulpit dates to 1626. A sculpture of St. Valentin, original to the church and dated circa 1510, is now in a collection in Dresden. From 1681 the manor and village of Gundorf were owned by the Leipzig publisher Johann Friedrich Gleditsch. There was a connection, too, with Leipzig University. In 1702 Professor Johann Burchard Mencke married Gleditsch's daughter, Katharina Margaretha. Although it is much closer to Leipzig than to Merseburg, Gundorf is nevertheless under the jurisdiction of the bishopric of Merseburg. In circa 1712, Scheibe built a new organ for the church, which was successfully examined on 17 December 1713 by Johann Wilhelm Böttiger, organist in Annaberg. A second examination was carried out by Kauffmann, court organist in Merseburg, on Thursday, 15 May 1716.

The church possessed a positive (its origins are unknown), but by 1711 it was deemed "completely useless and practically unable to be played,"[1] and money began to be collected for a new organ. Knowing very well how poor the congregation was, the superintendent in Merseburg only reluctantly allowed the new organ to be built and insisted that the contract for 154 taler include the provision that, should there not be enough funds to complete the organ, Scheibe would take back either the unused materials or the organ itself in lieu of payment. It was also agreed that, until the new instrument was fully paid for, salary payments would continue to be withheld from the schoolmaster-organist, an employee of the congregation who, because he "played only seldom and not well," had already not been paid for two years.[2]

As the superintendent feared, when the organ was finished, Scheibe could not be fully paid. Scheibe put the organ under lock and key and refused to give it over to the congregation until he received what he was owed. (Once an organ builder has signed a contract, the organ is under his care and fully his responsibility; at the end of the project and a successful examination, the organ is "turned over" again to its owner.) Six parishioners made a loan of approximately 26 taler,[3] Scheibe was paid, and, eight days before Christmas in 1713, the organ was successfully examined and the schoolmaster's organ skills tested and approved. It was agreed at the time that once the loan had been repaid, the organ would be reexamined and the schoolmaster's skills as organist retested.

The organ's dedication, delayed by the death of the superintendent, took place ten months later, on 21 October 1714. According to the pastor, who described the simple dedicatory service in a letter to the new superintendent, who did not attend, the sermon he preached was based on Psalm 150. The service began with the singing of Psalm 150 ("Praise God in his holiness") followed by the Kyrie and the German Gloria "Allein Gott in der Höh sei Ehr." Other hymns included "Nun lob mein Seel' den Herren" after the epistle lesson, "Es woll uns Gott gnädig sein" from the pulpit, "Herr Gott, Dich loben wir" (the German *Te Deum*) after the sermon and during communion, and "Nun danket alle Gott" at the conclusion of the service.[4]

The reexamination of the organ and the retesting of the schoolmaster-organist took place on 15 May 1716. Kauffmann carried out the examination in the presence of the pastor, the town magistrate from Schkeuditz, and, "at the request of the congregation," both Daniel Vetter and Scheibe. According to Kauffmann, who provided a report to the superintendent, Scheibe protested that he saw no reason for the organ to be reexamined as it had been "found to be good" when it was examined two and a half years earlier and he had a testimonial in hand that proved it.[5] Kauffmann convinced him no harm was meant, and Scheibe—no doubt reluctantly—acquiesced.

Kauffmann began by examining the bellows, the playing and stop actions, and other parts, and then went through the registers one by one, testing them "accurately and exactly." He found that the pipework was not evenly voiced, that there were runs (wind leakage from one tone channel to another), and that the instrument was badly out of tune. Since the previous examination had not revealed any problems, Kauffmann and Scheibe believed the problems had occurred naturally, over time. When very dry wood swells in humid weather, registers become difficult to pull. If the toeboards are not adjusted ("the screws are not opened") and the registers are simply left "in duress," then "the leather that covers the channels little by little gives way and rolls up, with the result that the tone channels are no longer perfectly closed" by the sliders. Scheibe claimed, and Kauffmann agreed, that the organ "should have been under the care of a knowledgeable organ builder who had annual oversight and was paid an annual fee, which is the norm in other places." Everyone agreed there was nothing to be done except to take the organ apart, make the necessary repairs "with great diligence," and retune the instrument from scratch.[6] Scheibe requested 24 taler for the repair and tuning but accepted the offer of 20 taler and agreed not to require payment until the organ once again had been reexamined. Unfortunately, as Pastor Carl Gottfried Jacobi later reported to his superintendent, after the organ was repaired the parishioners refused to pay the annual fee of 6 taler that Scheibe requested for carrying out annual maintenance.

Kauffmann next tested the organ skills of the schoolmaster, Friedrich Wilhelm Spillner. Even though he first played pieces of his own choosing, the preludes and other small pieces he had learned were performed miserably, Kauffmann reported. The playing was lackluster. Aware that "this way of playing [by memory] is very uncertain, and a man over 30 years of age cannot very well rely on his memory," Kauffmann suggested that the schoolmaster perform something "from his own fantasy." Improvisation, too, ended badly. The organist was not able to complete even one measure, using simple harmony, without immediately falling back into his memorized pieces again. Kauffmann apparently saw potential, however, because he recommended that the schoolmaster go to nearby Leipzig for instruction. "If he will give up drinking, especially brandy, which according to the pastor and the congregation, he is prone to," Kauffmann wrote, "it is just possible he will succeed in learning something, for he reads quite well, and was able to play the chorale 'Allein Gott in der Höh sei Ehr' without confusing the congregation, which had to sing along."[7]

It was not unusual for someone to be both schoolmaster and organist, and most often such individuals did not possess advanced skills. In his study of organs in villages near Leipzig, Hubert Henkel described a candidate in Wahren who could not play the pedal, could not read music, could play only one chorale, by ear, and did not even know how to register, let alone vary the registration.[8] In Gundorf, schoolmaster Spillner was not rejected altogether but was exhorted to work hard and give up drinking; he continued to teach and play the Gundorf organ for another 15 years.[9]

Scheibe's organ for Gundorf apparently was a one-manual organ with a pedal and 12 stops.[10] I have not been able to discover a contemporary description, the disposition, the contract, or the original examination report (if there was one). The organ and bellows suffered during a church fire in 1748. Whether Scheibe lived to witness this and whether he was able to make repairs is not known. By the mid-19th century, the organ had become so worm-eaten that it was decided to replace it, and a new organ was built by Leopold Kohl in 1869–73. The remains of the Scheibe organ were sold, and the case does not survive.[11]

As it turns out, the major renovation of the cathedral organ in Merseburg was just ending in the summer of 1716. A few weeks after his trip to evaluate the organ and organist in Gundorf, Kauffmann was joined by Kapellmeister Jacob Christian Hertel of Merseburg and Cantor Johann Kuhnau of Leipzig for the organ's nine-day examination. The initial renovation of the cathedral organ had cost 4,000 taler, but the examinations of Zacharias Thayssner's work were unfavorable and in July 1714 a contract was made with Johann Friedrich Wender for the organ's complete renovation and expansion. After a successful examination in June 1715, by Kuhnau and Gottfried Ernst Pestel, a further renovation by Wender was agreed to in September 1715. By the time the now 66-stop organ was successfully examined in July 1716, Wender's renovations had cost another 3,500 taler.[12] The dedication took place more than a year later, on 17 October 1717. The celebratory concerted work performed opened with a chorus set to a biblical text (Psalm 34:1–3), followed by three recitative-aria pairs and a closing chorus on an aria text,[13] and was performed by all the court musicians—17 singers and instrumentalists as well as trumpeters and timpani. Just as there can be no comparison between the 66-stop organ in Merseburg and the 12-stop organ in Gundorf, or between the competence and professionalism of court organist Kauffmann and that of schoolmaster-organist Spillner, so, too, there is no comparison between the festive celebration at the court in Merseburg and the simple service of hymns in the village of Gundorf.

Examination of a Competitor's Work in Leutzsch

In 1728 Scheibe's opinion was sought by the Leipzig city council regarding the organ in the church in Leutzsch, now a western suburb of Leipzig. The organ had been built in 1620–21 and repaired in 1671, but by 1728 it was "no longer usable."[14] Scheibe responded that even if the organ were repaired, which would cost as much as 180 taler, nothing good would come of it, so the council solicited proposals for a new organ—not only from Scheibe but also from David Apitzsch, another local builder.

Scheibe requested a fee of 250 taler 12 groschen and the old organ. Apitzsch requested a fee of 265 taler 8 groschen but said he would be willing to pay 24 taler for the old organ—in other words, his organ would cost the city 9 taler 4 groschen less than Scheibe's. Hoping to spend even less, the city council asked Apitzsch whether a smaller organ might serve the church just as well, and a visit to the church was arranged. Given the size of the congregation, Apitzsch agreed that it was not necessary to build all the stops he initially proposed. After all, the existing organ, described as a "patchwork" limited by its short-octave bass, amply filled the church with just nine manual stops and three pedal stops, including Subbass 8'. Apitzsch provided a drawing and a revised disposition for a small organ of eight stops, seven in the Manual and a Subbass 16' in the Pedal

that would provide "even more power and usefulness [than the Subbass 8']."[15]
In the end, Apitzsch reduced his fee even further, to 174 taler (less the 24 taler
he would pay for the old organ). The city's outlay would thus be only 150 taler,
approximately 100 taler less than what Scheibe had requested for an organ. (At
the same time, however, it was agreed to spend 48 taler 6 groschen to build an
organ gallery in the west end of the church.)

The completed organ was played and examined by Johann Gottlieb Görner—
organist at St. Nicholas's at the time—on Wednesday, 30 November 1729. No
report has survived, but a letter to the superintendent in Merseburg provides
details.[16] Görner consulted the contracted disposition, went through the organ
"part by part" (*Stück zu Stück*), including the seven Manual stops and the Subbass in the Pedal, and observed that, as regards materials, Apitzsch had provided two wedge bellows, had used brass wire, had built the manual keyboard
from boxwood and black ebony, and had built the wind chests from good oak.
Everything was "well and skillfully built" (*gut und tüchtig gearbeitet*). The tonal
character was "pleasant in the highest pitches but penetrating in the middle and
lowest pitches, resulting in an equal harmony [throughout], there was good balance in the registers, and the necessary order could be recognized."[17] Also, all
the manual keys spoke well. He noted that three stops had been added, namely
Violon 8', Bordun 16' ("from the top note down to g in the tenor range"),[18] and
a Tremulant, stops "that very much contribute to the instrument's overall perfection, in that these registers make it stronger and more robust. Furthermore,
[without these additions] the higher number of higher pitched stops would
have overwhelmed the smaller number of lower pitched stops and the instrument would thus have suffered a lack of penetrating strength, which [quality]
is necessary for accompanying the full congregation."[19]

Görner went to some length to defend Apitzsch's additions. He observed
that the instrument had been solidly and accurately built according to the contract and admitted that the contract had not provided for the addition of three
extra stops, nor had they been added with the knowledge or permission of any
authority. Although the builder hoped to be paid 50 taler for the additional
stops, he stood ready to remove the stops should the authorities not be willing
to pay for them. Görner recommended that the three additional stops be kept,
however, especially since, as he pointed out, at the end of the 1728–29 fiscal year,
the church had assets of 3,795 aßo 14 groschen 10 pfennig. Görner's appeal on
behalf of the organ builder was persuasive. (6 aßo was the equivalent of 5 taler.)
According to the payment records for 1729–30, Apitzsch was paid 185 taler for
the new organ, 35 taler more than the contract price.

Three years later, in fiscal year 1732–33, payments of 3 aßo 12 groschen were made to Scheibe "for inspecting the new organ" and to Görner "for examining and playing the new organ."[20] On the basis of these payments, Henkel assumed that both Görner and Scheibe examined the organ in 1729 and concluded that Scheibe must have returned to Leipzig at that time from a two- or three-year absence.[21] Görner is the only examiner mentioned in the report that was submitted to the superintendent in December 1729, however, and it is puzzling that the examiners were paid two or three years later. Perhaps the matter remained open while the organ remained under an extended warranty (and the organ builder's protection), and the organ was reexamined and dedicated at the end of a three-year warranty period.

Scheibe fulfilled three functions with respect to the organ in Leutzsch: he evaluated the existing organ and determined it was not worth repairing; he submitted a proposal to build a new organ, which was rejected in favor of a competing, more economical proposal; and, along with Görner, he inspected the instrument built by his competitor.

A Proposal for Gollma

In 1738 Scheibe sent a proposal to build a new organ in Gollma, a town 16 kilometers/10 miles northwest of Leipzig. He must have had a personal connection with the pastor, for in the letter to Adam Friedrich Trainer dated 26 August, in which he sent a drawing and two organ dispositions, Scheibe appended personal greetings to the pastor's wife and son.[22] Trainer had connections in Leipzig; he had attended the St. Nicholas and St. Thomas Schools, matriculated at Leipzig University in 1717, and defended two dissertations in 1723. He was a Vespers preacher at St. Paul's from 1723 to 1726 and by 1730 had moved to Gollma, serving first as substitute pastor and then, from 1740, as pastor.[23] The church in Gollma had been almost destroyed by fire in 1734; it was rebuilt in baroque style in the years 1737 to 1741.

Scheibe described the two proposed dispositions, either of which he was willing to build, as "sharp and penetrating as well as soft"[24] and invited the pastor to choose whichever pleased him. If the disposition was too large (*starck*), it could be amended, but Scheibe urged the pastor to keep the congregation's needs in mind: the organ must be "strong enough to keep the congregation in order during singing."[25] Scheibe included a carefully prepared, scaled drawing for the choir gallery and organ. (Neither the drawing nor the dispositions have survived.) According to his description, the organ would have three towers, the large middle tower 2 Elle wide, the two outer towers each 1½ Elle wide. He suggested he come to Gollma to discuss the drawing with the carpenter, and he implored the pastor to "please be a little careful with the drawing, that it is not folded." Scheibe also discussed the wood he would need to build the organ:

> If you were to succeed in having the woodcutter provide and prepare the wood while there is still good weather, it would be of great help in building the organ. It is better if the joinery and seasoning [of the wood] is done at the organ builder's rather than you having to do such things in the church. One can never acquire enough dry wood for such building projects, and it is always better, when building a new organ, that the wood is acquired, worked on, and prepared a year in advance—wood for the posts and boards, that is. As for the oak that the organ requires, it has been stored at my place for ten or eleven years, and well soaked [dried] wood for the wind chests is also in my inventory.[26]

Scheibe promised that an instrument built by him would last a long time, and he begged the pastor not to allow just anyone to take on the project, for he could guarantee that such a person would end up cheating the church. "If you are going to build," he urged, "then find a man whom you know has built a good instrument that has lasted, for it is perilous when churches are deceived and cheated by negligent bunglers. Not only is money wasted but one is stuck with a ruined instrument for as long as it stands and can do nothing to help it, while the church gets an asset it must continually maintain in good condition."[27]

Nothing came of Scheibe's proposal, even though he visited Gollma several times. Scheibe eventually learned that "a carpenter, apparently from Merseburg," was going to build the new organ, and he wrote the pastor in August 1741 requesting that the drawing, dispositions, and proposal be returned and that he be reimbursed for his trouble, travel costs, and time.[28] "I fear," replied the pastor, "that someone from Merseburg—whether a carpenter or an organ builder who learned the trade secondarily, as he claims, I do not know—offered to build the organ and . . . has made a proposal. But there is less money and less desire among the parishioners than before, so that it is not at all certain the instrument will be built." The pastor returned the proposal and drawing but would not satisfy Scheibe's request for reimbursement, pointing out that Scheibe had visited Gollma at the behest of a number of people—including Scheibe himself, the secretary of the city council, and the church inspector—and that he should seek reimbursement "from those places."[29]

Surviving documents do not tell us how it was that the church authorities turned to Johann Dietrich, "organ builder and *mechanicus* in Merseburg," but on 18 November 1741 a contract was made with Dietrich for the "rebuilding of the organ sacrificed in the latest fire." Dietrich had proposed a two-manual, 19-stop organ[30]—whether the same as, or similar to, Scheibe's own proposal(s) is not known—for a fee of 510 taler plus 12 taler for room and board. Dietrich specified the following materials: wind chests from oak and linden, the posts and beams of the bellows from fir (*Tanne*), keyboards from black ebony (naturals) and ivory (sharps), pedalboard from oak, the trackers from maple and linden. He would provide screws for adjusting the keyboard and use brass for the springs, pins, and hooks in the wind chests. In lieu of full payment in cash, Dietrich agreed to take the "tin" from the old organ, 170 pounds of material that was assessed at a value of approximately 16 taler, and he was required to post a bond. He promised to have three or four stops playing in just seven months, by the feast of St. John in 1742, and to complete the organ entirely by Michaelmas in 1743. At the organ's examination, it was determined that Dietrich had built far more stops of wood than had been agreed upon (wood is less expensive than metal).[31] It appears, then, that not only did it take much longer than anticipated for Dietrich to finish the organ—final payment from the congregation was not requested until March 1744—but the organ may have been just the sort of bungler's work about which Scheibe had warned.

The Positive Proposed for the Georgenhaus

The Georgenhaus in Leipzig was a hospital complex that served primarily orphans, the psychologically ill, and the poor. Founded as the St. George Hospital in 1212, it was the oldest social institution in Leipzig and survived, in various incarnations, until the 20th century. From 1701 the Georgenhaus was on the Brühl on Leipzig's northeast side; a well-furnished church was built in 1705. Hymns were sung in the church every morning and evening before and after prayers, as well as twice weekly during prayer hours, but otherwise music played a rather subordinate role in the daily life of the residents. In May 1742, however, an anonymous gift of 100 taler for an organ was received, and the director of the Georgenhaus informed the city council of the desire to acquire an organ. A drawing and disposition, as well as an estimate, had already been solicited from Scheibe.[32]

Scheibe's proposal, dated 22 May 1742, was for a 7-stop positive.[33] He requested 250 taler if he built the case and was responsible for the metalwork but only 210 taler if the case and metalwork were taken care of by others. The materials he specified included a "double bellows," well-boiled oak barrel staves for the wind chest[34]—drying wood by boiling it in water is quicker than air drying, results in less cracking, and kills microorganisms—and iron and brass for the

38. Drawing for the positive organ proposed by Scheibe for the
Georgenhaus, Leipzig, 1742. Stadtarchiv Leipzig, Georgenhaus Nr. 642,
fol. 5.

roller board, which would have iron rollers and brass loops, similar to the roller
board construction in Zschortau. As is clear from the very attractive drawing
(fig. 38), Scheibe proposed a reverse-console positive, its convex facade placed
on the balustrade; the dimensions were 3–3/4 Elle high, 2 Elle 6 Zoll wide, and
1 Elle 7 Zoll 2 deep (approximately 7′ × 4′ × 2½′).

The proposed disposition—Grob Gedackt 8′, Principal 4′, Gedackt 4′, Hohl
Quinta (Hohlflöte) 3′,[35] Octav 2′, Superoctav 1′, Mixtur III—is remarkably similar
to Tobias Gottfried Trost's organ at St. John's. As Scheibe received the St. John's

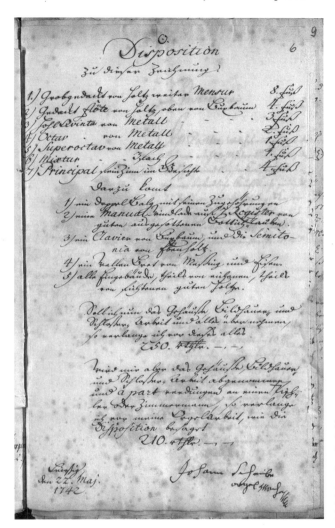

39. Disposition for the positive proposed by Scheibe for the Georgenhaus, 22 May 1742. Stadtarchiv Leipzig, Georgenhaus Nr. 642, fol. 6.

organ in partial payment for the new organ he built for St. John's in 1741–43, it is possible Scheibe imagined using pipework from Trost's organ for a positive at the Georgenhaus. (In 1748, or perhaps earlier, he offered the St. John's organ to the church in Stötteritz, an offer it refused; see below.)

The Leipzig city council refused to authorize the new instrument, however. Burgomaster Gottfried Lange noted that an organ would make it "necessary also to pay for an organist and a bellows pumper," and, with a lukewarm response from other board members as well, in August 1742 action was deferred. Even a further gift received a few weeks later—an additional 100 taler "from some good friends and benefactors, whose names shall all remain anonymous"—was not enough to get the project off the ground.[36] The monies were deposited in an interest-bearing account, Scheibe's proposal was filed, and he never did build the 7-stop positive he had recommended.

Two years later, however, the Georgenhaus was offered an 8-stop positive from the estate of Johann Benedict Belger, a spice merchant, for the sum of 62 taler 18 groschen. This time, on 14 May 1744, the city council approved the project, and Scheibe was hired to "repair and set up" the instrument in an arched niche in the lower gallery, to the right of the altar, beside a south-facing window.[37] The instrument was dedicated at Pentecost in 1744 by organist Johann Georg Hille, and Scheibe was paid 14 taler with his assistants receiving a 1-taler gratuity. Among other payments to guild workers, the painter received 2 taler 8 groschen for painting the organ and gilding the decorative carvings. The church was able to cover almost the entire cost of the positive with additional gifts and earnings, and further interest on the 200 taler set aside earlier—10 taler a year—was designated as salary for the organist. (Records show, however, that Hille actually received 12 taler a year, an amount equal to that paid to the organist at St. John's.)

The positive was repaired and enlarged in 1746—not by Scheibe but by Hille, the organist and, one might say, "occasional organ builder." Hille added a Pedal with two stops, Subbass 16' and Principal Bass 8', and built two new bellows. He requested a gratuity above the 25-taler fee he was paid on 29 September 1746 because of the "trouble of various kinds" he had taken to "raise the entire organ" and give it "an entirely different installation [*Einrichtung*]," and on 31 December 1746 Hille was paid an additional 10 taler 12 groschen.[38] All that remained, apparently, was the finishing and decorating of the case. As can be seen from the invoices received in May and October from the cabinetmaker and painter/gilder, this work took place in 1747. We do not know what organ-building experience Hille may have had when he took on this expansion at the age of approximately 30. Nor do we know whether Scheibe had been asked for a proposal or a cost estimate. What is certain, however, is that Hille would have underbid the older and more experienced Scheibe.

A Proposal to Renovate the Thayssner Organ in Köthen

In 1746–47 Scheibe evaluated the organ at St. Jacob's, Köthen, a two-manual, 25-stop instrument that had been built in 1674–76 by Zacharias and Andreas

Thayssner[39] that at the time was under an annual maintenance contract with Johann Christoph Zuberbier, privileged court instrument and organ maker in Köthen since his father's death in 1743.[40] (Zuberbier was the builder of the small organ now in Köthen's court chapel, a 6-stop instrument built for the church in Thurau in 1754.)

Scheibe's invitation may have come from Bernhard Christian Kayser, commissary to the prince of Anhalt-Köthen and, by 1747 at the latest, also court organist and chamber musician in Köthen.[41] Kayser was a student of Bach's, first in Köthen and then in Leipzig, where he was apparently one of Bach's closest associates in the period 1718–25. Andrew Talle has identified him as the scribe known as "Anonymous 5," well known especially for his copies of the English Suites BWV 806–811 and the first volume of the Well-Tempered Clavier BWV 846–869.

Scheibe knew Thayssner's style of organ building well. He took care of Thayssner's organ at St. Nicholas's for most of 25 years and was responsible for its major renovation in 1724–25. Zacharias Hildebrandt, on the other hand, maintained the St. Nicholas organ for only seven years, from 1737 to 1743. That Scheibe—rather than Hildebrandt—was invited to evaluate the Thayssner organ and make a proposal for its renovation suggests that someone in Köthen—perhaps Kayser—regarded Scheibe's fairly conservative renovation of Thayssner's organ at St. Nicholas's as successful.

Scheibe's undated evaluation report[42] is essentially a proposal for a major renovation. In 15 succinctly written points (many with helpful explanations inserted by Kayser), Scheibe dealt with problems associated with the organ's spring chests, winding, actions, and pipework. Scheibe first addressed the pipes that were not speaking in the Hauptwerk and Rückpositiv. The chests were too dirty for him to see the cause of the problem, but the origin was either the stop beam (also called guide rail, the piece running lengthwise across the chest that opens or closes all the individual pallets) or the wedge strips holding the top boards in place. If it was the stop beam, it would have to be replaced with a new piece of well-seasoned wood that would not shrink.

The second problem he addressed was "sticking"—which, Kayser explained, is when a note, or pitch, sounds in both the manual and the pedal at the same time. It appears Thayssner had placed the Manual (Hauptwerk) and Pedal stops on the same wind chest and that something was causing more than one pitch to sound at a time. Perhaps the stop pallets were not closing completely. Scheibe said that the problem could be corrected when each division was given its own wind chest. Further, Scheibe recommended that the hundreds of iron springs in the chests—in a spring chest, each pipe has its own pallet and spring—be replaced with brass springs. (As Kayser noted, the iron springs had been attacked by *Galmey*.)

Scheibe proposed correcting the organ's deep key dip and difficult playing action, problems that are exacerbated by changes in weather. He had encountered the same problems in Christoph Donat's organ at the New Church and had successfully corrected both the key dip and the playing action so that after his renovation the organ played easily. Also, Scheibe recommended that the actions be brought into perfect adjustment. A major cause of the ciphering were the too-short trackers, which Scheibe proposed lengthening.

Scheibe wanted to make changes to Thayssner's wind system—three bellows that were winded by pulling on ropes. He proposed altering the bellows so that they could be pumped by treading a bellows pole, which would result in a much more equal wind and no rattling or rumbling. The bellows would be releathered where necessary and their surfaces saturated with glue, and they would be provided with horse veins. The bellows would be turned in order to install the bellows poles, and at the same time the base frame would be enlarged by about 2 feet and the wind trunks relocated and lengthened by about 20 feet. This modification, too, would result in a more even wind supply.

The flue pipework needed to be cleaned. Further, in the upperwork, many of the languids had been cut up too much or had been attacked by *Salpeter*—primarily in the mixture, Octav 4′, Octav 2′, Quint 3′, and Tierce 1-3/5′. To restore brightness, Scheibe recommended replacing these pipes. With their higher cut-ups, Thayssner's stops had a more vocal sound, but now the desire was for "brilliance," a sound with a lot of overtones. (Again, this is similar to work Scheibe carried out two decades earlier at the New Church.) In the Pedal, the Posaunen Bass 16′ and the Subbass 16′ needed to be revoiced so that they spoke evenly, and the reed tongues in the Posaunen Bass and Trompete 8′ needed to be cleaned of *Galmey* and properly adjusted. After this, all the pipework would be revoiced and brought to a quick and easy speech, a good temperament set, and the organ tuned.

Finally, Scheibe strongly expressed his opinion that the repairs and adjustments would last longer, and the same problems would never recur, if the "evil spring chests" were replaced with new slider wind chests.[43] He argued that building new chests would be no more expensive than carrying out all the repairs the organ now required but that with new chests the organ would be both durable and reliable, whereas no organ builder worth his salt would be able to warranty the repairs carried out to this spring-chest organ. He warned that even if an organ builder were found who was foolhardy enough to provide a warranty, it would be useless because changes in weather inevitably led to problems in spring chests. Spring chests demanded an honest builder who understood how to maintain them—there was always something in a spring chest that required the assistance of an organ builder—but while there were many organ builders, few of them had occasion to look at spring chests or had any experience working on them. In short, if the spring chests were retained, nothing reliable would result. With slider chests, however, the organ would be durable and reliable.[44]

Scheibe requested 460 taler to carry out the repairs, as well as room and board for him and his workers, the services of a handyman and bellows pumper, and the cost of transporting his tools and equipment back and forth from Leipzig. He offered to build the slider chests for 560 taler, including the same conditions regarding room and board, a handyman, and transportation, but requested that the authorities be responsible for any work by a metal forger.[45]

Although Scheibe's report left no doubt as to the organ's poor condition, the authorities were not persuaded. Instead, Scheibe was hired to carry out what must have been rather basic repairs, for which he was paid just 16 taler.[46] More than 20 years later, the organ underwent a major rebuild by Zuberbier. (Zuberbier's proposal dated 27 July 1756 includes the earliest record of the organ's disposition.)[47]

Two Dispositions for Stötteritz

On 30 August 1748, only a few days before Scheibe's death, a letter was sent to the Leipzig Consistory requesting that the church in Stötteritz, a nearby village now part of the city of Leipzig, be allowed to purchase a new organ from Scheibe.[48] As the letter and previous correspondence explain, the initial gift for a new organ had been received in 1719, when the owner of the village's lower manor, Engelbrecht von der Burg, had made a testamentary gift of 50 taler. Even though the invested monies had grown considerably, the donor's wish had never been fulfilled.

Newly built in 1702–03, when it replaced a much smaller building, the church in Stötteritz had purchased a positive from Scheibe around 1709.[49] A tower was added in 1712–13, significantly increasing seating capacity, and by 1748 the congregation had expanded fivefold. Scheibe's positive, now "completely and utterly decrepit," no longer met the church's needs. Neither could it be heard over the congregation, nor could the organist prevent the congregation from losing the pitch it had been given, a situation that resulted in "considerable annoyance and dissonance."[50]

Scheibe first offered Stötteritz the "fine instrument that until now had stood at St. John's," which was "still good and serviceable" and could be obtained "for a fair price."[51] (Whether Scheibe made the offer around 1742, when the St. John's organ was dismantled, or later is unclear.) The "fine instrument" at St. John's was of course the small organ built by Tobias Gottfried Trost in 1694–95, an instrument valued at 75 taler when Scheibe had received it as partial payment for the organ he built at St. John's in 1741–43. But the St. John's organ was not acquired by Stötteritz. As church patron Christiana Clara Glafey and superintendent Salomon Deyling explained in a letter dated 30 August 1748, the option of purchasing the organ from Scheibe for 310 taler—almost twice the 175 taler Trost himself had been paid—had been rejected, "because if this organ had continued to meet the needs of St. John's just outside Leipzig it would not have been necessary to sell it."[52]

The church was still in need of an organ, however, and Scheibe was approached once again. As the letter from the patron and superintendent explains, "We therefore had the aforementioned organ builder Scheibe provide not only the organ drawing . . . but also two different proposals . . . , both of which were passed on to Court Composer and cantor H[err] Johann Sebastian Bach so that he could express his thoughts about them. He then chose the first disposition, but nevertheless suggested one thing or another for its improvement."[53] Neither the drawing nor the proposals nor Bach's comments have survived.

Scheibe died in September 1748, and it was another five years before Johann Christian Immanuel Schweinefleisch agreed to build a one-manual, 12-stop organ for a fee of 450 taler.[54] It was not Scheibe's disposition as emended by Bach that was built, however. The contract made on 17 October 1753 specifically states that Schweinefleisch would build "the disposition drawn up by him personally," which was included as Attachment A.[55] The Schweinefleisch organ was examined by Görner on Thursday, 24 October 1754, and dedicated the following Sunday in the presence of "a large crowd of people from Leipzig and other neighboring towns."[56] Görner judged the organ to be "good and serviceable" and offered Schweinefleisch his congratulations and "highest recommendation."[57]

11 Scheibe and Bach in Leipzig

Johann Scheibe was an excellent organ builder highly esteemed
by J. S. Bach.
—Paul Rubardt, 1963

[Bach's] sense of fairness was so strong that, if he found the work
really well done, and the builder's remuneration too small, so
that he was likely to be a loser, Bach endeavoured, and often
successfully, to procure for him an adequate addition to the
purchase price.
—Johann Nikolaus Forkel, 1802 (1920)

On 3 September 1748, at the age of 68, Scheibe died in Leipzig, almost
two years before Bach's death on 28 July 1750. For 25 years, beginning in 1723,
when Bach became Leipzig's Thomaskantor and director of music, Scheibe
and Bach were colleagues. Bach examined Scheibe's work, reviewed proposed
dispositions, and on several occasions acted on Scheibe's behalf to see that he
was properly paid. Bach certainly played Scheibe's organs, whether at Leipzig
University, at the principal churches of St. Thomas and St. Nicholas, at the New
Church, at St. John's, or in Zschortau. Bach wrote a recommendation on behalf
of Scheibe's son and on at least one occasion undertook an organ excursion
with him. According to Paul Rubardt, Scheibe "was an extraordinary character, a straight thinker, and a deft writer who well deserved J. S. Bach's esteem."[1]
Along with Zacharias Hildebrandt and lute and violin maker Johann Christian
Hoffmann, important instrument makers who also worked in Leipzig, Scheibe
probably enjoyed Bach's friendship.

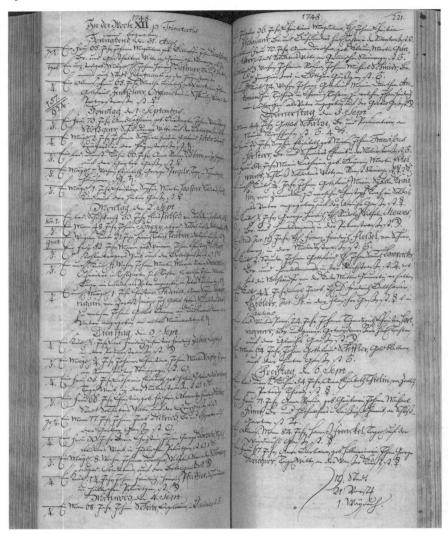

40. *Leichenbuch* entry (*bottom left*) for Johann Scheibe's burial in the St. Paul's churchyard on 4 September 1748. Stadtarchiv Leipzig, *Ratsleichenbuch* 1743–50, fol. 220v.

Three of Scheibe's new organs were "conscientiously and impartially"[2] examined by Bach, and we have two written reports, one of them extensive. Scheibe and Bach no doubt met for the first time in 1717, when Bach came from Köthen to examine Scheibe's magnum opus at the University Church of St. Paul's. (At the time, Bach was 32 years of age, Scheibe 37.) Bach's positive and thorough report described an instrument "well and carefully built" but with some flaws, none of which was considered a major defect, and Daniel Vetter, Leipzig's preeminent organist at the time and an advisor on the project, reported that Bach could not give enough praise to the organ's rare and unusual stops. Bach also examined Scheibe's organ for St. John's. No report survives, but city council minutes from December 1743 record that Bach (now 58) and Hildebrandt had found the organ well-built. With Bach and Hildebrandt's approval of the organ, Scheibe was able to successfully petition for a substantial additional payment. Later, the authors of Bach's earliest biographies would praise Bach for judging Scheibe's work impartially and would point out that Bach and Hildebrandt had undertaken a particularly painstaking examination. Bach also examined Scheibe's organ in Zschortau, which he declared in his report to be "skillfully, diligently, and well built." There is no evidence that Bach performed concerts on these occasions, but it is hard to imagine that he did not improvise in the presence of those gathered to demonstrate the possible registrations and the range of each organ's expressivity. In Zschortau, at least, there was the usual acknowledgment of the builder's diligent, good, and dependable work: Scheibe received an additional payment, his workers were given gratuities, and a celebratory meal took place. Dare we imagine Bach and Scheibe in attendance, with "toasts of recognition and wide-ranging and good conversation,"[3] as Andreas Werckmeister described such occasions?

Whether Bach officially examined Scheibe's overhauls and renovations is less certain. Only for the renovation of the St. Thomas organ in 1747 is there evidence that Bach participated, with Johann Gottlieb Görner, in the examination. Nothing reveals who examined Scheibe's major renovation of the St. Nicholas organ, undertaken shortly after Bach came to Leipzig. Most likely it was Bach and Görner, who was then the organist at St. Nicholas's, but there is no surviving report, and payment records mention only that the work was "well done." A glaring example of the university insisting on its autonomy and independence from the city is the major overhaul carried out at St. Paul's in 1736. Put off for several years despite Scheibe's repeated requests and Bach's approval of it, Scheibe's overhaul was overseen not by Bach, whose support of organ builders apparently led the university to distrust his ability to act on its behalf, but by a university professor serving on Council who had ties to an organ-building family. There is no record of an examination.

Less extensive than renovations, overhauls appear to have been examined by the organist of the church. But records are incomplete. Scheibe's overhaul at St. Thomas's, in 1730, which included setting a temperament, was examined by

Görner, the church's newly appointed organist. At St. Nicholas's, in 1733, Johann Schneider initiated the overhaul and examined Scheibe's work. At the New Church, in 1732, there is no record of who examined the organ after Scheibe set a temperament and retuned the instrument. That the decision regarding something as important as an instrument's temperament was made at the highest level, though, is obvious from the events in Altenburg, where Heinrich Gottfried Trost completed a new organ for the court chapel in 1739. In order to decide which temperament should be set, experiments and lengthy discussions took place among parties with, as it turned out, quite different opinions: the builder, the organist in Altenburg, the organist in Gotha, and the Kapellmeister in Gotha. (Altenburg was a minor court under the jurisdiction of Gotha.) The final decision was made by the Kapellmeister, although the Altenburg organist was allowed to suggest "corrections" during the tuning. Even without direct evidence, we can assume Bach's involvement in determining which temperament to set and tune in Leipzig's organs.

On several occasions, Bach acted on Scheibe's behalf to see that he was properly paid for his work. Bach unequivocally supported Scheibe's claim for a substantial additional payment for the organ at St. Paul's. In one of his many requests for payment, Scheibe referred to Bach's report, reminding the university that the various items he had added over and above the contract had been "acknowledged to be indispensable at the examination."[4] Indeed, in his report Bach had gone so far as to warn the university that Scheibe would honor the one-year warranty "as long as he is promptly and fully reimbursed for the costs he has incurred over and above the contract."[5] Scheibe requested an additional payment for the organ at St. John's, too. Nothing shows that Bach was directly involved, and no examination report survives, but it seems unlikely that Scheibe would have demanded more money without the support of the organ's examiners. Further, because the church director who had approved the additions had died and there was no record of his verbal agreement with Scheibe, the extremely thorough and fastidious examination by Bach and Hildebrandt probably was undertaken to provide support for Scheibe's claim. Finally, Bach's Zschortau examination report surely was taken into account when the church agreed to pay Scheibe an additional 60 taler at the conclusion of the project in 1746. It is perhaps surprising that, by claiming the Fleute-Travers 4′ was an additional stop, Bach exaggerated Scheibe's largesse. (Scheibe built only one 4-foot stop, the Flute douce.) On three occasions, then, Bach endeavored, as Johann Nikolaus Forkel put it, "to procure for him an adequate addition to the purchase price" so that Scheibe would not suffer financial loss.[6]

Bach played Scheibe's organs—a fact that requires emphasis. Obviously, he played Scheibe's organs when he examined them and demonstrated their tonal resources, and it is possible he played dedicatory recitals at St. Paul's, at St. John's, and in Zschortau. "When the examination was over, especially if the instrument pleased him, Bach liked to exhibit his splendid talent, both for his own pleasure and the gratification of those who were present," Forkel reported.[7] The evidence strongly suggests that on occasion Bach played the organ during the main worship services in the principal churches. Several times between 1725 and 1728, and probably afterward for repeat performances, at St. Nicholas's and St. Thomas's, Bach almost certainly played the solo organ part in his cantatas with obbligato organ.[8] He also may have played the organ for certain special services that took place at the University Church.[9] Some scholars have proposed that Bach used the organ at St. Paul's for public performances, while at least one commentator has suggested that Bach would have preferred a more traditional organ, such as the instrument at St. Nicholas's.[10] According to Christoph Wolff, "The best, if not the only suitable, place for the display of Bach's organistic art would have been St. Paul's. . . . We can take for granted that Leipzig audiences were exposed to the same exciting performances and innovative repertoires as concertgoers in Dresden, only more frequently."[11] Surely all of Leipzig's organs, each in its own way, were of interest to Bach.

Only a few details are known about Bach's public organ recitals. A visitor to Leipzig in 1729 reported hearing Bach play—presumably on the organ—at the Easter trade fair,[12] and it has been proposed that such performances for Leipzig visitors may have occurred annually.[13] Georg Heinrich Ludwig Schwanberg, who studied with Bach in the late 1720s, said of Bach's playing—whether in public or private is not specified—that he had "never heard anything like it," and he feared he "must completely change my whole style of playing."[14] J. A. Scheibe, who lived in Leipzig until 1735 and heard Bach play "on various occasions," described Bach as "an extraordinary artist on the clavier and on the organ. . . . One is amazed at his ability, and one can hardly conceive how it is possible for him to achieve such agility, with his fingers and with his feet, in the crossings, extensions, and extreme jumps that he manages, without mixing in a single wrong tone, or displacing his body by any violent movement."[15] Forkel, too, left us a description of Bach's public organ concerts:

> When John Seb. Bach seated himself at the organ when there was no divine service, which he was often requested to do by strangers, he used to choose some subject and to execute it in all the various forms of organ composition so that the subject constantly remained his material, even if he had played, without intermission, for

two hours or more. First, he used this theme for a prelude and a fugue with the full organ. Then he showed his art of using the stops for a trio, a quartet, &c., always upon the same subject. Afterwards followed a chorale, the melody of which was playfully surrounded in the most diversified manner by the original subject, in three or four parts. Finally, the conclusion was made by a fugue with the full organ.[16]

Although Bach was involved throughout his life with devising dispositions for new organs and advising on organ rebuilds and renovations, only one piece of evidence proves that he was consulted regarding the disposition of an organ to be built by Scheibe. A letter written in 1748 reports that Bach's thoughts were solicited regarding Scheibe's two proposals for a new organ in the village church in Stötteritz, near Leipzig, and that "he then chose the first disposition, but nevertheless suggested one thing or another for its improvement."[17] (Neither the dispositions nor Bach's comments survive.) However, it must be assumed that Bach provided input regarding organ projects that took place under his jurisdiction in Leipzig; the absence of written records points more to losses endured over time, and perhaps also to Bach's well-known distaste for correspondence, than it does to Bach's non-involvement. Bach must have given his approval for—and perhaps initiated—the removal of the second organ at St. Thomas's in 1740. He surely would have consulted with Scheibe about the disposition of the new organ for St. John's, which reused some of the pipework from the St. Thomas organ.

Bach's opinions remain mostly unknown—except insofar as we believe we recognize them in the dispositions that survive. We have no idea what Bach thought about Scheibe's means of creating forte and piano in an organ, and we look in vain for Bach's comments about Scheibe's innovative use of divided stops (to permit a greater number of registration possibilities in a small organ). And while it was common practice for a builder to add a (relatively inexpensive) high-pitched rank that was not part of the contracted disposition and then to ask for an additional fee, did Scheibe on his own decide to add a (quite a bit more expensive) Quintatön 16′ in Zschortau over and above the contract, or did Bach put him up to it, as some commentators claim? Can we see Bach's preference in the addition of a Nasat 2–2/3′ to the St. Nicholas organ in 1724–25? Nasat is one of the stops Bach requested be added during the organ renovation in Mühlhausen, and it can be found in the disposition Bach drew up for an organ in Bad Berka. On the other hand, the Nasat is not a rare stop. It combines with other flutes to make a particularly beautiful solo sound and can be found in many organs. The surviving archival record does not tell us much about Bach's involvement, and I am not suggesting that Bach put together, or determined, the dispositions for the organs at St. John's or Zschortau or St. Nicholas's—only that Bach's input as an organist, organ composer, and organ expert would have been solicited by his colleague Scheibe.

The authors of Bach's obituary describe the ironic situation that Bach—despite being "the greatest organist and clavier player that we have ever had," despite his mastery of organ playing, organ registration, and organ performance that displayed "each stop according to its character in the greatest perfection," despite his knowing "the construction of organs from one end to the other," and despite his unsurpassable ability to draw up and judge dispositions—"never enjoyed the good fortune, as he used to point out frequently with regret, of having a really large and really beautiful organ at his constant disposal."[18] The comment is interpreted to mean that Bach was dissatisfied with the modest instruments he worked with as organist—whether in Arnstadt, Mühlhausen, or Weimar, even though it was there that he composed most of his much-admired organ compositions. Peter Williams has gone one step further even, extending Bach's dissatisfaction to the organs in Leipzig.[19] Without question, the obituary comment reflects a deeply felt regret, but it appears to me to be a wistful regret, rather like that expressed by a city dweller who, while continuing to live happily in a large and bustling city for 30 or more years, nevertheless frequently rues not living in a beautiful and peaceful country home. Bach expressed his regret that he was never organist of a large and very fine organ with full knowledge that he had in fact turned down job opportunities in Halle and Hamburg, organist positions where he would indeed have had regular access to organs both large and beautiful. As Thomaskantor and director of music in Leipzig, Bach would not have possessed the keys to the city's organs, which were held by the appointed organists, but no doubt exists that Bach on occasion played, may even have been inspired by, the organs of Leipzig. Only that he might have composed more for the organ had he had *regular access* to a large and beautiful instrument is to be regretted.

A particularly vexing relationship that is difficult to untangle is that between Bach and Scheibe's son, Johann Adolph. No evidence exists that Johann Adolph studied with Bach,[20] but Bach nevertheless agreed to provide a reference letter when Johann Adolph applied, unsuccessfully, for the position of organist at Freiberg Cathedral in 1731. Johann Adolph had failed as well in his attempt to become organist at St. Nicholas's in 1729. As discussed in chapter 9, in Leipzig Johann Adolph's audition was overseen by Bach. Forkel reported that Johann Adolph was so "offended" at not being offered the position that he later attacked Bach in his music journal, sparking a controversy that went on for several years.

The "attack" on Bach has ensured that Johann Adolph Scheibe, who served as Kapellmeister at the court of King Christian VI of Denmark from 1740 to 1746 and was active in Leipzig, Hamburg, and Denmark as composer, educator, translator, and critic, holds an uneasy place in Bach scholarship. However, it is a well-known fact that Bach and Johann Adolph, and probably Johann Scheibe the builder as well, together visited the organ built by Heinrich G. Trost for the court chapel in Altenburg in 1739, not long before the organ was examined and two years after Johann Adolph published his views on Bach's compositional style. Johann Adolph's account of the visit, which appeared in September 1739 in a pseudonymously composed letter published in his journal, *Der Critische Musicus*, allows one to draw inferences about views possibly shared among Bach, Johann Adolph, and his father regarding designing organs, visiting organs, and setting temperaments in organs.[21]

Scheibe lived and worked in Leipzig for most of his career and enjoyed the esteem of Bach as well as of the organists with whom he worked. Perhaps he also enjoyed a collegial relationship with Hildebrandt, who also worked in Leipzig. Bach must have taken opportunities to play the clavichords and other keyboard instruments built in Scheibe's and Hildebrandt's workshops. Indeed, one imagines a lively and active engagement between Bach and the Leipzig organ builders. Scheibe's and Hildebrandt's career paths differed, however. Hildebrandt worked as an independent organ builder in numerous locations. Because he studied and worked with Gottfried Silbermann, because a good number of his organs have survived, and because his magnum opus in Naumburg was examined by Bach, many have seen a special relationship between Hildebrandt and Bach. Hildebrandt's decision to spend so much of his career in Leipzig, his stint as organ builder in Sangerhausen, his appointment in 1730 as court organ builder to Christian, Duke of Saxe-Weißenfels, and his having been chosen to build the large organ in Naumburg—all are seen as evidence of Bach's hand in Hildebrandt's career. Scheibe, on the other hand, worked almost exclusively in one place, the cosmopolitan city of Leipzig. Because Scheibe and Bach worked together for a quarter of a century, because Bach examined Scheibe's magnum opus at St. Paul's and wrote an extensive, supportive report, and because Bach examined the only Scheibe organ that has survived, it is now time to acknowledge the special relationship between them. Bach's hand also can be seen in Scheibe's career. From 1717, when he examined the university organ, to 1746, when he examined the Zschortau organ, from the renovation at St. Nicholas's in 1724–25 to Scheibe's regular maintenance of Leipzig organs throughout a 40-year career, Bach supported Scheibe's organ-building activity, even putting his own reputation at risk by siding with Scheibe when he demanded additional payments.

Two weeks after Bach's death in July 1750, Hildebrandt accepted Silbermann's invitation to oversee the building of the large new organ for Dresden's Hofkirche. Hildebrandt had lived and worked in and around Leipzig for almost 30 years and must have left Leipzig for Dresden (or Silbermann's shop in Freiberg) in early August. As Hildebrandt's biographer observed, the importance and appeal that Leipzig had exerted on him since he first met the *Director Musices* in 1723 must have died together with Bach.[22] Had Scheibe survived Bach, he surely would have experienced a similar loss. That we so ardently look for Bach's influence on the organs of Leipzig (and elsewhere) and that we are so intrigued by Scheibe's connection with the great composer is understandable. Yet surely it is now obvious: Scheibe's work and his reputation as an organ builder stand on their own merit.

Directory of Appendixes
on the Companion Website

The University of Illinois Press has created a website to accompany *Johann Scheibe: Organ Builder in Leipzig at the Time of Bach*, where materials that cannot be made available in this book, such as full texts of contracts and reports, minutes recorded by Leipzig University professors, and tables detailing organ maintenance, are provided. Readers are encouraged to consult this resource at https://go.press.uillinois.edu/scheibe-organ-builder.

Appendix A: Archival Documents and Selected Texts
   from Early Printed Sources (in English and German)
Appendix B: Expenditures for Wages and Materials, St. Paul's Organ, 1710–16
Appendix C: Selected Minutes, Leipzig University's Concilium Decemvirorum
   (in German and English)
Appendix D: Disposition Comparisons
Appendix E: Schedules of Maintenance and Repairs of Leipzig Organs

Appendix A: Archival Documents and Selected Texts
from Early Printed Sources (in English and German)

No.	Reference	Date	Description and Source
1	Scheibe 1710	6 September 1710	Johann Scheibe, estimate for moving and repairing the St. Paul's organ Source: UAL, Rep. I/XVI/I 15, fols. 65–67
2	Kuhnau and Vetter 1710	25 September 1710	Johann Kuhnau and Daniel Vetter, memorandum (including dispositions) regarding moving, repairing, and modifying the St. Paul's organ Source: UAL, Rep. II/III/B II 6, fols. 1r–7v

No.	Reference	Date	Description and Source
3	Vetter 1710	24 November 1710	Daniel Vetter, letter to Leipzig University's rector regarding Gottfried Silbermann's proposal Source: UAL, Rep. II/III/B II 6, fols. 9r–10v; also, UAL, Rep. II/III/B II 5, fols. 10r–12r.
4	Silbermann 1710	27 November 1710	Gottfried Silbermann, evaluation of the organ at St. Paul's and proposal for a new organ Source: UAL, Rep. II/III/B II 6, fols. 11r–16v
5	Contract 1710	ca. 17 December 1710	Unsigned and undated draft of contract with Johann Scheibe for the organ at St. Paul's Source: UAL, Rep. II/III/B II 5, fols. 28v–31r
6	Scheibe 1711	1 May 1711	Johann Scheibe, memorandum regarding his unsigned contract and difficulties with the St. Paul's project Source: UAL, Rep. II/III/B II 6, fols. 25r–27r
7	Registrar 1712 and 1715	5 April 1712 5 July 1715	Notes for the record regarding unused materials Source: UAL, Rep. II/III/B II 6, fols. 32r–33r
8	Contract 1712	16 April 1712	Contract with Johann Scheibe for rebuilding the bellows at St. Paul's Source: UAL, Rep. II/III/B I 5, fol. 641r–v
9	Scheibe 1713	8 February 1713	Johann Scheibe, memorandum and estimates for finishing the St. Paul's organ Source: UAL, Rep. II/III/B II 8, fols. 13r–15r
10	Report 1713	4 March 1713	Christoph Donat II, report on the condition of the New Church organ Source: Stadtarchiv Leipzig, New Church Accounts, 1713–14, fols. 69–71
11	Scheibe 1714	21 August 1714	Johann Scheibe, memorandum regarding having met the terms of contract and requesting payment Source: UAL, Rep. II/III/B I 25, fols. 15r–16v

No.	Reference	Date	Description and Source
12	Contract 1715	26 May 1715	Contract with Johann Scheibe for completing the facade pipework Source: UAL, Rep. II/III/B II 5, fols. 79r–83r
13	Oath 1715	16 July 1715	Oath signed by Johann Scheibe Source: UAL, Rep. II/III/B II 6, fol. 34r
14	Mencke 1715	3 December 1715	Johann Burchard Mencke, memorandum and accounting regarding building the remaining stops in the St. Paul's organ Source: UAL, Rep. II/III/B II 5, fols. 46r–52r
15	Scheibe 1716a	24 February 1716	Johann Scheibe, memorandum regarding charges for rent Source: UAL, Rep. II/III/B II 5, fols. 53r–54r
16	Report 1716	15 May 1716	Georg Friedrich Kauffmann, report after examining the Gundorf organ and organist Source: Landeskirchenarchiv Dresden, Bestand 31999, Sign. 1155, fols. 6r–9r
17	Scheibe 1716b	29 October 1716	Johann Scheibe, memorandum regarding completion and examination of the St. Paul's organ Source: UAL, Rep. II/III/B II 5, fols. 55r–v and 68r–69v
18	Mencke 1716	22 November 1716	Johann Burchard Mencke, memorandum regarding the need to reward Scheibe Source: UAL, Rep. II/III/B II 5, fols. 56r–59r
19	Scheibe 1717	before 24 November 1717	Johann Scheibe, undated memorandum regarding the organ project's costs, the need for a reliable organist, and his appointment as organ builder to Leipzig University Source: UAL, Rep. II/III/B II 5, fols. 70r–72r
20	Sicul 1718	1718	Excerpts from Christoph Ernst Sicul's *Leipziger Jahrbuch* regarding the Scheibe organ at Leipzig University Source: Sicul 1718, 549–51, 195–99, 59–60

No.	Reference	Date	Description and Source
21	Scheibe 1718a	17 January 1718	Johann Scheibe, memorandum regarding not having received payment from Leipzig University Source: UAL, Rep. II/III/B II 5, fols. 77r–78r
22	Vetter 1718	28 January 1718	Daniel Vetter, memorandum regarding his role in the St. Paul's organ project Source: UAL, Rep. II/III/B II 5, fols. 73r–76r
23	Scheibe 1718b	28 December 1718	Johann Scheibe, memorandum regarding still not having received all of the promised payment Source: UAL, Rep. II/III/B II 5, fols. 84r–87r
24	Scheibe 1719	undated	Johann Scheibe, estimate for repairs to the St. Paul's organ, which had been damaged by extreme summer heat Source: UAL, Rep. II/III/B I 12, fol. 146; cited in Glöckner 2008, 164
25	Release 1720	26 March 1720	Release signed by Johann Scheibe Source: UAL, Rep. II/III/B I 12, fol. 166
26	Contract 1721	19 December 1721	Contract with Johann Scheibe for renovation of the New Church organ Source: New Church Accounts, 1721–22, fols. 49–59
27	Report 1722	8 November 1722	Georg Balthasar Schott, Christian Gräbner, and Johann Gottlieb Görner, report on the examination of Scheibe's renovation of the New Church organ Source: New Church Accounts, 1721–22, fols. 61–67
28	Report 1730	27 February 1730	Johann Scheibe, report on the condition of the St. Thomas's organ Source: Stadtarchiv Leipzig, Stift IX A 2, fol. 70r–v; first cited in Richter 1908, 52–53
29	Report 1731	6 December 1731	Johann Scheibe, report on the condition of the New Church organ Source: New Church Accounts, 1731–32, fol. 6r

No.	Reference	Date	Description and Source
30	Affidavit 1732	20 March 1732	Johann Scheibe, affidavit for employee Christian Francke Source: Stadtarchiv Leipzig, II Sekt. T (F) Nr. 393, fol. 13
31	Scheibe 1732	November 1732	Johann Scheibe, article for *Neue Zeitungen von Gelehrten Sachen* regarding his inventions Source: *Neue Zeitungen von Gelehrten Sachen* 18 (1732): 833–34
32	Dresden Ms. 1736	29 September 1736	Description of the organ at St. Paul's Church on the occasion of a visit Source: Dresden Ms., 42–43 (no. 76)
33	Proposal 1738	26 August 1738	Johann Scheibe, proposal to build an organ for the church in Gollma Source: Pfarrarchiv Gollma, "Acta, die Erbauung und Reparatur der Orgel betr.," fols. 1r–2r
34	Scheibe 1740	undated	Johann Scheibe, evaluation of the small organ at St. Thomas's Source: Stadtarchiv Leipzig, Stift IX A 2, fol. 105r–v
35	Silbermann 1741	[March 1741]	Johann Andreas Silbermann, description of the organ at St. Paul's on the occasion of a visit Source: *Silbermann-Archiv*, 156–58
36	Scheibe 1741	4 August 1741	Johann Scheibe, letter regarding his proposal to the church in Gollma Source: Pfarrarchiv Gollma, "Acta, die Erbauung und Reparatur der Orgel betr.," fol. 9r–v
37	Proposal 1742	22 May 1742	Johann Scheibe, proposal for a positive organ in the Georgenhaus, Leipzig Source: Stadtarchiv Leipzig, Georgenhaus Nr. 642, fol. 6; see also Hübner 2013, 351–52
38	Proposal 1744	undated	Johann Scheibe, proposal for a new organ in Zschortau Source: Dänhardt 2000, 3–4, citing Pfarrarchiv Zschortau, "Acta die Kirchen und Geistlichen Gebäude betreffend," fols. 187r–88r; also cited in Kaufmann 2000, 406–7

No.	Reference	Date	Description and Source
39	Contract 1744	30 June 1744	Contract for a new organ in Zschortau Source: Pfarrarchiv Zschortau, "Acta die Kirchen und Geistlichen Gebäude betreffend," fols. 194r–98v
40	Receipt 1745	17 April 1745	Receipt for additional payment signed by Johann Scheibe Source: St. John Accounts, 1745, fols. 101–3
41	Report 1746	ca. 1 November 1746	Johann Scheibe, report on the condition of the New Church organ Source: New Church Accounts, 1746–47, fols. 6r–7r
42	Proposal 1746	ca. 1746–47	Johann Scheibe, undated proposal to renovate the St. Jacob's organ, Köthen, with insertions by Bernhard Christian Kayser Source: Stadtarchiv Köthen, 3/402/C20, fols. 1r–3v
43	Contract 1747	28 June 1747	Contract with Johann Scheibe for renovation of the organ at St. Thomas's Source: St. Thomas Accounts, 1747–48, fols. 76–81, as cited in Spitta (1884–85) 1951 (slightly amended), vol. 2, appendix 8, 305–7

Appendix B: Expenditures for Wages and Materials, St. Paul's Organ, 1710–16

1   Expenditures for the first phase of the organ project at St. Paul's, 1710–12

2   Expenditures for the second phase of the organ project at St. Paul's, 1715–16

Appendix C: Selected Minutes, Leipzig University's Concilium Decemvirorum (in German and English)

Appendix D: Disposition Comparisons

1   Disposition of the organ in Zschortau: 1744, 1746, 2000

2   Disposition of the large organ at St. Thomas's, Leipzig, ca. 1700 and 1757

3   Disposition of the New Church organ, Leipzig, 1703–1833

4   Disposition of the organ at St. Nicholas's, Leipzig, 1694 and 1741

5   Disposition of the small organ at St. Thomas's, ca. 1700 and 1740

6   Disposition of the organ at St. Paul's, ca. 1700 and 1710

Appendix E: Schedules of Maintenance and Repairs of Leipzig Organs

Notes

Preface

1. Dähnert 1962, 5.

Chapter 1. Bach's 1717 Visit to Leipzig

1. Marshall and Marshall 2016, xxvi.
2. Vogel Annals, 1033.
3. Hütter 1993, 128.
4. Hütter 1993, ix.
5. Stiehl 1984, 40; also St. Thomas Accounts, 1670–71, fol. 20r: "11 T. 18 gr. [paid 24 December 1670] to the carpenter's 2 apprentices, who worked 7 days on the three columns under the organ."
6. J. F. Doles, examination report dated 27 July 1772, Stadtarchiv Leipzig, Stift IX A 34, fol. 33r.
7. J. G. Mauer, memorandum dated 18 March 1772, Stadtarchiv Leipzig, Stift IX A 34, fol. 11v.
8. Vogel Chronicle, 110.
9. Vogel Chronicle, 130–31.

Chapter 2. The Life and Work of Johann Scheibe

1. Kinsky 1910, 310. Information provided by the Museum of Musical Instruments, Leipzig University.
2. Stadtarchiv Leipzig, *Leichenbuch* 1748, fol. 221.
3. "Johann Scheibe, der Zeit bei einer löbl. Universität Leipzig Orgelmacher anno 1742 den 22. Aug. verfertigt, im Mai 62 Jahr." "Vermischtes" 1867.
4. Bach-Dokumente II, 549; Henkel 1986, 50n37; Theobald 1986, 90n9.
5. Henkel 1986, 50n37.

6. Michler 2005, 39 and unpublished notes. My thanks to Frau Barbara Michler for generously giving me copies of her late husband's article "Die Scheibe-Orgel in der Kirche St. Nicolai zu Zschortau" and his handwritten research notes.

7. Michler 2005, 39; also, Pape and Hackel 2015, 224. For the organ's disposition, see Theobald 1986, 83; or Petzoldt 2000, 321.

8. Michler 2005, 39.

9. Henkel 1986, 47; Flade 1953, 93.

10. See Henkel 1988, 114 and 121n15.

11. Kaufmann 2000, 404; Michler 2005, 40. In the 1860s the organ was sold to the church in Zehmen, near Borna, where it was installed, and altered, in 1865 by Emil Wiegand. Hackel and Pape 2012, 432.

12. Michler 2005, 40. The organ was damaged in 1877 by lightning and replaced in 1885 by a completely new one by Offenhauer. Hackel and Pape 2012, 275.

13. According to the following receipt, "On the date indicated below, eighteen taler—that is, 18 T.—were paid to me in cash, receipt of which I hereby acknowledge, and promise to repay the same eighteen T. as soon after Pentecost as I receive the money for the contracted new organ in Glesien." Johann Scheibe, receipt dated 3 June 1718, UAL, Rep. II/III/B I 12, fol. 171. Wilhelm Rühlmann Orgelbau built a new organ in 1901, retaining an old case that appears to be from the eighteenth century. It is not known whether the surviving case is Scheibe's. (Information from J. Kocourek.)

14. Henkel (1986, 48) listed Zscheila as among places where Scheibe built new organs and thanked Herbert Heyde for providing the information, but nothing more is known about this organ. An excerpt from a letter written by the pastor in Zscheila, Christian Gottfried Petzsch, is preserved at Leipzig University. Although Petzsch praises Scheibe and the St. Paul's organ, he makes no mention of a Scheibe organ in Zscheila. Further, we know from records in the Sächsisches Staatsarchiv Dresden (Bestand 10058 Meißen Nr. 2395, fols. 1–14) that one Johann Martini repaired the organ in Zscheila in 1712 and that Johann Ernst Hähnel made further repairs in 1735.

15. Stadtarchiv Leipzig, II. Sekt. T (F) Nr. 393, fol. 5r. Cited in Heller 2010, 117.

16. Sicul 1718 (appendix A-20), 199.

17. Affidavit 1732 (appendix A-30).

18. "Johann Hinrich Jentz von Lübeck 1745" was found inscribed on the frame of the C-side Manual wind chest in Zschortau. Dänhardt 2000, 22–23, 55.

19. St. Nicholas Accounts (appendix E-3), 1748–49, fol. 42; St. Thomas Accounts (appendix E-2), 1749, fol. 47; St. John Accounts (appendix E-5), 1749, fol. 64, and 1750, fol. 68.

20. "The organ builder, Scheibe, has died and his apprentice, Jen[t]z, has applied for his position" (Wäre der Orgelmacher, Scheibe, verstorben und hätte deßen Gesell, Jen[t]z, um seine Stelle angesuchet). Minutes of meeting dated 28 September 1748, UAL, Rep. I/XI/I 39, fol. 42v.

21. Flade 1953, 138n365.

22. St. Nicholas Accounts (appendix E-3), 1725–26, fol. 53; St. Thomas Accounts (appendix E-2), 1725–26, fol. 41; New Church Accounts (appendix E-4), 1725–26, fol. 34.

23. Mattheson 1740, 313.

24. J. A. Scheibe 1748, 374.

25. In Koska's recent study of Bach's private students (Koska 2019), J. A. Scheibe is listed in Category C, among "those who have unjustifiably been treated as Bach students in the relevant literature." Bach's testimonial on behalf of Johann Adolph (*NBR* 153 [no. 153]) refers to him as a "most zealous student of music" but does not claim that he trained or taught him.

26. See Glöckner 1990, esp. 119–25 and 132–33.

27. Glöckner 1990, 159; also, Bach-Dokumente I, 137 (note C).

28. Bach-Dokumente I, 137 (note C).

29. J. A. Scheibe 1745, introduction, unnumbered p. 19.

30. See Edwards Butler 2020.

31. *NBR*, 153 (no. 153); for the German original, see Bach-Dokumente I, 136 (no. 68).

32. See Hauge 2018 for a catalog and description of J. A. Scheibe's compositions.

33. A positive is a modest-sized organ, usually without a pedal. It is fixed in position—that is, it cannot be carried about like a portative.

34. Stockigt 2016, 61–62; also Leaver 2018, 50. Whether this is the same Johann Christoph Hennig who built in Zschortau is unknown.

35. The Leipzig city council approved the purchase on 20 December 1719 and Ficker was paid 46 florins 14 groschen in fiscal year 1720–21 "for a positive that will be used at home wedding ceremonies, and whose cost will be offset each time by a 1-taler payment to the school." School Accounts, 1720–21, fol. 42. Ficker is considered to be the first in Germany to build a fortepiano not based on Bartolomeo Cristofori's action model. He was in Zeitz from 1705, where, in addition to undertaking various organ projects—mostly repairs—he apparently was very active as a stringed keyboard maker. For a description of Ficker's organ building activities, see Ahrens 2002, 140–45. (Ahrens was not aware of Ficker's activities in Leipzig.)

36. Organs "in Bach's surroundings" near Leipzig are discussed in Henkel 1988.

37. Henkel 1988, 115.

38. Heller 2010, 111.

39. Minutes A (appendix C), 21 April 1718, fols. 477–79; St. Paul Accounts A, 1719–20, fol. 158. Also Glöckner 2008, 163.

40. Rubardt 1948, 173.

41. Scheibe 1732, 833.

42. Scheibe 1732, 834.

43. Cited in Heyde 1985, 75. The organ is also described briefly in J. A. Scheibe's dedication to his father (see page 20).

44. Scheibe 1732, 834.

45. J. A. Scheibe 1738, unnumbered pp. 4–5.

46. Report 1722 (appendix A-27), fol. 65–66.

47. Proposal 1744 (appendix A-38), fol. 188r.

48. J. A. Scheibe 1748, 374.

49. Mencke 1716 (appendix A-18), fol. 59r.

50. Vetter 1718 (appendix A-22), fol. 75r.

51. Schering 1941, 112.

52. J. A. Scheibe 1738, dedication (see page 20).

53. Flade 1926, 50; Flade 1953, 94.

54. Klotz 1934, 229.

55. Williams 1984, 130.

56. Wolff 2000, 1.

57. See Bach's report on the organ in Zschortau (page 27).

58. Rubardt 1950, 105.

59. Becker 1842, col. 427.

60. Schering 1926, 257.

61. Kuhnau and Vetter 1710 (appendix A-2), fol. 3r.

Chapter 3. *The Organ for Zschortau*

1. Dänhardt 2000, 37.

2. Marshall and Marshall 2016, 208.

3. Theobald 1986, 83; Petzoldt 2000, 321; Michler 2005, 38; Pape and Hackel 2015, 224. According to Michler, Hennig was from Großschepa, a small village about 6 kilometers/3.5 miles from Wurzen; according to Pape and Hackel, he was from Hohenpießnitz. It is unknown whether he was the same Johann Christoph Hennig who may have been from Annaberg, according to Stockigt 2016, who in 1719 was contracted to build a 6-stop organ (with pull-down pedal) for Leipzig's Royal Catholic Chapel.

4. Andreas Christian Brandes, memorandum dated 1 June 1744, Superintendentur Archiv Delitzsch, "Acta Bau- und Reparatur-Sachen zu Zschortau betr . . . 1660–1756," unnumbered folio.

5. Henkel 1986, 48; Michler 2005, 38–39.

6. Proposal 1744 (appendix A-38).

7. Contract 1744 (appendix A-39).

8. Johann Christoph Cademann, letter dated 13 July 1746, Superintendentur Archiv Delitzsch, "Acta Bau- und Reparatur-Sachen zu Zschortau betr . . . 1660–1756," unnumbered folio. For the full letter, see Petzoldt 2000, 280; or Edwards Butler 2013, 2.

9. Johann Christoph Cademann, undated letter, Superintendentur Archiv Delitzsch, "Acta Bau- und Reparatur-Sachen zu Zschortau betr . . . 1660–1756," unnumbered folio.

10. Bach-Dokumente II, 424 (no. 545).

11. For Bach's organ examination reports, see Wolff and Zepf 2012, 139–48; or *NBR*, nos. 31, 42, 59, 62, 72, 235, and 236; also Williams 1984, 139–54.

12. Superintendentur Archiv Delitzsch, "Acta Bau- und Reparatur-Sachen zu Zschortau betr . . . 1660–1756," unnumbered folios. See Edwards Butler 2013, 2–3. The copy now in Delitzsch may be the copy mentioned by Theobald (1986, 81) as being in the Pfarrarchiv Zschortau.

13. Contract 1744 (appendix A-39), fol. 198v, reproduced in Theobald 1986, 82.

14. Superintendentur Archiv Delitzsch, "Zschortauische Kirch-Rechnung," 1745–46, fol. 220r–v; see also Michler 2005, 41–43.

15. "5 [taler] von H. Scheiben zu mahlung der Orgel." Superintendentur Archiv Delitzsch, "Zschortauische Kirch-Rechnung," 1745–46, fol. 218v.

16. See also Michler 2005, 43.

17. Information provided by Lothar Michler, Zschortau.

18. Dänhardt 2000. My thanks to Anne-Christin Eule for providing the report; additional details were provided in personal communications.

19. Rubardt 1950, 105–6.

20. Dänhardt 2000, 29.

21. Kuntze 1875, 7.

22. Cited in Friedrich 1989, 25.

23. Friedrich 1989, 25. Adlung (1768) 1961, § 59, 42 (cited in Krapf 1976, 2), describes horse veins as "either straps of horse skin or actual dried horse veins, leg tendons or sinews. They are more durable than common leather which has a tendency to crack."

24. Friedrich 1989, 25.

25. Dänhardt 2000, 29.

26. Scheibe 1732 (appendix A-31).

27. Sponsels are "in-set wooden strips on the top of the chest"; a bungboard or bung is "the air-tight panel clamped onto the front of a chest, allowing access to its innards when removed." Adlung (1768) 2011, 140.

28. My thanks to Konrad Dänhardt for this observation.

29. Dänhardt 2000, 22, 23 and 55.

30. Blanchard 1985, 178–79.

31. Cited in W. Müller 1982, 460.

32. See Friedrich 1989, 30–31, 181, and 214.

33. Silbermann used this construction when space between the keyboard and wind chest was extremely limited, but only for some notes, never for the whole compass.

34. M. Faulkner 2009, 18 (Boxberg 1704, 81).

35. Henkel 1986, 48.

36. Wolffheim 1911, 41–42.

37. Rubardt 1937. See companion website.

38. David 1951, 104; Bach-Dokumente I, 170 (no. 89).

39. Dähnert 1980, 285–86. Schrammek 1983a, 51, gives an identical version.

40. Theobald 1986, 84.

41. Blanchard 1985, 176–79.

42. Kaufmann 2000. Petzoldt's brief history of the organ and the associated table of its various dispositions were written before the 2000 restoration. See Petzoldt 2000, 280–85 and 322–23.

43. M. Faulkner 2009, 22 (Boxberg 1704, 87).

44. Praetorius (1619) 1976, 137.

45. Adlung (1768) 1961, § 180, 132. There are two examples of Bordun 16′ in a small organ: the organ Apitzsch built in Leutzsch in 1729 included a Bordun 16′ in the treble range (from g to c³), as did Hildebrandt's organ for Lindenau, built in 1732.

46. Flute douce 4′ was built by Casparini (Görlitz, 1697–1703), Johann Joshua Mosengel (Königsberg, 1698), Tobias G. Trost (Langensalza, 1697–1701), Georg Christoph Stertzing (Jena, 1706), Thayssner (Merseburg Cathedral, 1706–13), Scheibe (Leipzig, St. Paul's, 1710–16), Heinrich G. Trost (Waltershausen, 1724–30), Finke (Gera, St. John's, 1721–25), Schröter (Alach, 1726), and C. F. Wender (Mühlhausen, St. Mary's, 1734–38).

47. M. Faulkner 2009, 23 (Boxberg 1704, 88).

48. Adlung (1768) 1961, § 146, 96.

49. Greß 1989, 36. In his small two-manual organs, on the other hand, Silbermann most often placed Octav Bass 8′ as the third Pedal stop. Only one small two-manual organ has Trompete 8′ as its third Pedal stop.

50. Adlung (1768) 1961, § 205, 153.

51. Volckland built Violon 16′ and Violon 8′ in his organs for Elxleben near Erfurt, built 1749–51, and Elxleben near Arnstadt, built c. 1750. Adlung (1768) 1961, 216–27; Friedrich 2005, 212.

52. Adlung (1768) 1961, 264; Reichling 2000, 55.

53. The organ builder in 1727 was Johann George Gordt (also Görke), from Mittweida. Gernhardt and Börger 2006, esp. 11, 39, and 71. The suggestion that Bach may have requested or been consulted concerning the alterations to the organ—in addition to the Violon 8′, the temperament may have been altered (from meantone) and the pedal coupler changed from being permanent to switchable—has never been proved.

54. Kirchliches Archiv Leipzig, Sign. 1249, fol. 15r. See chapter 10.

55. Gernhardt 2011.

56. Eichler 2018, 29–30.

57. Eichler 2018, 42–44.

58. Dänhardt 2000, 7.

59. M. Faulkner 2009, 24 (Boxberg 1704, 89).

60. Greß 1989, 72–73.

61. Reichling 2000, 55.

62. Friedrich 1989, 42.

63. "C,D–c¹ original Becher Nadelholz; Köpfer und Stiefelspitzen Rotbuche; Stiefelmantel aus Weißblech; Kehlen Hartholz, beledert; Krücken Eisen, geschmiedet." H. Werner 1997, 49.

64. Adlung (1768) 1961, § 389, 47.

65. Adlung (1768) 1961, 230.

66. Hartmann 1841, 32.

67. Friedrich 1989, 157.

68. Dresden Ms., 39; Dähnert 1980, 148.

69. Albrecht emendation in Adlung (1768) 1961, § 389, 46.

70. Friedrich and Dietl 1995, 55.

71. Greß 2001, 60, 99, and 95; Dähnert 1980, 99, 101, 238, and 252.

72. Friedrich 1989, 154.

73. See Zavarsky 1975, 87.

74. Scheibe 1716b (appendix A-17), fol. 68r; Sicul 1718 (appendix A-20), 60.

75. Mattheson (1739) 1954, 469.

76. M. Faulkner 2009, 21 (Boxberg 1704, 85).

77. Friedrich 1989, 43.

78. Cited in Friedrich 1989, 94n270.

79. Heinrich G. Trost, Großengottern organ proposal dated 12 October 1714, in Friedrich 1989, 154.

80. See Mahrenholz 1942, 77.

81. Dänhardt 2000, 47.

82. For a discussion of mixture characteristics, see Vogel 2003; also Greß 1989, 51, and Klotz 1978.

83. In this period, the German term *Eingebäude* refered to all the organ's inner components, excluding the pipes: the pipe rack, keys and frames, trackers and roller boards, trace-rods, squares and trundles. Dähnert (1953) 1971, 89. See also Adlung (1768) 1961, § 47, 36.

84. Proposal 1744 (appendix A-38).

85. Praetorius and Compenius 1936, 23.

86. Krapf 1976, 29; Werckmeister (1698) 1970, 37.

87. Werckmeister 1715, 61–72. Werckmeister's *Kurzer Unterricht* was also published in Mizler 1737, pages 58–68. Descriptions of Werckmeister's system can be found in Arnold (1965, 204) and Poletti (2006, 115n16).

88. "Weil das Orgelwerck stärcker als er accordiret ausgefallen wäre und er mit dem accordirten quanto des Macherlohns nicht auskommen könnte, sondern großen Schaden hätte, also noch um einen Nachschuß und Zulage von 80. Thlr. gebethen haben wollte." British Library, London, Add. Ms. 33965, fol. 169r.

89. British Library, London, Add. Ms. 33965, fol. 169r. Also, Bach-Dokumente I, 169 (no. 89).

90. Theobald 1986, 85; also Michler 2005, 41.

91. Schrammek 1983a, 49.

92. Dänhardt 2000, 6.

93. Johann Lorenz Bach's disposition for an organ in Lahm, built 1730–32 by Heinrich Gottlieb Herbst, included Flute douce 4' in the Hauptwerk and Flute traversiere 4' in the Hinterwerk. Johann Lorenz was Bach's student, in Weimar, from 1713 to 1717.

94. Theobald 1986, 90.

95. Dänhardt 2000, 6.

96. Rubardt 1963.

97. Williams 1984, 154.

98. Greß 1989, 49.

99. Michler, handwritten notes kindly made available to the author by Frau Barbara Michler.

100. The new division had Flauto traverso 8', Rohrflöte 8', Flauto amabile 4', and Octave 2'. Offenhauer also built new keyboards and a pedalboard, replaced the stop labels with porcelain insets, and replaced the three existing wedge bellows with three box bellows. He removed the Tremulant and probably also the Super Octava 1'. Dänhardt 2000, 3.

101. Willy Strube, Magdeburg, was the advisor. Unfortunately, although original documents were available, incorrect conclusions were drawn, which affected the two divided stops (Viol di Gamba 8' and Hohlflöte 3', divided between c^1 and $c\sharp^1$) especially. The two treble sliders, from $c\sharp^1$ on, received the Quint 2–2/3' and Tierce 1–3/5 ', and the toeboards were altered accordingly. The disposition of the second division was changed to Quintatön 8', Rohrflöte 4', Spitzflöte 2', and Zimbel II, and Super Octava 1' was again

placed in the main division. The renovation was examined on 23 September 1954 by W. Strube. Dänhardt 2000, 3.

   102. Dänhardt 2000, 37.

Chapter 4. Building the Organ for St. Paul's

   1. Flade 1926, 50.

   2. Flade appears to have relied on an article published by Ernst Müller (1915), organist at St. Paul's. Without providing citations, Müller claimed that on 1 May 1711 Scheibe swore to build "a good instrument for the glory of God" and that the three-manual, 56-stop organ, for which Müller provided a disposition, "cost only 2,926 taler."

   3. Minutes B (appendix C), 10 September 1710, fols. 25–26.

   4. A. Q. Rivinus, "Die Ursachen Warum die Orgel weg zunehmen" (The reasons for removing the organ), Minutes B (appendix C), 10 October 1710, fols. 73–75.

   5. Kuhnau and Vetter 1710 (appendix A-2).

   6. Kuhnau and Vetter 1710 (appendix A-2), fols. 1v–2r.

   7. Kuhanu and Vetter 1710 (appendix A-2), fol. 3v.

   8. Vetter 1718 (appendix A-22), fol. 73v.

   9. Kuhnau and Vetter 1710 (appendix A-2), fol. 4r.

   10. Kuhnau and Vetter 1710 (appendix A-2), fol. 3r.

   11. Kuhnau and Vetter 1710 (appendix A-2), fol. 5r–v.

   12. Kuhnau and Vetter 1710 (appendix A-2), fols. 6r–7v.

   13. Vogel Chronicle, 118–19. See Schering 1926, 317; or Dähnert 1980, 183.

   14. Minutes B (appendix C), 13 October 1710, fol. 99.

   15. According to E. Müller (1915, 224), who did not cite specific sources, proposals were requested from organ builders Ritter—no first name is supplied—Silbermann, and Scheibe.

   16. Kuhnau's letter does not survive. Lehmann's letter of 29 September 1710 to Freiberg's city council, in which he describes Kuhnau's request, is cited in W. Müller 1982, 415.

   17. "Jener kam vor etlichen Jahren aus Straßburg mit guten *Attestatis,* daß er nicht nur in Straßburg, sondern auch an unterschiedenen Orten in Franckreich, herrliche Orgelwerk und *Clavecins* verfertiget. Daher ich ihm auch damahls eine *Recommendation* nach Freyberg mitgab, wo ihm gleich der Bau eines grossen Orgelwerkes anvertrauet wurde, das er mit grossen Ruhme verfertiget, und eine ganz ungemein saubere und *accurate* Arbeit geliefert." Kuhnau 1717, 235.

   18. "Seines gleichen an fundamentaler mathematisch mechanischer Scientz in *Organopoeia* nicht angetroffen zu haben." Reported by Lehmann in a letter to Freiberg's city council dated 29 September 1710; cited in W. Müller 1982, 415.

   19. W. Müller 1982, 415. For Müller's discussion of Silbermann's unsuccessful attempt to build an organ at St. Paul's, Leipzig, see W. Müller 1982, 365–67; also, W. Müller 1969, 67–72.

   20. For the contract and disposition, see W. Müller 1982, 416–18. As built, the organ had 44 stops.

   21. Minutes B (appendix C), 20 November 1710, fol. 133r.

   22. Silbermann 1710 (appendix A-4).

   23. Silbermann 1710 (appendix A-4), fols. 11r–12r.

24. Silbermann 1710 (appendix A-4), fols. 12v–13r.

25. Silbermann 1710 (appendix A-4), fol. 13r–v.

26. W. Müller 1969, 72n8.

27. Vetter 1718 (appendix A-22), fol. 74r.

28. Vetter 1718 (appendix A-22), fol. 74r.

29. Vetter 1710 (appendix A-3).

30. Vetter 1710 (appendix A-3), fol. 9r.

31. Vetter 1710 (appendix A-3), fol. 9r–v.

32. "In seventeenth-century and eighteenth-century organistic parlance," Krapf wrote, gravity (*gravitätisch*) "connotes not one single characteristic but a composite of qualities, such as: well-developed bass sound, majestic, dignified, noble, commanding respect, profound, solemn." Krapf 1976, 16n27.

33. Krapf 1976, 42; Werckmeister (1698) 1970, 51–52.

34. Adlung (1768) 1961, § 177, 125.

35. Adlung (1758) 1953, 443.

36. See Williams 1967, 152.

37. Krapf 1976, 43; Werckmeister (1698) 1970, 53.

38. M. Faulkner 2009, 19 (Boxberg 1704, 83).

39. Greß 1989, 40.

40. Minutes B (appendix C), 27 November 1710, fols. 144–47.

41. Minutes B (appendix C), 13 October 1710, fol. 99.

42. Minutes B (appendix C), 27 November 1710, fols. 145–47. According to Schering (1926, 318; also reported in David 1951, 45), a contract with Silbermann was drafted, but Silbermann refused to sign. I could find no evidence of a contract with Silbermann in any form. It seems that Schering consulted an index to Council minutes (UAL, Rep. II/III/B II 9) and misunderstood items that referred to Silbermann's arrival and to council's consideration of his proposal.

43. "Dem Herrn *Rectore Magnifico* H[err] D[octor] Schmid wider erstattet, so dieselbe dem Orgelbauer von Freyberg vor seine anhero Reise und Bemühung bezahlt, 20 [Taler]." St. Paul Renovation, week 2–7 February 1711, fol. 230.

44. Minutes B (appendix C), 4 December 1710, fol. 154.

45. Vetter 1718 (appendix A-22), fol. 74v.

46. Schering 1926, 318–19.

47. Flade 1926, 50; Flade 1953, 93.

48. W. Müller 1982, 367–68.

49. Leipzig University's own accounts differ slightly: expenses totaled 2,886 taler (plus the 200 taler paid to Scheibe when he demanded reimbursement for work done over the contract).

50. Scheibe 1717 (appendix A-19), fol. 71r–v; also draft in hand of Vetter, UAL, Rep. II/III/B II 5, fol. 61.

51. According to Praetorius ([1619] 1976, 115–16), organ-building improvements that had occurred approximately 90 years before—that is, around 1529—could be seen in instruments such as the organ at St. Paul's in Leipzig. The date of around 1528 is cited by Wustmann (1909, 40); David (1951, 44); and Dähnert (1980, 182–83).

52. "The old organ at St. Paul's in Leipzig, which was set up in the year 1537 and again brought into good order and built by Josias Ibach in the year 1627" (In der alten Orgel der Pauliner Kirche zu Leipzig, so Anno 1537 gesetzet, und Anno 1627 wiederum ganz neu von Josua Ibachin angerichtet und verfertiget worden). Fabricius 1756, 43–44. Regarding Fabricius's tenure as university music director, see Maul 2010, especially 35–41.

53. Heller 2010, 120–21. Ibach's work was examined by Georg Engelmann (organist at St. Thomas's and St. Paul's), Samuel Scheidt (court music director in Halle), and Caspar Schwarze (organist at the cathedral in Merseburg).

54. See the discussion in A. Werner (1900, 423–29), which includes transcriptions of the evaluations; also, more briefly, Heller 2010, 120–21.

55. Heller 2010, 121. Donat received 40 guilders in 1685–86 and 184 guilders 24 groschen in 1686–87; in the same year, the bellows pumper was paid 16 guilders 18 groschen. St. Paul Accounts A, fols. 3 and 6. Without citing a source, Dähnert (1980, 183) reports anonymous repairs in 1654 that cost 24 guilders and 44 guilders 18 groschen.

56. "There was also a small organ up high beside the large organ, but because it could no longer be used, about twenty years ago it was taken down and the case ripped apart. The pipes were melted down and used during the renovation of the large organ so that more registers could be added to it than were there before" (Neben dieser hat in der Höhe noch ein kleiner Orgelwerk gestanden, weil es aber nicht gebraucht werden können, ist es vor etlich zwanzig Jahren zernommen und das Gehäuse abgerissen, die Pfeiffen sind eingeschmeltzet und bey Renovirung der grossen Orgel verbraucht, und also mehr Stimmen, als hiebevor darinnen gesessen, darein gebracht worden). Vogel Chronicle, 119.

57. Scheibe 1710 (appendix A-1).

58. UAL, Rep. II/III/B I 6, fol. 37r–v; also, St. Paul Renovation.

59. Minutes B (appendix C), 18 October 1710, fol. 103.

60. See Scheibe 1714 (appendix A-11), fol. 15r; also, Mencke 1715 (appendix A-14), fol. 47v.

61. See Scheibe 1711 (appendix A-6), fol. 25r.

62. Contract 1710 (appendix A-5).

63. UAL, Rep. II/III/B I 6, fol. 37r–v.

64. Löffler 1931, 282. Trost worked with three organ apprentices. A carpenter's apprentice was paid only 18 groschen per week. Lodging for Trost and his four workers cost 15 groschen weekly.

65. UAL, Rep. II/III/B I 6, fols. 37r–v and 38v–39r.

66. Scheibe 1714 (appendix A-11), fol. 15v.

67. Minutes C (appendix C), 24 March 1712, fol. 9.

68. "Zum Schluß des Orgelbaues auff seinen recompens, 2 Taler." St. Paul Renovation, fol. 635.

69. Contract 1712 (appendix A-8).

70. Minutes C (appendix C), 26 June 1712, fol. 11v; St. Paul Renovation, fol. 645v.

71. UAL, Rep. II/III/B I 6, fols. 43–44.

72. Minutes B (appendix C), 18 December 1710, fol. 173.

73. Minutes B (appendix C), 16 May 1711, fol. 354. Likewise, concerning the project not undertaken by Silbermann in Leipzig, Flade (1931, 127) observed that Silbermann "never would have bound himself by an oath, as was desired in Leipzig."

74. Scheibe 1711 (appendix A-6), fol. 25r–v.

75. Scheibe 1711 (appendix A-6), fol. 25v.

76. Vetter 1718 (appendix A-22), fols. 74v–75r.

77. Scheibe 1711 (appendix A-6), fol. 26r; Minutes B (appendix C), 16 May 1711, fols. 359–60.

78. W. Müller 1982, 120–38.

79. Scheibe 1713 (appendix A-9).

80. Minutes D (appendix C), 7 February 1714, fol. 49r.

81. Minutes D (appendix C), 30 May 1714, fol. 53v.

82. Minutes D (appendix C), 18 June 1714, fol. 68r–v.

83. Minutes B (appendix C), 15 June 1713, fols. 545–46.

84. Bach-Dokumente I, 154 (no. 83).

85. Minutes B (appendix C), 15 June 1713, fol. 551.

86. Scheibe 1714 (appendix A-11), fols. 15r–16r.

87. "Legire ich der Pauliner Kirche 1,500, sage Fünffsehen Hundert Rathstaler, welche Sie zu ihrer Nothwendigkeit, insonderheit zu Ausbauung der Orgel gebrauchen mag," Gottlieb Gerhard Titius, Last Will and Testament dated 8 April 1714, UAL, Rep. II/III/B I 11, fol. 1v. Sicul (1718, 261) also mentioned the gift: "In his Last Will and Testament dated 8 April 1714, he [Titius] made a substantial gift for the completion [enlargement] of the beautiful St. Paul's organ" (Derselbe [Titius] in seinem Testament de dato den 8 Aprilis 1714 zu Ausbauung der schönen Pauliner-Orgel ein ansehnliches legiret hat).

88. Minutes D (appendix C), 21 February 1715, fol. 68v.

89. Minutes A (appendix C), 7 March 1715, fols. 167–68; also, Glöckner 2008, 160. There is no mention of the estimates Scheibe had provided in February 1713.

90. Minutes A (appendix C), 7 March 1715, fol. 171; also, Glöckner 2008, 160.

91. Contract 1715 (appendix A-12).

92. Contract 1715 (appendix A-12), fols. 79r, 79v, and 80r.

93. Contract 1715 (appendix A-12), fol. 80r–81r; Oath 1715 (appendix A-13).

94. Contract 1715 (appendix A-12), fol. 81v.

95. Minutes D (appendix C), 21 November 1715, fol. 69b.

96. Minutes D (appendix C), 21 November 1715, fol. 69b.

97. Minutes E (appendix C), 21 November 1715, fols. 263v–64r.

98. Mencke 1715 (appendix A-14).

99. Mencke 1715 (appendix A-14), fol. 47v.

100. As Gerhard Krapf (1976, 3fn9) explains, "tin and lead occasionally turn into a non-metallic white powder which looks somewhat like saltpeter."

101. Mencke 1715 (appendix A-14), fols. 48v–49r.

102. Mencke 1715 (appendix A-14), fol. 48r; Minutes A (appendix C), 5 December 1715, fol. 225r.

103. Mencke 1715 (appendix A-14), fol. 48v.

104. Draft of contract and list of materials required, UAL, Rep. II/III/B II 5, fols. 65r–67v. The wording of the contract is almost exactly the wording of the contract signed 26 May 1715.

105. Scheibe 1716b (appendix A-17).

106. Scheibe 1716b (appendix A-17).

107. Mencke 1716 (appendix A-18), fol. 56r.

108. Mencke 1716 (appendix A-18), fols. 58v–59r.

109. Minutes A (appendix C), 7 November 1715, fols. 206–7, 210.

110. Minutes D (appendix C), 21 November 1715, fol. 69b.

111. Minutes A (appendix C), 5 December 1715, fol. 225.

112. Scheibe 1716a (appendix A-15), fols. 53v–54r.

113. UAL, Rep. II/III/B I 12, fol. 91.

114. Sicul 1718 (appendix A-20), 550–51.

115. See appendix A-7 (memoranda dated 5 April 1712 and 5 July 1715).

116. "Dito ferner *anticipando*, auff Abschlag seiner zu hoffenhabenden *recompens* auf Befehl gegeben." St. Paul Renovation, fol. 353.

117. W. Müller 1982, 124n650.

118. Appendix B-1, fols. 635 and 573.

119. Appendix B-2, Ref. H.

120. Mencke 1716 (appendix A-18), fol. 59r.

121. W. Müller 1982, 134–35.

122. Scheibe 1718a (appendix A-21).

123. Scheibe 1717 (appendix A-19), fol. 72r. The undated memorandum was written after a severe storm in the summer of 1717 and before 24 November 1717, when Rechenberg requested reimbursement of 6 taler given to Scheibe as the first installment for repairing pipework before the organ's examination (UAL, Rep. II/III/B I 12, fol. 106).

124. Minutes A (appendix C), 28 January 1718, fols. 460–62; see Glöckner 2008, 161; and Bach-Dokumente II, 60 (no. 88), for partial transcriptions. Neither Glöckner nor Bach-Dokumente II includes the specific comments of council members, which are found in Minutes E (appendix C), 28 January 1718, fols. 363r–64r.

125. Minutes A (appendix C), 3 February 1718, fol. 469; also, Glöckner 2008, 161–62.

126. Settlement agreement with Scheibe dated 11 February 1718, UAL, Rep. II/III/B I 12, fol. 167r–v; for the complete text, see Glöckner 2008, 162–63.

127. Glöckner 2008, 163–64.

128. Scheibe 1718b (appendix A-23).

129. J. S. Bach, report on examining the St. Paul's organ (see pages 92–93).

130. Release 1720 (appendix A-25). Glöckner (2008, 164) read "inc. [inclusive]" as "nicht," which leads to the mistaken conclusion that the university did not waive Scheibe's rent.

131. Minutes A (appendix C), 3 February 1718, fols. 469–70.

132. Minutes A (appendix C), 21 April 1718, fols. 477–79; see also Glöckner 2008, 163.

133. "Organopoeo, laut concl. Decemv.: Michael. 1718, 12 [Taler]. Michael. 1719, 12 [Taler]. Michael. 1720, 12 [Taler]." St. Paul Accounts A, 1719–20, fol. 58 (see appendix E-1). Thus, Scheibe was paid retroactively from Michaelmas 1717—that is, from approximately the end of the one-year warranty period. (The date of 1713 given by Dähnert [1980, 308] should be corrected.)

Chapter 5. Bach's Examination of the St. Paul's Organ

1. This chapter expands on my article "Bach's Report on Johann Scheibe's Organ for St. Paul's Church, Leipzig: A Reassessment." See Edwards Butler 2016.

2. Minutes A (appendix C), 22 October 1717, fols. 440–41. There is no evidence that Lindner was an organ builder; he studied music, mathematics, and law and was appointed cathedral organist in Freiberg on 25 February 1711. See W. Müller 1982, 129n678.

3. Kuhnau told Mattheson how pleased everyone was with "the fine variety of stops, especially the soft ones, and with the light action of the four manual keyboards" (Mit jedermanns Vergnügen an der schönen Variation derer sonderlichen doucen Stimmen, und an dem leichten movement der Manual-Claviere, derer 4 sind). Kuhnau 1717, 235.

4. St. Paul Accounts B, 1717–18, fol. 47v (see appendix E-1); Bach-Dokumente I, 189 (no. 109).

5. Bach-Dokumente I, 189 (no. 109).

6. The edge of the page is bound here and the exact number illegible.

7. Scheibe 1717 (appendix A-19), fol. 70v.

8. UAL, Rep. II/III/B I 12, fols. 106 and 107.

9. UAL, Rep. II/III/B I 12, fol. 108.

10. Minutes A (appendix C), 7 December 1717, fol. 448.

11. Sicul 1718 (appendix A-20), 198–99.

12. UAL, Rep. II/III/B II 5, fols. 63r–64r (only Bach's signature is autograph). For the original German text, see Bach-Dokumente I, 163–65 (no. 87).

13. Bach-Dokumente I, 189 (no. 109); *NBR*, 86 (no. 73). See also Bach-Dokumente IX, 138 (no. 111), for a reproduction of Bach's handwritten receipt.

14. Although it has been proposed, there is no evidence that Bach performed the Weimar cantata *Nun komm, der heiden Heiland* BWV 61 during this visit to Leipzig. See Dürr and Jones 2006, 76.

15. Vetter 1718 (appendix A-22), fol. 75r; cited in Bach-Dokumente I, 166 (no. 87).

16. See Chrysander 1867, 235–41.

17. Chrysander 1867, 240.

18. Krapf 1976, 11, 9, 3; Werckmeister (1698) 1970, 15, 13, 4.

19. "It is a major fault to build organs too cramped" (Ein Hauptfehler ist, wenn man die Orgeln allzuenge bauet). Adlung (1768) 1961, § 347, 22.

20. See Wolff and Zepf 2012, 150.

21. W. Müller 1982, 129–30.

22. Vetter 1710 (appendix A-3), fol. 9v.

23. Scheibe 1710 (appendix A-1), fol. 66. Also, the surviving draft of the contract states that Scheibe would be responsible for "the entire organ—except the case, which will be made by the joiner." Contract 1710 (appendix A-5), fol. 30r.

24. See Edwards Butler 2016; also, Edwards Butler and Butler 2006, 301n21.

25. Silbermann 1710 (appendix A-4), fol. 11v.

26. Vetter 1710 (appendix A-3), fol. 9r.

27. For example, Glöckner refers to the "substantial faults in construction [*erhebliche Konstruktionsmängel*]," especially the "continuously unstable wind pressure [*vor allem den stets instabilen Winddruck*]." Glöckner 2008, 160–61.

28. Glöckner 2008, 165.

29. See Heller 2010, 125–26.

30. "Habe ich gefunden (1) daß das überaus starcke und dem Wercke höchst nach-theilige Windstossen gänzlich weggeschafft, und das Werck, bey allen angezogenen Stimmen, beständig hinreichenden, richtigen und gleichen Wind hat, und also auch gar nicht mehr Windseich ist." UAL, Rep. II/III/B II 10, fol. 74r.

31. See Werckmeister (1698) 1970, 42, 27–28, and 23; and Krapf 1976, 33, 21, and 27.

32. Adlung (1768) 1961, § 276, 193, referring to Werckmeister (1698) 1970, 42.

33. "Instead of a roller board one sometimes uses, when there is adequate space, an oak frame to which the rollers are attached" (Anstatt des Wellenbretts bedienet man sich bisweilen mit großer Commodität eines eichenen Rahmens, an welchen man die Wellen bevestiget). Adlung (1768) 1961, § 50, 38. "Our ancestors attached the rollers to a roller board, which has now been replaced by a frame" (Die Vorfahren befestigten die Wellen an dem Wellenbrete, an dessen Stelle bedient man sich ietzo eines Rahmens). Adlung (1758) 1953, § 111, 357.

34. "Some builders eliminate the roller board, mounting the rollers instead on a strong oaken frame; this seems to have the additional advantage of more permanent key align-ment. . . . Others experiment with a turned-around placement of the roller board. . . . It is best to retain conventional roller board construction. If the [trackers to the] keyboards are equipped with adjusting screws, they can be constantly maintained in good regula-tion." Krapf 1976, 11.

35. Kuhnau and Vetter 1710 (appendix A-2), fol. 3r.

36. "[The organ builder] already admitted that the organ bellows had suffered dam-age, yet it was his fault that this has happened." Minutes B (appendix C), 16 May 1711, fol. 357.

37. Scheibe 1718b (appendix A-23), fol. 86v.

38. Scheibe 1713 (appendix A-9), fol. 14v.

39. Scheibe 1716b (appendix A-17), fol. 68r.

40. Bach-Dokumente IX, 137 (no. 110).

41. Schalmey 4′ was added to the Pedal in 1755 by Schweinefleisch.

42. Scheibe 1716b (appendix A-17), fol. 68r.

43. Scheibe 1717 (appendix A-19), fol. 70v.

44. Quoted in Wolff and Zepf 2012, 152.

45. Scheibe 1718a (appendix A-21), fol. 77v.

46. J. A. Scheibe 1738, unnumbered introduction. Previously cited in Edwards Butler 2010, 90.

47. Flade 1953, 166.

48. The use of the term "Hinterwerk" is found nowhere in the documents relating to the organ project—it first appears in the disposition published by Sicul—and probably came to be used because it reflected the position of the division's pipes: at the back, with no facade pipes, functioning as an "echo" while providing its sound from a distance.

49. See Scheibe 1716b (appendix A-17), fol. 68r; and Scheibe 1717 (appendix A-19), fol. 70r.

50. Three slightly different versions exist of Scheibe's accounting of expenses over and above the contract. The earliest (see appendix A-17) was submitted on 29 October 1716,

shortly before Scheibe completed the organ in November; another version, undated (see appendix A-19), appears to have been written shortly before the organ's examination in 1717; yet another version, also undated (UAL, Rep. II/III/B I 12, fol. 168r, cited in Glöckner 2008, 163), provided the basis for the settlement agreement arrived at on 11 February 1718.

51. Mencke 1716 (appendix A-18), fol. 59r.

52. Minutes B (appendix C), 26 March 1711, fol. 292.

53. The bill, from Mattheus Weydlich, specifies 12 Schock (60 pieces each) of *Doppelscheiben* (large windowpanes) at 1 T. 7 gr. per Schock, and 12 Schock of *Spiegelscheiben* (small windowpanes) at 13 gr. 6 pf. a Schock. On the same day, the glazier was paid for placing windowpanes in the window near the altar, which had 21 panes. The large window behind the organ had 42 panes. St. Paul Renovation, fols. 353, 369, 370, 493, and 496.

54. Scheibe 1711 (appendix A-6), fol. 26r; also cited in Heller 2010, 122–23.

55. Minutes B (appendix C), 16 May 1711, fol. 359.

56. Scheibe 1717 (appendix A-19), fol. 70v.

57. Minutes A (appendix C), 28 September 1717, fols. 430–31.

58. Scheibe 1718a (appendix A-21), fol. 78r.

59. Minutes A (appendix C), 21 April 1718, fol. 479.

60. *Silbermann-Archiv*, 158; also, Bach-Dokumente V, 162 (no. B 485a).

61. Scheibe's struggle with the university over payment is described in Glöckner 2008, 161–64.

62. Heller 2010, 116–19.

63. *NBR*, 441.

64. Adlung (1768) 1961, § 287, 212.

65. Scheibe 1718a (appendix A-21), fol. 77v.

66. "Noch nicht reine ausgespielet" is the phrase used by the scribe. This translates directly as "not yet properly played in," which suggests that the new organ needed time to settle in before its tuning became stable. This is no doubt one reason why organs were generally tuned and corrected before the official examination, which often did not take place until after a one-year warranty period.

67. Minutes A (appendix C), 28 January 1718, fols. 460–61; also, Bach-Dokumente II, 69 (no. 88).

68. See Vetter 1718 (appendix A-22), fol. 75r; Wolff and Zepf 2012, 46, citing Bach-Dokumente I, 166–67 (no. 87).

69. Sicul 1718 (appendix A-20), 199, cited in Bitter 1881, 4:101, and Bach-Dokumente I, 166 (no. 87).

70. Sicul 1718 (appendix A-20), 199. "Complet," the French word used by Sicul in its superlative form, meant "complete" or "vollständig." One talked of "the fullness, completeness, perfection, achievement or accomplishment of a piece of work." See Ludwig 1716, s.v. "Vollständigkeit."

71. "Die alte Orgel wurde von der Mittags-Seite weggenommen, und nach der Abend-Seite gebracht, die Pfeiffen umgegossen, und ein *incomparables* Werk aufs neue aufgeführet." Weiz 1728, 10–11.

72. J. A. Scheibe 1738, unnumbered introductory pages.

73. Adlung (1768) 1961, § 307, 251.

74. "Certainly, the organ's concept was excellent and it contained a profusion of sweet, strong, very unusually timbered registers. For this reason, among the organs in Leipzig, the most important organists chose the one from Scheibe, for it was here that they liked to display their virtuosity and prove that in fact an organ built properly in all its parts is solely and alone the king of all instruments" (Die Orgel war allerdings ihrer Anlage nach ein treffliches Werk und enthielt liebliche, kräftige, ganz eigenthümliche Stimmen der Klangfarbe nach in Fülle. Die bedeutendsten Orgelspieler wählten daher meistens unter den in Leipzig befindlichen Orgeln die von Scheibe, denn hier vermochten sie ihre Virtuosität geltend zu machen und zu beweisen, dass in der That eine in allen ihren Theilen tüchtig gebaute Orgel einzig und allein die Königen sämmtlicher Instrument sei). Becker 1842, 427.

75. Flade 1953, 93–94.

76. David 1951, 45.

77. Busch 1995, 130.

78. See *Silbermann-Archiv*.

79. *Silbermann-Archiv*, 156–58.

80. Glöckner 2008, 160–61.

81. Ahrens 2007, 57.

82. Spitta (1884–85) 1951, 2:287.

83. Flade 1931, 127.

84. Flade 1926, 50.

85. Schering 1926, 317.

86. Klotz 1934, 229.

87. Keller 1967, 23.

88. Matthaei 1950, 144.

89. Rubardt 1961, 496.

90. Dähnert 1986, 11.

91. David 1951, 49.

92. Flade 1953, 93–94.

93. See Schering 1941, 112.

Chapter 6. Disposition and Tonal Character of the St. Paul's Organ

1. Sicul 1718, 195–97; also cited in Bach-Dokumente I, 167 (no. 87). For Sicul's complete account, see appendix A-20 (Sicul 1718).

2. The drawing is reproduced as well in Bach-Dokumente IX, 137 (no. 110); and Wolff and Zepf 2012, 90–91. The drawing of the stop knobs was originally between pp. 13 and 14 of volume 1 (1714–37) of the Riemer Chronicle but has been missing since about 1972 (communication from Carla Calov, Stadtarchiv Leipzig).

3. Dresden Ms., 42–43 (no. 76). Edited by Paul Smets, with contributions from Christhard Mahrenholz and Ernst Flade, the collection was published in 1931 and is known variously as *Orgeldispositionen*, Smets, and Dresden Hs. (or Dresden Ms.).

4. *Silbermann-Archiv*, 156–58.

5. Contract with Gottlob Göttlich dated 5 December 1780, UAL, Rep. II/III/B II 10, fols. 1r–3v.

6. *Silbermann-Archiv*, 157–58.

7. Adlung (1768) 1961, vol. 1, 251n58 (footnote added by Johann Lorenz Albrecht).

8. Spitta (1873–80) 1964, 2:117–19; Spitta (1884–85) 1951, 2:287–88.

9. See David 1951, 94–95.

10. Dähnert 1980, 182–83.

11. Harmon 1981, 358–59.

12. Williams 1984, 129.

13. See Silbermann 1741 (appendix A-35).

14. Wolff and Zepf 2012, 90–91.

15. Rubardt 1961, 496 and 505n5, citing Stieda 1938; Rubardt 1963.

16. Stieda 1938, 79.

17. "Einen Species-Ducaten vor H. Casparini, Orgelbauern in Breßlau zum Gratial, wegen des überschickten Orgel-Rißes und Einen [Guilder] vor aufgewendetes porto zu unterschiedenen mahlen hin und wieder zu schreiben." St. Paul Renovation, 28 January 1711, fol. 224.

18. Boxberg's treatise (1704) is available in facsimile, with translation and commentary by Mary Murrell Faulkner (2009).

19. The organ was built in the years 1708 to 1711. Its disposition is included in *SeN*.

20. Stadtarchiv Leipzig, Stift IX A 34, fols. 74r-75r. There are discrepancies with the disposition as published in Boxberg's monograph.

21. "For the costs he incurred, 16 florins [paid] 18 November 1702 [to] Johann Heinrich Gräbner, who was brought here from Dresden and consulted regarding building a new instrument" (16 fl. [an] Johann Heinrich Gräbnern, so von Dresden anhero verschrieben und umb Verfertigung eines Neuen Werks consultiret worden, vor ufgewandte Kosten bezahlet, den 18. Novembris ao: 1702). New Church Accounts, 1702–3, fol. 39. The case drawing Gräbner submitted is preserved in the City History Museum Leipzig under the call number K IV/329. The context suggests that Gräbner was not hired as consultant for the new organ (built by Donat) but was one of the builders who made a proposal.

22. See Scheibe 1713 (appendix A-9).

23. Busch 1995, 130.

24. Williams 1984, 130.

25. J. A. Scheibe 1738, unnumbered introduction.

26. Scheibe may have built a new Octav 2′ (see Scheibe 1713, appendix A-9).

27. Vogel Chronicle, 118–19.

28. Vetter 1718 (appendix A-22), fol. 75r.

29. Dähnert 1980, 92.

30. Dresden Ms. 1736 (appendix A-32).

31. Eberlein 2009, 76, citing Burgemeister 1973, 225, and *SeN*, 6.

32. Dresden Ms., 87 and 89.

33. Silbermann included Chalumeau in the 1742 proposal for a new organ in Zwickau, too, but the funds could not be raised for the project.

34. Dähnert 1962, 90.

35. It may be that Hildebrandt had previously added the Chalumeau to the cathedral organ in Merseburg when he carried out a renovation in 1734–35. See Dresden Ms., 67–68, for the disposition.

36. Ingrid Elizabeth Pearson, "Delicacy, Sentimentality, and Intimacy: The Chalumeau as 'Signifier,'" paper presented at 1998 Clarinet Fest Symposium, Ohio State University.

37. Lawson 1992, 83–84.

38. See Lawson 1981.

39. Lawson 1981, 312.

40. Flade 1953, 138n366.

41. M. Faulkner 2009, 23 (Boxberg 1704, 88).

42. Fock 1974, 189, cited in Greß 1989, 53.

43. "Cornett 5fach . . . giebt dem Vollenwerke, eine schöne Force, ist auch nebst dem Principal 8. Fuß, zu tractirung eines Chorals schön zu gebrauchen." J. F. Walther 1727, 18, cited in Bergelt 2012, 114.

44. M. Faulkner 2009, 23 (Boxberg 1704, 88).

45. Heinrich Compenius II and his son Esaias II renovated the organ in 1627–30. Heller 2010, 121. According to T. Schneider (1937, 48) a signature stop of the Compenius family was the Rohrflöte.

46. Inexplicably, in later dispositions recorded in proposals or contracts for repairing or renovating the organ, whether by Göttlich (1780, UAL, Rep. II/III/B II 10, fol. 3r–v) or Jehmlich (1834, UAL, Rep. II/III/B II 11, fols. 29r–30r), there is absolutely no mention of the Brust-Pedal stops.

47. For the disposition, see Adlung (1768) 1961, vol. 1, 237–39.

48. According to Agricola (1758, 502, cited in Q. Faulkner 1993, 60), a plenum registration based on Principal 8′ had to include a 16-foot flute: "If the Principal is only an 8′, then a 16-foot Gedackt, Bordun, Quintadena or Rohrflöte can and must be drawn with it" (Das Flötenwerk wird bey dem vollen Werke nicht mit gezogen. Ausser wenn das Principal nur achtfüßig ist; so kann und muß ein 16 füßig Gedackt, Bordun, Quintadena oder Rohrflöte dazu gezogen werden).

49. Untersatz 32′ was added in 1822 by Mende. UAL, Universitäts-Rentamt 454I–454II, Film 357, Aufnahme 8; also, Heller 2010, 127.

50. See, for example, dispositions for Schnitger's organ (1695) in St. John's, Magdeburg (Adlung [1768] 1961, vol. 1, 254–55); Stertzing's organ (1706) at St. Michael's, Jena (Adlung [1768] 1961, vol. 1, 244–45); Contius's organ (1716) for the Market Church in Halle (Adlung [1768] 1961, vol. 1, 239–40); and Hildebrandt's organ at St. Wenceslas, Naumburg (Adlung [1768] 1961, vol. 1, 263–64).

51. "In dem Hinter Werckgen," St. Paul Renovation, fol. 632; Sicul 1718, 196.

52. UAL, Rep. II/III/B II 10, fol. 3r–3v.

53. Adlung ([1768] 1961, § 146, 96) reported that "organ builders prefer to make the pipes of wood . . . in order to imitate as far as possible the characteristic recorder sound."

54. "Sertin 8′ is a reed that, even though it is stopped, because of its sharp intonation and beating, nevertheless imitates the muted trumpet called Sertin. Most organ builders call the stop Sordun [Sordino]." Dresden Ms. 1736 (appendix A-32), 43. The mention of the stop "beating" suggests that the stop was played with tremulant.

55. "In place of the Vox humana, however, another register called Sordino" (an der Stelle Vox humana aber, ein ander Register Sourdine genannt). Contract 1721 (appendix A-26), fol. 53.

56. Praetorius (1619) 1976, 199; T. Schneider 1937, 49–50.

57. "Die gedämpffte Trompeta von Metall ist ein gedackt Rohrwerk, und hat einen gar angenehmen, doch nicht allzustillen resonanz." Dresden Ms., 50. In 1713 the organ was repaired and renovated by Johann Gottfried Brumme.

58. Christian Heinrich Wolf, memorandum presented 20 December 1794, UAL, Rep. II/III/B II 10, fol. 20r–v. The tin from the old Vox humana weighed 8½ pounds.

59. "Sordino 8′, dessen Corpora von weißem Blech mit zinnernen Hütchen, welches die *Vocem humanum* präsentiren kann." Engel 1855, 14.

60. "Mit jedermans Vergnügen, an der schönen *Variation* derer sonderlichen *doucen* Stimmen." Kuhnau 1717, 235.

61. Adlung (1768) 1961, vol. 1, 257.

62. Bach consulted with Wender during a visit to Mühlhausen in 1735. Wolff and Zepf 2012, 112.

63. Dresden Ms. 1736 (appendix A-32), 43.

64. M. Faulkner 2009, 23 (Boxberg 1704, 88).

65. For the Görlitz disposition, see Wolff and Zepf 2012, 26–27; or M. Faulkner 2009, 11–15 (Boxberg 1704, 74–77). For the contract disposition, see Flade 1953, 18–19; or M. Faulkner 2009, 53–56.

66. Mahrenholz 1942, 45.

67. Stadtarchiv Leipzig, Stift IX A 34, fols. 74r–75v.

68. Dresden Ms. 1736 (appendix A-32), 43. For later references to the stop, see UAL, Rep. II/III/B II 10, fol. 3r–v (1780); UAL, Rep. I/X/62, fol. 9v–11r (1790); and UAL, Rep. II/III/B II 11, fols. 29r–30r (1834). (See appendix D-6.)

69. In later records of the disposition, Helle Cymbel II becomes Tertian II (in 1780 and 1790) and then Cimbel III (in 1824). UAL, Rep. II/III/B II 10, fol. 3r–v; UAL, Rep. I/X/62, fols. 9v–11r; UAL, Rep. II/III/B II/11, fols. 29r–30r. (See appendix D-6.)

70. "Einen lieblichen, scharfen und Violenklang." Adlung (1758) 1953, 461; also, Adlung (1768) 1961, § 188, 140–41.

71. Sicul 1718 (appendix A-20), 60.

72. Scheibe 1716b (appendix A-17), fol. 68r.

73. Mahrenholz 1942, 77.

74. Thayssner also built Viol di Gamba 8′ stops for the organs he renovated in Naumburg (St. Wenceslas, 1695–1705; see Dähnert 1962, 191–92; also, Adlung [1768] 1961, vol. 1, 262) and Merseburg (cathedral, 1706–13; see W. Schneider 1829, 19).

75. "One wished to imitate the sound of this elegant instrument also in organs; but this demands a good master" (In den Orgeln hat man den Klang dieses lieblichen Instruments auch nachäffen wollen; es wird aber ein guter Meister dazu erfordert). Niedt (1721) 1976, 115. Adlung ([1768] 1961, § 206, 153) remarked, "The stop depicts the Violdigamba well if one succeeds in making it right [if the nail is hit on the head]" (Es stellt die Violdigamba wohl vor, wenn es recht getroffen ist).

76. Friedrich 1989, 43.

77. "Ein ausnehmend Register und vor andern sehr schön ausgearbeitet." Report dated 14 October 1739, cited in Friedrich 1989, 175.

78. "At the last, its tone exceeds in beauty that of many other so-called Violas da Gamba in organs" (Wenigstens übertrift dieser Klang an Schönheit den Klang vieler andern sogenannten Orgel-Viola da Gamben). Adlung (1758) 1953, 497; Q. Faulkner 1993, 60.

79. "Silbermann was an enemy of strongly stringy stops—especially the narrow-scaled *Gambe naturelle* (cf. organ in Greiz) with cylindrical scaling, which he characterized as 'saccharine, not worth the trouble, and dry'" (Silbermann war ein Feind der stark streichenden Stimmen. Besonders die engmensurierte *Gambe naturelle* (vgl. Orgel zu Greiz) mit zylinderförmiger Mensur bezeichnete er als 'süßlich, unwürdig und dürr'). Flade 1953, 187, citing Wolfgang Hilf, "Gottfried Silbermanns letzte Orgel," *Wissenschaftliche Beilage der Leipziger Zeitung*, Nr. 4 (14.1.1883) and Nr. 5 (18.1.1883).

80. Mahrenholz 1942, 89–90. In Dresden's Frauenkirche, for example, the Hauptwerk had a stop called "Viol di gamba oder Spiel-Flöte 8." Dresden Ms., 27.

81. Mattheson ([1739] 1954, 469), for example, recommended that "for solo melodies played on a separate organ keyboard, one does well to use the stop that is called Viola da Gamba" (Zu einzeln Melodien auf einem besondern Orgel-Clavier bedienet man sich mit guter Art eines Stimmwerks, welches Viola da Gamba heisset).

82. According to Greß (1989, 46), it served this double role in the organs of Silbermann.

83. Viol di Gamba 8' "lends itself well to playing continuo and gives a special gravity to the Ripieno or full organ" (läst sich gut zum General-Bass gebrauchen, und giebt dem Ripieno oder vollem Werke eine sonderbahre Gravität). M. Faulkner 2009, 21 (Boxberg 1704, 85).

84. On the basis of the Mühlhausen proposal, Dähnert (1962, 97) made the assumption that it was at Bach's instigation that Hildebrandt built two string stops (Viol di Gamba 8' and Fugara 4') for the organ in Naumburg.

85. Flade n.d., s.v. "Stertzing." If Flade's information is correct, the disposition recorded by the organist Christoph Herthum in 1708 that is cited in Wolff and Zepf (2012, 44) must reflect the organ *before* G. C. Stertzing's renovation.

86. My thanks to Markus Zepf (Leipzig Bach Archive) for suggesting this cautionary observation.

87. The three-manual organ was built by Johann Stephan Schmaltz in 1758–60. Johann Andreas Bach, owner of the Andreas Bach Book, and possibly the Möller Manuscript as well, was the church's organist beginning in 1744, and the new organ was built according to his plans. Wolff and Zepf 2012, 78–79.

88. Schlimbach 1801, 191–92:

Viola di Gamba. Violdigambe. Eine der feinsten und zärtlichsten Orgelstimmen, wenn sie von einem Meister gearbeitet ist. Sie gibt in langsamen gebundenen Sachen, vorzüglich von f oder g bis c^2–e^2—einen schmelzenden, schmeichelnden Ton an, erfordert aber eine ihr ganz anpassende Spielart, und verträgt nichts weniger als geschwinde bunte Sätze. Sie ist ein Flötenwerk von 8 und 4 Fuß, doch ist 8 Fuß ihre gehörige eigenthümliche Größe, wenn sie vollkommen sein soll. Schade wäre es, ein so schönes Register von holz oder schlechtem Metall zu machen, es ist schon gutes Zinn werth. Manche Orgelbauer machen die Gambe cylinderförmig, manche auf Gemshornart, oben enger als unten. Ich ziehe die letzte Art vor. Noch muß ich bemerken, daß sie eng mensuriert wird. Am besten hat mir die Gambe in der Orgel zu St. Michaelis in Ohrdruff gefallen. Und o wie schön behandelte sie mein mir unvergeßlicher Lehrer, der selige [Johann Andreas] Bach!

89. UAL, Rep. II/III/B II 10, fol. 3r–v; UAL, Rep. I/X/62, fols. 9v–11r.

90. Scheibe 1732 (appendix A-31), 833. Scheibe refers to the organ's six transmission stops—Principal 16′, Quintatön 16′, Octav 8′, Octav 4′, Quint 3′, and Mixtur V–VI—as stops "at 16′, 8′, 4′, 3′ and 2′," which indicates that the Mixtur V–VI in the Hauptwerk was based on 2′.

91. J. A. Scheibe 1745, unnumbered introduction:

Es müssen daher, um die Kirchen besser auszufüllen, und die Gemeine zu unterstützen, Mixturen, Quinten- und Terzenregister mit angebracht werden. . . . Wenn ich den Accord C anschlage, und ich habe zur völligen *Harmonie* das Principal 8 Fuß, die Octav 4 Fuß, die Octav 2 Fuß, Quinte-Nasat 3 Fuß und die Mixtur 4 Fach von 1 Fuß, so klingen bey diesem Accorde C, c, c¹, g, c², e², g², c³. In der Mixtur klingt zugleich bey dem c, auch e, g, c, bey dem e, auch gis, h, e, bey dem g auch h, d, g. Folglich höret man bey dem einzigen Accorde C: c, d, e, g, gis und h . . . [etc.] . . . erhielt auch das ganze Werk mehr Nachdruck und Schärfe, und war alsdann einer grossen Gemeine zur Genüge gewachsen.

92. Adlung (1768) 1961, § 267, 187 (emendation by Agricola); cited in Wolff and Zepf 2012, 72–73.

93. "Next are the reeds, or 'fool's pipes,' as some call them, since they often go out of tune and thus cause a lot of fuss and bother for the organist" (Es folgen die Schnarrwerke oder Narrwerke, wie sie andere nennen, weil sie sich oft verstimmen, und daher dem Organisten viel Mühe and Verdruß machen). Adlung (1768) 1961, § 104, 66. "I would nevertheless advise against putting too many reeds into an organ because of the dreadful task of tuning them" (So wollte ich doch nicht rathen, allzuviel Schnarrwerke in eine Orgel zu setzen, wegen der gräulichen Arbeit, die deren Stimmung verursacht). Adlung (1768) 1961, § 267, 187.

94. Thanks to Martin Pasi for this clarification.

95. "Die Corpora des Posaunen Baßes, sind recht langer, und gehöriger proportional Weite-Mensur, die Stöcke und Pfannen aber von guten, harten, recht glatt gearbeiteten Holtze, die Blätter oder Zungen von Meßing in recht gehöriger Stärcke, daher es den ganz gut und pompös sonirt, wegen der höltzernen Pfannen aber nicht so laut schreyet, sondern einen recht scharff gestrichenen Violon im Sono gleichet." Dresden Ms., 39.

96. "Weil der Posaunen Bass in der Neuen Dom Orgel ungefüttert, und dahero so sehr grollet, auch wegen den kleinen Mundstücken keine rechte gravität hat, und welches das vornehmste, solcher nur zum vollen Werke, und nicht zu eintzeln Stimmen, welches doch nothwendig wegen der Music seyn solte, und sonderlich bey einem Tutti ungemein wohlklingen würde, kan gebrauchet werden." Cited in Greß 1989, 76.

97. Bergelt 2012, 66–67.

98. Biermann (1738) 1981, 20–21; also, Vogel, Lade, and Borger-Keweloh 1997, 338–39.

99. The frontispiece appeared in *Eisenachisches neurevidirtes und beständiges Gesangbuch*, 10th ed. (Eisenach, 1763). For a reproduction, see Edwards Butler 2004, 59; or Edwards Butler 2008, 269.

100. W. Müller 1982, 120n620.

101. See Wolff and Zepf 2012, 109.

102. "Daß das alte Rück-Positiv, zu gewinnung mehreren Raumes auf dem Chor, nunmehro ins Haupt-Werk gebracht, mithin das Chor zu Aufführung starker musiquen

bequem gemacht werde." Buchstab 2002, unnumbered page, n. 482, citing Staatsarchiv Gotha, "Geh. Archiv XXVI, 148a," fol. 26.

103. "Das Rückpositiv sei wegzunehmen . . . so gewinne man Platz, daß die ganze fürstliche Kapelle am Chore musiciren könne." Löffler 1932, 172, citing a memorandum submitted by Gottfried Heinrich Stölzel dated 24 September 1734.

104. Wolff 2000, 312.

105. Glöckner 2008, 186.

106. Although it has been suggested that Bach assigned direction of these motets to a prefect, Reinhard Szeskus (2003) has shown that Bach was paid for quarterly oration performances throughout most of his time in Leipzig.

107. Wolff 2000, 313.

108. Bach-Dokumente II, 175 (no. 232); see also *NBR*, 136–37 (no. 136).

109. Sicul 1718, 71–73 and 116–17.

110. See Bach-Dokumente I, 166–67 (no. 87), where Vetter's comment is cited in the explanatory text to Bach's report.

111. Edwards Butler 2018, 61.

112. J. A. Scheibe 1738, unnumbered introduction.

Chapter 7. Construction Details of the St. Paul's Organ

1. *Silbermann-Archiv*, 158.

2. The width of the choir, between pillars, was 13½ Elle. This and other measurements in this paragraph were taken by Jehmlich, who made a detailed appraisal and proposal dated 27 January 1834. UAL, Rep. II/III/B II 11, fols. 28r–45v.

3. Praetorius (1619) 1976, 2–3.

4. Sicul 1718 (appendix A-20), 60.

5. Dresden Ms. 1736 (appendix A-32), 43.

6. *Silbermann-Archiv*, 158.

7. "Vor die Strahlen an der Orgel zu vergolden." St. Paul Renovation, fol. 515.

8. St. Paul Renovation, fols. 548r and 547v.

9. "At St. Paul's, I have built the organ case, which is joiner work, according to the drawing. It was contracted for 200 T., of which I have received 70. There remain therefore 130 T. owing. Johannes Gerlach, master joiner, 29 April 1711" (In der Pauliner Kirche habe ich das Orgelgehäuse was Tischler arbeit nach den Riß anbelanget gemacht, ist verdungen vor 200 T., darauf habe ich empfangen seibenzich rthl. Bleibt also 130 T. zu empfangen. Johannes Gerlach, Tischler Meister, den 29 April 1711). St. Paul Renovation, fol. 367.

10. Gerlach was paid 20 T. on 1 November 1710, 50 T. on 20 December 1710, 50 T. on 9 May 1711, 50 T. on 4 July 1711, and the remaining 30 T. on 15 June 1712. UAL, Rep. II/III/B I 6, fol. 40; also St. Paul Renovation, fols. 77, 152, 353, 429, and 669.

11. St. Paul Renovation, fol. 387.

12. "For 2½ Schock [a Schock is 60 pieces] of wool ticking, which are to be painted and used as curtains for the organ, 9 T. 9 gr." (Vor 2½ Schock wolle Zwilch bezahlt so zu Vorhängen vor die Orgel verbraucht und bemahlt worden, 9 T. 9 gr.). St. Paul Renovation, week 14–19 September 1711, fol. 493.

13. "Reimbursement of 8 gr. to M. Hüffner [who paid] the woman who sewed together the cloth for the organ. 2 gr. to the same for two paintbrushes" (Einer Frauen so das Gewant an der Orgel zusammen genahet, Mons. Hüffnern restitiret, 8 gr. Demselben vor 2 Pinsel, 2 gr.). St. Paul Renovation, week 14–19 September 1711, fol. 493.

14. "The decoration over the pipes in the organ, which consists of a cloth, the lowest side of which was contracted for 15 T., is delivered 27 June 1711, David Näther, sculptor" (Die Verzihrung an der Orgel über die Pfeiffen wegen angewießen so in Gewand bestehet, die underste Seite verfertiget betungen vor 15 T. geliefert den 27. Jun. 1711, Davidt Nather, Bilthauer). St. Paul Renovation, fol. 433.

15. Minutes A (appendix C), 24 September 1715, fols. 190, 192–93.

16. St. Paul Renovation, fol. 614.

17. Thanks to Markus Zepf (Leipzig Bach Archive) for this observation.

18. Scheibe 1716b (appendix A-17), fol. 68r–v.

19. "A piece of sculpture made for the organ, which was attached over the keyboard ... delivered 23 December ... David Näther, sculptor" (Ein Stück Bilthauer Arbeit verfertiget an die Orgel welches wo das Clavier ist oben drüber befestiget worden ... geliefert den 23. December ... Davidt Näther, Bilthauer). St. Paul Renovation, fol. 613.

20. St. Paul Renovation, fols. 353, 369, 370, 493, and 496.

21. Minutes B (appendix C), 16 May 1711, fols. 350 and 359.

22. Scheibe 1711 (appendix A-6), fol. 26r–v.

23. "To the handyman for hanging canvas on the window in the middle of the organ, 2 gr. For nails, 2 gr." (Das Fenster zwischen der Orgel mit Packleinwand behengen laßen, dem Handlanger so geholffen, 2 gr. Vor Nägel dazu, 2 gr.). St. Paul Renovation, week 13–18 July 1711, fol. 439.

24. St. Paul Renovation, fol. 493.

25. St. Paul Renovation, fol. 494.

26. *Silbermann-Archiv*, 157.

27. Contract 1710 (appendix A-5), fol. 30r.

28. Dresden Ms. 1736 (appendix A-32), 43.

29. Flade 1953, 26–27. "The stops ... are differentiated by certain colors on the knobs, each according to the manual or pedal windchest to which it belongs" (Die Register ... sind mit gewissen Farben an denen Knöpffen, jedes nach seiner Clavir- oder Pedal-Lade, worzu es gehöret, unterschieden). M. Faulkner 2009, 19 (Boxberg 1704, 82).

30. Minutes D (appendix C), 30 May 1714, fol. 53v.

31. "Schwartzgebeitzte Register Züge mit weißen Helffenbeinern Knöpffgens." St. Paul Renovation, fol. 350; Mencke 1715 (appendix A-14), fol. 52r.

32. Scheibe 1716b (appendix A-17), fol. 69r.

33. *Silbermann-Archiv*, 158.

34. "Alle Registerzüge sind falsch angelegt, die Wellenbretter ebenso unbequem, und die Abstracten entbehren der nöthigen Sauberkeit und Leichtigkeit, auch sind an den Enden nicht mit Pergament, sondern mit bloßen Bindfaden verwahret." Johann Gotthold Jehmlich, appraisal and proposal dated 27 January 1834, UAL, Rep. II/III/B II 11, fol. 36r.

35. Flade 1953, 27n76, with reference to Mattheson (1739) 1954, 460 [*recte* 466]. (Mattheson expresses the opinion that it is better to have an action that is "too hard, too sluggish, or has too great a key dip" and is "harder to play" than one that is "too easy to play" and where a key often stays down or does not easily return to its height, often resulting in ciphers.)

36. "Ich kan fast nicht mehr, helffen Sie mir trücken." *Silbermann-Archiv*, 158.

37. On the other hand, Boxberg claimed the pedalboard was "somewhat hard to play because seven springs [*Federn oder Scheren*] stand under each key." M. Faulkner 2009, 19 (Boxberg 1704, 82).

38. *Silbermann-Archiv*, 170; also, Bach-Dokumente II, 389 (no. 486).

39. "Große Orgelkenner beklagen daran, daß sie, was die Claviere anlanget, so gar schwer zu spielen ist" (Eminent organ experts complain about it that, as regards the keyboard [action], it is so very heavy to play). Adlung (1768) 1961, vol. 1, 233.

40. M. Faulkner 2009, 58.

41. Flade 1953, 27n76, citing (without page number) David Traugott Nicolai, *Kurze doch zuverlässige Beschreibung der großen Orgel in der Hauptkirche zu Görlitz* (Görlitz, 1797).

42. Dähnert 1962, 114.

43. Kuhnau and Vetter 1710 (appendix A-2), fol. 7v.

44. Vetter 1710 (appendix A-3), fol. 9r.

45. St. Paul Renovation, fol. 249.

46. Contract 1712 (appendix A-8).

47. Scheibe 1714 (appendix A-11), fol. 15r.

48. *Silbermann-Archiv*, 157.

49. St. Paul Renovation, fol. 280.

50. The glazier received 2 T. on 1 July 1711 for providing "good glass panes in the oval window in the bellows room" (ein Ovalfenster mit guten Glaß Taffeln in die Balge Kammer verglast, ist 2 T. bedungen und bezahlet, Leipzig den 1. Julius Anno 1711). St. Paul Renovation, fol. 445. "For panes in the organ window in the bellows room that goes into the alleyway" (Vor das Orgel Fenster mit Taffeln in die Balge Cammer so in das Gäßgen gehet). St. Paul Renovation, fol. 439.

51. Scheibe 1710 (appendix A-1), fol. 65; also, Vetter 1710 (appendix A-3), fol. 9r.

52. Werckmeister 1705.

53. "Daß also das volle Werk seinen gebührenden Zufall des Windes hat." Werckmeister 1705, § 38.

54. Sicul 1718 (appendix A-20), 196.

55. Scheibe 1732 (appendix A-31), 833–34.

56. This description is taken from Friedrich 1989, 30.

57. Scheibe 1732 (appendix A-31), 833.

58. Transmissions were built for Compenius organs in Kroppenstedt, Kloster Riddagshausen, Markranstädt (near Leipzig), Brüderkirche Altenburg, Predigerkirche Erfurt, Johanniskirche Gera, and in the Weimar castle organ. See T. Schneider 1937.

59. Heller 2010, 121.

60. Friedrich 1989, 29.

61. Dresden Ms. 1736 (appendix A-32), 43.

62. "Ferner taugen die Koppeln in den Manualen nichts und die Pedalkoppel für alle Manualstimmen fehlt und ist blos für 6. Stimmen im Hauptwerke, als Principal 16. Fuß, Octave 8. Fuß, Octave 4. Fuß, Quintatön 16. Fuß, Quinte 3. Fuß und Mixtur 6. fach, angewendet." Johann Gotthold Jehmlich, evaluation and proposal dated 27 January 1834, UAL, Rep. II/III/B II 11, fol. 36v.

63. St. Paul Renovation, fols. 191 and 187.

64. "4. Aus dem Posaunen Bass 16 Fuß, 21 Pfeiffen von guten Zinn, worunter 3 von Blech und 3 zerschnittene von Zinn." Registrar 1712 and 1715 (appendix A-7), fol. 32r–v.

65. "For soldering one needs bismuth" (Zum Löthen muß Wißmuth kommen). Scheibe 1713 (appendix A-9), fol. 14v.

66. Johann Scheibe, receipt dated 5 March 1712, St. Paul Renovation, fol. 632.

67. Contract 1715 (appendix A-12), fol. 79v.

68. Contract 1715 (appendix A-12), fol. 83r.

69. W. Müller 1982, 126.

70. Scheibe's estimate, "What further materials are required for the missing 18 registers," cited the following: "3 hundredweight of tin @ 26 T. per cwt., 78 T.; 3 hundredweight of lead @ 4 T. per cwt., 12 T.; ¼ hundredweight of bismuth for soldering, 5 T.; 1 cord of wood for [the] melting [pot], 4 T. 12 gr.; 45 boards, 3 T.; 4 lbs. brass wire for the Angehänge [connections between the trackers and the keys] of the 18 registers @ 8 gr. per lb., 1 T. 8 gr.; 4 lbs. *Dalch* for casting, 14 gr.; Oak for trackers for the registers, 2 T.; [total =] 106 T. 10 gr." UAL, Rep. II/III/B II 5, fol. 66r. According to organ builder Martin Pasi, *Dalch* may be chalk or *Kalk*, which is used for the sizing (paint) to prepare the metal sheets for soldering and is also used to size the casting cloth—that is, to seal it and keep it from burning too fast.

71. Appendix B-2, fol. 51r, G.

72. Contract 1715 (appendix A-12), fol. 83r.

73. Dähnert (1953) 1971, 91.

74. Thanks to Markus Zepf (Leipzig Bach Archive) for this observation.

75. "A tin pipe obviously costs more than a lead one of the same size, since a hundredweight of lead (according to prevailing economic conditions) will not cost over 4 taler, while the same amount of tin will cost 10 taler." Adlung (1768) 1961, § 319, 4.

76. Arp Schnitger's organ for St. John's in Magdeburg, built 1690–95, had four Principal stops in the facade, all "from English tin." Adlung (1768) 1961, vol. 1, 254–55. Stertzing's organ for St. George's in Eisenach, built 1697–1707, had "four beautiful pure tin Principal stops." Edwards Butler 2008, 237. The organ that the Casparinis built for the Church of St. Peter and Paul in Görlitz, in 1697–1703, had four facade Principals, all "from English tin." Adlung (1768) 1961, vol. 1, 232–33; also, M. Faulkner 2009, 11–13 (Boxberg 1704, 74–75).

77. Wolff and Zepf 2012, 142.

78. Cited in Greß 1989, 88.

79. Bendeler (1690) 1972, 2.

80. Werckmeister (1698) 1970, 67; Krapf 1976, 55.

81. Contract 1721 (appendix A-26), fol. 54.

82. "Das Materiale des zinnernen und metallnen Pfeifwerks ist im Allgemeinen schlecht und die Principalpfeifen im Gesicht können, wegen ihrer Mischung oder Legierung, gar nicht als *Principalia*, gelten, sondern müssen durch ganz neue, von reinen englischen Zinn ersetzt werden." Johann Gotthold Jehmlich, evaluation and proposal dated 27 January 1834, UAL, Rep. II/III/B II 11, fols. 37v–38r.

83. The list of materials required for making the pipes during the second building phase includes "sand for the casting table, 5 wheelbarrows from Thonberg, 1 T. 6 gr." Contract 1715 (appendix A-12), fol. 83r.

84. The process of casting on sand is described by Bendeler ([1690] 1972, 3–5), for example, in his chapter "On Pipes." See also descriptions in Yokota 2003 and Shull 2021.

85. Friedrich 1989, 41.

86. Greß 1989, 90.

87. M. Faulkner 2009, 17 (Boxberg 1704, 79).

88. Scheibe 1716b (appendix A-17), fol. 69r–v.

89. Scheibe 1714 (appendix A-11), fol. 16r.

90. "Das gantze werk, so itzo ein *Semiton* zuhoch, und daher weder *Cornet, Trombon* noch *Flauten* rein darinn zugebrauchen, tiefer auf Chorton zu bringen, wie auch nach einem heutzutage erheischenden und erträglichen *Temperament* zustimmen." Johann Christoph Bach, memorandum dated 16 March 1696, cited in Edwards Butler 2008, 260.

91. Scheibe 1716b (appendix A-17), fol. 69r–v.

92. "Die Pracht, der Nachdruck und die überaus bequeme und wohlklingende Temperatur dieses grossen Werks und aller andern von Ihm erbauten Orgeln zeigen die gröste Erfahrung und keine gemeine Geschicklichkeit." J. A. Scheibe 1738, unnumbered introduction.

93. See Edwards Butler 2020.

94. Wolff (2000, 316) claimed that this organ part could not have been performed on the Scheibe organ because he mistakenly believed at the time that the organ was set in Cammerton.

95. "Das gantze Werk, welches vorher in unrichtigen Cammer Ton gestanden, nunmehro in richtigen Chor Ton, mithin durch aus höher, und für die Kirchen-Musik bequemer den blasenden Instrumenten gleich, mit vieler Mühe umgestimmet habe." UAL, Rep. II/III/B II 10, fol. 11, cited in Heller 2010, 126.

96. "Auch ist die Temperatur und Stimmung neu im richtigen Chorton, und so, daß in allen 24 Tonarten rein gespielt werden kann." UAL, Rep. II/III/B II 10, fol. 16r., cited in Heller 2010, 126. Heller assumes that at the very least the organ was set in a well-tempered system, although a tuning approaching equal temperament would not have been out of the question.

97. "Das ganze Werk, so nach den Cammerton zu hoch und nach dem Chor Ton zu tief stehet, neu temperiren und in richtigen Chor-Ton, damit die blasenden Instrumente mit der Orgel harmonieren." UAL, Rep. II/III/B II 10, fol. 59r–v; cited in Heller 2010, 126. (Heller incorrectly gives fol. 54v as the source.)

98. Scheibe 1713 (appendix A-9), fol. 13r–v.

99. Scheibe 1711 (appendix A-6), fol. 26v.

100. Scheibe 1714 (appendix A-11), fol. 15v.

101. "Des alten Tremulantens, welcher aussen an dem Canale angebracht ist, und also die Bälge *ruini*ret, einen neuen fertigen, und solchen inwendig in die Hauptröhre legen." Contract with Johann Gottlob Trampeli dated 3 July 1801, UAL, Rep. II/III/B II 10, fols. 58v–59r.

102. Scheibe 1716b (appendix A-17), fol. 68v; also, *Silbermann-Archiv*, 158.

Chapter 8. Renovations and Maintenance

1. Cited in Schumann 1973, 374.
2. Dresden Ms. 1736 (appendix A-32), 42.
3. Contract 1721 (appendix A-26), fol. 49.
4. St. Thomas Accounts (appendix E-2), 1721–22, fol. 46.
5. St. Nicholas Accounts (appendix E-3), 1724–25, fol. 49.
6. According to Krapf (1976, 3n9), "most so-called corrosion is 'tin pest.' Tin and lead occasionally turn into a non-metallic white powder which looks somewhat like saltpeter."
7. Report 1713 (appendix A-10).
8. New Church Accounts, 1713–14, fol. 71.
9. New Church Accounts, 1703–4, fols. 96–99.
10. Mattheson (1740) 1969, 366; cited in Glöckner 1985, 26.
11. Contract 1721 (appendix A-26).
12. Resolution dated 14 December 1721, New Church Accounts, 1721–22, fols. 69–70.
13. "Es habe ein Orgelmacher von Merseburg die Orgel in der Neuen Kirche angesehen u. wolle über 1,000 T. haben, dargegen der hiesige Scheibe nur 600 T. verlange, auch gebe der Cantor diesem ein gut Zeugnis." Council minutes dated 14 November 1721, Stadtarchiv Leipzig, Tit. VIII 60a, fol. 113r.
14. Report 1722 (appendix A-27).
15. Haupt 1981, 17.
16. Report 1722 (appendix A-27), fol. 62.
17. Contract 1721 (appendix A-26), fol. 50.
18. Vogel, Lade, and Borger-Keweloh 1997, 288.
19. "He was particularly artful with the Pedal, which now, without making a fuss, can be used separately from the [Unter] Werck, and with the Klein Werck's soft stops. Before, it [the Pedal] was permanently attached to the full Werck." Report 1722 (appendix A-27), fol. 66.
20. Report 1722 (appendix A-27), fol. 63.
21. Contract 1721 (appendix A-26), fol. 51.
22. Werckmeister (1698) 1970, 20; Krapf 1976, 16.
23. Report 1722 (appendix A-27), fols. 65–66.
24. Mahrenholz 1942, 77n1.
25. Mattheson (1739) 1954, 469.
26. Agricola 1758, 497; cited in Q. Faulkner 1993, 60.
27. Nothing in the contract or report mentions the material Scheibe used, but during the organ's renovation in 1773–74 Mauer replaced "the old Posaunen Bass, which had tinplate resonators, but shallots made from wood" (den alten Posaunen Bass, denen die

Pfeifen von verzinnten Bleche, die Mund-Stücken aber aus Holtze bestanden, heraus genommen). Johann Carl Matthiesen, report dated 30 May 1774, New Church Accounts, 1774–75, fol. 11v.

28. Report 1722 (appendix A-27), fol. 64.

29. Cited in Greß 1989, 76.

30. Report 1722 (appendix A-27), fol. 62.

31. "Into this [Donat] organ, however, according to Herr Johann Scheibe's own statement and the attached Specification A, prepared by him, there have now been placed 1,034 new pipes, whereas the sum of the entire organ's pipework consists altogether in 1,372 pieces" (Zu solchen Orgelwercke aber sind annoch von Herrn Johann Scheiben laut seiner eigenen Aussage und hierbey selbst eigenen Specification sub Lit: A noch 1034 neue Pfeiffen gebracht worden, die Haupt Summa aber der gantzen Orgel- und Pfeiffen-Wercks bestehen ingesambt in 1372 Stücken). City History Museum Leipzig, A/3667/2006, unnumbered folio. (Specification A has not been preserved.) According to Scheibe's condition report dated 6 December 1731 (appendix A-29), the instrument had "almost 2,000 pipes."

32. St. Thomas Accounts (appendix E-2), 1721–22, fol. 46.

33. St. Nicholas Accounts (appendix E-3), 1724–25, fol. 49.

34. Organists Schott, Gräbner and Görner signed the report, but Michael Steinert, organist at St. John's, also took part in the examination. City History Museum Leipzig, A/3667/2006, unnumbered folio.

35. Report 1722 (appendix A-27), fols. 64–65.

36. Stadtarchiv Leipzig, Stift IX A 2, vol. 1, fol. 45.

37. Petzoldt 2000, 145; also, Stiehl 1984, 19; or Magirius et al. 1995, 1:209.

38. St. Thomas Accounts (appendix E-2), 1720–21, fol. 42.

39. "400. neue zur Mixtur gehörige Pfeiffen." St. Thomas Accounts (appendix E-2), 1721–22, fol. 46.

40. St. Thomas Accounts (appendix E-2), 1721–22, fol. 46.

41. Vogel Annals, 113. According to an inscription discovered in 1772 by Mauer (memorandum dated 18 March 1772, Stadtarchiv Leipzig, Stift IX A 34, fol. 10v), the large organ was at that time already 366 years old—that is, it had been built in 1406. Without citing a source, several authors (Wustmann 1909, 21; David 1951, 51; Dähnert 1980, 209; and Wolff 2005, 10) report that the organ was built as a *Blockwerk* by Joachim Schmid (or Schund) in 1356. Stiehl (1984, 40) dated the Eicha organ to 1420.

42. Wustmann 1909, 147; Stiehl 1984, 35; St. Thomas Accounts, 1619–20, fol. 21.

43. St. Thomas Accounts 1657–58, fol. 34; 1670–71, fols. 18v, 21v; 1671–72, fol. 20v; 1702–3, fol. 45; also, Stadtarchiv Leipzig, Stift IX A 34, fol. 1; and Vogel Annals, 742.

44. Vogel Chronicle, 111.

45. Report 1722 (appendix A-27), fol. 65.

46. St. Thomas Accounts (appendix E-2), 1721–22, fol. 46.

47. Rust 1875, xvi.

48. Spitta (1884–85) 1951, 2:282–83.

49. Dähnert 1980, 185.

50. The date given for the Vogel Chronicle by the Universitäts- und Landesbibliothek Sachsen-Anhalt, which has made the chronicle available online, is "ca. 1710." According

to Schrammek (1983b, 46), Vogel wrote and published his chronicle "between 1696 and 1714." From the content, however, it is clear that the section on the churches (and their organs) was written over a period of years: Vogel knew about Thayssner's renovation of St. Nicholas's organ in 1691–94 but not that the New Church was rebuilt and dedicated in 1699 or that an organ was commissioned in 1703 and dedicated in 1704; further, he referred to the 1686–87 renovation of the St. Paul's organ as having occurred about 20 years earlier. A date of circa 1700 thus appears appropriate for the Vogel Chronicle, but no matter what the exact date, Vogel recorded the large organ's disposition *before* Scheibe's renovation in 1720–21.

51. I first identified these changes and discussed their importance in Edwards Butler 2010.

52. The term "Schallflöte" appears to have been a variation, or corruption, of Hohlflöte. See Eberlein 2009, 540.

53. Vogel 2003, 295. Vogel is describing a Cymbel III, but it seems likely that Scheibe's Cymbel II had a similar effect. For a detailed discussion of mixture construction, see Vogel 2003.

54. The pitch of mutations is usually given for the 2′ octave—that is, the pitches at middle C. According to Werckmeister and Adlung, the Tertian is composed of principal-scaled pipes, usually of two ranks, either 3–1/5′ + 2–2/3′ or 1–3/5′ + 1–1/3′. Adlung assumed that when a third rank was added it would have been the lower sounding octave, just as the Octav 4′ was sometimes added to make a three-ranked Sesquialtera (4′ + 2–2/3′ + 1–3/5′). Werckmeister (1698) 1970, 74; Adlung (1758) 1953, 468–69; Adlung (1768) 1961, § 190, 458. J. G. Walther ([1732] 1953, 600) described only the higher-pitched Tertian (1–3/5′ + 1–1/3′).

55. Adlung (1768) 1961, § 190, 143.

56. The Tertien-Zug (Tierce combination): Gedackt 8′, Rohrflöte 4′, Nasat 3′, Octav 2′, Tierce 1–3/5′. For Silbermann's registrations, see, for example, Q. Faulkner 2008, 49–53.

57. "Aber es ist besser wann ein jede Pfeiffe auff ein sonderlich *Register* gesetzet würde durch alle *Claves*, denn so kann man mehr Veränderungen haben." Werckmeister (1698) 1970, 74.

58. Adlung (1768) 1961, § 228, 167.

59. "Damit in diesem Orgel-Wercke alles anzutreffen was zum vollen Concent- und Registerirung gehöret." Werckmeister 1705, § 27.

60. "Damit auch der Accord complet, und die Registeratur zum vollen Wercke richtig sey." Werckmeister 1705, § 28.

61. See Adlung (1768) 1961, vol. 1, for the dispositions (Halle on p. 239, Glaucha on p. 231).

62. "Weil sie zur Ausfüllung der *Harmonie* und guter *Variation* dienet." Cited in W. Müller 1982, 431.

63. Adlung (1758) 1953, 484n*b*. Adlung's reference is to Claude F. Milliet de Chales's *Cursus seu mundus mathematicus* (five editions published between 1674 and 1690).

64. Flade n.d., s.v. "Scheibe."

65. "Eine Orgel wird allemahl schwach und ohne Nachdruck seyn, wenn alle Stimmen bloß aus Principalstimmen bestehen, und nur eine oder mehrerer Octaven von einander entfernet sind. Es müssen daher, um die Kirchen besser auszufüllen, und die

Gemeine zu unterstützen, Mixturen, Quinte- und Terzenregister mit angebracht werden, doch mit dieser Vorsicht, daß diese Stimmen theils durch eine gute Einrichtung." J. A. Scheibe 1745, introduction, unnumbered p. 19.

66. Wustmann 1909, 145.

67. Praetorius (1619) 1976, 179–80.

68. Zacharias Thayssner, "Complete Description of Repairs to the Organ at St. Nicholas's," insert in memorandum dated 1 March 1694, Stadtarchiv Leipzig, Stift IX A 2, vol. 1, fols. 17r–18v. For a detailed description of the project, see Edwards Butler 2019.

69. *Silbermann-Archiv*, 173.

70. St. Nicholas Accounts (appendix E-3), 1724–25, fol. 49.

71. "Den 14. dieses Monats wurde der Orgel-Bau zu St. Nicolai angefangen, die Pfeiffen herausgenommen u. ist mit 150. Pfeiffen vermehret worden. Man hat doch *continuir*lich darauf gespielet, ohngeacht fortgebauet worden, u. habe es der Herr Scheibe, der Orgelbauer, in guten Standt gebracht." Riemer Chronicle, vol. 1, 161. The contract is dated December 1724, so a July 1725 starting date is unlikely. Perhaps Riemer is referring to when the pipes were actually removed, after preparatory work.

72. Scheibe was paid 250 taler in 1724–25 and the remaining 350 taler in 1725–26. St. Nicholas Accounts (appendix E-3), 1724–25, fol. 49; 1725–26, fol. 53.

73. Spitta (1884–85) 1951, 2:286.

74. Schering 1941, 72.

75. Proposal 1746 (appendix A-42), first discussed in Henkel 1985.

76. Proposal 1746 (appendix A-42), fols. 2r–3r.

77. "Octav:bass. stunde vor dem Cornet, 2 Schuh über der Windlade, und waren viereckigte Rohre herauf geführt und zwischen dem Rohrwerck hervor gekröpfft." *Silbermann-Archiv*, 173.

78. Agricola 1758, 503; cited in Q. Faulkner 1993, 61.

79. Agricola 1758, 505; cited in Q. Faulkner 1993, 61.

80. "[Tertian II] is quite useful, but it would be even better if each [of its two] ranks were available as a separate stop throughout the keyboard. In this way, one would have greater flexibility. Otherwise, one might as well combine many ranks in one single stop in the manner of the very earliest builders. But what would then happen to flexibility and variability in registration?" ([Tertian II] gehet nun wohl an, aber es ist besser wann ein jeder Pfeiffe auff ein sonderlich Register gesetzt würde durch alle *Claves,* denn so kann man mehr Veränderungen haben. Sonst könnten wohl nach der Uhralten Arth viel Stimmen auff ein Register gesetzt warden, aber wo bliebe die Veränderung und Abwechselung im Registeriren). Werckmeister (1698) 1970, 74–75; Krapf 1976, 61.

81. *Silbermann-Archiv*, 173.

82. Adlung (1768) 1961, § 30, 27.

83. Adlung (1768) 1961, § 345, 20. According to Adlung, however, the two horizontal rows were Hauptwerk (14 stops) and Rückpositiv (12 stops), the rings belonged to the Pedal (10 stops plus 4 accessories), and the metal stops in oblique notches were for the Brustwerk (8 stops).

84. "Sonsten gehet vor eine alte Orgel das Werck recht gut." *Silbermann-Archiv*, 173.

85. "Mehr daran verdorben weder gut gemacht." *Silbermann-Archiv*, 158.

86. Koska 2019, 74, citing Maul 2017.

87. Thayssner reported that he had built "four new large wedge bellows" (*4. neue Große Span Bälge*). Zacharias Thayssner, memorandum received 3 March 1694, Stadtarchiv Leipzig, Stift IX A 2, fol. 17r. The bellows are described by Vogel (Chronicle, 97) as "4 large wedge bellows with one fold" (*vier grossen Span-Bälgen mit einer Falten*) but by J. A. Silbermann (*Silbermann-Archiv*, 173) as bellows "which are tread, with many folds" (*werden getretten, mit vielen Falten*).

88. Report 1730 (appendix A-28).

89. St. Thomas Accounts (appendix E-2), 1730–31, fol. 36.

90. Rust 1875, xvi.

91. Spitta (1884–85) 1951, 2:282.

92. Richter 1908, 52–54.

93. Report 1730 (appendix A-28), fol. 70r.

94. Franklin 1991, 1–6 and 12–14. Franklin adopted Mark Lindley's definition that an irregular temperament was constructed with "no wolf fifth but with the thirds in the C major scale tempered lightly. . . . As a modulation of triadic harmonies moved about the circle of fifths the amount of tempering in the thirds would thus change, [but] in a fairly unabrupt fashion." See Lindley n.d.

95. "Die überaus bequeme und wohlklingende Temperatur." J. A. Scheibe 1738, introduction.

96. "Und daher meynen sie vollkommen berechtiget zu seyn, von 12. Quinten eine, und von 12. grossen Terzen viere aufzuopffern, damit die übrigen, und zwar nur die Terzen, nicht aber die Quinten, desto besser wären. Allein: Ist es gleich in vorigen Zeiten so ziemlich thunlich gewesen, da man sich in so engen Grenzen der Tonarten hat behelffen müssen und können; so ist es doch bey heutiger *Praxi* durchaus nicht mehr *practicable*." Sorge 1748, 26.

97. "Heutiger Manier nach, da alle musicalischen Stücke mehrentheilß fict gesetzt, durch alle modos, so wohl regular, als irregular, harmonisch können gebrauchet werden, nach accurater Temperatur abgefaßet und gestimmet seyn [und befunden werden sollen]." Moser 1994, 193.

98. See Edwards Butler 2019, especially 118–23.

99. Kuhnau 1717.

100. Neidhardt's first publication of 1706 recommended equal temperament, but Kuhnau describes a Neidhardt system that alters each pitch by 1/12, 2/12, or, at the most, 3/12 of a comma. This suggests that Neidhardt's theories circulated before his later publications of 1724 and 1732.

101. According to Rathey (2001, 166) Wender employed a well-tempered system that may have been based on or was similar to Werckmeister's proposals. Lindley (1988, 110 and 117, citing Sorge 1748) concluded that Silbermann used a 1/6-comma meantone system, but according to Greß (2010), Silbermann later changed to a well-tempered system.

102. *NBR*, 368 (no. 363).

103. J. F. Agricola in Adlung (1768) 1961, vol. 1, 212, as translated by Williams (1984, 118).

104. Greß 2010.

105. Sorge 1748, 21, as translated by Lindley (1988, 117–18).

106. Sorge 1748, 10–11. As noted above, according to recent research, Silbermann employed a well-tempered system after 1716. See Greß 2010.

107. Sorge 1748, 26–27:

So ist es doch bey heutiger Praxi durchaus nicht mehr *practicable*. Denn da kömmt ja so offt ein General-Baß aus dem As als aus dem G vor, wie es alle heutige Componisten bejahen werden, und ihre *Compositiones* die Sache bezeugen. Man muß dahero wissen, daß man sich an das Schweben der grossen Terzen, so ein viertheil, drittheil oder 5/12-einer *Diesis* aufwerts schweben müssen, nicht zu kehren hat, den eine Terz kan weit mehr vertragen als eine Quint, wie Werckmeister und Neidhardt zur Gnüge gezeiget haben. . . . Ich mache dahero den andern Schluß: Weil keine von den 12 grossen Terzen zu entrathen, wenn man sie auch gleich nicht *pro Triade fundamentali* setzet; so ist es weit besser, sie schweben alle 1/3 *Diesis*, oder einige etwa weniger, als ¼ oder 7/24 oder mehr, als 3/8 oder 5/12, und werden also alle brauchbar, ja recht gewürzt, frisch und munter, als daß der dritte Theil (man bedencke es doch) unbrauchbar, wenigstens allzu rauh und unfreundlich, ja recht versalzen werden, und 2/3 *Diesis*, d.i. weit über ein *Comma*, schweben soll.

108. "Also: Lasse keine einzige Quint, wohl aber alle grosse Terzen, aufwärts schweben, jedoch keine über 5/12 und also nicht gar eine halbe *Diesin*, so wird die Sache getroffen werden. Das ist kurz und deutlich genug." Sorge 1748, 47.

109. "Denn wenn man sich an keinen *Modum* in Stimmen will binden lassen, so kan man nur alle *Tertias majores* in die Höhe schweben lassen." Werckmeister (1691) 1983, 75.

110. Report 1731 (appendix A-29).

111. New Church Accounts (appendix E-4), 1731–32, fol. 33.

112. *NBR*, 184 (no. 186); Bach-Dokumente II, 275 (no. 383).

113. This was the so-called Telemannisches Collegium founded by Telemann in 1701.

114. See Glöckner 1990, 106.

115. St. Nicholas Accounts (appendix E-3), 1733–34, fol. 53.

116. Glöckner 2008, 164–65, citing Minutes F (appendix C), 31 March 1730, fol. 119r–v.

117. Glöckner 2008, 165, citing Minutes F (Appendix C), 28 September 1730, fols. 133v–34r. It was not possible to find a copy of Bach's report in the archives.

118. Glöckner 2008, 165.

119. Minutes F (appendix C), 7 November 1730, fols. 136 and 137.

120. Glöckner 2008, 165–66.

121. Minutes G (appendix C), 21 April 1735, fol. 55r.

122. Minutes G (appendix C), 21 April 1735, fol. 55v.

123. Minutes G (appendix C), 8 March 1736, fols. 68v–69r.

124. Minutes G (appendix C), 5 April 1736, fols. 74v–75r.

125. "[Paid to] Johann Scheibe, organ builder, for renovation of the organ, according to the contract, attachment A, signed 13 April 1736 between the Most Honorable Academy and the aforesaid: 60 taler on 17 April 1736, 50 taler on 27 June 1736, 50 taler on 31 August 1736." St. Paul Accounts A, fol. 265; also, Glöckner 2008, 167.

126. Report 1746 (appendix A-41), fols. 6r–6v.

127. "Das Orgel-Wergk in besagter Kirche einer starcken *Reparatur* bedürfftig." New Church Accounts, 1746–47, fol. 5r.

128. Report 1746 (appendix A-41).

129. Report 1746 (appendix A-41), fols. 6v–7r.

130. Contract 1747 (appendix A-43). Cited in Spitta (1873–80) 1964, 2:870–72; and Spitta (1884–85) 1951, 2:305–7.

131. This point was overlooked by Schering (1954, 90–91) and Dreyfus (1987, 27), who believed the organ would have been totally unplayable for approximately four months in 1747.

132. St. Thomas Accounts, 1747–48, fols. 81–82.

133. St. Thomas Accounts (appendix E-2), 1747–48, fol. 52; also, Bach-Dokumente II, 439 (no. 561).

134. St. Nicholas Accounts (appendix E-3), 1750–51, fol. 44.

135. Schweinefleisch received 280 taler in 1751 (50 taler on 25 January, 50 taler on 5 April, 30 taler on 22 May, 75 taler on 30 June, and 75 taler on 27 August); the following fiscal year he was paid another 70 taler in arrears, for a total of 350 taler. St. Paul Accounts C, fols. 74, 82, and 90.

136. There is no payment in the records of the university that corresponds to work done in 1755; it appears that Riemer was reporting changes that Schweinefleisch had carried out in 1751.

137. "Zu dieser Zeit [1755] ist die schöne *Pauliner* Orgel *repariret*, und durch Herrn Johann Christian Immanuel Schweinefleischen, Orgelbauern, mit 3. Registern, als *Principal* 8. Fuß, *Schalmey Bass*. 4. Fuß ins *Pedal*, und *Principal* 4. Fuß ins Ober Werck vermehret worden." Riemer Chronicle, vol. 3, 917–18.

138. Schweinefleisch was paid 250 taler on 26 February 1767, 150 taler on 15 May 1767, 150 taler on 25 July 1767, 50 taler on 28 September 1767, and 142 taler on 9 November 1767. St. Paul Accounts C, fol. 228.

139. Schering 1926, 257.

140. Scheibe 1717 (appendix 19), fol. 72r.

141. Johann Christoph Bach, memorandum dated 30 December 1697, cited in Edwards Butler 2004, 54.

142. "Er möchte auf die Orgel Acht haben, daß wann etwas schadhafftes daran wäre, man solchem bey Zeiten vorkommen möchte." Stadtarchiv Leipzig, Stift IX, Tit. VII B, Nr. 108, fol. 109.

143. *NBR*, 41 (no. 16); Bach-Dokumente II, 11 (no. 8).

144. *NBR*, 68 (no. 48); Bach-Dokumente II, 50 (no. 63).

145. Werckmeister (1698) 1970, 75–76; Krapf 1976, 62–63.

146. See chapter 4; also, Heller 2010, 111–15.

147. "Davor er die Orgel beständig im bräuchlichen Wesen erhalten wolle." Minutes G (appendix C), 3 December 1739, fol. 145v.

148. St. Paul Accounts C (appendix E-1), 1744–45, fol. 28.

149. Council minutes dated 28 September 1748, UAL, Rep. I/XVI/I 39, fol. 42v.

150. The history of repairs and renovations to the St. Paul's organ from circa 1717 to 1755 was reported by Andreas Glöckner (2008, 159–68); see also Heller 2010, 123–24.

151. Scheibe 1719 (appendix A-24).

152. UAL, Rep. II/III/B I 12, fol. 144; also, St. Paul Accounts B, 1719–20, fol. 73v (see appendix E-1).

153. "Es wird freylich Hülffe geschehen müßen, jedoch auch in Zukunft zustegen, daß der Organiste die Orgel nicht so streng angreiffe, und die Balgentreter das Fenster zu den Windladen, wodurch die Hitze hinein dringt, nicht offen stehen laßen." UAL, Rep. II/III/B I 12, fol. 145.

154. Minutes F (appendix C), 31 March 1730, fol. 119r–v; St. Paul Accounts A, 1729–30, fol. 229.

155. Minutes F (appendix C), 31 July 1731, fols. 151v–52r; St. Paul Accounts A, 1730–31, fol. 236.

156. Minutes G (appendix C), 3 December 1739, fols. 145r and 146r; also, Glöckner 2008, 167.

157. St. Paul Accounts B, 1741–42, fol. 348v (see appendix E-1).

158. In Andreas Glöckner's view, the "ongoing repairs" are proof that the organ's bellows, among other items, were not built to the highest standard and that the maintenance record confirms J. A. Silbermann's "damning review"—that "Der Thon und Arbeit trifft mit dem Gutachten des H[errn] Kapellmeisters Bach nicht wohl überein." Glöckner 2008, 167; and Silbermann 1741 (appendix A-35), 158.

159. St. Thomas Accounts (appendix E-2), 1712–13, fol. 41; 1713–14, fol. 40.

160. "9 guilders 3 groschen [8 taler] to the organ builder Christoph Donat, who repaired both organs in the church and the regal in the Thomas School, paid 19 March 1678" (9 fl. 3 gr. dem Orgelmacher Christoph Donaten, so beyde Orgelwercke in der Kirche und das Regal auf der Thomas Schul ausgebeßert, bezahlt den 19 Martÿ 1678). St. Thomas Accounts, 1678–79, fol. 29. Although Schering (1954, 55) reported a similar repair in 1683 (also cited in Dähnert 1980, 186), I could not verify this in the payment records.

161. St. Thomas Accounts (appendix E-2), 1720–21, fol. 42; 1727–28, fol. 41.

162. St. Nicholas Accounts (appendix E-3), 1718–19, fol. 45.

163. He was paid a fee of 42 taler on 22 September 1716 but requested a supplement because the project had required more time and effort than he had anticipated. Ahrens 2002, 145.

164. Krapf 1976, 62–63; Werckmeister (1698) 1970, 76.

165. Administrator Johann Carl Matthiesen, memorandum dated 23 February 1773, Stadtarchiv Leipzig, Stift IX A 2, fol. 138v.

166. Schrammek 1983b.

167. According to Geck (2003, 566), Telemann was appointed as organist and director of music at the New Church in 1704 "in order systematically to establish a modern church practice which now clearly stood against that of the St. Thomas cantor, possibly deemed too traditionally based."

168. See Spitta (1884–85) 1951, 281–86.

Chapter 9. An Innovative Organ for St. John's

1. Spitta (1873–80) 1964, 2:501; Spitta (1884–85) 1951, 3:21.

2. Glöckner 2013, 335.

3. Kevorkian 2007, 30.

4. Vogel Chronicle, 128–31.

5. Trost was paid 100 taler in 1694 and the remaining 75 taler in 1695. St. John Accounts (appendix E-5), 1694, fol. 139; 1695, fol. 135.

6. For an assessment of Tobias Gottfried Trost's work, see Friedrich 1989, 13–18.

7. Magirius et al. 1995, 2:838.

8. Henkel 1986, 44. Some sources indicate Lausitz as the town that received the organ, but Henkel proved it to be Laußick (near Geithain).

9. St. John Accounts, 1694, fols. 187–89.

10. St. John Accounts, 1694, fol. 187; Stadtarchiv Leipzig, RRA(F) No. 657. See also Vogel Chronicle, 130; Dähnert 1980, 177; or Wolff and Zepf 2012, 54.

11. Council meeting dated 6 December 1740. Stadtarchiv Leipzig, Tit. VIII. 63, fol. 383.

12. Vogel Chronicle, 110.

13. Wustmann 1909, 147.

14. St. Thomas Accounts, 1639–40, fol. 41.

15. Vogel Annals, 562; Magirius et al. 1995, 1:205; Wustmann 1909, 147.

16. Vogel Chronicle, 110.

17. St. Thomas Accounts, 1665–66, fol. 28v.

18. Donat was paid 68 florins 12 groschen for the bellows, 80 florins "for the 6 new registers with which this organ has been enlarged to its better perfection," and 171 florins 9 groschen "for all the work done by him and his workers, including materials." (1 florin or guilder was equal to 21 groschen; 1 taler was equal to 24 groschen.) The bellows pumper was paid for 11½ days in May, 6 days in June, 4 days in July, and 6½ days in August. St. Thomas Accounts, 1665–66, fols. 28v–30r.

19. "Das ganze gesprenge von feingolde ufs neue zu vergulden." St. Thomas Accounts, 1665–66, fol. 30r.

20. St. Thomas Accounts, 1665–66, fols. 28v–30r.

21. St. Thomas Accounts, 1678–79, fol. 29. Schering (1954, 55) reported a similar repair in 1683 (see also Dähnert 1980, 186), but I could not verify this in the payment records. Schering (1926, 109) also reported, without citing a source, that organist Jacob Weckmann had complained in 1675 that the pipework was out of tune and the Subbass was very weak, because it was made from wood (rather than metal) and really only there "pro forma."

22. "Vor Reparirung der kleinen Orgel, welche gantz unbrauchbar gewesen." St. Thomas Accounts (appendix E-2), 1720–21, fol. 42.

23. "Vor 8. Register in den kleinen Orgelwerck in brauchbaren Stand zusezen, ingl. vor Reise-Kosten." St. Thomas Accounts (appendix E-2), 1727–28, fol. 41; also cited in Dähnert 1962, 220n231.

24. Stadtarchiv Leipzig, Tit. VIII. 63, 352; cited in Bitter (1881) 1978, 4:178. Bitter incorrectly read Stötteritz as Kötteritz.

25. Scheibe was paid 15 taler "for tuning the large organ this year as well as examining the small old organ, assessing its value, and, along with a laborer, removing it." St. Thomas Accounts (appendix E-2), 1740–41, fol. 52.

26. Scheibe 1740 (appendix A-34).

27. Adlung (1768) 1961, § 323, 6.

Notes to Chapter 9

28. Adlung (1768) 1961, § 323, 6.

29. See Adlung (1768) 1961, § 181, 132–33 (Rancket); § 201, 150 (Trichterregal); and § 183, 134–35 (Regal).

30. Schering 1926, 111.

31. Vogel Chronicle, 110.

32. Stiehl 1984, 35.

33. Resolution dated 22 December 1702, New Church Accounts, 1703–4, fol. 103.

34. St. John Accounts (appendix E-5), 1741, fol. 86.

35. The date and terms of the contract are revealed in the receipt for additional payment signed by Johann Scheibe on 17 April 1745. Henkel 1986, 45. See appendix A-40 (Receipt 1745).

36. St. John Accounts (appendix E-5), 1741, fol. 86, and 1742, fol. 77.

37. "Vor die bey obersagten Orgelbau gehabte viele Bemühung." St. John Accounts (appendix E-5), 1745, fol. 92.

38. "On the 1st [of June 1742] the organ at St. John's started to be removed, which Herr Scheibe, the organ builder, had been given so that he could rebuild and perfect it" (Den 1. [Juni] ist die Orgel zu St. Johannis abzureizen angefangen worden, welche Hr. Scheiben der Orgel Bauer wiederum zu bauen und zuverfertigen, übergeben worden). Riemer Chronicle, vol. 2, 526–27.

39. Cited in *Neue Zeitschrift für Musik* 63 (1867): 333.

40. St. John Accounts (appendix E-5), 1742 (January to August), fol. 77.

41. Henkel 1986, 45.

42. "Den Rest, so ihm vermöge Contracts bei völliger Verfertigung der Neuen Orgel zu zahlen versprochen worden." St. John Accounts (appendix E-5), 1742 (January to August), fol. 77.

43. "6 [taler to] Johann Got[t]lob Reinicke, organist, for playing the organ on Sundays and feastdays for the 2 quarters Michaelmas and Christmas 1742 . . . 1 [taler to] the bellows pumper for the 2 quarters Michaelmas and Christmas 1742." St. John Accounts (appendix E-5), 1742 (September to December), fols. 42 and 43.

44. "On this very day [2 June 1743] the new organ at St. John's was played for the first time, even though not yet entirely finished" (An eben diesen Tage ist das erste mahl die neue Orgel zu St. Johannis zum ersten mahle, jedoch noch nicht gantz verfertiget, gespielet worden). Riemer Chronicle, vol. 2, 548; also cited in Wit 1900, 990.

45. St. John Accounts (appendix E-5), 1743, fols. 84 and 85.

46. "2. große Vasen 1. Schild mit Palmen Zweigen und 4. Gehencke [Schnitzwerk] über und an die Orgel zu machen." St. John Accounts (appendix E-5), 1743, fol. 85.

47. The collection was reviewed by Agricola in Friedrich Wilhelm Marpurg, *Historisch-Kritische Beyträge zur Aufnahme der Musik*, vol. 3 (Berlin, 1758), 486–87 (see Q. Faulkner 1993), and Agricola added a reference to the disposition in *SeN* in his emendations in Adlung (1768) 1961, vol. 1, 251: "In this book [*SeN*] is also on p. 56 the disposition of the organ at St. John's just outside of Leipzig, of 22 stops, which the aforesaid Johann Scheibe built from 1742 to 1744."

48. Reported in Oehme 1978, 115.

49. Wit 1900, 990.

50. Kinsky 1910, 327.

51. Niedt (1721) 1976, 121–22, based on a translation by Thomas Braatz ("Documentary evidence revealing the contemporary performance practices for Bach's *Organo* (*basso continuo*) parts," published online in 2012).

52. Dänhardt 2000, 44.

53. *SeN*, 56.

54. Letter from Christoph Gottlieb Schröter dated Nordhausen, 22 September 1738, in Mizler 1747, 476.

55. See Mizler 1747, 578–79, for the description; a drawing of the invention is on p. 608.

56. Adlung (1758) 1953, 505–6.

57. Mizler (1747, 579) wrote, "My personal wish is that Herr Schröter's newly discovered organ is soon produced and that Herr Inventor partakes in the reward he deserves."

58. See Koster 1994. Other "expressive" keyboards were also being developed. Adlung reported that Michael Steinert, organist at St. John's from 1694 to 1731, had bought a Geigenwerk, a bowed-stringed-keyboard instrument, "and copied it such that it sounded much better than before." Adlung (1758) 1953, 566.

59. Adlung (1758) 1953, 560–61; cited in Koster 1994 (8, no. 1): 3.

60. Adlung (1768) 1961, vol. 1, 251.

61. Henkel 1986, 45.

62. By contract, Hildebrandt was obligated to begin construction of the new organ at St. Wenceslas's by St. Martin's Day, 11 November 1743.

63. Bach-Dokumente II, 408 (no. 519). Also, Dähnert 1960, 86; and Henkel 1986, 48, citing Stadtarchiv Leipzig, Tit. VIII. 64, fol. 205b (13 December 1743).

64. C. P. E. Bach and Johann Agricola, obituary [1754], *NBR*, 297 (no. 306).

65. See *NBR*, "Criticism and Defense: A Controversy," 337–53 (nos. 343–48); also Buelow 1974. More recently, the dispute has been considered by Jerold (2011) and Maul (2013).

66. This point was eloquently argued by Buelow (1974).

67. Buelow 1974, 85.

68. Bach-Dokumente I, 136–37 (no. 68); *NBR*, 153 (no. 153). Johann Adolph was unsuccessful in Freiberg as well and afterward stopped pursuing a career as organist and instead devoted himself to composition and musical criticism. For a brief biography and a catalog and description of J. A. Scheibe's compositions, see Hauge 2018.

69. Buelow 1974, 89.

70. Bach-Dokumente II, 368 (no. 453) and 372 (no. 460). Regarding J. A. Scheibe's description of the visit to Altenburg, see Edwards Butler 2020.

71. Henkel 1986, especially 44 and 47.

72. Krapf 1976, 2; Werckmeister (1698) 1970, 2.

73. For Bach's report, see pages 92–93.

74. Forkel (1802) 1920, 68–69.

75. The dispute is described briefly by Wit (1900, 990) and in detail by Henkel (1986, 46–47).

76. The director was Johann Georg Sieber, lord of the Rittergut Plaußig, near Delitzsch, who died 24 August 1742.

77. Cited in Henkel 1986, 46. See also Bach-Dokumente II, 408 (no. 519).

78. See Greß 1989, 49.

79. Henkel 1986, 46 and 50n28.

80. Henkel 1986, 46.

81. Henkel 1986, 46 and 50n31.

82. Receipt 1745 (appendix A-40), fol. 102.

83. Wit 1900, 989; Kinsky 1910, 319–23 and 327. The leather covering and shape of the organ bench suggest it dates to the 19th century.

84. Henkel 1986, 48.

85. Schumann and Schumann 2007, 101.

Chapter 10. Small Projects and Proposals

1. "Ganz unbrauchbar worden, und fast nicht mehr darauf gespielet werden können." Landeskirchenarchiv Dresden, Bestand 31999, Sign. 1155, unnumbered fol. 12r.

2. "Der Schulmeister . . . doch selten oder wohl gar nicht darauf gespielet und spielen können." Letter dated 15 July 1715 from members of the congregation in Gundorf to Superintendent Polycarp Leyser, Landeskirchenarchiv Dresden, Bestand 31999, Sign. 1155, unnumbered fol. 12r.

3. No mention is made of the Gleditsch family, who owned the *Gut* or manor in Gundorf but who do not appear to have contributed toward the cost of the organ.

4. Letter from Pastor Carl Gottfried Jacobi to Superintendent Polycarp Leyser dated 4 December 1714, Landeskirchenarchiv Dresden, Bestand 31999, Sign. 1155, unnumbered fols. 4r–v and 11r–v.

5. Pastor Carl Gottfried Jacobi provides a report on the examination in a letter dated 25 May 1716 to Superintendent Polycarp Leyser in Merseburg (Landeskirchenarchiv Dresden, Bestand 31999, Sign. 1155, unnumbered fols. 5r–v and 10r–v), as does Georg Friedrich Kauffmann in his letter report to Superintendent Polycarp Leyser dated 15 May 1716 (Report 1716, appendix A-16).

6. "Das gantze Orgel-Werck von einander genommen, mit großen Fleiße corrigiret, und von neuen wieder gestimmet worden müste." Report 1716 (appendix A-16), unnumbered fols. 7v–8r.

7. Report 1716 (appendix A-16), unnumbered fols. 8v–9r.

8. Henkel 1988, 117.

9. See www.grundschule-gundorf.de, accessed 10 February 2015.

10. This information is reported by Sylvia Kolbe, citing no reference, at www.home .uni-leipzig.de/kolbe/KirchenorgelnLeipzig.html. Also, see www.kirchgemeinde -gundorf.de. According to Jiri Kocourek (of Hermann Eule Orgelbau), in notes now deposited in the Sächsische Landes- und Universitätsbibliothek in Dresden, Paul Rubardt wrote that the Scheibe organ in Gundorf was a one-manual, 12-stop instrument and that Scheibe had reused Principal 4′ and Octav 2′ from the previous organ.

11. See www.kirchgemeinde-gundorf.de, accessed 11 February 2015; information also was provided by Jiri Kocourek (of Hermann Eule Orgelbau).

12. See W. Schneider 1829.

13. For the text, see Engel 1855, 15–17.

14. Letter dated 2 February 1728 from the Leipzig City Council to Heinrich Gottlieb Schneider, superintendent in Merseburg. Kirchliches Archiv Leipzig, Sign. 1249, fol. 1r–3r (here, fol. 1v).

15. Kirchliches Archiv Leipzig, Sign. 1249, fol. 2v.

16. Letter dated 15 December 1729 from the Leipzig City Council to Heinrich Gottlieb Schneider, superintendent in Merseburg. Kirchliches Archiv Leipzig, Sign. 1249, fols. 14r–16v.

17. "Den Klang und die Krafft des *Tons* betreffend, wäre derselbe in denen Ober Stimmen angenehm, in denen mittlern und *Bässen* aber durchdringend, so daß die *Harmonie egal,* und eine gute *proportion* derer Registern, wie nicht weniger die behörige Ordnung zu verspüren gewesen." Kirchliches Archiv Leipzig, Sign. 1249, fol. 15r.

18. "Ein Portun von 16. Fuß von oben bis in das ungestrichene g." Kirchliches Archiv Leipzig, Sign. 1249, fol. 15r. It is possible that, like the organ in Lindenau, which also had a treble Bordun 16′, the disposition was based on Principal 4′.

19. "So zu mehrerer Vollkommenheit des Wercks sehr vieles beytrage, indem diese Register daßelbe kräfftiger und stärcker machten, außerdem auch die kleinen Stimmen, so an der Anzahl ungleich größer, denen tiefen weit überlagen gewesen, folglich das Werck an durch dringender Stärcke, so bey dem Gesang einer ganze Gemeinde allerdings nöthig sey, Mangel gelitten haben würden." Kirchliches Archiv Leipzig, Sign. 1249, fol. 15v.

20. Cited in Henkel 1988, 121–22n16.

21. Henkel 1988, 121–22n16.

22. Proposal 1738 (appendix A-33). Scheibe's bid to build an organ for Gollma is described briefly by Wilfried Stüven (1964, 96–97).

23. *Acta historico ecclesiastica, oder Gesammlete Nachrichten von den neuesten Kirchen-Geschichten,* vol. 5 (1743), part 30, 946–47.

24. Proposal 1738 (appendix A-33), fol. 1r.

25. Proposal 1738 (appendix A-33), fol. 1v.

26. Proposal 1738 (appendix A-33), fol. 1v.

27. Proposal 1738 (appendix A-33), fol. 1r–v.

28. Scheibe 1741 (appendix A-36).

29. "Es ist anden, daß sich einer von Merseburg, er sey nun ein Tischler, welches mir nicht bekannt, oder ein Orgel-Bauer, der es ex professo gelernet, wofür er sich ausgiebt, zur Erbauung der Gollmischen Kirchen-Orgel gemeldet, so auff des H. Cammerherr Heils Verlangen einen Anschlag übergeben hatt, es ist aber weniger Geld u. Lust der Eingepfarrten vorhanden, als vorher, folgends noch gar nicht gewiß, wenn u. von wem dieses Wercke werde gefertiget werden. Inzwischen übersende durch der H. Stadt-Schreiber in Landsberg die übergebende disposition nebst Anschlag u. Riß nach Verlangen." Response from Pastor A. F. Trainer to Scheibe's inquiry dated 4 August 1741, Pfarrarchiv Gollma, "Acta, die Erbauung und Reparatur der Orgel betr.," fol. 10r.

30. The contracted disposition was as follows:

Hauptmanual (9 stops): Bordun 16′ (lowest 2 octaves of wood, rest *Metall*), Principal 8′ (good tin in the facade, well polished), Quintatön or Viol 8′, Grob Gedackt 8′ (lowest octave of wood), Octav 4′, Klein Gedackt 4′, Quint 3′, Spitzflöte 2′, Mixtur IV 2′.

Oberwerk (6 stops): Mittel Gedackt 8' (lowest octave wood), Viol di Gamba 8', Principal 4' (tin, well polished), Offen Flöte 4', Octav 2', Sifflöte 1'.

Pedal (4 stops): Subbass 16', Posaunen Bass 16', Principal Bass 8', Octav Bass 4'. In addition, Tremulant, Cymbelstern, and ventils for each division.

Contract with Johann Dietrich dated 18 November 1741, Pfarrarchiv Gollma, "Bau u. Reparaturen der Orgel der Kirche," fols. 5r–6r.

31. Stüven 1964, 99.

32. Maria Hübner (Leipzig Bach Archive) discovered this hitherto unknown organ proposal, and the following account is based primarily on her report. See Hübner 2013.

33. Proposal 1742 (appendix A-37); see also Hübner 2013, 351–52.

34. According to Krünitz's *Oekonomische Encyklopädie* (1773–1858), barrel staves were 3½ to 4 feet long and 2 inches thick and the best were made from red oak, which had the tightest and hardest wood. The trees were felled in the winter months, when they had no sap, because the wood had a better appearance and was less likely to become worm-eaten.

35. As Adlung ([1768] 1961, § 160) explains, Hohl Quinta is a Hohlflöte at three-foot pitch.

36. Hübner 2013, 352.

37. Hübner 2013, 353.

38. Hübner 2013, 355.

39. For the disposition and a brief history of the St. Jacob's organ, see Wolff and Zepf 2012, 42. For a detailed history, including its maintenance history and eventual rebuild by Zuberbier in 1765–71, see Henkel 1985.

40. Henkel 1985, 10.

41. See Talle 2003, 161.

42. Proposal 1746 (appendix A-42).

43. For a description of a spring chest, see Werckmeister (1698) 1970, 19–20; or Krapf 1976, 14–15. Illustrations of a spring chest can be found in Sumner 1952, 64; Williams and Owen 1988, 13; and Winter 1979, 35–36. Organs built with spring chests included Förner's organs in Halle and Weißenfels; the Junge organs in Weimar, Sondershausen, and Erfurt; and Thayssner's organs in Quedlinburg and Köthen.

44. Scheibe's views were not unique. Werckmeister (1681, 20) described the difficulties associated with spring chests—and he expanded the list of problems in the revised edition ([1698] 1970, 38–39; Krapf 1976, 30–31).

45. Henkel 1985, 12.

46. Cited in Henkel 1985, 10.

47. Henkel 1985, 12–13; also, Wolff and Zepf 2012, 42.

48. Letter from patron Christiana Clara Glafey nee Rinck and superintendent Salomon Deyling to the Leipzig Consistory, Stadtarchiv Leipzig, AHM 775, fols. 31v–35v. The letter was mentioned but not cited in Wünsche 2003, 36.

49. Henkel (1988, 114 and 121) made the attribution, noting that an additional payment (*Zugeldt*) of 15 taler 18 groschen was paid in 1710–11. Records for the immediately

previous years are missing, but the *Zugeldt* payment suggests a new instrument had just been constructed.

50. "Die starcken Gemeinden nicht überschreÿen und zwingen kan, daß sie beÿ den angegebenen Thone bleiben solten, sondern geschehen laßen muß, daß selbige beÿ denen Liedern herunter fallen, wodurch ein recht ärgerl. Übelstand und Dissonanz entstehet." Stadtarchiv Leipzig, AHM 775, fol. 34r.

51. "So haben wir bereits ein feines Werck, so bis anhero in der St. Joh: Kirche zu Leipzig gestanden, und noch gut und tüchtig ist, in Vorschlage und können solches . . . vor ein billiges erhalten." Stadtarchiv Leipzig, AHM 775, fol. 5r–v. Scheibe's Stötteritz proposal and its evaluation by Bach was first discussed in Edwards Butler 2011; see Edwards Butler 2013 for the article in English.

52. "Weil diese Orgel, wenn solche der Kirche zu Sct Johann: vor Leipzig ferner gedienet hätte, nicht würde haben verkaufft werden sollen." Stadtarchiv Leipzig, AHM 775, fol. 33v. Although this suggests that in 1748 Scheibe apparently still owned, and was trying to sell, the Trost organ from St. John's, Scheibe's offer could have been made anytime between 1742, when he acquired the St. John's organ, and 1748, the date of the letter that describes the offer.

53. Cited in Edwards Butler 2013, 4–5.

54. Schweinefleisch's contract called for the following stops: in the Manual (CD–c^3), Principal 4′ (tin), Grob Gedackt 8′ (wood), Quintatön 8′ (metal), Rohrflöte 4′ (metal), Quint 3′ (tin), Octav 2′ (tin), Tierce 2′ [1–3/5′] (tin), Cornet III (discant), and Mixtur IV 1′; in the Pedal (CD–c^1), Subbass 16′, Violon Bass 8′, and Posaunen Bass 16′, all of wood. The organ also had a Tremulant and a *Windkoppel*. Stadtarchiv Leipzig, AHM 775, fol. 55r–v.

55. "Said Herr Schweinefleisch shall and wants to provide a new organ, well and skillfully built according to the disposition attached to this contract as Attachment A, drawn up by him personally and undersigned by him today" (Es soll und will benannter Herr Schweinefleisch nach der diesen *Contract*e beygefügten von ihm selbst auffgesezten und unter heutigen *dato* eigenhändig unterschriebenen *Disposition Sub A*. eine neue Orgel . . . gut und tüchtig). Contract with Schweinefleisch dated 17 October 1753, Stadtarchiv Leipzig, AHM 775, fols. 51v–52r.

56. "So traff in der Kirche eine grose Menge Volcks an, das sich von Leipzig und andern benachtbarten Orten mit eingefunden." Stadtarchiv Leipzig, AHM 775, fol. 59r.

57. "Said organ has been found to be good and serviceable, built not only according to the contract but also all of its parts according to the organ builder's craft. I extend to him not only this courtesy but also give the praise he deserves to the maker Herr Schweinefleisch and, on the basis of truth, can give him my highest recommendation" (Gedachte Orgel nicht nur den *Contract* gemäß, sondern auch nach allen Theilen der Orgel-Macher Kunst gut und tüchtig befunden, so bezeige nicht er alleine solches hiermit, sondern gebe dem Verfertiger H. Schweinifleischen dabeÿ, daß ihm gehörigen Lob, und kan ihm auch mit Grund der Vahrheit aufs beste dabeÿ *recommendi*ren). Johann Gottlieb Görner, examination report dated 24 October 1754, Stadtarchiv Leipzig, AHM 775, fol. 58r–v.

Chapter 11. Scheibe and Bach in Leipzig

1. Rubardt 1963.

2. According to Forkel, when Bach gave his opinion of young organist candidates and of new organs, he "proceeded, in both cases, with so much conscientiousness and impartiality that he seldom added to the number of his friends by it." *NBR*, 440.

3. Krapf 1976, 58; Werckmeister (1698) 1970, 71.

4. Scheibe 1718a (appendix A-21), fol. 77r.

5. See pages 92–93.

6. Forkel (1802) 1920, 69.

7. Forkel (1802) 1920, 69.

8. See Dreyfus 1985; and also Wolff 2016.

9. Butler (2007) proposes one such occasion, for example.

10. David 1951, 49–50.

11. Wolff 2000, 318.

12. *NBR*, 325 (no. 321).

13. See Stauffer 1980, 152.

14. *NBR*, 325 (no. 320).

15. *NBR*, 338 (no. 343).

16. *NBR*, 440.

17. Edwards Butler 2013, 5. Scheibe died before the organ could be built.

18. *NBR*, 306–7 (no. 306).

19. Williams 2007, 277–78; Williams 2016, 501–3.

20. See Koska 2019, where J. A. Scheibe is categorized as someone who has been erroneously designated a Bach student.

21. See Edwards Butler 2020.

22. Dähnert 1962, 120–21.

Bibliography

Archival Sources (also see Abbreviations in the front matter)

The British Library, London
 Add. Ms. 33965

Kirchliches Archiv Leipzig
 Sign. 1249, "Die Orgel zu Leutzsch betr. 1728"

Landeskirchenarchiv Dresden
 Bestand 31999, Sign. 1155, "Den Orgelbau zu Gundorf betr. 1711"

Pfarrarchiv Gollma
 "Acta, die Erbauung und Reparatur der Orgel betr."
 "Bau u. Reparaturen der Orgel der Kirche"

Pfarrarchiv Zschortau
 "Acta die Kirchen und Geistlichen Gebäude betreffend"

Sächsisches Staatsarchiv Dresden
 Bestand 10058 Meißen Nr. 2395, "Acta, den Orgelbau in der Kirche zu Zscheyla betr.
  1712, 1735"

Stadtarchiv Köthen
 3/402/C20, "Reparaturen an der Orgel 1765–1852"

Stadtarchiv Leipzig
 II. Sekt. T (F) Nr. 393, "Acta, Das Tischer-Handwerck alhier contra Christian Francken,
  wegen Stöhrerey, Anno 1732"
 AHM 775, "Acta die Anschaffung eines Orgel-Wercks in der Kirche zu Stötteriz betr.
  Anno. 1753"
 Cap. 41 C. Nr. 4, "Acta, Die Orgel an der Neukirchen betreffend"
 Georgenhaus Nr. 642
 Leichenbücher der Stadt Leipzig
 Stift IX A 2, vol. 1, "Die Kirche zu St. Thomas betr."

Stift IX A 34, "Acten, die Orgel, die musikalischen Instrumente, den Organisten und den Calcanten an der Thomaskirche betr. 1657–1802"
Stift IX, Tit. VII. B Nr. 108, "Ersetzung derer Organisten u. Küsterdienste in denen Kirchen zu St. Thomae und St. Nicolai it: St. Johannis, vol. I [from 1699]"
Tit. VIII. 60a, "Protokoll in die Enge," from 31 May 1720 to 5 May 1725
Tit. VIII. 63, "Protokoll in die Enge," from 8 January 1735 to 19 April 1741
Tit. VIII. 64, "Protokoll in die Enge," from 24 April 1741 to 6 May 1747

Stadtgeschichtliches Museum Leipzig (City History Museum Leipzig)
A/3667/2006, "Die Reparatur der Orgel bey der Neuen Kirche betr."

Superintendentur Archiv Delitzsch
"Acta Bau- und Reparatur-Sachen zu Zschortau betr . . . 1660–1756"
"Zschortauische Kirch-Rechnung von Martini 1745 biß dahin 1746"

Universitätsarchiv Leipzig (UAL)
Rep. I/X/62, "Acta, die Bestallung des Stimmens der Orgel in der Pauliner Kirche betr. 1790"
Rep. I/XVI/I 39, "Acta, Protocoll. Concilii Dnn. Decemvirorum. 1744"
Rep. II/III/B I 6, "Conten Buch über die Pauliner Kirchbau Rechnung, von Anfang als mens: 7br: Anno 1710 bis dahin Anno 1713"
Rep. II/III/B I 11, "Acta, das vom Herrn Dr. Glieb. Gerhard Titius . . . der Paulinerkirche verordnete Legat . . . betr. 1714"
Rep. II/III/B I 12, "Acta, Belege zu der neuen Kirchrechnung von Neujahr 1714 bis dahin 1726"
Rep. II/III/B I 25, "Acta, etliche Projecte, Anschläge, durch Wochenzettel wegen des Kirchbaues, Verlosing, Capellen und Stühlen, auch Orgelbau betr., 1710–28"
Rep. II/III/B II 5, "Acta, den Orgel- und anderen Bau, ingleichen Verschreibung der Capellen, Verlosung der Stühle u.w.d.a. in der Paulinerkirche betr., 1710-"
Rep. II/III/B II 6, "Acta, den Orgel- und anderen Bau, ingleichen Verschreibung der Capellen, Verlosung der Stühle u.w.d.a. in der Paulinerkirche betr., 1710–15"
Rep. II/III/B II 9, "Index über die gesammten Acten, den Gottesdienst in der Paulinerkirche betr. [1712]"
Rep. II/III/B II 10, "Acta, die Reparatur an der Orgel in der Pauliner Kirche betr. [1780–1811]"
Rep. II/III/B II 11, "Acta, die Herstellung der Orgel in der Pauliner Kirche betr. [1833–1921]"

Universitäts-Rentamt, Leipzig
454I–454II, Film 357

Books, Articles, and Manuscripts

Acta historico ecclesiastica, oder Gesammlete Nachrichten von den neuesten Kirchen-Geschichten. 1736–66. 24 vols. Weimar: Siegm. Heinrich Hoffmann.
Adlung, Jacob. (1758) 1953. *Anleitung zur musikalischen Gelahrtheit.* Erfurt: J. D. Jungnicol, Sen. Facsimile reprint, Kassel: Bärenreiter.

————. (1768) 1961. *Musica mechanica organoedi*. 2 vols. Edited posthumously by Johann Lorenz Albrecht with contributions also by Johann Friedrich Agricola. Berlin: F. W. Birnstiel. Facsimile reprint, with afterword by Christhard Mahrenholz, Kassel: Bärenreiter, 1931 and 1961. Translated (and annotated) by Quentin Faulkner as *Musical Mechanics for the Organist*. Lincoln, Nebr.: Zea E-Books, 2011.

Agricola, Johann Friedrich. 1758. Review of *Sammlung einiger Nachrichten von berühmten Orgelwerken in Teutschland* (Breslau, 1757). In *Historisch-Kritische Beyträge zur Aufnahme der Musik*, vol. 3 part 6, edited by Friedrich Wilhelm Marpurg, 486–518. Berlin: Lange. [See also Q. Faulkner 1993.]

Ahrens, Christian. 2002. "Der 'Orgel- und Instrumentmacher' Wahlfried Ficker (1676–1770) aus Zeitz." *Ars Organi* 50, no. 3: 140–45.

————. 2007. "Gottfried Silbermanns Bekanntenkreis." In *"Wir loben deine Kunst, Dein Preiß ist hoch zu schätzen . . .": Der Orgelbauer Gottfried Silbermann (1683–1753); Symposium im Rahmen der 28. Tage Alter Musik in Herne 2003*, edited by Christian Ahrens and Gregor Klinke, 53–67. München-Salzburg: Musikverlag Katzbichler.

Arnold, Frank Thomas. 1965. *The Art of Accompaniment from a Thorough-Bass as Practised in the XVIIth and XVIIIth Centuries*. Oxford: Oxford University Press.

Becker, Carl Ferdinand. 1842. "Ueber die Orgeln in der Universitäts- (Pauliner-) Kirche zu Leipzig, nebst ihren Dispositionen." *Allgemeine musikalische Zeitung* 44:425–30.

Bendeler, Johann Philipp. (1690) 1972. *Organopoeia, oder Unterweisung, wie eine Orgel nach ihren Hauptstücken . . . zu erbauen*. Frankfurt und Leipzig: Calvisius. Facsimile reprint, Buren: F. Knuf.

Bergelt, Wolf. 2012. *Joachim Wagner, Orgelmacher (1690–1749)*. Regensburg: Schnell and Steiner.

Biermann, Johann Hermann. (1738) 1981. *Organographia Hildesiensis Specialis*. Hildesheim. Facsimile reprint, Buren: F. Knuf.

Bitter, Carl Hermann. (1881) 1978. *Johann Sebastian Bach*. 2nd ed., 4 vols. Berlin: W. Baensch. Reprint, Leipzig: Zentralantiquariat der DDR.

Blanchard, Homer D. 1985. *The Bach Organ Book*. Delaware, Ohio: Praestant Press.

Boxberg, Christian Ludwig. 1704. *Ausführliche Beschreibung der großen neuen Orgel in der Kirchen zu St. Petri und Pauli allhie zu Görlitz*. Görlitz: Johann Gottlob Laurentio. Facsimile reprint in Mary Murrell Faulkner, *C. L. Boxberg's 1704 Description of Casparini's Sun Organ in Görlitz: Translation and Commentary*, 70–92. Saarbrücken: VDM Verlag Dr. Müller, 2009.

Buchstab, Bernhard. 2002. *Orgelwerke und Prospektgestaltung in Thüringer Schlosskapellen: Visualisierung sakraler Musikinstrumente im höfischen Kontext*. PhD diss., Philipps University, Marburg.

Buelow, George J. 1974. "In defense of J. A. Scheibe against J. S. Bach." *Proceedings of the Royal Musical Association* 101:85–100.

Burgemeister, Ludwig. 1973. *Der Orgelbau in Schlesien*, 2nd ed. Frankfurt: Verlag Wolfgang Weidlich.

Busch, Hermann J. 1995. "Orgeln um Johann Sebastian Bach." In *Zur Interpretation der Orgelmusik Johann Sebastian Bachs*, by Ewald Kooiman, Gerhard Weinberger, and Hermann J. Busch, 119–40. Berlin: Merseburger.

Butler, Gregory. 2007. "Bach's Preluding for a Leipzig Academic Ceremony." In *Music and Theology: Essays in Honor of Robin A. Leaver,* edited by Daniel Zager, 51–68. Lanham, Md.: Scarecrow Press.

Chrysander, Friedrich. 1867. "Johann Sebastian Bach und sein Sohn Friedemann Bach in Halle, 1713–1768." *Jahrbücher für musikalische Wissenschaft* 2:235–48.

Dähnert, Ulrich. (1953) 1971. *Die Orgeln Gottfried Silbermanns in Mitteldeutschland.* Leipzig: Koehler and Amelang. Reprint, Amsterdam: Frits Knuf.

———. 1962. *Der Orgel- und Instrumentenbauer Zacharias Hildebrandt.* Leipzig: Breit-kopf and Härtel.

———. 1980. *Historische Orgeln in Sachsen: Ein Orgelinventar.* Frankfurt am Main: Verlag das Musikinstrument.

———. 1986. "Organs Played and Tested by J. S. Bach." In *J. S. Bach as Organist: His Instruments, Music, and Performance Practices,* edited by George Stauffer and Ernest May, 3–24. Bloomington: Indiana University Press.

Dänhardt, Konrad. 2000. "Dokumentation des 1999/2000 vorgefundenen Zustand und der 2000 ausgeführten Arbeiten an der von Johann Scheibe erbauten Orgel in der evangelischen Kirche zu Zschortau." Unpublished report prepared for Hermann Eule Orgelbau Bautzen.

David, Werner. 1951. *Johann Sebastian Bachs Orgeln.* Berlin: Berliner Musikinstrumenten-Sammlung.

Dreyfus, Laurence. 1985. "The Metaphorical Soloist: Concerted Organ Parts in Bach's Cantatas." *Early Music* 13:237–47.

———. 1987. *Bach's Continuo Group: Players and Practices in His Vocal Works.* Cambridge, Mass.: Harvard University Press.

Dürr, Alfred, and Richard D. P. Jones. 2006. *The Cantatas of J. S. Bach: With Their Libret-tos in German–English Parallel Text.* Oxford: Oxford University Press.

Eberlein, Roland. 2009. 2nd ed. *Orgelregister, ihre Namen und ihre Geschichte.* Köln: Siebenquart.

Edwards Butler, Lynn. 2004. "Johann Christoph Bach's New Organ for Eisenach's Georgenkirche." *Bach: Journal of the Riemenschneider Bach Institute* 25, no. 1: 42–60.

———. 2008. "Johann Christoph Bach und die von Georg Christoph Stertzing erbaute große Orgel der Georgenkirche in Eisenach." *Bach-Jahrbuch* 94:229–69.

———. 2010. "Leipzig Organs in the Time of Bach." *Keyboard Perspectives* 3:87–101.

———. 2011. "Bach, Johann Scheibe und die Orgeln in Zschortau und Stötteritz—Vier neue Quellen." *Bach-Jahrbuch* 97 (2011): 265–68.

———. 2013. "Four Sources Relating to Bach, Organ Builder Johann Scheibe, and the Organs in Zschortau and Stötteritz." *Bach: Journal of the Riemenschneider Bach Insti-tute* 44, no. 2: 1–5. Originally published as "Bach, Johann Scheibe und die Orgeln in Zschortau und Stötteritz—Vier neue Quellen." *Bach-Jahrbuch* 97 (2011): 265–68.

———. 2016. "Bach's Report on Johann Scheibe's Organ for St. Paul's Church, Leipzig: A Reassessment." *Bach Perspectives* 10:1–15.

———. 2018. "Innovation in Early Eighteenth-Century Central German Organ Build-ing." *Keyboard Perspectives* 11:61–73.

———. 2019. "Zacharias Thayssner: Organ Builder at the End of an Era." *Organ Year-book* 48:110–31.

———. 2020. "J. S. Bach in Altenburg: Ein bisher unbeachtetes Dokument." *Bach-Jahrbuch* 106:227–34.

Edwards Butler, Lynn, and Gregory Butler. 2006. "'Rare, Newly Invented Stops': Scheibe's Organ for St. Paul's Church, Leipzig." In *Orphei Organi Antiqui: Essays in Honor of Harald Vogel,* edited by Cleveland Johnson, 285–306. Seattle: Westfield Center.

Eichler, Ulrich. 2018. *Der sächsische Orgelbauer Johann Ernst Hähnel (1697–1777).* Markkleeberg: Sax-Verlag.

Engel, David Hermann. 1855. *Beitrag zur Geschichte des Orgelbauwesens: Denkschrift zur Einweihung der durch Fr. Ladegast erbauten Domorgel zu Merseburg nebst Disposition derselben.* Erfurt: G. W. Körner.

Fabricius, Werner. 1756. *Unterricht, wie man ein neu Orgelwerk, obs gut und beständig sey, nach allen Stücken, in- und auswendig examiniren, und so viel wie möglich probiren soll.* Frankfurt and Leipzig.

Faulkner, Mary Murrell. 2009. *C. L. Boxberg's 1704 Description of Casparini's Sun Organ in Görlitz: Translation and Commentary* [translation and commentary, pp. 1–69; facsimile reprint, pp. 70–92]. Saarbrücken: VDM Verlag Dr. Müller.

Faulkner, Quentin. 1993. "Information on Organ Registration from a Student of J. S. Bach." *American Organist* 27:58–63. Also in *Early Keyboard Studies Newsletter* 8 (1993): 1–10.

———. 2008. *The Registration of J. S. Bach's Organ Works.* Colfax, N.C.: Wayne Leupold Editions.

Flade, Ernst. 1926. *Der Orgelbauer Gottfried Silbermann.* Leipzig: Fr. Kistner and C. W. Siegel.

———. 1931. "Geschichtliches über die sächsischen Orgeln und die Autoren der 'Dresdener Handschrift.'" In *Orgeldispositionen: Eine Handschrift aus dem XVIII. Jahrhundert, im Besitz der Sächsischen Landesbibliothek, Dresden,* edited by Paul Smets, 102–27. Kassel: Bärenreiter.

———. 1953. *Gottfried Silbermann: Ein Beitrag zur Geschichte des deutschen Orgel- und Klavierbaus im Zeitalter Bachs.* Leipzig: Breitkopf and Härtel.

———. n.d. "Orgelbauer Lexikon." Typewritten ms., preserved in the Staatsbibliothek zu Berlin-Preußischer Kulturbesitz, Musikabteilung mit Mendelssohn-Archiv.

Fock, Gustav. 1974. *Arp Schnitger und seine Schule.* Kassel: Bärenreiter.

Forkel, Johann Nikolaus. (1802) 1920. *Johann Sebastian Bach: His Life, Art, and Work,* translated and notated by Charles Sanford Terry. Originally published as *Ueber Johann Sebastian Bachs Leben, Kunst und Kunstwerke.* Leipzig: Hoffmeister und Kühnel. Reprint, New York: Harcourt, Brace and Howe; e-book published by Project Gutenberg, 2011.

Franklin, Don O. 1991. "Bach's Keyboard Music in the 1730s and 1740s: Organs and Harpsichords, Hildebrandt and Neidhardt." *Early Keyboard Studies Newsletter* 6:1–14.

Friedrich, Felix. 1989. *Der Orgelbauer Heinrich Gottfried Trost.* Wiesbaden: Breitkopf and Härtel.

———. 2005. "Der Orgelbauer Franciscus Volckland." In *Dulce Melos Organorum: Festschrift Alfred Reichling zum 70. Geburtstag,* edited by Roland Behrens and Christoph Grohmann, 191–216. Mettlach: Gesellschaft der Orgelfreunde.

Friedrich, Felix, and Albrecht Dietl. 1995. *Orgeln im Altenburger Land*. Altenburg: Kamprad.

Geck, Martin. 2003. "Bach's Art of Church Music and His Leipzig Performance Forces: Contradictions in the System." *Early Music* 31:558–71.

Gernhardt, Klaus. 2011. "Die Orgel in der romanischen Dorfkirche zu Klinga: Zur Baugeschichte, geplanten Rekonstruktion und Restaurierung." Unpublished paper.

Gernhardt, Klaus, and Roland Börger, eds. 2006. *Die Orgel zu Pomssen: Festschrift zur Wiederweihe*. Beucha: Sax-Verlag.

Glöckner, Andreas. 1985. "Johann Kuhnau, Johann Sebastian Bach und die Musikdirektoren der Leipziger Neukirche." *Beiträge zur Bach-Forschung* 4:23–32.

———. 1990. "Die Musikpflege an der Leipziger Neukirche zur Zeit Johann Sebastian Bachs." *Beiträge zur Bach-Forschung* 8:1–170.

———. 2008. "Johann Sebastian Bach und die Universität Leipzig—Neue Quellen." *Bach-Jarhbuch* 94:159–201.

———. 2013. "'Zu besser Bequemlichkeit der Music': Über einige neue Quellen zur Leipziger Kirchenmusik." *Bach-Jahrbuch* 99:335–48.

Greß, Frank-Harald. 1989. *Die Klanggestalt der Orgeln Gottfried Silbermanns*. Leipzig: Deutsche Verlag für Musik.

———. 2001. *Die Orgeln Gottfried Silbermanns*. 2nd ed. Dresden: Sandstein.

———. 2010. *Die Orgeltemperaturen Gottfried Silbermanns: Ein Beitrag zur Theorie und Praxis der Orgeldenkmalpflege*. Freiberger Studien zur Orgel, no. 12. Altenburg: Kamprad.

Hackel, Wolfram, and Uwe Pape, eds. 2012. *Lexikon norddeutscher Orgelbauer*. Vol. 2, *Sachsen und Umgebung*. Berlin: Pape Verlag.

Harmon, Thomas Fredric. 1981. *The Registration of J. S. Bach's Organ Works*. 2nd ed. Buren: Knuf.

Hartmann, Carl. 1841. *Populäres Handbuch der allgemeinen und speziellen Technologie*. Vol. 2. Berlin: Carl Friedrich Amelang.

Hauge, Peter. 2018. *Johann Adolph Scheibe: A Catalogue of His Works*. Danish Humanist Texts and Studies, vol. 58. Copenhagen: Danish Centre for Music Editing, Royal Danish Library, and Museum Tusculanum Press.

Haupt, Hartmut. 1981. *Die Orgel der Kapelle im Schloß Eisenberg, ein bedeutendes Denkmal der barocken Orgelbaukunst in Thüringen*. Eisenberg: Rat des Kreises Eisenberg.

Heller, Veit. 2010. "'Eine kleine Ehr'—Zum Status der Orgelbauer an der Universität Leipzig zwischen 1685 und 1850." In *600 Jahre Musik an der Universität Leipzig*, edited by Eszter Fontana, 111–30. Leipzig: Janos Stekovics.

Henkel, Hubert. 1985. "Die Orgeln der Köthener Kirchen zur Zeit Johann Sebastian Bachs und ihre Geschichte (Teil I)." *Cöthener Bach-Hefte* 3:5–28.

———. 1986. "Zur Geschichte der Scheibe-Orgel in der Leipziger Johannis-Kirche." *Bach-Studien* 9:44–50.

———. 1988. "Orgeln im Umfeld Bachs." In *Bericht über die Wissenschafftliche Konferenz zum 5. Internationalen Bachfest der DDR,* edited by W. Hoffmann, 113–24. Leipzig: Deutscher Verlag für Musik.

Heyde, Herbert. 1985. "Der Instrumentenbau in Leipzig zur Zeit Johann Sebastian Bachs." In *Dreihundert Jahre Johann Sebastian Bach . . . eine Ausstellung der Internationalen Bachakademie in der Staatsgalerie Stuttgart, 14.9 bis 27.10.1985,* edited by Ulrich Prinz and Konrad Küster, 73–78. Tutzing: H. Schneider.

Hübner, Maria. 2013. "Johann Scheibe und die Orgel in der Kirche des Leipziger Georgenhauses." *Bach-Jahrbuch* 99:349–58.

Hütter, Elisabeth. 1993. *Die Pauliner-Universitätskirche zu Leipzig: Geschichte und Bedeutung.* Weimar: Verlag Hermann Böhlaus Nachfolger.

Jerold, Beverly. 2011. "The Bach-Scheibe Controversy: New Documentation." *Bach: Journal of the Riemenschneider Bach Institute* 42, no. 1: 1–45.

Kaufmann, Michael Gerhard. 2000. "' . . . alles tüchtig, fleißig und wohl erbauet . . . ;' Johann Sebastian Bachs Prüfung der Scheibe-Orgel in Zschortau." *Orgel International* 4:404–9.

Keller, Hermann. 1967. *The Organ Works of Bach: A Contribution to Their History, Form, Interpretation and Performance.* Translated from the German by Helen Hewitt. New York: C. F. Peters. Originally published in 1948.

Kevorkian, Tanya. 2007. *Baroque Piety: Religion, Society, and Music in Leipzig, 1650–1750.* Aldershot: Ashgate.

Kinsky, Georg. 1910. *Katalog. Musikhistorisches Museum von Wilhelm Heyer in Cöln. I: Besaitete Tasteninstrumente, Orgeln und orgelartige Instrumente, Friktionsinstrumente.* Leipzig: Breitkopf and Härtel.

Klotz, Hans. 1934. *Über die Orgelkunst der Gotik, der Renaissance und des Barock.* Kassel: Bärenreiter-Verlag.

———. 1978. "Historische Orgelbauschulen und ihre Mixturmodelle." *Ars organi* 26:326–30.

Koska, Bernd. 2019. "Bachs Privatschüler." *Bach-Jahrbuch* 105:13–82.

Koster, John. 1994. "Pianos and Other 'Expressive' *Claviere* in J. S. Bach's Circle." *Early Keyboard Studies Newsletter,* 7, no. 4: 1–11; 8, no. 1: 1–7; and 8, no. 2: 8–15.

Kraft, Günther. 1957. "Neue Ergebnisse der Thüringer Bachforschung." In *34. Deutsches Bachfest der Neuen Bachgesellschaft (1957),* Beiträge zum Programm, 74–90. Eisenach: Erich Röth.

Krapf, Gerhard, trans. 1976. *Werckmeister's "Erweiterte und verbesserte Orgel-Probe" in English.* Raleigh, N.C.: Sunbury Press.

Kuhnau, Johann. 1717. Letter to Johann Mattheson dated 8 December 1717. Published in *Critica musica,* 2:233–35. Hamburg, 1725.

Kuntze, C., ed. 1875. *Die Orgel und ihr Bau. Dritte gänzlich umgearbeitete Auflage von Joh. Julius Seidel's gleichnamigem Werke.* Leipzig: Verlag F. E. C. Leuckart.

Lawson, Colin. 1981. "Telemann and the Chalumeau." *Early Music* 9:312–19.

———. 1992. "The Chalumeau in the Works of Fux." In *Johann Joseph Fux and the Music of the Austro-Italian Baroque,* edited by Harry White, 78–94. Brookfield, Vt.: Ashgate.

Leaver, Robin. 2018. "A Catholic Hymnal for Use in Lutheran Leipzig: Catholisches Gesang-Buch (Leipzig 1724)." *Bach Perspectives* 12:36–62.

Lindley, Mark. 1988. "A Suggested Improvement for the Fisk Organ at Stanford." *Performance Practice Review* 1:107–32.

———. n.d. "Temperaments." In *Grove Music Online, Oxford Music Online*. Accessed 29 June 2011. http://www.oxfordmusiconline.com/subscriber/article/grove/music /27643.

Löffler, Hans. 1931. "Ein unbekanntes Thüringer Orgelmanuscript von 1798." *Musik und Kirche* 3:140–43 and 280–85.

———. 1932. "G. H. Trost und die Altenburger Schlossorgel." *Musik und Kirche* 4:171–76.

Ludwig, Christian. 1716. *Teutsch-Englisches Lexicon*. Leipzig: Thomas Fritzsch. https:// archive.org/details/teutschenglischeooleipuoft/page/n5/mode/2up?view=theater.

Magirius, Heinrich, Hartmut Mai, Thomas Trajkovits, and Winfried Werner, eds. 1995. *Stadt Leipzig—Die Sakralbauten*. 2 vols. Munich: Deutscher Kunstverlag.

Mahrenholz, Christhard. 1942. *Die Orgelregister*. 2nd ed. Kassel: Bärenreiter.

Marshall, Robert L., and Traute M. Marshall. 2016. *Exploring the World of J. S. Bach: A Traveler's Guide*. Urbana: University of Illinois Press.

Matthaei, Karl. 1950. "Johann Sebastian Bachs Orgel." In *Bach-Gedenkschrift 1950*, edited by K. Matthaei, 118–49. Zürich: Atlantis-Verlag.

Mattheson, Johann. (1739) 1954. *Der vollkommene Capellmeister*. Facsimile reprint edited by Margarete Reimann. Kassel: Bärenreiter.

———. (1740) 1969. *Grundlage einer Ehrenpforte*. Facsimile reprint edited by Max Schneider. Kassel: Bärenreiter, and Graz (Austria): Akademische Druck- u. Verlags-anstalt.

Maul, Michael. 2010. "Musikpflege in der Paulinerkirche im 17. Jahrhundert bis hin zur Einführung des 'neuen Gottesdienstes' (1710)." In *600 Jahre Musik an der Universität Leipzig: Studien anlässlich des Jubiläums*, ed. Eszter Fontana, 33–56. Wettin: Verlag Janos Stekovics.

———. 2013. "Bach versus Scheibe: Hitherto Unknown Battlegrounds in a Famous Conflict." *Bach Perspectives* 9:20–143.

———. 2017. "Homilius: Wirklich ein Schüler Bachs? Überlegungen zu seiner Leipziger Zeit." In *Ohne Widerrede unser größter Kirchenkomponist: Annäherungen an Gottfried August Homilius*, Forum Mitteldeutsche Barockmusik, vol. 7, edited by Gerhard Poppe and Uwe Wolf, 67–80. Beeskow: Ortus Musikverlag.

Michler, Lothar. 2005. "Die Scheibe-Orgel in der Kirche St. Nicolai zu Zschortau." *Delitzscher Heimatkalender 2000* 5:38–46.

Mizler, Lorenz Christoph. 1737. *Neu eröffnete Musikalische Bibliothek*, vol. 1, pt. 2. Printed in Leipzig by the author.

———. 1747. *Musikalische Bibliothek*, vol. 3, pt. 3. Printed in Leipzig by the author.

Moser Dietz-Rüdiger. 1994. *Tausend Jahre Musik in Quedlinburg*. Quedlinburg: Ehrenwirth.

Müller, Ernst. 1915. "Die neue Orgel in der Universitäts-Kirche St. Paul zu Leipzig." *Zeitschrift für Instrumentenbau* 36:224–26 and 238–42.

Müller, Werner. 1969. *Auf den Spuren von Gottfried Silbermann: Ein Lebensbild des berühmten Orgelbauers*. Berlin: Evangelische Verlagsanstalt.

———. 1982. *Gottfried Silbermann, Persönlichkeit und Werk: Eine Dokumentation*. Leipzig: Deutscher Verlag für Musik.

Niedt, Friedrich Erhardt. (1721) 1976. *Musicalische Handleitung*. Edited by Johann Mattheson. Hamburg. Facsimile reprint, Buren, The Netherlands: Fritz Knuf.

Oehme, Fritz. 1978. *Handbuch über ältere, neuere und neueste Orgelwerke im Königreiche Sachsen vom Jahre 1640–1890.* Facsimile reprint of vol. 2 with a supplement and index edited by Wolfram Hackel with assistance from Ulrich Dähnert. Leipzig: Peters. First published in 1889–97.

Pape, Uwe, and Wolfram Hackel, eds. 2015. *Lexikon norddeutscher Orgelbauer,* vol. 3, *Sachsen-Anhalt und Umgebung.* Berlin: Pape Verlag.

Petzoldt, Martin. 2000. *Bachstätten: Ein Reiseführer zu Johann Sebastian Bach.* Frankfurt am Main: Insel-Verlag.

Poletti, Paul. 2006. "Temperament and Intonation in Ensemble Music of the Late Eighteenth Century: Performance Problems Then and Now." In *Music of the Past—Instruments and Imagination* (Proceedings of the Harmoniques International Congress, Lausanne, 2004), edited by Michael Latcham, 109–32. Bern: Peter Lang.

Praetorius, Michael. (1619) 1976. *Syntagma Musicum II: De Organographia.* Wolfenbüttel. Facsimile reprint, edited by Wilibald Gurlitt. Kassel: Bärenreiter.

Praetorius, Michael, and Esaias Compenius. 1936. *Orgeln Verdingnis.* Kieler Beiträge zur Musikwissenschaft 4, edited by Friedrich Blume. Wolfenbüttel and Berlin: Kallmeyer Verlag.

Rathey, Markus. 2001. "Die Temperierung der Divi Blasii-Orgel in Mühlhausen." *Bach-Jahrbuch* 87:163–71.

Reichling, Alfred, ed. 2000. *Die Hildebrandt-Orgel zu Naumburg, St. Wenzel: Festschrift anlässlich der Wiedereinweihung nach vollendeter Restaurierung am 3. Dezember 2000.* Naumburg: Stadt Naumburg, Evangelisches Kirchspiel Naumburg, Förderkreis Hildebrandt-Orgel.

Richter, Bernhard Friedrich. 1908. "Über Seb. Bachs Kantaten mit obligater Orgel." *Bach-Jahrbuch* 5:49–63.

Rubardt, Paul. 1937. "Die Bach-Orgel in Zschortau." *Die Musik* 24, no. 4: 272–74.

———. 1948. "Johann Scheibe zu seinem 200. Todestag." *Musik und Kirche* 18, nos. 5/6: 173–74.

———. 1950. "Bachorgeln in Leipzigs Umgebung." In *Johann Sebastian Bach: Das Schaffen des Meisters im Spiegel einer Stadt,* edited by Richard Petzoldt, 102–8. Leipzig: Volk und Buch Verlag.

———. 1961. "Zwei originale Orgeldispositionen J. S. Bachs." In *Festschrift Heinrich Besseler zum sechzigsten Geburtstag,* 495–503. Leipzig: Deutscher Verlag für Musik.

———. 1963. S.v. "Scheibe." In *Die Musik in Geschichte und Gegenwart,* vol. 11. Kassel: Bärenreiter.

Rust, Wilhelm. 1875. Introduction to vol. 22, *Johann Sebastian Bachs Werke* (Bach-Gesellschaft ed.). Leipzig: Breitkopf and Härtel.

Scheibe, Johann. 1732. "Leipzig [November 1732]." In *Neue Zeitungen von Gelehrten Sachen* 18:833–34.

Scheibe, Johann Adolph. 1738. *Der Critische Musicus, Erster Theil.* Hamburg: Thomas von Weiring's Heirs.

———. 1745. *Der Critische Musicus: Neue, vermehrte und verbesserte Auflage.* Leipzig: Bernhard Christoph Breitkopf.

———. 1748. Evaluation dated 31 January 1748 of a proposal to renovate the organ in the Castle Church in Gottorf. Cited in Schumann 1973, 374–78.

Schering, Arnold. 1926. *Musikgeschichte Leipzigs,* vol. 2, *Von 1650 bis 1723.* Leipzig: Fr. Kistner and C. F. W. Siegel.

———. 1941. *Musikgeschichte Leipzigs,* vol. 3, *Johann Sebastian Bach und die Musikleben Leipzigs im 18. Jahrhundert.* Leipzig: Fr. Kistner and C. F. W. Siegel.

———. 1954. *Johann Sebastian Bachs Leipziger Kirchenmusik.* 2nd ed. Leipzig: Breitkopf and Härtel.

Schlimbach, Georg Christian Friedrich. 1801. *Ueber die Structur, Erhaltung, Stimmung, Prüfung etc. der Orgel.* Leipzig: Breitkopf and Härtel.

Schneider, Thekla. 1937. "Die Orgelbauerfamilie Compenius." *Archiv für Musikforschung* 2:8–76.

Schneider, Wilhelm. 1829. *Ausführliche Beschreibung der grossen Dom-Orgel zu Merseburg.* Halle: Carl August Kümmel.

Schrammek, Winfried. 1975. "Fragen des Orgelgebrauchs in Bachs Aufführungen der Matthäus-Passion." *Bach-Jahrbuch* 61:114–23.

———. 1983a. *Bach-Orgeln in Thüringen und Sachsen,* vol. 11, *Beiträge zur Bachpflege der DDR.* Leipzig: Nationale Forschungs- und Gedenkstätten Johann Sebastian Bach der DDR.

———. 1983b. "Zur Geschichte der großen Orgel in der Thomaskirche zu Leipzig von 1601 bis 1885." *Beiträge zur Bachforschung* 2:46–55.

———. 1985. "Johann Sebastian Bachs Stellung zu Orgelpedalregistern im 32-Fuß-Ton." *Bach-Jahrbuch* 71:147–54.

Schumann, Otto. 1973. *Quellen und Forschungen zur Geschichte des Orgelbaus im Herzogtum Schleswig vor 1800,* vol. 23, *Schriften zur Musik,* edited by Walter Kolneder. Munich: Musikverlag Emil Katzbichler.

Schumann, Robert, and Clara Schumann. 2007. *Ehetagebücher 1840–1844.* Edited by Gerd Nauhaus and Ingrid Bodsch. Bonn: Stroemfeld Verlag und StadtMuseum.

Shull, Bruce. 2021. "Casting Pipe Metal on Sand." *Vox Humana,* 25 April 2021. http://voxhumanajournal.com/shull2021.html.

Sicul, Christoph Ernst. 1718. *Neo-Annalium Lipsiensium Prodromus oder Des mit dem 1715ten Jahre Neu-angehenden Leipziger Jahrbuchs Vierte Probe [1718]* and *Anderen Beylage zu dem Leipziger Jahrbuche, aufs Jahr 1718.* Leipzig: Author.

Sorge, Georg Andreas. 1748. *Gespräch . . . von der Prätorianischen, Prinzischen, Werckmeisterischen, Neidhardtischen und Silbermannischen Temperatur.* Printed in Lobenstein by the author.

Spitta, Philipp. (1873–80) 1964. *Johann Sebastian Bach.* 2 vols. Leipzig: Breitkopf and Härtel. Reprint, Wiesbaden: Breitkopf and Härtel.

———. (1884–85) 1951. *Johann Sebastian Bach: His Work and Influence on the Music of Germany, 1685–1750.* Translated by Clara Bell and John Alexander Fuller-Maitland. 3 vols. London. Reprint, New York: Dover.

Stauffer, George. 1980. *The Organ Preludes of Johann Sebastian Bach.* Studies in Musicology, no. 27, edited by George Buelow. Ann Arbor, Mich.: UMI Research Press.

Stieda, Wilhelm. 1938. "Der Neubau der Paulinerkirche in den Jahren 1710–12: Aktenmäßige Forschungen über die Mitarbeit der Leipziger Gewerken." *Schriften des Vereins für Geschichte Leipzigs* 22:75–89.

Stiehl, Herbert. 1984. "Das Innere der Thomaskirche zur Amtszeit Johann Sebastian Bachs." *Beiträge zur Bachforschung* 3:5–96.

Stockigt, Janice B. 2016. "The Music of Leipzig's Royal Catholic Chapel during the Reign of August II." *Understanding Bach* 11:57–66.

Stüven, Wilfried. 1964. *Orgel und Orgelbauer im halleschen Land vor 1800*. Wiesbaden: Breitkopf and Härtel.

Sumner, William Leslie. 1952. *The Organ: Its Evolution, Principles of Construction and Use*. London: Macdonald.

Szeskus, Reinhard. 2003. "Bach und die Leipziger Universitätsmusik." In *Bach in Leipzig: Beiträge zu Leben und Werk von Johann Sebastian Bach*, Taschenbücher zur Musik-wissenschaft 146, 217–31. Wilhelmshaven: Florian Noetzel.

Talle, Andrew. 2003. "Nürnberg, Darmstadt, Köthen: Neuerkenntnisse zur Bach-Überlieferung in der ersten Hälfte des 18. Jahrhunderts." *Bach-Jahrbuch* 89:143–72.

Theobald, Hans Wolfgang. 1986. "Zur Geschichte der 1746 von Johann Sebastian Bach geprüften Johann-Scheibe Orgel in Zschortau bei Leipzig." *Bach-Jahrbuch* 72:81–90.

"Vermischtes." 1867. *Neue Zeitschrift für Musik* 63:333.

Vogel, Harald. 2003. "The Mixtures of the Örgryte Organ." In *The North German Organ Research Project at Göteborg University*, edited by Joel Speerstra, 283–99. Göteborg: Göteborg Organ Art Center.

Vogel, Harald, Günter Lade, and Nicola Borger-Keweloh. 1997. *Orgeln in Niedersachsen*. Bremen: Verlag H. M. Hauschild.

Walther, Johann Friedrich. 1727. *Die in der Königl. Garnison-Kirche zu Berlin befindliche neue Orgel*. Berlin: Carl Gottfried Möller.

Walther, Johann Gottfried. (1732) 1953. *Musicalisches Lexicon*. Leipzig: Wolffgang Deer. Facsimile reprint, Kassel: Bärenreiter.

Weiz, Anton. 1728. *Verbessertes Leipzig, oder Die vornehmsten Dinge, so von Anno 1698 an bis hiehern bey der Stadt Leipzig verbessert worden*. Leipzig: Lancke.

Werckmeister, Andreas. 1681. *Orgel-Probe*. Quedlinburg.

———. (1691) 1983. *Musicalische Temperatur*. 2nd ed. Frankfurt and Leipzig: Theodor Philipp Calvisi. Facsimile reprint, Utrecht: Diapason Press.

———. (1698) 1970. *Erweiterte und verbesserte Orgel-Probe*. 2nd enlarged ed. Quedlin-burg. Facsimile reprint, Kassel: Bärenreiter.

———. 1705. *Organum Gruningense Redivium*. Quedlinburg and Aschersleben. Reprint, Paul Smets, Mainz: Rheingold, 1932.

———. 1715. *Die nothwendigsten Anmerckungen und Regeln, wie der Bassus continuus oder General-Baß wohl könne tractiret werden*. 2nd ed. Aschersleben: Gottlob Ernst Struntz.

Werner, Arno. 1900. "Samuel und Gottfried Scheidt: Neue Beiträge zu ihrer Biographie." *Sammelbände der Internationalen Musikgesellschaft* 1:401–45.

Werner, Helmut. 1997. *Festschrift zur Weihe der Trost-Orgel in der Walpurgiskirche zu Großengottern am 14. September 1997*. Bad Homburg and Leipzig: Verlag Ausbildung + Wissen.

Williams, Peter. 1967. *The European Organ, 1450–1850*. Nashau, N.H.: Organ Literature Foundation.

———. 1984. *The Organ Music of J. S. Bach*, vol. 3, *A Background*. Cambridge: Cambridge University Press.

———. 2007. *J. S. Bach: A Life in Music*. Cambridge: Cambridge University Press.

———. 2016. *Bach: A Musical Biography*. Cambridge: Cambridge University Press.

Williams, Peter, and Barbara Owen. 1988. *The Organ*. New York: W. W. Norton.

Winter, Helmut, ed. 1979. *Die Huß-Orgel in Stade St. Cosmae*, vol. 1, *Orgel-Studien*. Hamburg: Musikalienhandlung Karl Dieter Wagner.

Wit, Paul de. 1900. "Die Bach-Orgel der alten Johanniskirche in Leipzig." *Zeitschrift für Instrumentenbau* 20:989–90.

Wolff, Christoph. 2000. *Johann Sebastian Bach: The Learned Musician*. New York: Norton.

———, ed. 2005. *Die Orgeln der Thomaskirche zu Leipzig*. Leipzig: Evangelische Verlagsanstalt.

———. 2016. "Did J. S. Bach Write Organ Concertos?" *Bach Perspectives* 10:60–75.

Wolff, Christoph, and Markus Zepf. 2012. *The Organs of J. S. Bach: A Handbook*. Translated by Lynn Edwards Butler. Urbana: University of Illinois Press. Originally published in German as *Die Orgeln J. S. Bachs: Ein Handbuch*. Leipzig: Evangelische Verlagsanstalt, 2006; rev. ed., 2008.

Wolffheim, Werner. 1911. "Bachiana." *Bach-Jahrbuch* 8:41–42.

Wünsche, Frieder. 2003. *Marienkirche Stötteritz: Die Ausstattung und ihre Funktion im Gottesdienst*. Delitzsch: Edition Akanthus.

Wustmann, Rudolf. 1909. *Musikgeschichte Leipzigs, 1. Band: bis zur Mitte des 17. Jahrhunderts*. Leipzig and Berlin: B. G. Teubner.

Yokota, Munetaka. 2003. "Historical Pipe Metal Casting Techniques in Seventeenth-Century North Germany." In *The North German Organ Research Project at Göteborg University*, edited by Joel Speerstra, 165–86. Göteborg: Göteborg Organ Art Center.

Zavarsky, Ernest. 1975. "J. S. Bachs Entwurf für den Umbau der Orgel in der Kirche Divi Blasii und das Klangideal der Zeit." In *Bach-Studien 5: Eine Sammlung von Aufsätzen*, edited by Rudolf Eller and Hans-Joachim Schulze, 83–92. Leipzig: VEB Breitkopf and Härtel Musikverlag.

———. 1977. "Die temperierte Stimmung, Bachs Klangideal der Orgel und die Entwicklungstendenzen der Zeit." In *Bericht über die Wissenschaftliche Konferenz zum III. Internationalen Bach-Fest der DDR*, edited by Werner Felix, Winfried Hoffmann, and Armin Schneiderheinze, 141–45. Leipzig: VEB Deutscher Verlag für Musik.

Index

LYNN EDWARDS BUTLER is an organist and harpsichordist, and the cofounder and former director of the Westfield Center. She is the translator of *The Organs of J. S. Bach: A Handbook*.

The University of Illinois Press
is a founding member of the
Association of University Presses.

———————————————

Composed in 10.5/14 Minion Pro
by Kirsten Dennison
at the University of Illinois Press
Manufactured by Sheridan Books

University of Illinois Press
1325 South Oak Street
Champaign, IL 61820-6903
www.press.uillinois.edu